ONE TO (

Bilingual Di

English-Spanish
Spanish-English
Dictionary

Compiled by
Cristina Rodriguez

STAR Foreign Language BOOKS

First Edition : 2014
This Edition : 2022

Published by
STAR Foreign Language BOOKS
a unit of
Star Books
56, Langland Crescent
Stanmore HA7 1NG, U.K.
info@starbooksuk.com
www.bilingualbooks.co.uk

Printed in India at
Star Print-O-Bind, New Delhi-110 020

About this Dictionary

Developments in science and technology today have narrowed down distances between countries, and have made the world a small place. A person living thousands of miles away can learn and understand the culture and lifestyle of another country with ease and without travelling to that country. Languages play an important role as facilitators of communication in this respect.

To promote such an understanding, **STAR Foreign Language BOOKS** has planned to bring out a series of bilingual dictionaries in which important English words have been translated into other languages, with Roman transliteration in case of languages that have different scripts. This is a humble attempt to bring people of the word closer through the medium of language, thus making communication easy and convenient.

Under this series of *one-to-one dictionaries*, we have published almost 57 languages, the list of which has been given in the opening pages. These have all been compiled and edited by teachers and scholars of the relative languages.

Publishers

ONE TO ONE

Bilingual Dictionaries in this Series

English-Afrikaans / Afrikaans-English	Abraham Venter
English-Albanian / Albanian-English	Theodhora Blushi
English-Amharic / Amharic-English	Girun Asanke
English-Arabic / Arabic-English	Rania-al-Qass
English-Bengali / Bengali-English	Amit Majumdar
English-Bosnian / Bosnian-English	Boris Kazanegra
English-Bulgarian / Bulgarian-English	Vladka Kocheshkova
English-Burmese (Myanmar) / Burmese (Myanmar)-English	Kyaw Swar Aung
English-Cambodian / Cambodian-English	Engly Sok
English-Cantonese / Cantonese-English	Nisa Yang
English-Chinese (Mandarin) / Chinese (Mandarin)-Eng	Y. Shang & R. Yao
English-Croatian / Croatain-English	Vesna Kazanegra
English-Czech / Czech-English	Jindriska Poulova
English-Danish / Danish-English	Rikke Wend Hartung
English-Dari / Dari-English	Amir Khan
English-Dutch / Dutch-English	Lisanne Vogel
English-Estonian / Estonian-English	Lana Haleta
English-Farsi / Farsi-English	Maryam Zaman Khani
English-French / French-English	Aurélie Colin
English-Georgian / Georgina-English	Eka Goderdzishvili
English-Gujarati / Gujarati-English	Sujata Basaria
English-German / German-English	Bicskei Hedwig
English-Greek / Greek-English	Lina Stergiou
English-Hindi / Hindi-English	Sudhakar Chaturvedi
English-Hungarian / Hungarian-English	Lucy Mallows
English-Italian / Italian-English	Eni Lamllari
English-Japanese / Japanese-English	Miruka Arai & Hiroko Nishimura
English-Korean / Korean-English	Mihee Song
English-Latvian / Latvian-English	Julija Baranovska
English-Levantine Arabic / Levantine Arabic-English	Ayman Khalaf
English-Lithuanian / Lithuanian-English	Regina Kazakeviciute
English-Malay / Malay-English	Azimah Husna
English-Nepali / Nepali-English	Anil Mandal
English-Norwegian / Norwegian-English	Samuele Narcisi
English-Pashto / Pashto-English	Amir Khan
English-Polish / Polish-English	Magdalena Herok
English-Portuguese / Portuguese-English	Dina Teresa
English-Punjabi / Punjabi-English	Teja Singh Chatwal
English-Romanian / Romanian-English	Georgeta Laura Dutulescu
English-Russian / Russian-English	Katerina Volobuyeva
English-Serbian / Serbian-English	Vesna Kazanegra
English-Sinhalese / Sinhalese-English	Naseer Salahudeen
English-Slovak / Slovak-English	Zuzana Horvathova
English-Slovenian / Slovenian-English	Tanja Turk
English-Somali / Somali-English	Ali Mohamud Omer
English-Spanish / Spanish-English	Cristina Rodriguez
English-Swahili / Swahili-English	Abdul Rauf Hassan Kinga
English-Swedish / Swedish-English	Madelene Axelsson
English-Tagalog / Tagalog-English	Jefferson Bantayan
English-Tamil / Tamil-English	Sandhya Mahadevan
English-Thai / Thai-English	Suwan Kaewkongpan
English-Tigrigna / Tigrigna-English	Tsegazeab Hailegebriel
English-Turkish / Turkish-English	Nagme Yazgin
English-Ukrainian / Ukrainian-English	Katerina Volobuyeva
English-Urdu / Urdu-English	S. A. Rahman
English-Vietnamese / Vietnamese-English	Hoa Hoang
English-Yoruba / Yoruba-English	O. A. Temitope

STAR Foreign Language BOOKS

ENGLISH-SPANISH

A

a *a.* un/una
aback *adv.* desconcertado
abandon *v.t.* abandonar
abase *v.* humillarse
abashed *adj.* avergonzado
abate *v.t.* moderarse
abbey *n.* abadía
abbot *n.* abad
abbreviate *v.t.* abreviar
abbreviation *n.* abreviación
abdicate *v.t,* abdicar
abdication *n.* abdicación
abdomen *n.* abdomen
abdominal *a.* abdominal
abduct *v.t.* secuestrar
abduction *n.* secuestro
aberrant *adj.* aberrante
aberration *n.* aberración
abet *v.* incitar
abeyance *n.* en desuso
abhor *v.* aborrecer
abhorrence *n.* aberración
abhorent *adj.* aborrecible
abide *v.i* aguantar
abiding *adj.* perdurable
ability *n.* habilidad
abject *adj.* lamentable
abjure *v.* renunciar
ablaze *adv.* ardiendo
able *adj.* capaz
ablutions *n.* ablución
abnormal *adj.* anormal
aboard *adv.* a bordo
abode *n.* domicilio
abolish *v.t* abolir
abolition *v.* abolición
abominable *adj.* abominable
abominate *v.* abominar

aboriginal *adj.* aborigen
abort *v.i* abortar
abortion *n.* aborto
abortive *adj.* abortivo
abound *v.i.* abundar
about *adv.* más o menos
about *prep.* sobre
above *adv.* arriba
above *prep.* encima de
abrasion *n.* abrasión
abrasive *adj.* abrasivo
abreast *adv.* de frente
abridge *v.t* abreviar
abroad *adv.* en el extranjero
abrogate *v.* derogar
abrupt *adj.* brusco
abscess *n.* absceso
abscond *v.* fugarse
absence *n.* ausencia
absent *adj.* ausente
absentee *n.* ausente
absolute *adj.* absoluto
absolution *n.* absolución
absolve *v.* absolver
absorb *v.* absorber
abstain *v.* abstenerse
abstinence *n.* abstinencia
abstract *adj.* abstracto
abstruse *adj.* abstruso
absurd *adj.* absurdo
absurdity *n.* absurdo
abundance *n.* abundancia
abundant *v.t.* abundar
abuse *v.* abusar
abusive *adj.* abusivo
abut *v.* lindar
abysmal *adj.* abismal
abyss *n.* abismo
academic *adj.* académico
academy *n.* academia
accede *v.* acceder
accelerate *v.* acelerar

accelerator *n.* acelerador
accent *n.* acento
accentuate *v.* acentuar
accept *v.* aceptar
acceptable *adj.* aceptable
acceptance *n.* aceptación
access *n.* acceso
accessible *adj.* accesible
accession *n.* accesión
accessory *n.* accesorio
accident *n.* accidente
accidental *adj.* accidental
acclaim *v.* aclamar
acclimatise *v.t* aclimatar
accolade *n.* elogio
accommodate *v.* acomodar
accommodation *n.* acomodación
accompaniment *n.* acompañamiento
accompany *v.* acompañar
accomplice *n.* cómplice
accomplish *v.* acabar
accomplished *adj.* experto
accomplishment *n.* realización
accord *v.* acordar
accordance *n.* acuerdo
according *adv.* acordado
accordingly *adv.* por consiguiente
accost *v.* abordar
account *n.* cuenta
accountable *adj.* responsable
accountancy *n.* contabilidad
accountant *n.* contable
accoutrement *n.* guarnición
accredit *v.* acreditar
accredited *adj.* acreditado
accretion *n.* aumento
accrue *v.t.* aumentar
accumulate *v.* acumular
accumulation *n.* acumulación
accurate *adj.* acertado
accusation *n.* acusación

accuse *v.* acusar
accused *v.t.* acusado
accustom *v.* acostumbrar
accustomed *adj.* acostumbrado
ace *n.* as
acerbic *adj.* acerbo
acetate *n.* acetato
acetone *n.* acetona
ache *n.* dolor
achieve *v.* lograr
achievement *n.* logro
acid *n.* ácido
acidity *n.* acidez
acknowledge *v.* conocer
acknowledgement *n.* conocimiento
acme *n.* apogeo
acne *n.* acné
acolyte *n.* acólito
acorn *n.* bellota
acoustic *adj.* acústico
acquaint *v.* avisar
acquaintance *n.* conocimiento
acquiesce *v.* conformarse
acquiescence *n.* consentimiento
acquire *v.* adquirir
acquisition *n.* adquisición
acquit *v.* absolver
acquittal *n.* absolución
acre *n.* dolor
acrid *adj.* acre
acrimony *n.* acrimonia
acrobat *n.* acróbata
acrobatic *adj.* acrobático
across *adv.* a través
acrylic *adj.* acrílico
act *v.* acto
acting *n.* hacer teatro
acting *adj.* interino
actinium *n.* actinio
action *n.* acción
actionable *adj.* procesable

activate *v.* activar
active *adj.* activo
activist *n.* activista
activity *n.* actividad
actor *n.* actor
actress *a.* actriz
actual *adj.* actual
actually *adv.* actualmente
actuary *n.* actuario
actuate *v.* impulsar
acumen *n.* sagacidad
acupuncture *n.* acupuntura
acute *adj.* agudo
adamant *adj.* inflexible
adapt *v.* adaptar
adaptation *n.* adaptación
add *v.* añadir
addendum *n.* apéndice
addict *n.* adicto
addicted *adj.* adictivo
addiction *n.* adicción
addition *n.* adición
additional *adj.* adicional
additive *n.* aditivo
addled *adj.* aturdido
address *n.* dirección
addressee *n.* destinatario
adduce *v.* aducir
adept *adj.* adepto
adequacy *n.* suficiencia
adequate *adj.* adecuado
adhere *v.* adherir
adherence *n.* adherencia
adhesive *n.* adhesivo
adieu *n.* adiós
adjacent *adj.* adyacente
adjective *n.* adjetivo
adjoin *v.* adjuntar
adjourn *v.* aplazar
adjournment *n.* aplazamiento
adjudge *v.t.* declarar
adjudicate *v.* sentenciar

adjunct *n.* adjunto
adjust *v.* ajustar
adjustment *n.* modificación
administer *v.* administrar
administration *n.* administración
administrative *adj.* administrativo
administrator *adj.* administrador
admirable *adj.* admirable
admiral *n.* almirante
admiration *n.* admiración
admire *v.* admirar
admissible *adj.* admisible
admission *n.* admisión
admit *v.* admitir
admittance *n.* entrada
admonish *v.* amonestar
ado *n.* sin más
adobe *n.* adobe
adolescence *n.* adolescencia
adolescent *adj.* adolescente
adopt *v.* adoptar
adoption *n.* adopción
adoptive *adj.* adoptivo
adorable *adj.* adorable
adoration *n.* adoración
adore *v.t.* adorar
adorn *v.* adornar
adrift *adj.* a la deriva
adroit *adj.* hábil
adsorb *v.* absorber
adulation *n.* adulación
adult *n.* adulto
adulterate *v.* adulterar
adulteration *n.* adulteración
adultery *n.* adulterio
advance *v.* avanzar
advance *n.* avance
advancement *n.* progreso
advantage *v.t.* aventajar
advantage *n.* ventaja
advantageous *adj.* aventajado

advent *n.* advenimiento
adventure *n.* aventura
adventurous *adj.* aventurero
adverb *n.* adverbio
adversary *n.* adversario
adverse *adj.* adverso
adversity *n.* adversidad
advertise *v.* anunciar
advertisement *n.* anuncio
advice *n.* consejo
advisable *adj.* aconsejable
advise *v.* aconsejar
advocate *n.* abogado
advocate *v.* abogar por
aegis *n.* tutela
aerial *n.* antena
aeon *n.* eón
aerobatics *n.* aerobático
aerobics *n.* aerobics
aerodrome *n.* aeródromo
aeronautics *n.* aeronáutica
aeroplane *n.* avión
aerosol *n.* aerosol
aerospace *n.* aeroespacial
aesthetic *adj.* estético
aesthetics *n.* estética
afar *adv.* desde lejos
affable *adj.* afable
affair *n.* aventura
affect *v.* afectar
affectation *n.* afectación
affected *adj.* afectado
affection *n.* afecto
affectionate *adj.* afectuoso
affidavit *n.* declaración jurada
affiliate *v.* afiliar
affiliation *n.* afiliación
affinity *n.* afinidad
affirm *v.* afirmar
affirmation *n.* afirmación
affirmative *adj.* afirmativo
affix *v.t.* añadir

afflict *v.* afligir
affliction *n.* aflicción
affluence *n.* opulencia
affluent *adj.* opulento
afford *v.t.* costear
afforestation *n.* forestación
affray *n.* reyerta
affront *n.* afrenta
afield *adv.* muy lejos
aflame *adj.* encendido
afloat *adj.* a flote
afoot *adv.* algo se esta tramando
afraid *adj.* temeroso
afresh *adv.* de nuevo
african *adj.* africano
aft *adv.* en popa
after *adv.* después
after *conj.* después de que
after *prep.* después de
again *adv.* otra vez
against *prep.* en contra de
agate *n.* ágata
age *n.* edad
aged *adj.* anciano
ageism *n.* edad
ageless *adj.* siempre joven
agency *n.* agencia
agenda *n.* agenda
agent *n.* agente
agglomerate *v.* aglomerarse
aggravate *v.* agravar
aggravation *n.* agravación
aggregate *n.* conjunto
aggression *n.* agresión
aggressive *adj.* agresivo
aggressor *n.* agresor
aggrieve *v.* ofender
aghast *adj.* horrorizado
agile *adj.* ágil
agility *n.* agilidad
agitate *v.* agitar
agitation *n.* agitación

agnostic *n.* agnóstico
ago *adv.* hace
agog *adj.* ansiado
agonize *v.* agonizar
agony *n.* agonía
agrarian *adj.* agrario
agree *v.* acordar
agreeable *adj.* agradable
agreement *n.* acuerdo
agricultural *adj.* agrícola
agriculture *n.* agricultura
aground *adj.* encallado
ahead *adv.* delante de
aid *n.* ayuda
aide *n.* edecán
aids *n.* sida
ail *v.* aquejar
ailing *adj.* enfermizo
ailment *n.* achaque
aim *v.i.* apuntar
aim *n.* puntería
aimless *adj.* sin proposito
air *n.* aire
aircraft *n.* avión
airy *adj.* ventilado
aisle *n.* pasillo
ajar *adv.* entreabierto
akin *adj.* relacionado con
alacrity *n.* presteza
alarm *n* alarma
alarm *v* asustar
alas *conj.* desgraciadamente
albeit *conj.* aunque
album *n* álbum
albumen *n.* albúmina, albumen
alchemy *n.* alquimia
alcohol *n.* alcohol
alchoholic *adj.* alcohólico
alcove *n.* nicho
ale *n.* cerveza
alert *adj.* alerta
algebra *n.* algebra

alias *adv.* alias
alias *n.* alias
alibi *n.* coartada
alien *adj.* extranjero
alienate *v.i.* enajenar
alight *v.t.* ardiendo
align *v.* alinear
alignment *n.* alineación
alike *adj.* semejantes
alimony *n.* alimentos
alive *adj.* vivo
alkali *n.* álcali
all *adj.* todos, todas
allay *v.* aliviar
allegation *n.* alegación
allege *v.* afirmar
allegiance *n.* lealtad
allegory *n.* alegoría
allergen *n.* alérgeno
allergic *adj.* alérgico
allergy *n.* alergia
alleviate *v.* aliviar
alleviation *n.* alivio
alley *n.* callejuela
alliance *n.* alianza
allied *adj.* aliado
alligator *n.* caimán
alliterate *v.* aliterar
alliteration *n.* aliteración
allocate *v.* repartir
allocation *n.* reparto
allot *v.* asignar
allotment *n.* ración
allow *v.* permitir
allowance *n.* subsidio
alloy *n.* mezcla
allude *v.t.* aludir
allure *n.* encanto
alluring *adj.* seductor
allusion *n.* alusión
ally *n.* aliado
almanac *n.* almanaque

almighty *adj.* todopoderoso
almond *n.* almendra
almost *adv.* casi
alms *n.* limosna
aloft *adv.* en alto
alone *adv.* solo
along *prep.* a lo largo de
alongside *prep.* junto a
aloof *adj.* reservado
aloud *adv.* en voz alta
alpha *n.* alfa
alphabet *n.* alfabeto
alphabetical *adj.* alfabético
alpine *adj.* alpino
already *adv.* ya
also *adv.* también
altar *n.* altar
alter *v.* modificar
alteration *n.* modificación
altercation *n.* altercado
alternate *v.t.* alternarse
alternative *adj.* alternativo
although *conj.* aunque
altitude *n.* altitud
altogether *adv.* enteramente
altruism *n.* altruismo
aluminium *n.* aluminio
alumnus *n.* alumno graduado
always *adv.* siempre
amalgam *n.* amalgama
amalgamate *v.* amalgamar
amalgamation *n.* amalgamación
amass *v.* amontonar
amateur *n.* aficionado
amateurish *adj.* de aficionado
amatory *adj.* amatorio
amaze *v.* asombrar
amazement *n.* asombro
amazon *n.* amazonas
ambassador *n.* embajador
amber *n.* ámbar
ambient *adj.* ambiental

ambiguity *n.* ambigüedad
ambiguous *adj.* ambiguo
ambit *n.* ámbito
ambition *n.* ambición
ambitious *adj.* ambicioso
ambivalent *adj.* ambivalente
amble *v.* deambular
ambrosia *n.* ambrosia
ambulance *n.* ambulancia
ambush *n.* emboscada
ameliorate *v.* mejorar
amelioration *n.* mejora
amend *v.* enmendar
amendment *n.pl.* enmienda
amenable *adj.* sensible
amiable *adj.* amable
amicable *adj.* amistoso
amid *prep.* entre
amiss *adj.* equivocado
amity *n.* cordialidad
ammunition *n.* municiones
amnesia *n.* amnesia
amnesty *n.* amnistía
amok *adv.* enloquecerse
among *prep.* entre, en medio de
amoral *adj.* amoral
amorous *adj.* amoroso
amorphous *adj.* amorfo
amount *n.* cantidad
ampere *n.* amperio
ampersand *n.* signo &
amphibian *n.* anfibio
amphitheatre *n.* anfiteatro
ample *adj.* amplio
amplification *n.* amplificación
amplifier *n.* amplificador
amplify *v.* amplificar
amplitude *n.* amplitud
amulet *n.* amuleto
amuse *v.* entretener
amusement *n.* diversión
an *adj.* un, una

anachronism *n.* anacronismo
anaemia *n.* anemia
anaesthesia *n.* anestesia
anaesthetic *n.* anestésica
anal *adj.* anal
analgesic *n.* analgésico
analogous *adj.* análogo
analogue *adj.* analógico
analogy *n.* analogía
analyse *v.* analizar
analysis *n.* análisis
analyst *n.* analista
analytical *adj.* analítico
anarchism *n.* anarquismo
anarchist *n.* anarquista
anarchy *n.* anarquía
anatomy *n.* anatomía
ancestor *n.* ancestro
ancestral *adj.* ancestral
ancestry *n.* ancestro
anchor *n.* ancla
anchorage *n.* anclaje
ancient *adj.* antiguo
ancillary *adj.* auxiliar
and *conj.* y
android *n.* androide
anecdote *n.* anécdota
anew *adv.* de nuevo
angel *n.* angel
anger *n.* rabia
angina *n.* angina
angle *n.* ángulo
angry *adj.* enfadado
anguish *n.* angustia
angular *adj.* angular
animal *n.* animal
animate *v.* animar
animated *adj.* animado
animation *n.* animación
animosity *n.* animosidad
aniseed *n.* anís
ankle *n.* tobillo

anklet *n.* cadenita para el tobillo
annals *n.* anales
annex *v.* anexo
annexation *n.* anexión
annihilate *v.* aniquilar
annihilation *n.* aniquilación
anniversary *n.* aniversario
annotate *v.* anotar
announce *v.* anunciar
announcement *n.* comunicado
annoy *v.* molestar
annoyance *n.* enojo
annual *adj.* anual
annuity *n.* renta
annul *v.* anular
anode *n.* ánodo
anoint *v.* untar
anomalous *adj.* anómalo
anomaly *n.* anomalía
anonymity *n.* anonimato
anonymous *adj.* anónimo
anorexia *n.* anorexia
another *adj.* otro
answer *n.* respuesta
answerable *adj.* responsable
ant *n.* hormiga
antacid *adj.* antiácido
antagonism *n.* antagonismo
antagonist *n.* antagonista
antagonize *v.* enemistarse con
antarctic *adj.* Antártico
antecedent *n.* antecedente
antedate *v.* anteceder
antelope *n.* antílope
antenna *n.* antena
anthem *n.* himno nacional
anthology *n.* antología
anthropology *n.* antropología
anthrax *n.* ántrax
anti *n.* anti
antibiotic *n.* antibiótico
antibody *n.* anticuerpo

antic *n.* bufonerías
anticipate *v.* anticipar
anticipation *n.* anticipación
anticlimax *n.* decepción
antidote *n.* antídoto
antioxidant *n.* antioxidante
antipathy *n.* antipatía
antiperspirant *n.* antiperspirante
antiquarian *adj.* anticuario
antiquated *adj.* anticuado
antique *n.* antigüedad
antiquity *n.* antigüedad
antiseptic *adj.* antiséptico
antisocial *adj.* antisocial
antithesis *n.* antítesis
antler *n.* cuerno
antonym *n.* antónimo
anus *n.* ano
anvil *n.* yunque
anxiety *n.* ansiedad
anxious *adj.* inquieto
any *adj.* algún, algunos, algunas
anyhow *adv.* de cualquier manera
anyone *pron.* alguien
anything *pron.* algo,alguna cosa
anywhere *adv.* en cualquier sitio
apace *adv.* rápidamente
apart *adv.* aparte
apartheid *n.* apartheid
apartment *n.* apartamento
apathy *n.* apatía
ape *n.* mono
aperture *n.* abertura
apex *n* ápice
aphorism *n.* aforismo
apiary *n.* colmenar
aplomb *n.* aplomo
apocalypse *n.* apocalipsis
apologize *v.* disculparse
apology *n.* disculpa
apoplectic *adj.* apoplético

apostate *n.* apóstata
apostle *n.* apóstol
apostrophe *n.* apostrofe
appal *v.* horrorizar
apparatus *n.* aparato
apparel *n.* atavío
apparent *adj.* aparente
appeal *v.t.* apelar
appear *v.* aparecer
appearance *n.* aparición
appease *v.* apaciguar
append *v.* añadir
appendage *n.* añadidura
appendicitis *n.* apendicitis
appendix *n.* apéndice
appetite *n.* apetito
appetizer *n.* aperitivo
applaud *v.* aplaudir
applause *n.* aplauso
apple *n.* manzana
appliance *n.* aparato
applicable *adj.* aplicable
applicant *n.* candidato
application *n.* aplicación
apply *v.t.* presentarse a
appoint *v.* nombrar
appointment *n.* nombramiento
apportion *v.t.* repartir
apposite *adj.* oportuno
appraise *v.* evaluar
appreciable *adj.* sensible
appreciate *v.* apreciar
appreciation *n.* apreciación
apprehend *v.* percibir
apprehension *n.* aprensión
apprehensive *adj.* aprensivo
apprentice *n.* aprendiz
apprise *v.* informar
approach *v.* acercarse
appropriate *adj.* apropiado
appropriation *n.* apropiación
approval *n.* aprobación

approve *v.* aprobar
approximate *adj.* aproximado
apricot *n.* albaricoque
apron *n.* delantal
apt *adj.* acertado
aptitude *n.* aptitud
aquarium *n.* acuario
aquatic *adj.* acuático
aqueous *adj.* acuoso
Arab *n.* Árabe
Arabian *n.* Arábigo
Arabic *n.* Arábico
arable *adj.* cultivable
arbiter *n.* árbitro
arbitrary *adj.* arbitrario
arbitrate *v.* arbitrar
arbitration *n.* arbitraje
arbitrator *n.* árbitro
arbour *n.* cenador
arc *n.* arco
arcade *n.* arcada
arch *n.* arco
archaeology *n.* arqueología
archaic *adj.* arcaico
archangel *n.* arcángel
archbishop *n.* arzobispo
archer *n.* arquero
architect *n.* arquitecto
architecture *n.* arquitectura
archives *n.* archivos
Arctic *adj.* Ártico
ardent *adj.* ardiente
ardour *n.* ardor
arduous *adj.* peligroso
area *n.* área
arena *n.* ruedo
argue *v.* discutir
argument *n.* argumento
argumentative *adj.* argumentativo
arid *adj.* árido
arise *v.* surgir

aristocracy *n.* aristocracia
aristocrat *n.* aristócrata
arithmetic *n.* aritmética
arithmetical *adj.* aritmético
ark *n.* arca
arm *n.* brazo
armada *n.* armada
Armageddon *n.* Armagedón
armament *n.* armamento
armistice *n.* armisticio
armour *n.* armadura
armoury *n.* armería
army *n.* ejército
aroma *n.* aroma
aromatherapy *n.* aromaterapia
around *adv.* alrededor
arouse *v.* suscitar, excitar
arrange *v.* arreglar
arrangement *n.* arreglo, plan
arrant *adj.* redomado
array *n.* selección
arrears *n.* atrasos
arrest *v.* arrestar
arrival *n.* llegada
arrive *v.* llegar
arrogance *n.* arrogancia
arrogant *adj.* arrogante
arrogate *v.* atribuirse
arrow *n.* flecha
arsenal *n.* arsenal
arsenic *n.* arsénico
arson *n.* incendio provocado
art *n.* arte
artefact *n.* artefacto
artery *n.* arteria
artful *adj.* taimado
arthritis *n.* artritis
artichoke *n.* alcachofa
article *n.* artículo
articulate *adj.* articulado
artifice *n.* artificio
artificial *adj.* artificial

artillery *n.* artillería
artisan *n.* artesano
artist *n.* artista
artistic *adj.* artístico
artless *adj.* tosco
as *adv.* como
asbestos *n.* asbesto
ascend *v.* ascender
ascendant *adj.* ascendente
ascent *n.* ascenso
ascertain *v.* determinar
ascetic *adj.* ascético
ascribe *v.* atribuir
aseptic *adj.* aséptico
asexual *adj.* asexual
ash *n.* ceniza
ashamed *adj.* avergonzado
ashore *adv.* en tierra
Asian *adj.* asiático
aside *adv.* a un lado
asinine *adj.* necio
ask *v.* preguntar
askance *adv.* con desconfianza
askew *adv.* de forma retorcida
asleep *adj.* dormido
asparagus *n.* esparrago
aspect *n.* aspecto
asperity *n.* aspereza
aspersions *n.* en entredicho
asphyxiate *v.* asfixiar
aspirant *n.* aspirante
aspiration *n.* aspiración
aspire *v.* aspirar
ass *n.* asno,idiota, culo
assail *v.* atacar
assassin *n.* asesino
assassinate *v.* asesinar
assassination *n.* asesinato
assault *n.* asalto
assemblage *n.* ensamblaje
assemble *v.* ensamblar
assembly *n.* asamblea, montaje

assent *n.* asentimiento
assert *v.* afirmar
assess *v.* calcular
assessment *n.* evaluación
asset *n.* recurso, activo
assiduous *adj.* asiduo
assign *v.* asignar
assignation *n.* asignación
assignment *n.* misión, tarea
assimilate *v.* asimilar
assimilation *n.* asimilación
assist *v.* asistir
assistance *n.* asistencia
assistant *n.* asistente
associate *v.* asociarse
association *n.* asociación
assonance *n.* asonancia
assorted *adj.* surtido
assortment *n.* selección
assuage *v.* saciar
assume *v.* asumir
assumption *n.* suposición
assurance *n.* seguridad, garantía
assure *v.* asegurar
assured *adj.* seguro
asterisk *n.* asterisco
asteroid *n.* asteroide
asthma *n.* asma
astigmatism *n.* astigmatismo
astonish *v.* asombrar
astonishment *n.* asombro
astound *v.* sorprender
astral *adj.* astral
astray *adv.* extraviarse
astride *prep.* a horcajadas en
astrologer *n.* astrologo
astrology *n.* astrológica
astronaut *n.* astronauta
astronomer *n.* astrónomo
astronomy *n.* astronomía
astute *adj.* astuto
asunder *adv.* por separado

asylum *n.* asilo
at *prep.* en
atavistic *adj.* atávico
atheism *n.* ateísmo
atheist *n.* ateo
athlete *n.* atleta
athletic *adj.* atlético
atlas *n.* atlas
atmosphere *n.* atmosfera
atoll *n.* atolón
atom *n.* átomo
atomic *adj.* atómico
atone *v.* expiar
atonement *n.* expiación
atrium *n.* atrio
atrocious *adj.* atroz
atrocity *n.* atrocidad
attach *v.* atar, adjuntar
attache *n.* agregado
attachment *n.* accesorio, apego
attack *v.* atacar
attain *v.* alcanzar
attainment *n.* logro
attempt *v.* intentar
attempt *n.* intento
attend *v.* atender
attendance *n.* asistencia
attendant *n.* encargado
attention *n.* atención
attentive *adj.* atento
attest *v.* atestiguar
attic *n.* ático
attire *n.* atuendo
attitude *n.* actitud
attorney *n.* abogado
attract *v.* atraer
attraction *n.* atracción
attractive *adj.* atractivo
attribute *v.* atribuir
aubergine *n.* berenjena
auction *n.* subasta
audible *adj.* audible

audience *n.* audiencia
audio *n.* audio
audit *n.* auditoría
audition *n.* audición
auditorium *n.* auditorio
augment *v.* aumentar
August *n* Agosto
aunt *n.* tía
aura *n.* aura
auspicious *adj.* propicio
austere *adj.* austero
Australian *n.* Australiano
authentic *adj.* autentico
authenticity *n.* autenticidad
author *n.* autor
authoritative *adj.* autoritario
authority *n.* autoridad
authorize *v.* autorizar
autism *n.* autismo
autobiography *n.* autobiografía
autocracy *n.* autocracia
autocrat *n.* autócrata
autocratic *adj.* autocrático
autograph *n.* autógrafo
automatic *adj.* automático
automobile *n.* automóvil
autonomous *adj.* autónomo
autopsy *n.* autopsia
autumn *n.* otoño
auxiliary *adj.* auxiliar
avail *v.* aprovechar
available *adj.* disponible
avalanche *n.* avalancha
avarice *n.* avaricia
avenge *v.* vengar
avenue *n.* avenida
average *n.* promedio
averse *adj.* contrario
aversion *n.* aversión
avert *v.* apartar
aviary *n.* aviario
aviation *n.* aviación

aviator *n.* aviador
avid *adj.* ávido
avidly *adv.* ávidamente
avocado *n.* aguacate
avoid *v.* evitar
avoidance *n.* evitación
avow *v.* confesar
avuncular *adj.* paternal
await *v.* esperar
awake *v.* despertar
awaken *v.* despertarse
award *v.* premiar
aware *adj.* informado
away *adv.* lejos
awe *n.* sobrecogimiento
awesome *adj.* formidable
awful *adj.* espantoso
awhile *adv.* un rato
awkward *adj.* torpe
awry *adv.* mal
axe *n.* hacha
axis *n.* eje
axle *n.* eje

B

babble *v.* barbullar
babe *n.* criatura, nena
babel *n.* babel
baboon *n.* mandril
baby *n.* bebe
bachelor *n.* soltero
back *n.* espalda, reverso
backbone *n.* columna vertebral
backdate *v.* fecha atrasada
backdrop *n.* trasfondo
backfire *v.* fallar, salir al revés
background *n.* fondo, antecedentes

backhand *n.* revés
backing *n.* apoyo
backlash *n.* reacción
backlog *n.* atrasos
backpack *n.* mochila
backside *n.* trasero, culo
backstage *adv.* entre bastidores
backtrack *v.* retroceder
backward *adj.* atrasado
backwater *n.* lugar apartado
bacon *n.* bacón
bacteria *n.* bacteria
bad *adj.* malo
badge *n.* insignia, chapa
badly *adv.* mal
badminton *n.* bádminton
baffle *v.* desconcertar
bag *n.* balsa
baggage *n.* equipaje
baggy *adj.* holgado
baguette *n.* barra de pan
bail *n.* fianza
bailiff *n.* alguacil
bait *n.* cebo
bake *v.* hornear
baker *n.* panadero
bakery *n.* panadería
balance *n.* equilibrio
balcony *n.* balcón
bald *adj.* calvo
bale *n.* fardo
ball *n.* pelota
ballad *n.* balada
ballet *n.* ballet
balloon *n.* globo
ballot *n.* votación
balm *n.* bálsamo
balsam *n.* bálsamo
bamboo *n.* bambú
ban *v.* prohibir
banal *adj.* banal
banana *n.* plátano

band *n.* banda, tira
bandage *n.* vendaje
bandit *n.* bandido
bane *n.* pesadilla, ruina
bang *n.* estallido
banger *n.* chatarra
bangle *n.* brazalete
banish *v.* desterrar
banishment *n.* destierro
banisters *n.* pasamanos
banjo *n.* banjo
bank *n.* banco
banker *n.* banquero
bankrupt *adj.* quebrado
bankruptcy *n.* bancarrota
banner *n.* pancarta
banquet *n.* banquete
banter *n.* bromas
baptism *n.* bautismo
baptist *n.* bautista
baptize *v.* bautizar
bar *n.* bar
barb *n.* lengüeta, púa
barbarian *n.* bárbaro
barbaric *adj.* bárbaro
barbecue *n.* barbacoa
barbed *adj.* mordaz
barber *n.* barbero
bard *n.* bardo
bare *adj.* desnudo, descubierto
barely *adv.* apenas
bargain *n.* pacto, negocio, ganga
barge *n.* barcaza
bark *n.* corteza
barley *n.* cebada
barn *n.* granero
barometer *n.* barómetro
baron *n.* barón
barrack *n.* cuartel
barracuda *n.* barracuda
barrage *n.* descarga, bombardeo
barrel *n.* barril, tonel

barren *adj.* árido
barricade *n.* barricada
barrier *n.* barrera
barring *prep.* excepto, salvo
barrister *n.* abogado
barter *v.* cambiar, trocar
base *n.* base
baseless *adj.* infundado
basement *n.* sótano
bashful *adj.* tímido
basic *n.* básico
basil *n.* albahaca
basilica *n.* basílica
basin *n.* cuenco, palangana
basis *n.* base
bask *v.* disfrutar
basket *n.* cesta, cesto
bass *n.* contrabajo
bastard *n.* bastardo, cabrón
baste *v.* pringar
bastion *n.* baluarte
bat *n.* murciélago, palo
batch *n.* hornada, lote
bath *n.* baño
bathe *v.* bañarse
bathos *n.* trivialidad
batik *n.* batik
baton *n.* batuta
battalion *n.* batallón
batten *n.* sable
batter *n.* bateador
battery *n.* pila
battle *n.* batalla
bauble *n.* bola de navidad
baulk *v.* negarse
bawl *v.* chillar
bay *n.* bahía
bayonet *n.* bayoneta
bazaar *n.* bazar
bazooka *n.* bazuca
be *v.* ser, estar
beach *n.* playa

beacon *n.* faro
bead *n.* cuenta
beady *adj.* malvado
beagle *n.* Beagle
beak *n.* pico
beaker *n.* jarra
beam *n.* viga
bean *n.* judía
bear *v.t* aguantar
bear *n.* oso
beard *n.* barba
bearing *n.* dirección, relevancia, comportamiento
beast *n.* bestia
beastly *adj.* bestial
beat *v.* golpear
beautician *n.* esteticista
beautiful *adj.* guapo, bello
beautify *v.* embellecer
beatitude *n.* beatitud
beauty *n.* belleza
beaver *n.* castor
becalmed *adj.* inmóvil
because *conj.* porque
beck *n.* disposición, arroyo
beckon *v.* hacer señas
become *v.* convertirse
bed *n.* cama
bedding *n.* ropa de cama
bedlam *n.* confusión, manicomio, belén
bedraggled *adj.* desaliñado
bee *n.* abeja
beech *n.* haya
beef *n.* ternera
beefy *adj.* fornido
beep *n.* pitido
beer *n.* cerveza
beet *n.* remolacha
beetle *n.* escarabajo
beetroot *n.* remolacha
befall *v.* suceder

befit *v.* convenir
before *adv.* antes, anteriormente
beforehand *adv.* ancipadamente
befriend *v.* favorecer
befuddled *adj.* aturdido
beg *v.* rogar
beget *v.* engendrar
beggar *n.* mendigo
begin *v.* empezar, comenzar
beginning *n.* principio
beguile *v.* engañar
behalf *n.* beneficio
behave *v.* comportarse
behaviour *n.* comportamiento
behead *v.* decapitar
behemoth *n.* gigante, monstruo
behest *n.* petición
behind *prep.* detrás
behold *v.* mirar, contemplar
beholden *adj.* deudor
beige *n.* beis
being *n.* existencia
belabour *v.* apalear
belated *adj.* retrasado, tardío
belay *v.* amarrar
belch *v.* eructar
beleaguered *adj.* asediado
belie *v.* desmentir
belief *n.* creencia
believe *v.* creer
belittle *v.* empequeñecer
bell *n.* campana, timbre
belle *n.* belleza
bellicose *adj.* belicoso
belligerent *adj.* beligerante
bellow *v.* bramar
bellows *n.* fuelle
belly *n.* vientre
belong *v.* pertenecer
belongings *n.* pertenencias
beloved *adj.* amado
below *prep.* debajo

belt *n.* cinturón
bemoan *v.* lamentar
bemused *adj.* desconcertado
bench *n.* banco
bend *v.* doblar
beneath *adv.* abajo, debajo
benediction *n.* bendición
benefactor *n.* benefactor
benefice *n.* beneficio
beneficent *adj.* benéfico
beneficial *adj.* beneficioso
benefit *n.* beneficio
benevolence *n.* benevolencia
benevolent *adj* benévolo
benign *adj.* benigno
bent *adj.* encorvado
bequeath *v.* legar algo a alguien
bequest *n.* legado
berate *v.* reprender
bereaved *v.* desposeer
bereavement *n.* privación
bereft *adj.* privado de, desprovisto
bergamot *n.* bergamota
berk *n.* imbécil
berry *n.* baya
berserk *adj.* frenético
berth *n.* amarradero
beseech *v.* suplicar
beset *v.* asediar
beside *prep.* al lado de
besiege *v.* sitiar
besmirch *v.* manchar
besom *n.* escoba hecha de ramas
besotted *adj.* perdidamente en-
  amorado
bespoke *adj.* hecho de encargo
best *adj.* mejor
bestial *adj.* bestial
bestow *v.* conferir
bestride *v.* montar a horcajadas
bet *v.* apostar

betake *v.* recurrir
betray *v.* traicionar
betrayal *n.* traición
better *adj.* mejor
between *adv.* entre
bevel *n.* bisel
beverage *n.* refresco
bevy *n.* grupo, bandada
bewail *v.* lamentar
beware *v.* tener cuidado
bewilder *v.t* desconcertar
bewitch *v.* hechizar
beyond *adv.* más allá
bi *comb.* bi-
biannual *adj.* semestral, dos
  veces al año
bias *n.* sesgo
biased *adj.* sesgado, parcial
bib *n.* babero
Bible *n.* biblia
bibliography *n.* bibliografía
bibliophile *n.* bibliófilo
bicentenary *n.* bicentenario
biceps *n.* bíceps
bicker *v.* pelear, discutir
bicycle *n.* bicicleta
bid *v.* ofertar
biddable *adj.* dócil
bidder *n.* postor
bide *v.* aguardar
bidet *n.* bidé
biennial *adj.* bienal
bier *n.* féretro
bifocal *adj.* bifocal
big *adj.* grande
bigamy *n.* bigamia
bigot *n.* intolerante, fanático
bigotry *n.* intolerancia, fanatismo
bike *n.* moto, bici
bikini *n.* bikini
bilateral *adj.* bilateral
bile *n.* bilis

bilingual *adj.* bilingüe
bill *n.* cuenta
billet *n.* alojamiento
billiards *n.* billar
billion *n.* billón
billionaire *n.* multimillonario
billow *v.* hincharse
bin *n.* cubo
binary *adj.* binario
bind *v.* atar, amarrar
binding *n.* tapa, cubierta, fijación
binge *n.* juerga
binocular *adj.* binocular
biochemistry *n.* bioquímica
biodegradable *adj.* biodegradable
biodiversity *n.* biodiversidad
biography *n.* biografía
biologist *n.* biólogo
biology *n.* biología
biopsy *n.* biopsia
bipartisan *adj.* de dos partidos
birch *n.* abedul
bird *n.* pájaro
bird flu *n.* gripe aviar
birth *n.* nacimiento
biscuit *n.* galleta
bisect *v.* bisecar
bisexual *adj.* bisexual
bishop *n.* obispo
bison *n.* bisonte
bit *n.* bit, trozo
bitch *n.* perra, bruja, puta
bite *v.* morder, picar
biting *adj.* cortante
bitter *adj.* amargo
bizarre *adj.* extraño, singular
blab *v.* descubrir
black *adj.* negro
blackberry *n.* mora
blackboard *n.* pizarra
blacken *v.* ennegrecer
blacklist *n.* lista negra

blackmail *n.* chantaje
blackout *n.* desvanecimiento, desmayo
blacksmith *n.* herrero
bladder *n.* vejiga
blade *n.* hoja, cuchilla
blain *n.* ampolla, llaga
blame *v.* echar la culpa, culpar
blanch *v.* blanquear
bland *adj.* soso, insulso
blank *adj.* liso, virgen, pedido, de fogueo
blanket *n.* manta
blare *v.* atronar
blarney *n.* labia, paparruchas
blast *n.* ráfaga, chorro, explosión
blatant *adj.* descarado, ostensible
blaze *n.* llamarada, fogata, fuego, resplandor
blazer *n.* chaqueta
bleach *adj.* blanquear
bleak *adj.* inhóspito, sombrío, miserable
bleat *v. i* balar, quejarse
bleed *v.* sangrar
bleep *n.* pitido
blemish *n.* imperfección, marca
blench *v.* recular
blend *v. t* mezclar
blender *n.* licuadora
bless *v.* bendecir
blessed *adj.* bendecido
blessing *n.* bendición
blight *n.* tizón, plaga
blind *adj.* ciego
blindfold *v.* vendar los ojos
blindness *n.* ceguera
blink *v.* parpadear, pestañear
blinkers *n.* anteojeras
blip *n.* pitidito, señal luminosa, accidente
bliss *n.* dicha, felicidad

blister *n.* ampolla
blithe *adj.* despreocupado
blitz *n.* bombardeo aéreo
blizzard *n.* ventisca
bloat *v.* hinchar
bloater *n.* arenque ahumado, distensión abdominal
blob *n.* gota, mancha
bloc *n.* bloque
block *n.* bloque
blockade *n.* bloqueo
blockage *n.* obstrucción
blog *n.* blog
bloke *n.* tío
blonde *adj.* rubio
blood *n.* sangre
bloodshed *n.* derramamiento de sangre
bloody *adj.* ensangrentado, puñetero
bloom *v.* florecer
bloomers *n.* bombachos
blossom *n.* flor
blot *n.* borrón, mancha de tinta
blotch *n.* erupción
blouse *n.* blusa
blow *v.* soplar
blowzy *adj.* desaliñado
blub *v.* lloriquear
bludgeon *n.* porra
blue *adj.* azul
bluff *v.* engañar
blunder *n.* error garrafal
blunt *adj.* desafilado
blur *v.* desdibujar
blurb *n.* propaganda
blurt *v.* espetar o soltar algo
blush *v.* ruborizarse
blusher *n.* colorete
bluster *v.* bravuconear
boar *n.* cerdo macho, jabalí
board *n.* tabla, tablero, tribunal

boast *v.* presumir
boat *n.* barco
bob *v.* agitar, sacudir
bobble *n.* pompón
bode *v.* presagiar
bodice *n.* corpiño
bodily *adv.* enteramente
body *n.* cuerpo
bodyguard *n* guardaespaldas
bog *n.* ciénaga
bogey *n.* cuco, moco, bogey (golf)
boggle *v.* quedarse atónito
bogus *adj.* falso
boil *v.i.* hervir
boiler *n.* caldera
boisterous *adj.* bullicioso
bold *adj.* atrevido
boldness *n.* atrevimiento
bole *n.* tronco
bollard *n.* bolardo
bolt *n.* tornillo
bomb *n.* bomba
bombard *v.* bombardear
bombardment *n.* bombardeo
bomber *n.* bombardero, terrorista
bonafide *adj.* genuino
bonanza *n.* bonanza, mina
bond *n.* lazo, vinculo
bondage *n.* cautiverio
bone *n.* hueso
bonfire *n.* hoguera
bonnet *n.* capota, sombrero
bonus *n.* prima, bono, bonifi-cación
bony *adj.* huesudo
book *n.* libro
booklet *n.* folleto
bookmark *n.* marcador
bookseller *n.* librero
bookish *adj.* libresc

boom *n.* boom
boon *n.* gran ayuda
boor *n.* zafio
boost *v.* estimular, fomentar, impulsar, potenciar
booster *n.* repetidor
boot *n.* bota
booth *n.* cabina, taquilla
bootleg *adj.* de contrabando, pirata
booty *n.* botín
border *n.* frontera
bore *v.* agujerear
born *adj.* nato
borough *n.* municipio
borrow *v.* prestar
bosom *n.* seno
boss *n.* jefe
bossy *adj.* mandón
botany *n.* botánica
both *adj. & pron.* ambos
bother *v.* molestar
bottle *n.* botella
bottom *n.* fondo, trasero
bough *n.* rama
boulder *n.* roca
boulevard *n.* bulevar
bounce *v.* lanzar, botar
bouncer *n.* gorila, bouncer
bound *v.* saltar
boundary *n.* limite
boundless *adj.* ilimitado
bountiful *adj.* abundante
bounty *n.* generosidad
bouquet *n.* ramo
bout *n.* tanda, ronda
boutique *n.* boutique
bow *n.* reverencia, arco
bow *v.* arquear
bowel *n.* intestino
bower *n.* enramada
bowl *n.* bol

box *n.* caja
boxer *n.* boxeador
boxing *n* boxeo
boy *n.* niño
boycott *v.* boicotear
boyhood *n* niñez
bra *n.* sujetador
brace *n.* abrazadera
bracelet *n.* pulsera
bracket *n.* paréntesis
brag *v.* alardear
braille *n.* braille
brain *n.* cerebro
brake *n.* freno
branch *n.* rama, sucursal
brand *n.* marca
brandish *v.* blandir
brandy *n.* brandy, coñac
brash *adj.* desenvuelto
brass *n.* latón
brave *adj.* valiente
bravery *n.* valentía
brawl *n.* pelea
bray *v.* rebuznar
breach *v.* infringir, violar
bread *n.* pan
breadth *n.* anchura
break *v.* romper
breakage *n.* rotura
breakfast *n.* desayuno
breast *n.* pecho
breath *n.* respiro
breathe *v.* respirar
breech *n.* recámara
breeches *n.* bombachos
breed *v.* criar
breeze *n.* brisa
brevity *n.* brevedad
brew *v.* preparar, hacer
brewery *n.* cervecería, fabrica de cerveza
bribe *v. t.* sobornar

brick *n.* ladrillo
bridal *adj.* nupcial
bride *n.* novia
bridegroom *n.* novio
bridge *n.* puente
bridle *n.* brida
brief *adj.* breve
briefing *n.* instrucciones
brigade *n.* brigada
brigadier *n.* brigadier
bright *adj.* brillante
brighten *v.* alegrar, iluminar
brilliance *n.* brillantez
brilliant *adj.* brillante
brim *n.* ala, borde
brindle *adj.* atigrado, pinto
brine *n.* salmuera
bring *v.* traer, llevar
brink *n.* borde
brisk *adj.* rápido, enérgico
bristle *n.* cerda
British *adj.* británico
brittle *adj.* quebradizo
broach *v.* mencionar
broad *adj.* amplio
broadcast *v. t* emitir
brocade *n.* brocado
broccoli *n.* brócoli
brochure *n.* folleto
broke *adj.* pelado
broken *adj.* roto
broker *n.* correrdor,agente
bronchial *adj.* bronquial
bronze *n.* bronce
brood *n.* nidada, camada
brook *n.* arroyo
broom *n.* escoba
broth *n.* caldo
brothel *n.* burdel
brother *n.* hermano
brotherhood *n.* fraternidad,
hermandad

brow *n.* ceja
brown *n.* marrón
browse *v.* mirar
browser *n.* navegador, explorador
bruise *n.* cardenal
brunch *n.* almuerzo
brunette *n.* morena
brunt *n.* choque
brush *n.* cepillo
brusque *adj.* brusco
brutal *adj.* brutal
brute *n.* bestia, bruto
bubble *n.* pompa, burbuja
buck *n.* ciervo
bucket *n.* cubo
buckle *n.* hebilla
bud *n.* brote
budge *v.* moverse
budget *n.* presupuesto
buffalo *n.* búfalo
buffer *n.* parachoques
buffet *n.* buffet
buffoon *n.* bufón
bug *n.* bicho
buggy *n.* calesa, sillita de paseo
bugle *n.* clarín
build *v.* construir
building *n.* edificio
bulb *n.* bulbo
bulge *n.* bulto
bulimia *n.* bulimia
bulk *n.* bulto, volumen
bulky *adj.* voluminoso
bull *n.* toro
bulldog *n.* bulldog
bullet *n.* bala
bulletin *n.* boletín
bullion *n.* lingotes de plata u oro
bullish *adj.* optimista
bullock *n.* buey
bully *n.* matón
bulwark *n.* baluarte

bum *n.* vago, trasero, vagabundo
bumble *v.* trastabillar
bump *n.* chichón, golpe
bumper *n.* parachoques
bumpkin *n.* campesino
bumpy *adj.* desigual
bun *n.* bollo
bunch *n.* manojo, grupo
bundle *n.* lio, paquete
bung *n.* tapón
bungalow *n.* bungalow
bungle *v.* echar a perder
bunk *n.* litera
bunker *n.* búnker
buoy *n.* boya
buoyant *adj.* flotante
buoyancy *n.* flotabilidad
burble *v.* borbotear
burden *n.* carga
bureau *n.* agencia
bureaucracy *n.* burocracia
bureaucrat *n.* burócrata
burgeon *v.* prosperar
burger *n.* hamburguesa
burglar *n.* ladrón
burglary *n.* robo
burial *n.* entierro
burlesque *n.* parodia
burn *v.* quemar
burner *n.* quemador
burning *adj.* ardiente
burrow *n.* madriguera
bursar *n.* tesorero
bursary *n.* tesorería
burst *v.* estallar, explotar
bury *v.* enterrar
bus *n.* autobús
bush *n.* arbusto
bushy *adj.* espeso, poblado
business *n.* negocios
businessman *n.* hombre de
  negocios

bust *n.* busto
bustle *v.* bullir
busy *adj.* ocupado,
but *conj.* pero
butcher *n.* carnicero
butler *n.* mayordomo
butter *n.* mantequilla
butterfly *n.* mariposa
buttock *n.* nalga
button *n.* botón
buy *v.* comprar
buyer *n.* comprador
buzz *n.* zumbido, rumor
buzzard *n.* águila ratonera
buzzer *n.* timbre, chicharra
by *prep.* por, de, según
bygone *adj.* pasado
byline *n.* línea de meta
bypass *n.* circunvalación
byre *n.* establo
bystander *n.* transeúnte
byte *n.* byte

C

cab *n.* taxi
cabaret *n.* cabaret
cabbage *n.* col
cabin *n.* camarote
cabinet *n.* armario, vitrina
cable *n.* cable
cacao *n.* cacao
cache *n.* alijo
cachet *n.* distinción
cackle *n.* cacareo
cactus *n.* cactus
cad *n.* bellaco
cadaver *n.* cadáver
caddy *n.* carrito, cajita, caddie

cadet *n.* cadete
cadmium *n.* cadmio
cadre *n.* cuadro
caeserean *n.* cesárea
cafe *n.* café
cafeteria *n.* cafetería
cage *n.* jaula
cahoots *n.* acuerdo, arreglo
cajole *v.* engatusar
cake *n.* pastel
calamity *n.* calamidad
calcium *n.* calcio
calculate *v.* calcular
calculator *n.* calculadora
calculation *n.* cálculo
calendar *n.* calendario
calf *n.* becerro, pantorrilla
calibrate *v.* calibrar
calibre *n.* calibre
call *v.* llamar
calligraphy *n.* caligrafía
calling *n.* vocación
callous *adj.* insensible
callow *adj.* inmaduro
calm *adj.* calmado
calorie *n.* caloría
calumny *n.* calumnia
camaraderie *n.* camaradería
camber *n.* peralte
cambric *n.* batista
camcorder *n.* videocámara
camel *n.* camello
cameo *n.* cameo
camera *n.* cámara
camp *n.* campamento
campaign *n.* campaña
camphor *n.* alcanfor
campus *n.* campus
can *n.* lata, bote, tarro
can *v.* poder
canal *n.* canal
canard *n.* bulo

cancel *v.* cancelar
cancellation *n.* cancelación
cancer *n.* cáncer
candela *n.* candela
candid *adj.* franco
candidate *n.* candidato
candle *n.* vela
candour *n.* franqueza
candy *n.* golosina
cane *n.* caña
canine *adj.* canino
canister *n.* lata, bote
cannabis *n.* cannabis
cannibal *n.* caníbal
cannon *n.* cañón
canny *adj.* astuto
canoe *n.* canoa
canon *n.* canon
canopy *n.* dosel
cant *n.* hipocresía
cantankerous *adj.* atravesado
canteen *n.* cantina
canter *n.* medio galope
canton *n.* cantón
cantonment *n.* acantonamiento
canvas *n.* lona
canvass *v.* solicitar votos
canyon *n.* cañón
cap *n.* gorra
capability *n.* capacidad, competencia
capable *adj.* competente
capacious *adj.* capaz, amplio
capacitor *n.* condensador
capacity *n.* capacidad
caparison *v.* engualdrapar
cape *n.* capa
capital *n.* capital
capitalism *n.* capitalismo
capitalist *n. &adj.* capitalista
capitalize *v.* capitalizar
capitation *n.* capitulación

capitulate *v.* capitular
caprice *n.* capricho
capricious *adj.* caprichoso
capsicum *n.* pimentón
capsize *v.* volcar
capstan *n.* cabrestante
capsule *n.* capsula
captain *n.* capitán
captaincy *n.* capitanía
caption *n.* leyenda, pie de letra, título
captivate *v.* cautivar
captive *n.* cautivo
captivity *n.* cautividad
captor *n.* captor
capture *v.* capturar
car *n.* coche
caramel *n.* caramelo
carat *n.* quilate
caravan *n.* caravana
carbohydrate *n.* carbohidrato, hidrato de carbono
carbon *n.* carbono
carbonated *adj.* carbonatado, gaseoso
carboy *n.* garrafón
carcass *n.* armazón, esqueleto, carcasa
card *n.* tarjeta
cardamom *n.* cardamomo
cardboard *n.* cartón
cardiac *adj.* cardíaco
cardigan *n.* rebeca
cardinal *n.* cardenal
cardiograph *n.* cardiógrafo
cardiology *n.* cardiología
care *n.* cuidado
career *n.* carrera
carefree *adj.* despreocupado
careful *adj.* cuidadoso
careless *adj.* descuidado
carer *n.* cuidador

caress *v.* acariciar
caretaker *n.* conserje
cargo *n.* cargamento
caricature *n* caricatura
carmine *n.* carmín
carnage *n.* carnicería, matanza
carnal *adj.* carnal
carnival *n.* carnaval
carnivore *n.* carnívoro
carol *n.* villancico
carpal *adj.* carpiano
carpenter *n.* carpintero
carpentry *n.* carpintería
carpet *n.* moqueta
carriage *n.* carruaje
carrier *n.* transportista
carrot *n.* zanahoria
carry *v.* llevar, traer
cart *n.* carreta
cartel *n.* cartel
cartilage *n.* cartílago
carton *n.* envase de cartón
cartoon *n.* dibujo animado
cartridge *n.* cartucho
carve *v.* esculpir
carvery *n.* asador
casanova *n.* casanova
cascade *n.* cascada
case *n.* caso
casement *n.* marco de la ventana, cubierta
cash *n.* efectivo, metálico
cashew *n.* anacardo
cashier *n.* cajero
cashmere *n.* cachemir
casing *n.* cubierta
casino *n.* casino
cask *n.* barril
casket *n.* cofre
casserole *n.* cazuela
cassock *n.* sotana, túnica
cast *v.* tirar, vaciar, repartir

castaway *n.* náufrago
caste *n.* casta
castigate *v.* castigar
casting *n.* reparto, vaciado
castle *n.* castillo
castor *n.* ruedecilla
castrate *v.* castrar
castor oil *a.* aceite de ricino
casual *adj.* despreocupado, deportivo
casualty *n.* casualidad
cat *n.* gato
cataclysm *n.* cataclismo
catalogue *n.* catalogo
catalyse *v.* catalizar
catalyst *n.* catalítico
cataract *n.* catarata
catastrophe *n.* catástrofe
catch *v.* coger, agarrar
catching *adj.* contagioso
catchy *adj.* pegadizo
catechism *n.* catequesis
categorical *adj.* categórico
catagorize *v.* clasificar
category *n.* categoría
cater *v.* abastecer
caterpillar *n.* oruga
catharsis *n.* catarsis
cathedral *n.* catedral
catholic *adj.* católico
cattle *n.* ganado
catty *n.* malicioso
caucasian *adj.* caucásico
cauldron *n.* caldero
cauliflower *n.* coliflor
causal *adj.* causal
causality *n.* casualidad
cause *n.* causa
causeway *n.* calzada
caustic *adj.* cáustico
caution *n.* cautela
cautionary *adj.* advertido, cautelar, de precaución
cautious *adj.* cauto, cauteloso
cavalcade *n.* cabalgata
cavalier *adj.* autoritario
cavalry *n.* caballería
cave *n.* cueva
caveat *n.* advertencia
cavern *n.* caverna
cavernous *adj.* cavernoso
cavity *n.* cavidad
cavort *v.* cabriolar
cease *v.* cesar
ceasefire *n.* alto el fuego
ceaseless *adj.* incesante
cedar *n.* cedro
cede *v.* ceder
ceiling *n.* techo
celandine *n.* celidonia
celebrant *n.* celebrante
celebrate *v.* celebrar
celebration *n.* celebración
celebrity *n.* celebridad
celestial *adj.* celestial
celibacy *n.* celibato
celibate *adj.* célibe
cell *n.* celda
cellar *n.* sótano
cellphone *n.* teléfono celular, móvil
cellular *adj.* celular
cellulite *n.* celulitis
celluloid *n.* celuloide
cellulose *n.* celulosa
celsius *n.* centígrados
Celtic *adj.* celta
cement *n.* cemento
cemetery *n.* cementerio
censer *n.* incensario
censor *n.* censor
censorship *n.* censura
censorious *adj.* censurado
censure *v.* censurar

census *n.* censor
cent *n.* céntimo, centavo
centenary *n.* centenario
centennial *n.* centenario
center *n.* centro
centigrade *adj.* centígrado
centimetre *n.* centímetro
centipede *n.* ciempiés
central *adj.* central
centralize *v.* centralizar
centre *n.* centro
century *n.* siglo
ceramic *n.* cerámica
cereal *n.* cereal
cerebral *adj.* cerebral
ceremonial *adj.* ceremonial
ceremonious *adj.* ceremonioso
ceremony *n.* ceremonia
certain *adj.* seguro
certainly *adv.* ciertamente, por
   supuesto
certifiable *adj.* demente
certificate *n.* certificado
certify *v.* certificar
certitude *n.* certidumbre
cervical *adj.* cervical, de cuello
   uterino
cessation *n.* cese
cession *n.* cesión
chain *n.* cadena
chair *n.* silla
chairman *n.* presidente
chaise *n.* diván, tumbona, carruaje
chalet *n.* chalet
chalice *n.* cáliz
chalk *n.* tiza, creta
challenge *n.* desafío, reto
chamber *n.* cámara, aposento
chamberlain *n.* chambelán
champagne *n.* champan
champion *n.* campeón
chance *n.* oportunidad

chancellor *n.* canciller
Chancery *n.* cancillería
chandelier *n.* araña de luces
change *v.* cambiar
channel *n.* canal
chant *n.* canto, salmodia
chaos *n.* caos
chaotic *adj.* caótico
chapel *n.* capilla
chaplain *n.* capellán
chapter *n.* capítulo
char *v.* carbonizar, chamuscar
character *n.* carácter, figura,
   personaje
characteristic *n.* característica
charcoal *n.* carbón de leña, car-
   boncillo
charge *v.* acusar, cobrar
charge *n.* carga, coste
charger *n.* cargador
chariot *n.* carro de guerra
charisma *n.* carisma
charismatic *adj.* carismático
charitable *adj.* caritativo
charity *n.* caridad
charlatan *n.* charlatán
charm *n.* encanto, hechizo
charming *adj.* encantador
chart *n.* tabla, carta de navegación
charter *n.* estatuto, fuero, carta
chartered *adj.* colegiado
chary *adj.* reacio
chase *v.* perseguir
chasis *n.* chasis
chaste *adj.* casto, puro
chasten *v.* escarmentar, aleccionar
chastise *v.* reprender
chastity *n.* castidad
chat *v. i.* charlar
chateau *n.* castillo
chattel *n.* propiedad

chatter v. charlar
chauffeur n. chofer
chauvinism n. chovinismo
chauvinist n. &adj. chovinista
cheap adj. barato
cheapen v. t. degradar
cheat v. engañar, timar
cheat n. estafador, fraude
check v. revirar
checkmate n jaque mate
cheek n. mejilla
cheeky adj. atrevido, pícaro, caradura
cheep n. piído, gorjeo
cheer v. t. animar, aclamar
cheerful adj. alegre
cheerless adj. triste
cheery adj. risueño, grato
cheese n. queso
cheetah n. guepardo
chef n. chef
chemical adj. químico
chemist n. químico, farmacéutico, farmacia
chemistry n. química
chemotherapy n. quimioterapia
cheque n. cheque
cherish v. querer, apreciar
chess n. ajedrez
chest n. arca, cofre, tórax
chestnut n. castaña
chevron n. galón
chew v. masticar
chic adj. elegante, chic
chicanery n. argucia
chicken n. pollo
chickpea n. guisante
chide v. reprender
chief n. jefe
chiefly adv. principalmente
chieftain n. cacique, jefe
child n. niño

childhood n. infancia, niñez
childish adj. infantil
chill n. frio, fresco
chilli n. guindilla
chilly adj. frio
chime n. repique, campaneo
chimney n. chimenea
chimpanzee n. chimpancé
chin n. barbilla
china n. loza, porcelana
chip n. astilla, ficha
chirp v. gorjear
chisel n. cincel
chit n. recibo, resguardo, nota
chivalrous adj. caballeroso
chivalry n. caballerosidad
chlorine n. cloro
chloroform n. cloroformo
chocolate n. chocolate
choice n. elección
choir n. coro
choke v. sofocar, estrangular, obstruir
cholera n. cólera
choose v. t elegir
chop v. golpe, hachazo, chuleta
chopper n. desmenuzador, hacha, helicóptero
chopstick n. palillo
choral adj. coral
chord n. acorde
chorus n. coro
Christ n. Cristo
Christian adj. cristiano
Christianity n. cristianismo
Christmas n. navidad
chrome n. cromo
chronic adj. crónico
chronicle n. crónica
chronology n. cronología
chronograph n. cronógrafo
chuckle v. reírse

chum *n.* amigo
chunk *n.* trozo, pedazo
church *n.* iglesia
churchyard *n.* cementerio, camposanto
churn *v.* agitar
chutney *n.* chutney
cider *n.* sidra
cigar *n.* puro
cigarette *n.* cigarro
cinema *n* cine
cinnamon *n.* canela
circle *n.* circulo
circuit *n.* circuito
circular *adj.* circular
circulate *v.* circular
circulation *n.* circulación
circumcise *v.* circuncidar
circumference *n.* circunferencia
circumscribe *v.* circunscribir
circumspect *adj.* circunspecto
circumstance *n.* circunstancia
circus *n.* circo
cist *n.* arquilla
cistern *n.* cisterna
citadel *n.* ciudadela
cite *v.* citar
citizen *n.* ciudadano
citizenship *n.* ciudadanía
citrus *n.* cítricos
citric *adj.* cítrico
city *n.* ciudad
civic *adj.* cívico
civics *n.* cívica
civil *adj.* cortés
civilian *n.* civil
civilization *n.* civilización
civilize *v.* civilizar
clad *adj.* vestido
cladding *n.* revestimiento
claim *v.* reclamar
claimant *n.* demandante

clammy *adj.* bochornoso
clamour *n.* clamor
clamp *n.* abrazadera
clan *n.* clan
clandestine *adj.* clandestino
clap *v.* aplaudir
clarify *v.* aclarar
clarification *n.* aclaración
clarion *n.* clarín
clarity *n.* claridad
clash *v.* chocar
clasp *v.* apretar, abrazar, agarrar
class *n.* clase
classic *adj.* clásico
classical *adj.* clásico
classification *n.* clasificación
classify *v.* clasificar
clause *n.* cláusula
claustrophobia *n.* claustrofobia
claw *n.* zarpa, garra
clay *n.* arcilla
clean *adj.* limpio
cleanliness *n.* limpieza
cleanse *v.* limpiar
clear *adj.* despejado, claro
clearance *n.* autorización, liquidación
clearly *adv.* claramente
cleave *v.* hender, partir
cleft *n.* hendedura
clemency *n.* clemencia
clement *adj.* clemente
clementine *n.* clementina
clench *v.* apretar
clergy *n.* clero
cleric *n.* clérigo
clerical *adj.* clerical
clerk *n.* administrativo
clever *adj.* inteligente
click *n.* chasquido, clic
client *n.* cliente
cliff *n.* precipicio

climate *n.* clima
climax *n.* clímax
climb *v.i* escalar
clinch *v.* cerrar, ganar
cling *v.* aferrar
clinic *n.* clínica
clink *n.* tintineo
clip *n.* clip, gancho
cloak *n.* capa
clock *n.* reloj
cloister *n.* claustro
clone *n.* clon
close *adj.* cercano, próximo
closet *n.* armario
closure *n.* cierre
clot *n.* coágulo
cloth *n.* tela, tejido
clothe *v.* vestir
clothes *n.* ropa
clothing *n.* ropa
cloud *n.* nube
cloudy *adj.* nublado
clove *n.* clavo
clown *n.* payaso
cloying *adj.* empalagoso
club *n.* club
clue *n.* pista
clumsy *adj.* torpe, patoso
cluster *n.* grupo, racimo
clutch *v. t.* agarrar
coach *n.* entrenador, autocar, coche de caballos
coal *n.* carbón
coalition *n.* coalición
coarse *adj.* grueso, basto
coast *n.* costa
coaster *n.* posavasos, barco de cabotaje
coat *n.* abrigo
coating *n.* capa, baño
coax *v.* convencer
cobalt *n.* cobalto

cobble *n.* adoquín
cobbler *n.* zapatero
cobra *n.* cobra
cobweb *n.* telaraña
cocaine *n.* cocaína
cock *n.* gallo, verga
cockade *n.* escarapela
cockpit *n.* cabina de mando
cockroach *n.* cucaracha
cocktail *n.* coctel
cocky *adj.* gallito, chulo
cocoa *n.* cacao
coconut *n.* coco
cocoon *n.* capullo
code *n.* código
co-education *n.* coeducación
coefficient *n.* coeficiente
coerce *v.* coaccionar
coeval *adj.* coetáneo
coexist *v.* coexistir
coexistence *n.* coexistencia
coffee *n.* café
coffer *n.* cofre
coffin *n.* ataúd
cog *n.* diente, piñón
cogent *adj.* convincente
cogitate *v.* cavilar
cognate *adj.* afín
cognizance *n.* conocimiento
cohabit *v.* cohabitar
cohere *v.* adherirse
coherent *adj.* coherente
cohesion *n.* cohesión
cohesive *adj.* cohesivo
coil *n.* cofia
coin *n.* moneda
coinage *n.* acuñación
coincide *v.* coincidir
coincidence *n.* coincidencia
coir *n.* fibra de coco
coke *n.* coque
cold *adj.* frio

colic *n.* cólico
collaborate *v.* colaborar
collaboration *n.* colaboración
collage *n.* collage
collapse *v.* colapsar
collar *n.* collarín, collar
collate *v.* recopilar
collateral *n.* colateral
colleague *n.* compañero
collect *v.* reunir
collection *n.* colección
collective *adj.* colectivo
collector *n.* coleccionista
college *n.* colegio universitario
collide *v.* chocar
colliery *n.* mina de carbón
collision *n.* colisión
colloquial *adj.* coloquial
collusion *n.* colusión
cologne *n.* colonia
colon *n.* colon, dos puntos
colonel *n.* coronel
colonial *adj.* colonial
colony *n.* colonia
colossal *adj.* colosal
colossus *n.* coloso
column *n.* columna
colour *n.* color
colouring *n.* colorido
colourless *n.* incoloro, sin color, anodino
coma *n.* coma
comb *n.* peine
combat *n.* combate
combatant *n* combatiente
combination *n.* combinación
combine *v.* combinar
combustible *adj.* combustible
combustion *n.* combustión
come *v.* venir
comedian *n.* cómico
comedy *n* comedia

comet *n.* cometa
comfort *n.* confort, comodidad
comfort *v.* confortar
comfortable *adj.* confortable, cómodo
comic *adj.* cómico
comma *n.* coma
command *v.* mandar
commandant *n.* comandante
commander *n.* comandante
commando *n.* comando
commemorate *v.* conmemorar
commemoration *n.* conmemoración
commence *v.* comenzar
commencement *n.* comienzo
commend *v.* recomendar, encarecer
commendable *adj.* recomendable
commendation *n.* recomendación
comment *n.* comentario
commentary *n.* comentario
commentator *n.* comentarista
commerce *n.* comercio
commercial *adj.* comercial
commiserate *v.* compadecer, acompañar en el sentimiento
commission *n.* comisión
commissioner *n.* comisionado
commissure *n.* comisura
commit *v.* comprometerse, cometer
commitment *n.* compromiso
committee *n.* comité
commode *n.* cómoda
commodity *n.* artículo
common *adj.* común
commoner *n.* plebeyo
commonplace *adj.* común
commonwealth *n.* Commonwealth

commotion *n.* conmoción
communal *adj.* comunal
commune *n.* comuna
communicable *adj.* comunicable
communicant *n.* comulgante
communicate *v.* comunicar
communication *n.* comunicación
communion *n.* comunión
communism *n.* comunismo
community *n.* comunidad
commute *v.* conmutar
compact *adj.* compacto
companion *n.* compañero
company *n.* compañía, empresa
comparative *adj.* comparativo
compare *v.* comparar
comparison *n.* comparación
compartment *n.* compartimiento
compass *n.* brújula
compassion *n.* compasión
compatible *adj.* compatible
compatriot *n.* compatriota
compel *v.* compeler
compendious *adj.* compendioso
compendium *n.* compendio
compensate *v.* compensar
compensation *n.* compensación
compere *n.* presentador
compete *v.* competir
competence *n.* competencia
competent *adj.* competente
competition *n.* competición
competitive *adj.* competitivo
competitor *n.* competidor, participante
compile *v.* recopilar
complacent *adj.* complaciente
complain *v.* quejarse, reclamar
complaint *n.* queja, reclamo
complaisant *adj.* sumiso
complement *n.* complemento

complementary *adj.* complementario
complete *adj.* completo
completion *n.* finalización, terminación
complex *adj.* complejo
complexity *n.* complejidad
complexion *n.* cutis, naturaleza
compliance *n.* conformidad
compliant *adj.* conforme
complicate *v.* complicar
complication *n.* complicación
complicity *n.* complicidad
compliment *n.* cumplido, halago
compliment *v. i* felicitar por, hacer cumplidos
comply *v.* acatar
component *n.* componente
comport *v.* comportarse
compose *v.* componer
composer *n.* compositor
composite *adj.* compuesto
composition *n.* composición
compositor *n.* cajista
compost *n.* abono
composure *n.* compostura
compound *n.* compuesto de
comprehend *v.* comprender
comprehensible *adj.* comprensible
comprehension *n.* comprensión
comprehensive *adj.* exhaustivo
compress *v.* comprimir
compression *n.* compresión
comprise *v.* comprender, constar
compromise *n.* compromiso
compulsion *n.* compulsión
compulsive *adj.* compulsivo
compulsory *adj.* obligatorio
compunction *n.* compunción
computation *n.* computación
compute *v.* computar

computer *n.* ordenador
computerize *v.* computerizar
comrade *n.* camarada
concatenation *n.* concatenación
concave *adj.* cóncavo
conceal *v.* ocultar
concede *v.* reconocer
conceit *n.* presunción
conceivable *adj.* imaginable
conceive *v. t* concebir
concentrate *v.* concentrar
concentration *n.* concentración
concept *n.* concepto
conception *n.* concepción
concern *v.* asunto, interés, preocupación
concerning *prep.* en cuanto a,
respecto a
concert *n.* concierto
concerted *adj.* concertado
concession *n.* concesión
conch *n.* concha
conciliate *v.* conciliar
concise *adj.* conciso
conclude *v.* concluir
conclusion *n.* conclusión
conclusive *adj.* conclusivo
concoct *v.* preparar
concoction *n.* mezcolanza
concomitant *adj.* concomitante
concord *n.* concordia
concordance *n.* concordancia
concourse *n.* concurrencia
concrete *n.* hormigón
concubine *n.* concubina
concur *v.* concurrir
concurrent *adj.* concurrente
concussion *n.* concusión
condemn *v.* condenar
condemnation *n.* condenación
condense *v.* condensar
condescend *v.* dignarse

condiment *n.* condimento
condition *n.* condición
conditional *adj.* condicional
conditioner *n.* acondicionador
condole *v.* expresar condolencias
condolence *n.* condolencia
condom *n.* condón
condominium *n.* apartamento
condone *v.* aprobar
conduct *n.* conducta
conduct *v.* realizar
conductor *n.* director de orquesta
cone *n.* cono
confection *n.* creación, dulce
confectioner *n.* pastelero
confectionery *n.* confitería
confederate *adj.* confederado
confederation *n.* confederación
confer *v.* conferir
conference *n.* conferencia
confess *v.* confesar
confession *n.* confesión
confidant *n.* confidente
confide *v.* confiar
confidence *n.* confianza
confident *adj.* seguro
confidential *adj.* confidencial
configuration *n.* configuración
confine *v.* limitar, recluir
confinement *n.* reclusión
confirm *v.* confirmar
confirmation *n.* confirmación
confiscate *v.* confiscar
confiscation *n.* confiscación
conflate *v.* refundir
conflict *n.* conflicto
confluence *n.* confluencia
confluent *adj.* confluente
conform *v.* conformar
conformity *n.* conformidad
confront *v.* confrontar
confrontation *n.* confrontación

confuse *v.* confundir
confusion *n.* confusión
confute *v.* refutar
congenial *adj.* simpático
congenital *adj.* congénito
congested *adj.* congestionado, abarrotado
congestion *n.* congestión
conglomerate *n.* conglomerado
conglomeration *n.* aglomeración
congratulate *v.* felicitar
congratulation *n.* felicitación
congregate *v.* congregar
congress *n.* congreso
congruent *adj.* congruente
conical *adj.* cónico
conjecture *n. &v.* conjetura & conjeturar
conjugal *v.t. & i.* conyugal
conjugate *v.* conjugar
conjunct *adj.* conjunto
conjunction *n.* conjunción
conjunctivitis *n.* conjuntivitis
conjuncture *n.* coyuntura
conjure *v.* conjurar
conker *n.* castaña
connect *v.* conectar
connection *n.* conexión
connive *v.* confabularse
conquer *v.* conquistar
conquest *n.* conquista
conscience *n.* conciencia
conscious *adj.* consciente
consecrate *v.* consagrar
consecutive *adj.* consecutivo
consecutively *adv.* sucesivamente
consensus *n.* consenso
consent *n.* consentimiento
consent *v.t.* consentir
consequence *n.* consecuencia
consequent *adj.* consiguiente
conservation *n.* conservación

conservative *adj.* conservador
conservatory *n.* conservatorio
conserve *v. t* conservar
consider *v.* considerar
considerable *adj.* considerable
considerate *adj.* considerado
consideration *n.* consideración
considering *prep.* teniendo en cuenta
consign *v.* consignar
consignment *n.* remesa
consist *v.* constar, consistir
consistency *n.* consistencia
consistent *adj.* consistente
consolation *n.* consolación
console *v. t.* consolar
consolidate *v.* consolidar
consolidation *n.* consolidación
consonant *n.* consonante
consort *n.* consorte
consortium *n.* consorcio
conspicuous *adj.* conspicuo
conspiracy *n.* conspiración
conspirator *n.* conspirador
conspire *v.* conspirar
constable *n.* agente de policía
constabulary *n.* policía, guardia civil
constant *adj.* constante
constellation *n.* constelación
consternation *n.* consternación
constipation *n.* estreñimiento
constituency *n.* distrito electoral
constituent *adj.* constitutivo
constitute *v.* constituir
constitution *n.* constitución
constitutional *adj.* constitucional
constrain *v.* limitar, obligar
constraint *n.* coacción
constrict *v.* apretar
construct *v.* construir
construction *n.* construcción

constructive *adj.* constructivo
construe *v.* interpretar
consul *n.* cónsul
consular *n.* consular
consulate *n.* consulado
consult *v.* consultar
consultant *n.* asesor
consultation *n.* consultar
consume *v.* consumir
consumer *n.* consumidor
consummate *v.* consumar
consumption *n.* consumo
contact *n.* contacto
contagion *n.* contagio
contagious *adj.* contagioso
contain *v.t.* contener
container *n.* contenedor
containment *n.* contención
contaminate *v.* contaminar
contemplate *v.* contemplar
contemplation *n.* contemplación
contemporary *adj.* contemporáneo
contempt *n.* desprecio
contemptuous *adj.* despreciativo
contend *v.* sostener, afirmar
content *adj.* contento
content *n.* contenido
contention *n.* contención
contentment *n.* satisfacción
contentious *adj.* contencioso
contest *n.* contienda
contestant *n.* contendiente
context *n.* contexto
contiguous *adj.* contiguo
continent *n.* continente
continental *adj.* continental
contingency *n.* contingencia
continual *adj.* continuo
continuation *n.* continuación
continue *v.* continuar
continuity *n.* continuidad

continuous *adj.* continuado
contort *v.* retorcer
contour *n.* contorno
contra *prep.* contra
contraband *n.* contrabando
contraception *n.* anticoncepción
contraceptive *n.* anticonceptivo
contract *n.* contrato
contract *v.* contratar
contractual *adj.* contractual
contractor *n.* contratista
contraction *n.* contracción
contradict *v.* contradecir
contradiction *n.* contradicción
contrary *adj.* contrario
contrast *n.* contraste
contravene *v.* contravenir
contribute *v.* contribuir
contribution *n.* contribución
contrivance *n.* inventiva
contrive *v.* inventar, tramar
control *n.* control
controller *n.* inspector
controversial *adj.* polémico
controversy *n.* controversia
contusion *n.* contusión
conundrum *v. t* adivinanza
conurbation *n.* conurbación
convene *v.* convocar
convenience *n.* conveniencia
convenient *adj.* conveniente
convent *n.* convento
convention *n.* convención
converge *v.* converger
conversant *adj.* versado
conversation *n.* conversación
converse *v.* departir
conversion *n.* conversión
convert *n.* converso
convert *v.* convertir
convey *v.* transportar
conveyance *n.* transporte

convict *n.* convicto
convict *v.* condenar
conviction *n.* convicción
convince *v.* convencer
convivial *adj.* jovial
convocation *n.* convocación
convoy *n.* convoy
convulse *n.* convulsionar
convulsion *n.* convulsión
cook *n.* cocinero
cook *v.* cocinar
cooker *n.* cocina
cookie *n.* galleta
cool *adj.* fresco, guay
coolant *n.* refrigerante
cooler *n.* refrigerador
cooper *n.* tonelero
cooperate *v.* cooperar
cooperation *n.* cooperación
cooperative *adj.* cooperativo
coordinate *v. t* coordinar
coordination *n.* coordinación
cope *v.* poder hacerlo, poder hacer frente
copier *n.* copista
copious *adj.* copioso
copper *n.* cobre
copulate *v.* copular
copy *n.* copia
copy *v.* copiar
coral *n.* coral
cord *n.* cordón
cordial *adj.* cordial
cordon *n.* cordón
core *n.* centro, núcleo
coriander *n.* cilantro
cork *n.* corcho, tapón
corn *n.* maíz, grano
cornea *n.* cornea
corner *n.* esquina
cornet *n.* corneta
coronation *n.* coronación

coroner *n.* juez de instrucción
coronet *n.* corona
corporal *n.* cabo
corporate *adj.* corporativo
corporation *n.* corporación, sociedad
corps *n.* cuerpo
corpse *n.* cadáver
corpulent *adj.* corpulento
correct *adj.* correcto
correct *v.* corregir
correction *n.* corrección
corrective *adj.* correctivo
correlate *v.* correlacionar
correlation *n.* correlación
correspond *v.* corresponder
correspondence *n.* correspondencia
correspondent *n.* correspondiente
corridor *n.* pasillo
corroborate *v.* corroborar
corrode *v.* corroer
corrosion *n.* corrosión
corrosive *adj.* corrosivo
corrugated *adj.* ondulado
corrupt *adj.* corrupto
corrupt *v.* corromper
corruption *n.* corrupción
cortisone *n.* cortisona
cosmetic *adj.* cosmético
cosmetic *n.* cosmético
cosmic *adj.* cósmico
cosmology *n.* cosmología
cosmopolitan *adj.* cosmopolita
cosmos *n.* cosmos
cost *v.* costar, valer
costly *adj.* costoso
costume *n.* disfraz, traje
cosy *adj.* acogedor
cot *n.* cuna
cottage *n.* casita de campo

cotton *n.* algodón
couch *n.* sofá
couchette *n.* litera
cough *v.* toser
council *n.* concilio, ayuntamiento
councillor *n.* concejal
counsel *n.* consejo
counsel *v.* aconsejar
counsellor *n.* consejero
count *v.* contar
countenance *n.* semblante
counter *n.* contador, ventanilla
counter *v.t.* oponerse a
counteract *v.* contrarrestar
counterfeit *adj.* falsificado
counterfoil *n.* talón
countermand *v.* revocar
counterpart *n.* equivalente, correspondiente
countless *adj.* incontable
country *n.* país
county *n.* provincia
coup *n.* golpe
coupe *n.* cupé
couple *n.* pareja
couplet *n.* pareado
coupon *n.* vale, cupón
courage *n.* valor, coraje
courageous *adj.* valiente
courier *n.* guía, mensajero, correo
course *n.* curso
court *n.* patio, tribunal, juzgado
courteous *adj.* cortés
courtesan *n.* cortesana
courtesy *n.* cortesía
courtier *n.* cortesano
courtly *adj.* distinguido
courtship *n.* noviazgo
courtyard *n.* patio
cousin *n.* primo
cove *n.* cala

covenant *n.* pacto, cláusula
cover *n.* tapa, cubierta
cover *v.* cubrir, recorrer, abarcar
covert *adj.* cubierto
covet *v.* codiciar
cow *n.* vaca
coward *n.* cobarde
cowardice *n.* cobardía
cower *v.* acurrucarse
coy *adj.* vergonzoso
cozy *adj.* acogedor
crab *n.* cangrejo
crack *n.* crujido, grieta, rotura
crack *v.* quebrar, romper
cracker *n.* galleta salada, petardo
crackle *v.* crujir
cradle *n.* cuna
craft *n.* oficio, destreza
craftsman *n.* artesano
crafty *adj.* astuto
cram *v.* meter, memorizar
cramp *n.* calambre, rampa
crane *n.* grúa
crankle *v.* serpentear
crash *v.* estrellarse, chocar
crass *adj.* grosero
crate *n.* caja, cajón, cesto
cravat *n.* corbata
crave *v. t* ansiar
craven *adj.* cobarde
crawl *v.* arrastrarse
crayon *n.* lápiz de color
craze *n.* manía, locura
crazy *adj.* loco
creak *n.* crujido
creak *v.* crujir
cream *n.* nata, crema
crease *n.* arruga, pliegue
create *v.* crear
creation *n.* creación
creative *adj.* creativo
creator *n.* creador

creature *n.* criatura
creche *n.* orfanato
credentials *n.* credenciales
credible *adj.* creíble
credit *n.* crédito
creditable *adj.* encomiable
creditor *n.* acreedor
credulity *n.* credulidad
creed *n.* credo
creek *n.* cala
creep *v.* deslizarse
creeper *n.* reptil
cremate *v.* incinerar
cremation *n.* incineración
crematorium *n.* crematorio
crescent *n.* creciente
crest *n.* cresta
crew *n.* tripulación, pandilla
crib *n.* cuna, pesebre
cricket *n.* grillo, cricket
crime *n.* crimen
criminal *n.* criminal
criminology *n.* criminología
crimson *n.* carmesí
cringe *v.* encogerse
cripple *n.* lisiado
crisis *n.* crisis
crisp *adj.* crujiente
criterion *n.* criterio
critic *n.* crítico
critical *adj.* crítico
criticism *n.* crítica
criticize *v.* criticar
critique *n.* crítica
croak *n.* croar, canto, gruñido
crochet *n.* ganchillo
crockery *n.* vajilla
crocodile *n.* cocodrilo
croissant *n.* croissant
crook *n.* gancho, curva
crooked *adj.* torcido, deshonesto
crop *n.* cosecha

cross *n.* cruz
crossing *n.* travesía, cruce
crotchet *n.* negra, antojo
crouch *v.* agacharse
crow *n.* cuervo
crowd *n.* multitud, gentío
crown *n.* corona
crown *v.* coronar
crucial *adj.* crucial
crude *adj.* ordinario
cruel *adj.* cruel
cruelty *adv.* crueldad
cruise *v.* cruzar, patrullar, ir a
  velocidad de crucero
cruiser *n.* crucero
crumb *n.* miga
crumble *v.* desmigajar
crumple *v.* arrugar, abollar
crunch *v.* mascar, aplastar
crusade *n.* cruzada
crush *v.* aplastar, machacar
crust *n.* corteza, costra
crutch *n.* muleta
crux *n.* esencial
cry *n.* lloro
cry *v.* llorar
crypt *n.* cripta
crystal *n.* cristal
cub *n.* cachorro
cube *n.* cubo
cubical *adj.* cúbico
cubicle *n.* cubículo
cuckold *n.* cornudo
cuckoo *n.* cuco, cucú
cucumber *n.* pepino
cuddle *v.* abrazar
cuddly *adj.* mimoso
cudgel *n.* garrote, porra
cue *n.* taco de billar
cuff *n.* puño
cuisine *n.* cocina
culinary *adj.* culinario

culminate v. culminar
culpable adj. culpable
culprit n. inculpado
cult n. culto
cultivate v. cultivar
cultural adj. cultural
culture n. cultura
cumbersome adj. pesado, torpe
cumin n. comino
cumulative adj. acumulativo
cunning adj. astuto, malicioso
cup n. taza
cupboard n. armario
cupidity n. codicia
curable adj. curable
curative adj. curativo
curator n. conservador, comisario
curb v. t reducir, refrenar
curd n. cuajada
cure v. t. curar
curfew n. toque de queda
curiosity n. curiosidad
curious adj. curioso
curl v. rizar
currant n. pasa de Corinto
currency n. moneda
current adj. actual
current n. corriente
curriculum n. curriculum, currículo
curry n. curry
curse n. maldición
cursive adj. cursivo
cursor n. cursor
cursory adj. rápid, somero
curt adj. cortante
curtail v. abreviar
curtain n. cortina
curve n. curva
cushion n. cojín
custard n. natillas
custodian n. guardián

custody n. custodia
custom n. costumbre
customary adj. habitual
customer n. cliente
customize v. personalizar
cut v. cortar
cute adj. mono, rico
cutlet n. chuleta
cutter n. tenazas, corta vidrios
cutting n. recorte
cyan n. azul verdoso
cyanide n. cianuro
cyber comb. ciber
cyberspace n. ciberespacio
cycle n. ciclo
cyclic adj. cíclico
cyclist n. ciclista
cyclone n. ciclón
cylinder n. cilindro
cynic n. cínico
cynosure n. foco de atención
cypress n. ciprés
cyst n. quiste
cystic adj. cístico

D

dab v. toque, gota
dabble v. chapotear, tener escarceos,
dacoit n. ladrón
dad n papa
daffodil n. narciso
daft adj. tonto, bobo
dagger n. daga, puñal
daily adj. diario
dainty adj. delicado
dairy n. lácteo
dais n. tarima

daisy *n.* margarita
dale *n.* valle
dally *v.* perder el tiempo, coquetear
dalliance *n.* escarceo
dam *n.* presa
damage *n.* daño
dame *n.* dama
damn *v.* maldecir
damnable *adj.* deplorable
damnation *n.* condenación, maldición
damp *adj.* húmedo
dampen *v.* humedecer
damper *n.* amortiguador
dampness *n.* humedad
damsel *n.* damisela
dance *v.* bailar
dancer *n.* bailarín
dandelion *n.* diente de león
dandle *v.* mecer sobre ruedas
dandruff *n.* caspa
dandy *n.* dandy
danger *n.* peligro
dangerous *adj.* peligroso
dangle *v. i.* colgar
dank *adj.* frio, húmedo
dapper *adj.* atildado
dappled *adj.* moteado, rodado
dare *v.* atreverse
daring *adj.* osado
dark *adj.* oscuro
darkness *n.* oscuridad
darken *v.* oscurecer
darling *n.* querido, amado
darn *v.* zurcir
dart *n.* dardo
dash *v.* arrojar, golpear, salpicar
dashboard *n.* diana
dashing *adj.* elegante
dastardly *adj.* ruin
data *n.* datos

database *n.* base de datos
date *n.* fecha
date *v.* fechar, salir con
datum *n.* dato
daub *v.* embadurnar
daughter *n.* hija
daughter-in-law *n.* nuera
daunt *v.* amilanar
dauntless *adj.* intrépido
dawdle *v.* entretenerse
dawn *n.* amanecer
day *n.* día
daze *v.* aturdir
dazzle *v. t.* deslumbrar
dead *adj.* muerto
deadline *n.* fecha limite, plazo de entrega
deadlock *n.* punto muerto
deadly *adj.* mortal
deaf *adj.* sordo
deafening *adj.* ensordecedor
deal *n.* acuerdo
deal *v. i* dar, repartir
dealer *n.* comerciante, traficante, repartidor
dean *n.* decano
dear *adj.* querido
dearly *adv.* caro
dearth *n.* escasez
death *n.* muerte
debacle *n.* debacle
debar *v. t.* excluir
debase *v.* degradar
debatable *adj.* discutible
debate *n.* debate
debate *v. t.* debatir
debauch *v.* pervertir
debauchery *n.* disipación
debenture *n.* obligación
debilitate *v.* debilitar
debility *n.* debilidad
debit *n.* débito

debonair *adj.* elegante
debrief *v.* dar parte
debris *n.* escombros
debt *n.* deuda
debtor *n.* deudor
debunk *v.* demoler, desacreditar
debut *n.* debut
debutante *n.* debutante
decade *n.* década
decadent *adj.* decadente
decaffeinated *adj.* descafeinado
decamp *v.* esfumarse
decant *v.* decantar
decanter *n.* licorera
decapitate *v.* decapitar
decay *v. i* descomponerse
decease *n.* fallecimiento
deceased *adj.* difunto
deceit *n.* engaño
deceitful *adj.* embustero
deceive *v.* engañar
decelerate *v.* aminorar
december *n.* diciembre
decency *n.* decencia
decent *adj.* decente
decentralize *v.* descentralizar
deception *n.* decepción
deceptive *adj.* engañoso
decibel *n.* decibelio
decide *v.* decidir
decided *adj.* decidido
decimal *adj.* decimal
decimate *v.* diezmar
decipher *v.* descifrar
decision *n.* decisión
decisive *adj.* decisivo
deck *n.* cubierta
deck *v* engalanar
declaim *v.* declamar
declaration *n.* declaración
declare *n* declarar
declassify *v.* desclasificar

decline *v. t.* decaer, declinar
declivity *n.* declive
decode *v.* descodificar
decompose *n.* descomponerse
decomposition *v. t* descomposición
decompress *v.* descomprimir
decongestant *n.* descongestionante
decontaminate *v.* descontaminar
decor *n.* decoración
decorate *v.* decorar
decoration *n.* decoración
decorative *adj.* decorativo
decorous *adj.* decoroso
decorum *n.* decoro
decoy *n.* señuelo
decrease *v.* disminuir
decree *n.* decreto
decrement *v. t.* decremento
decrepit *adj.* decrépito
decriminalize *v.* despenalizar
decry *v.* condenar
dedicate *v.* dedicar
dedication *n.* dedicación
deduce *v.* deducir
deduct *v.* deducir, descontar
deduction *n.* deducción
deed *n.* acto, escritura
deem *v.* considerar
deep *adj.* profundo
deer *n.* ciervo
deface *v.* pintarrajear
defamation *n.* difamación
defame *v.* difamar
default *n.* omisión
defeat *v. t.* derrotar, vencer
defeatist *n.* derrotista
defecate *v.* defecar
defect *n.* defecto
defective *adj.* defectuoso
defence *n.* defensa

defend *v.* defender
defendant *n.* demandado
defensible *adj.* defendible
defensive *adj.* defensivo
defer *v.* diferir
deference *n.* deferencia
defiance *n.* desafío
deficiency *n.* deficiencia
deficient *adj.* deficiente
deficit *n.* déficit
defile *v. t* profanar
define *v.* definir
definite *adj.* definitivo
definition *n.* definición
deflate *v.* desinflar
deflation *n.* deflación
deflect *v.* desviar
deforest *v.* deforestar
deform *v.* deformar
deformity *n.* deformidad
defraud *v.* estafar
defray *v.* sufragar
defrost *v.* congelar
deft *adj.* hábil
defunct *adj.* caduco
defuse *v.* desactivar
defy *v.* desafiar
degenerate *v.* degenerar
degrade *v.* degradar
degree *n.* grado
dehumanize *v.* deshumanizar
dehydrate *v.* deshidratar
deify *v.* deificar
deign *v.* dignarse
deity *n.* deidad
deja vu *n.* deja vu
deject *v.* abatir
dejection *n.* abatimiento
delay *v. t* retrasar
delectable *adj.* delicioso
delectation *n.* deleite
delegate *n.* delegado

delegation *n.* delegación
delete *v. i* suprimir
deletion *n.* eliminación
deleterious *adj.* nocivo
deliberate *adj.* deliberado
deliberation *n.* deliberación
delicacy *n.* delicadeza
delicate *adj.* delicado
delicatessen *n.* tienda de comestibles finos
delicious *adj.* delicioso
delight *v. t.* deleitar
delightful *adj.* exquisito
delineate *v.* delinear
delinquent *adj.* delincuente
delirious *adj.* delirante
delirium *n.* delirio
deliver *v.* entregar
deliverance *n.* liberación
delivery *n.* entrega
dell *n.* hondonada
delta *n.* delta
delude *v.* engañar
deluge *n.* inundación
delusion *n.* inundar
deluxe *adj.* de lujo
delve *v.* ahondar
demand *n.* demanda
demanding *adj.* exigente, difícil
demarcation *n.* delimitación
demean *v.* degradar
demented *adj.* demente
dementia *n.* demencia
demerit *n* sanción
demise *n.* defunción
demobilize *v.* desmovilizar
democracy *n.* democracia
democratic *adj.* democrático
demography *n.* demografía
demolish *v.* demoler
demon *n.* demonio
demonstrate *v.* demonstrar

demonstration *n.* demonstración
demoralize *v.* desmoralizar
demote *v.* degradar
demur *v.* objetar
demure *adj.* recatado
demystify *v.* desmitificar
den *n.* guarida
denationalize *v.* desnacionalizar
denial *n.* desmentido, negación, abnegación
denigrate *v.* denigrar
denomination *n.* denominación
denominator *n.* denominador
denote *v. t* denotar
denounce *v.* denunciar
dense *adj.* denso
density *n.* densidad
dent *n.* abolladura
dental *adj.* dental
dentist *n.* dentista
denture *n.* dentadura
denude *v.* denudar
denunciation *n.* denuncia
deny *v. i.* negar
deodorant *n.* desodorante
depart *v.* partir
department *n.* departamento
departure *n.* salida
depend *v.* depender
dependant *n.* dependiente, persona a cargo
dependency *n.* dependencia
dependent *adj.* dependiente, necesitado
depict *v.* retratar
depilatory *adj.* depilatorio
deplete *v.* agotar
deplorable *adj.* deplorable
deploy *v.* desplegar
deport *v. t* deportar
depose *v.* deponer

deposit *n.* depósito
depository *n.* depósito
depot *n.* almacén
deprave *v.* depravar
deprecate *v.* reprobar
depreciate *v.* depreciar
depreciation *n.* depreciación
depress *v.* deprimir
depression *n.* depresión
deprive *v.* privar
depth *n.* profundidad
deputation *n.* delegación
depute *v.* delegar
deputy *n.* adjunto
derail *v. t.* descarrilar
deranged *adj.* desarreglado
deregulate *v.* desregular
deride *v.* ridiculizar
derivative *adj.* derivativo
derive *v.* derivar
derogatory *adj.* despectivo
descend *v.* descender
descendant *n.* descendiente
descent *n.* descenso
describe *v.* describir
description *n.* descripción
desert *v.* desertar
deserve *v. t.* merecerse
design *n.* diseño
designate *v.* designar
desirable *adj.* deseable
desire *n.* deseo
desirous *adj.* deseoso
desist *v.* desistir
desk *n.* pupitre
desolate *adj.* desolado
despair *n.* desesperación
desperate *adj.* desesperado
despicable *adj.* despreciable
despise *v.* despreciar
despite *prep.* a pesar de
despondent *adj.* desalentado

despot *n.* déspota
dessert *n.* postre
destabilize *v.* desestabilizar
destination *n.* destinación
destiny *n.* destino
destitute *adj.* indigente, desposeído
destroy *v.* destruir
destroyer *n.* destructor
destruction *n.* destrucción
detach *v.* separar, quitar
detachment *n.* desapego, indiferencia
detail *n.* detalle
detain *v. t* detener
detainee *n.* detenido
detect *v.* detectar
detective *n.* detective
detention *n.* detención
deter *v.* disuadir
detergent *n.* detergente
deteriorate *v.* deteriorarse
determinant *n.* determinante
determination *n.* determinación
determine *v. t* determinar
deterrent *n.* disuasivo
detest *v.* detestar
dethrone *v.* destronar
detonate *v.* detonar
detour *n.* desvío
detoxify *v.* desintoxicar
detract *v.* detraer
detriment *n.* detrimento
detritus *n.* detrito
devalue *v.* devaluar
devastate *v.* devastar
develop *v.* desarrollar
development *n.* desarrollo
deviant *adj.* desviado
deviate *v.* desviarse
device *n.* dispositivo, aparato
devil *n.* diablo

devious *adj.* taimado
devise *v.* proyectar, idear
devoid *adj.* desprovisto
devolution *n.* devolución
devolve *v.* transmitir
devote *v.* dedicar
devotee *n.* devoto
devotion *n.* devoción
devour *v.* devorar
devout *adj.* devoto, piadoso
dew *n.* rocío
dexterity *n.* destreza
diabetes *n.* diabetes
diagnose *v.* diagnosticar
diagnosis *n.* diagnostico
diagram *n.* diagrama
dial *n.* esfera
dialect *n.* dialecto
dialogue *n.* diálogo
dialysis *n.* diálisis
diameter *n.* diámetro
diamond *n.* diamante
diaper *n.* pañal
diarrhoea *n.* diarrea
diary *n.* diario
diaspora *n.* diáspora
dice *n.* dado
dictate *adj.* dictar
dictation *n.* dictado
dictator *n.* dictador
diction *n.* dicción
dictionary *n.* diccionario
dictum *n.* sentencia
didactic *adj.* didáctico
die *v.* morir
diesel *n.* diesel
diet *n.* dieta
dietitian *n.* dietista
differ *v.* diferir
difference *n.* diferencia
different *adj.* diferente
difficult *adj.* difícil

difficulty *n.* dificultad
diffuse *v.* difundir
dig *v.* cavar
digest *v.* digerir
digestion *n.* digestión
digit *n.* digito
digital *adj.* digital
dignified *adj.* digno
dignify *v.* dignificar
dignitary *n.* dignatario
dignity *n.* dignidad
digress *v.* divagar
dilapidated *adj.* ruinoso
dilate *v.* dilatarse
dilemma *n.* dilema
diligent *adj.* diligente
dilute *v.* dilatarse
dim *adj.* oscuro
dimension *n.* dimensión
diminish *v.* disminuir
diminution *n.* disminución
din *n.* barullo
dine *v.* cenar
diner *n.* comensal
dingy *adj.* lúgubre
dinner *n.* cena
dinosaur *n.* dinosaurio
dip *v.* *t* mojar en algo
diploma *n.* diploma
diplomacy *n.* diplomacia
diplomat *n.* diplomático
diplomatic *adj.* diplomático
dipsomania *n.* dipsomanía
dire *adj.* nefasto, atroz
direct *adj.* directo
direction *n.* dirección
directive *n.* directriz
directly *adv.* directamente
director *n.* director
directory *n.* directorio
dirt *n.* suciedad
dirty *adj.* sucio

disability *n.* discapacidad
disable *v.* inutilizar, dejar invalido
disabled *adj.* discapacitado
disadvantage *n.* desventaja
disaffected *adj.* desafecto
disagree *v.* no estar de acuerdo
disagreeable *adj.* desagradable
disagreement *n.* desacuerdo
disallow *v.* rechazar
disappear *v.* desaparecer
disappoint *v.* decepcionar
disapproval *n.* desaprobación
disapprove *v.* no aprobar, desaprobar
disarm *v.* desarmar
disarmament *n.* desarme
disarrange *v.* desarreglar
disarray *n.* desorden
disaster *n.* desastre
disastrous *adj.* desastroso
disband *v.* disolver, desbandar
disbelief *n.* incredulidad
disburse *v.* desembolsar
disc *n.* disco
discard *v.* desechar
discern *v.* distinguir
discharge *v.* liberar, dar de alta
disciple *n.* discípulo
discipline *n.* disciplina
disclaim *v.* rechazar, negar
disclose *v.* revelar
disco *n.* disco
discolour *v.* decolorar
discomfit *v.* desconcertar
discomfort *n.* incomodidad
disconcert *v.* desconcertar
disconnect *v.* desconectar
disconsolate *adj.* desconsolado
discontent *n.* descontento
discontinue *v.* suspender
discord *n.* discordia

discordant *adj.* discordante
discount *n.* descuento
discourage *v.* desalentar, desanimar
discourse *n.* disertación
discourteous *adj.* descortés
discover *v.* descubrir
discovery *n.* descubrimiento
discredit *v.* desacreditar
discreet *adj.* discreto
discrepancy *n.* discrepancia
discrete *adj.* discreto
discriminate *v.* discriminar
discursive *adj.* fluido
discuss *v.* hablar, debatir
discussion *n.* discusión, debate
disdain *n.* desdén
disease *n.* enfermedad
disembark *v.* desembarcar
disembodied *adj.* incorpóreo
disempower *v.* despojar de sus derechos a
disenchant *v.* desilusionar
disengage *v.* soltar
disentangle *v.* desenredar
disfavour *n.* desaprobación
disgrace *n.* vergüenza
disgruntled *adj.* contrariado
disguise *v.* disfrazar
disgust *n.* disgusto
dish *n.* plato, antena parabólica
dishearten *v.* desanimar
dishonest *adj.* deshonesto
dishonour *n.* deshonor
disillusion *v.* desilusión
disincentive *n.* desincentivo
disinfect *v.* desinfectar
disingenuous *adj.* insincero
disinherit *v.* desheredar
disintegrate *v.* desintegrar
disjointed *adj.* inconexo
dislike *v.* desagradar

dislocate *v.* dislocar
dislodge *v.* sacar
disloyal *adj.* desleal
dismal *adj.* sombrío
dismantle *v.* desmontar
dismay *n.* consternación
dismiss *v.* despedir
dismissive *adj.* desdeñoso
disobedient *adj.* desobediente
disobey *v.* desobedecer
disorder *n.* desorden
disorganized *adj.* desorganizado
disorientate *v.* desorientar
disown *v.* renegar
disparity *n.* disparidad
dispassionate *adj.* desapasionado
dispatch *v.* enviar
dispel *v.* desvanecer
dispensable *adj.* prescindible
dispensary *n.* dispensario
dispense *v.* ofrecer
disperse *v.* dispersar
dispirited *adj.* desanimado
displace *v. t* desplazar
display *v.* exponer
displease *v.* desagradar
displeasure *n.* desagrado
disposable *adj.* desechable
disposal *n.* disposición, eliminación
dispose *v. t* disponer
dispossess *v.* desposeer
disprove *v.* refutar
dispute *v. i* disputar, discutir
disqualification *n.* descalificación
disqualify *v.* descalificar
disquiet *n.* inquietud
disregard *v. t* descuidar
disrepair *n.* deterioro
disreputable *adj.* desacreditado
disrepute *n.* deshonra

disrespect *n.* desacato
disrobe *v.* desnudar, desvestir
disrupt *v.* perturbar, interrumpir
dissatisfaction *n.* descontento
dissect *v.* diseccionar
dissent *v.* discrepar
dissertation *n.* disertación, tesis
dissident *n.* disidente
dissimulate *v.* disimular
dissipate *v.* disipar
dissolve *v. t* disolver
dissuade *v.* disuadir
distance *n.* distancia
distant *adj.* distante
distaste *n.* desagrado
distil *v.* destilar
distillery *n.* destilería
distinct *adj.* distinto, definido
distinction *n.* distinción
distinguish *v. t* distinguir
distort *v.* deformar
distract *v.* distraer
distraction *n.* distracción
distress *n.* angustia, aflicción
distribute *v.* distribuir
distributor *n.* distribuidor
district *n.* zona, región, barrio, distrito
distrust *n.* desconfianza
disturb *v.* molestar
ditch *n.* zanja, cuneta
dither *v.* vacilar, titubear
ditto *n.* ídem
dive *v.* zambullirse
diverge *v.* divergir
diverse *adj.* diverso
diversion *n.* desviación
diversity *n.* diversidad
divert *v. t* desviar
divest *v.* despojar
divide *v.* dividir
dividend *n.* dividendo

divine *adj.* divino
divinity *n.* divinidad
division *n.* división
divorce *n.* divorcio
divorcee *n.* divorciado
divulge *v.* divulgar, revelar
do *v.* hacer
docile *adj.* dócil
dock *n.* muelle
docket *n.* rótulo, lista de casos pendientes
doctor *n.* doctor
doctorate *n.* doctorado
doctrine *n.* doctrina
document *n.* documento
documentary *n.* documental
dodge *v. t* esquivar
doe *n.* hembra
dog *n.* perro
dogma *n.* dogma
dogmatic *adj.* dogmático
doldrums *n.* calmas ecuatoriales, capa caída
doll *n.* muñeca
dollar *n.* dólar
domain *n.* dominio
dome *n.* cúpula
domestic *adj.* doméstico
domicile *n.* domicilio
dominant *adj.* dominante
dominate *v.* dominar
dominion *n.* dominio
donate *v.* donar
donkey *n.* burro
donor *n.* donante
doom *n.* sino, condena
door *n.* puerta
dormitory *n.* dormitorio
dose *n.* dosis
dossier *n.* dossier, expediente
dot *n.* punto
dote *v.* adorar

double *adj.* doble
doubt *n.* duda
dough *n.* masa, pasta
down *adv.* abajo, bajo
downfall *n.* perdición, ruina
download *v.* descargar
downpour *n.* aguacero, chaparrón
dowry *n.* dote
doze *v. i* dormitar
dozen *n.* docena
drab *adj.* monótono
draft *n.* borrador, esbozo
drag *v. t* arrastrar
dragon *n.* dragón
drain *v. t* drenar
drama *n.* drama
dramatic *adj.* dramático
dramatist *n.* dramaturgo
drastic *adj.* drástico
draught *n.* tiro, corriente de aire, dibujo
draw *v.* dibujar, sacar, atraer,
drawback *n.* inconveniente
drawer *n.* cajón
drawing *n.* dibujo
dread *v.t* temer
dreadful *adj.* terrible
dream *n.* sueño
dreary *adj.* melancólico
drench *v.* empapar
dress *v.* vestido
dressing *n.* apósito, vendaje
drift *v.* ir a la deriva
drill *n.* taladro, taladradora
drink *v. t* beber
drip *v. i* gotear
drive *v.* conducir
driver *n.* conductor
drizzle *n.* llovizna
droll *adj.* gracioso, ocurrente
droop *v.* decaer

drop *v.* caer, derribar, gotear
dross *n.* basura
drought *n.* sequía
drown *v.* ahogar
drowse *v.* dormitar
drug *n.* droga
drum *n.* tambor
drunkard *adj.* borracho
dry *adj.* seco
dryer *n.* secador
dual *adj.* dual, doble
dubious *adj.* dudoso
duck *n.* pato
duct *n.* conducto
dudgeon *n.* enojo
due *adj.* vencido
duel *n.* duelo
duet *n.* dúo
dull *adj.* apagado, aburrido
dullard *n.* zopenco
duly *adv.* débilmente
dumb *adj.* mudo, tonto
dummy *n.* maniquí
dump *n.* basurero, vertedero
dung *n.* estiércol, cagada
dungeon *n.* mazmorra
duo *n.* dúo
dupe *v.* engañar
duplex *n.* dúplex
duplicate *adj.* duplicado
duplicity *n.* duplicidad
durable *adj.* durable
duration *n.* duración
during *prep.* durante
dusk *n.* anochecer
dust *n.* polvo
duster *n.* plumero, trapo, borrador
dutiful *adj.* obediente, respetuoso
duty *n.* deber
duvet *n.* edredón
dwarf *n.* enano
dwell *v.* vivir, morar

dwelling *n.* morada, vivienda
dwindle *v. t* disminuir, menguar
dye *n.* tinte
dynamic *adj.* dinámico
dynamics *n.* dinámica
dynamite *n.* dinamita
dynamo *n.* dinamo
dynasty *n.* dinastía
dysentery *n.* disentería
dysfunctional *adj.* disfuncional
dyslexia *n.* dislexia
dyspepsia *n.* dispepsia

E

each *adj.* cada uno
eager *adj.* impaciente, entusiasta
eagle *n.* águila
ear *n.* oído, oreja
earl *n.* conde
early *adj.* temprano
earn *v.* ganar
earnest *adj.* serio, concienzudo
earth *n.* tierra
earthen *adj.* de tierra
earthly *adj.* terrenal
earthquake *n.* terremoto
ease *n.* facilidad
east *n.* este
easter *n.* Pascua
eastern *adj.* oriental
easy *adj.* fácil
eat *v.* comer
eatery *n.* restaurante
eatable *adj.* comible
ebb *n.* reflujo
ebony *n.* ébano
ebullient *adj.* vivaz
eccentric *adj.* excéntrico

echo *n.* eco
eclipse *n.* eclipse
ecology *n.* ecología
economic *adj.* económico
economical *adj.* económico
economics *n.* economía
economy *n.* economía
ecstasy *n.* éxtasis
edge *n.* filo
edgy *adj.* tenso
edible *adj.* comestible
edict *n.* edicto
edifice *n.* edificio
edit *v.* editar
edition *n.* edición
editor *n.* editor
editorial *adj.* editorial
educate *v.* educar
education *n.* educación
efface *v.* borrar
effect *n.* efecto
effective *adj.* efectivo
effeminate *adj.* afeminado
effete *adj.* amanerado
efficacy *n.* eficacia
efficiency *n.* eficiencia
efficient *adj.* eficiente
effigy *n.* efigie
effort *n.* esfuerzo
egg *n.* huevo
ego *n.* ego
egotism *n.* egotismo
eight *adj. & n.* ocho
eighteen *adj. & n.* dieciocho
eighty *adj. & n.* ochenta
either *adv.* tampoco
ejaculate *v.* eyacular
eject *v. t* expulsar
elaborate *adj.* complicado
elapse *v.* transcurrir
elastic *adj.* elástico
elbow *n.* codo

elder *adj.* mayor
elderly *adj.* anciano
elect *v.* elegir
election *n.* elecciones
elective *adj.* electo
electorate *n.* electorado
electric *adj.* eléctrico
electrician *n.* electricista
electricity *n.* electricidad
electrify *v.* electrificar
electrocute *v.* electrocutar
electronic *adj.* electrónico
elegance *n.* elegancia
elegant *adj.* elegante
element *n.* elemento
elementary *adj.* elemental
elephant *n.* elefante
elevate *v.* subir, elevar, conceder,
elevator *n.* ascensor
eleven *adj. & n.* once
elf *n.* elfo
elicit *v.* provocar
eligible *adj.* adecuado
eliminate *v.* eliminar
elite *n.* elite
ellipse *n.* elipse
elocution *n.* elocución
elongate *v.* alargar
elope *v.* fugarse
eloquence *n.* elocuencia
else *adv.* otro, más, demás
elucidate *v. t* dilucidar
elude *v.* eludir
elusion *n.* escapatoria
elusive *adj.* escurridizo
emaciated *adj.* escuálido
email *n.* correo electrónico
emancipate *v. t* emancipar
emasculate *v.* castrar
embalm *v.* embalsamar
embankment *n.* terraplén, muro
    de contención

embargo *n.* embargo
embark *v. t* embarcar
embarrass *v.* pasar vergüenza
embassy *n.* embajada
embattled *adj.* asediado
embed *v.* enterrar
embellish *v.* adornar
embitter *v.* amargar
emblem *n.* emblema
embodiment *v. t.* encarnación
embolden *v.* envalentonar
emboss *v.* repujar
embrace *v.* abrazar
embroidery *n.* bordado
embryo *n.* embrión
emend *v.* enmendar
emerald *n.* esmeralda
emerge *v.* aparecer
emergency *n.* emergencia
emigrate *v.* emigrar
eminence *n.* eminencia
eminent *adj.* eminente
emissary *n.* emisario
emit *v.* despedir
emollient *adj.* emoliente
emolument *n.* emolumento,
    honorario
emotion *n.* emoción
emotional *adj.* emocional
emotive *adj.* emotivo
empathy *n.* empatía
emperor *n.* emperador
emphasis *n.* énfasis
emphasize *v.* enfatizar
emphatic *adj.* enfático
empire *n.* imperio
employ *v.* contratar
employee *n.* empleado
employer *n.* empleador
empower *v.* otorgar poderes
empress *n.* emperatriz
empty *adj.* vacío

emulate v. t emular

enable v. permitir a alguien hacer algo

enact v. promulgar

enamel n. esmalte

enamour v. t enamorar

encapsulate v. encapsular

encase v. revestir

enchant v. cautivar

encircle v. t rodear

enclave n. enclave

enclose v. encerrar

enclosure n. recinto

encode v. codificar, cifrar

encompass v. abarcar

encore n. bis, repetición

encounter v. encuentro

encourage v. animar

encroach v. invadir

encrypt v. cifrar

encumber v. cargar

encyclopaedia n. enciclopedia

end n. fin, final, punta, extremo

endanger v. poner en peligro

endear v. hacerse querer

endearment n. expresión de cariño

endeavour v. intentar

endemic adj. endémico

endorse v. aprobar

endow v. dotar, dotar de

endure v. aguantar, soportar

enemy n. enemigo

energetic adj. energético

energy n. energía

enfeeble v. debilitar

enfold v. envolver

enforce v. hacer cumplir

enfranchise v. conceder el voto

engage v. participar, comprometer

engagement n. compromiso

engine n. motor

engineer n. ingeniero

English n. inglés

engrave v. grabar

engross v. absorber

engulf v. envolver

enigma n. enigma

enjoy v. disfrutar

enlarge v. agrandar

enlighten v. iluminar, aclarar

enlist v. alistar

enliven v. animar

enmity n. enemistad

enormous adj. enorme

enough adj. suficiente, bastante

enquire v. preguntar

enquiry n. pregunta, investigación, indagación

enrage v. enfurecer

enrapture v. cautivar

enrich v. enriquecer

enrol v. matricularse, inscribirse

enshrine v. consagrar

enslave v. esclavizar

ensue v. seguir

ensure v. asegurar, garantizar

entangle v. t enredar

enter v. entrar

enterprise n. empresa

entertain v. entretener

entertainment n. entretenimiento

enthral v. embelesar

enthrone v. entronizar

enthusiasm n. entusiasmo

enthusiastic n. entusiasta

entice v. atraer

entire adj. entero

entirety n. completamente, totalmente

entitle v. dar derecho a, autorizar

entity n. entidad

entomology n. entomología

entourage *n.* séquito
entrails *n.* entradas
entrance *n.* entrada
entrap *v. t.* atrapar
entreat *v.* suplicar
entreaty *v. t* rogar, suplicar
entrench *v.* afianzar
entrepreneur *n.* empresario
entrust *v.* confiar
entry *n.* entrada
enumerate *v. t* enumerar
enunciate *v.* enunciar
envelop *v.* envolver
envelope *n.* sobre
enviable *adj.* envidiable
envious *adj.* envidioso
environment *n.* medio ambiente
envisage *v.* prever
envoy *n.* enviado
envy *n.* envidia
epic *n.* épico
epicure *n.* sibarita
epidemic *n.* epidémico
epidermis *n.* epidermis
epigram *n.* epigrama
epilepsy *n.* epilepsia
epilogue *n.* epílogo
episode *n.* episodio
epistle *n.* epístola
epitaph *n.* epitafio
epitome *n.* epítome, muestra
epoch *n.* época
equal *adj.* igual
equalize *v. t* empatar, igualar
equate *v.* equiparar
equation *n.* ecuación
equator *n.* ecuador
equestrian *adj.* ecuestre
equidistant *adj.* equidistante
equilateral *adj.* equilátero
equilibrium *n.* equilibrio
equip *v.* equipar

equipment *n.* equipo
equitable *adj.* equitativo
equity *n.* equidad
equivalent *adj.* equivalente
equivocal *adj.* equívoco
era *n.* era
eradicate *v.* erradicar
erase *v.* borrar
erect *adj.* erguido, derecho
erode *v.* erosionar
erogenous *adj.* erógeno
erosion *n.* erosión
erotic *adj.* erótico
err *v.* errar
errand *n.* recado
errant *adj.* descarriado
erratic *adj.* errático
erroneous *adj.* erróneo
error *n.* error
erstwhile *adj.* antiguo
erudite *adj.* erudito
erupt *v.* estallar, entrar en
erupción
escalate *v.* intensificar, escalar
escalator *n.* escalera mecánica
escapade *n.* escapada, aventura
escape *v.i* escapar
escort *n.* escolta
esoteric *adj.* esotérico
especial *adj.* especial
especially *adv.* especialmente,
particularmente
espionage *n.* espionaje
espouse *v.* apoyar
espresso *n.* expreso
essay *n.* ensayo, redacción
essence *n.* esencia
essential *adj.* esencial
establish *v.* establecer
establishment *n.* establecimiento
estate *n.* propiedad, estado
esteem *n.* estima

estimate *v. t* calcular
estranged *adj.* separado
et cetera *adv.* etcétera
eternal *adj.* eterno
eternity *n.* eternidad
ethic *n* ética
ethical *n.* ético
ethnic *adj.* étnico
ethos *n.* valores
etiquette *n.* etiqueta, protocolo
etymology *n.* etimología
eunuch *n.* eunuco
euphoria *n.* euforia
euro *n.* euro
European *n.* europeo
euthanasia *n.* eutanasia
evacuate *v.* evacuar
evade *v. t* evadir, eludir
evaluate *v. i* evaluar
evaporate *v.* evaporar
evasion *n.* evasión
evasive *adj.* evasivo
eve *n.* víspera
even *adj.* plano, igual
evening *n.* tarde
event *n.* evento
eventually *adv.* finalmente, al
   final
ever *adv.* alguna vez
every *adj.* todo, todos
evict *v.* desahuciar
eviction *n.* desalojo
evidence *n.* evidencia
evident *adj.* evidente
evil *adj.* malvado
evince *v.* mostrar, manifestar
evoke *v.* provocar, suscitar
evolution *n.* evolución
evolve *v.* evolucionar
exact *adj.* exacto
exaggerate *v.* exagerar
exaggeration *n.* exageración

exalt *v.* exaltar
exam *n.* examen
examination *n.* examen
examine *v.* examinar
examinee *n.* examinador
example *n.* ejemplo
exasperate *v.* exasperar
excavate *v.* excavar
exceed *v.* exceder, sobrepasar
excel *v.* sobresalir
excellence *n.* excelencia
excellency *n.* Excelencia
excellent *adj.* excelente
except *prep.* menos, excepto,
   salvo
exception *n.* excepción
excerpt *n.* pasaje
excess *n.* exceso
excessive *adj.* excesivo
exchange *v. t* intercambiar
exchequer *n.* tesoro público
excise *n.* impuestos
excite *v.i* excitar
excitement *n.* excitación
exclaim *v.* exclamar
exclamation *n.* exclamación
exclude *v.* excluir
exclusive *adj.* exclusivo
excoriate *v.* vilipendiar
excrete *v.* excretar
excursion *n.* excursión
excuse *v.* disculpar, perdonar
execute *v.* ejecutar
execution *n.* ejecución
executive *n.* ejecutivo
executor *n.* albacea, testamentario
exempt *adj.* exento
exercise *n.* ejercicio
exert *v.* ejercer
exhale *v.* exhalar
exhaust *v.* agotar

exhaustive *adj.* exhaustivo
exhibit *v.* exponer
exhibition *n.* exposición
exhilarate *v.* ilusionar, estimular
exhort *v.* exhortar
exigency *n.* exigencia
exile *n.* exilio
exist *v.* existir
existence *n.* existencia
exit *n.* salida
exonerate *v.* exonerar
exorbitant *adj.* exorbitante
exotic *adj.* exótico
expand *v.* expandir
expanse *n.* extensión
expatriate *n.* expatriado
expect *v.* esperar
expectant *adj.* expectante
expedient *adj.* conveniente
expedite *v.* acelerar
expedition *n.* expedición
expel *v. t* expulsar
expend *v.* gastar, consumir
expenditure *n.* gasto
expense *n.* gasto
expensive *adj.* caro
experience *n.* experiencia
experiment *n.* experimento
expert *n.* experto
expertise *n.* pericia
expiate *v.* expiar
expire *v.* caducar
expiry *n.* vencimiento
explain *v.* explicar
explicit *adj.* explícito
explode *v.* explotar, estallar
exploit *v. t* explotar
exploration *n.* exploración
explore *v.* explorar
explosion *n.* explosión

explosive *adj.* explosivo
exponent *n.* exponente
export *v. t.* exportar
expose *v.* exponer
exposure *n.* exposición
express *v.* expresar
expression *n.* expresión
expressive *adj.* expresivo
expropriate *v.* expropiar
expulsion *n.* expulsión
extant *adj.* existente
extend *v.* extender
extension *n.* extensión
extent *n.* extensión
exterior *adj.* exterior
external *adj.* externo
extinct *adj.* extinto
extinguish *v.* extinguir, apagar, destruir
extirpate *v.* extirpar
extort *v.* extorsionar
extra *adj.* extra
extract *v. t* extraer
extraction *n.* extracción
extraordinary *adj.* extraordinario
extravagance *n.* extravagancia
extravagant *adj.* extravagante
extravaganza *n.* extravagancia
extreme *adj.* extremo
extremist *n.* extremista
extricate *v.* sacar, librar, extraer
extrovert *n.* extrovertido
extrude *v.* expulsar
exuberant *adj.* exuberante
exude *v.* rezumar
eye *n.* ojo
eyeball *n.* globo ocular
eyesight *n.* vista
eyewash *n.* colirio
eyewitness *n.* testigo

F

fable *n.* fábula
fabric *n.* tejido
fabricate *v.* fabrica
fabulous *adj.* fabuloso
facade *n.* fachada
face *n.* cara
facet *n.* faceta
facetious *adj.* chistoso
facial *adj.* facial
facile *adj.* superficial
facilitate *v.* facilitar
facility *n.* facilidad
facing *n.* entretela
facsimile *n.* facsímil
fact *n.* hecho
faction *n.* facción
factitious *adj.* faccioso
factor *n.* factor
factory *n.* fábrica
faculty *n.* facultad
fad *n.* moda pasajera
fade *v.i* desteñirse
faherenheit *n.* Fahrenheit
fail *v.* suspender
failling *n.* falta, defecto
failure *n.* fracaso
faint *adj.* débil
fair *adj.* justo, rubio
fairing *n.* carenado
fairly *adv.* limpiamente
fairy *n.* hada
faith *n.* fe
faithful *adj.* fiel
faithless *adj.* desleal
fake *adj.* falso
falcon *n.* halcón
fall *v.* caer
fallacy *n.* falacia

fallible *adj.* falible
fallow *adj.* barbecho
false *adj.* falso
falsehood *n.* mentira
falter *v.* vacilar
fame *n.* fama
familiar *adj.* familiar
family *n.* familiar
famine *n.* hambre
famished *adj.* hambriento
famous *adj.* famoso
fan *n.* fan
fanatic *n.* fanático
fanciful *adj.* fantástico, extravagante
fancy *n.* capricho
fanfare *n.* platillo, verbena
fang *n.* colmillo
fantasize *v.* fantasear
fantastic *adj.* fantástico
fantasy *n.* fantasía
far *adv.* lejos
farce *n.* farsa
fare *n.* tarifa
farewell *interj.* adiós
farm *n.* granja
farmer *n.* granjero
fascia *n.* faja, salpicadero
fascinate *v.* fascinar
fascism *n.* fascismo
fashion *n.* moda
fashionable *adj.* de moda
fast *adj.* rápidamente
fasten *v.* abrochar
fastness *n.* rapidez
fat *n.* gordo
fatal *adj.* fatal, mortal
fatality *n.* fatalidad
fate *n.* destino
fateful *adj.* fatídico
father *n.* padre
fathom *n.* braza

fatigue *n.* fatiga
fatuous *adj.* necio
fault *n.* error
faulty *adj.* defectuoso
fauna *n.* fauna
favour *n.* favor
favourable *adj.* favorable
favourite *adj.* favorito
fax *n.* fax
fear *n.* miedo
fearful *adj.* miedoso
fearless *adj.* sin miedo
feasible *adj.* factible
feast *n.* banquete
feat *n.* hazaña
feather *n.* pluma
feature *n.* característica
febrile *adj.* febril
February *n.* Febrero
feckless *adj.* irresponsable
federal *adj.* federal
federate *v.* federar
federation *n.* federación
fee *n.* tarifa, precio, cuota
feeble *adj.* débil
feed *v.* alimentar
feeder *n.* comedero
feel *v.* sentir
feeling *n.* sentimiento
feign *v.* fingir
feisty *adj.* animado
felicitate *v.* felicitar
felicitation *n.* felicitación
felicity *n.* felicidad
fell *v.* talar
fellow *n.* compañero
fellowship *n.* compañerismo
felon *n.* criminal
female *adj.* femenino
feminine *adj.* femenino
feminism *n.* feminismo
fence *n.* cerca

fencing *n.* esgrima
fend *v.* defenderse
feng shui *n.* feng shui
fennel *n.* hinojo
feral *adj.* salvaje
ferment *v.* fermentar
fermentation *n.* fermentación
fern *n.* helecho
ferocious *adj.* feroz
ferry *n.* ferry
fertile *adj.* fértil
fertility *n.* fertilidad
fertilize *v.* fertilizar
fertilizer *n.* fertilizante
fervent *adj.* ardiente
fervid *adj.* ferviente
fervour *n.* fervor
fester *v.* ulcerarse
festival *n.* festival
festive *adj.* festivo
festivity *n.* festividad
fetch *v.* buscar
fete *n.* fiesta
fetish *n.* fetiche
fettle *n.* de buen ánimo
fetus *n.* feto
feud *n.* enemistad
feudalism *n.* feudalismo
fever *n.* fiebre
few *adj.* pocos
fey *adj.* mágico
fiance *n.* prometido
fiasco *n.* fiasco
fibre *n.* fibra
fickle *adj.* inconstante
fiction *n.* ficción
fictitious *adj.* ficticio
fiddle *n.* violín
fidelity *adj.* fidelidad
field *n.* campo
fiend *n.* demonio
fierce *adj.* fiero

fiery *adj.* ardiente
fifteen *adj. & n.* quince
fifty *adj. & n.* cincuenta
fig *n.* higo
fight *v.t* pelear
fighter *n.* combatiente
figment *n.* invención
figurative *adj* figurativo
figure *n.* figura
figurine *n.* estatuilla
filament *n.* filamento
file *n.* carpeta, lima
filings *n.* fichero
fill *v.* llenar
filler *n.* relleno, masilla
filling *n.* relleno, empaste
fillip *n.* impulso
film *n.* película
filter *n.* filtro
filth *n.* quinto
filtrate *n.* filtrado
fin *n.* aleta
final *adj.* final
finalist *n.* finalista
finance *n.* finanzas
financial *adj.* financiero
financier *n.* financiero
find *v.* encontrar
fine *adj.* bueno, bonito, fino
finesse *n.* sutileza
finger *n.* dedo
finial *n.* florón
finicky *adj.* delicado
finish *v.* terminar
finite *adj.* finito
fir *n.* abeto
fire *n.* fuego
firewall *n.* cortafuegos
firm *adj.* firme
firmament *n.* firmamento
first *adj. & n.* primero
first aid *n.* primeros auxilios

fiscal *adj.* fiscal
fish *n.* pez, pescado
fisherman *n.* pescador
fishery *n.* pesca
fishy *adj.* sospechoso
fissure *n.* fisura
fist *n.* puño
fit *adj.* en forma, adecuado
fitful *adj.* irregular
fitter *n.* instalador
fitting *n.* adecuado
five *adj. & n.* cinco
fix *v.* seis
fixation *n.* fijación
fixture *n.* instalación, accesorio, elemento
fizz *v.* burbujear
fizzle *v.* apagarse
fizzy *adj.* gaseoso
fjord *n.* fiordo
flab *n.* michelines, molla
flabbergasted *adj.* pasmado
flabby *adj.* gordo, flojo
flaccid *adj.* flácido
flag *n.* bandera
flagellate *v.* flagelar
flagrant *adj.* flagrante
flair *n.* especial
flake *n.* escama, copo
flamboyant *adj.* extravagante
flame *n.* llama
flammable *adj.* inflamable
flank *n.* flanco
flannel *n.* franela
flap *v.* solapa
flapjack *n.* tortas, pastelitos de avena
flare *n.* llamarada, bengala
flash *v.* destellar
flash light *n.* linterna
flask *n.* frasco
flat *adj.* plano

flatten *v.t.* aplanar
flatter *v.* adular, halagar
flatulant *adj.* flatulento
flaunt *v.* ostentar, lucir
flavour *n.* sabor
flaw *n.* defecto
flea *n.* pulga
flee *v.* huir
fleece *n.* vellón, lana
fleet *n.* flota
flesh *n.* carne
flex *v.* flexionar
flexible *adj.* flexible
flexitime *n.* horario flexible
flick *v.* golpecito, chasquido
flicker *v.t* parpadear
flight *n.* vuelo, fuga
flimsy *adj.* muy ligero, débil
flinch *v.* acobardarse
fling *v.* arrojar
flint *n.* pedernal, piedra
flip *v.* tirar,
flippant *adj.* poco serio
flipper *n.* aleta
flirt *v.i* flirtear
flit *v.* revolotear
float *v.* flotar
flock *n.* rebaño, bandada
floe *n.* témpano
flog *v.* azotar
flood *n.* inundación
floodlight *n.* foco
floor *n.* suelo
flop *v.* fracasar
floppy *adj.* flojo
flora *n.* flora
floral *adj.* floral
florist *n.* florista
floss *n.* hilo dental
flotation *n.* flotación
flounce *v.* moverse de manera
  ostentosa

flounder *v.* tropezar
flour *n.* harina
flourish *v.* florecer
flow *v.i* fluir
flower *n.* flor
flowery *adj.* florido
flu *n.* gripe
fluctuate *v.* fluctuar
fluent *adj.* con fluidez, elocuente
fluff *n.* pelusa
fluid *n.* fluido
fluke *n.* chiripa
flourescent *adj.* fluorescente
flouride *n.* flúor
flurry *n.* ráfaga, agitación
flush *v.* ruborizarse, enjuagar
fluster *v.* poner nervioso
flute *n.* flauta
flutter *v.* revolotear
fluvial *adj.* fluvial
flux *n.* flujo
fly *v.i* volar
foam *n.* espuma
focal *adj.* focal
focus *n.* foco
fodder *n.* pienso
foe *n.* enemigo
fog *n.* niebla
foil *v.* frustrar
fold *v.t* plegar
foliage *n.* follaje
folio *n.* folio
folk *n.* folklore, gente
follow *v.* seguir
follower *n.* seguidor
folly *n.* locura
fond *adj.* cariñoso, tiene cariño a
fondle *v.* acariciar
font *n.* fuente, pila
food *n.* comida
fool *n.* tonto
foolish *adj.* estúpido

foolproof *adj.* infalible
foot *n.* pie
footage *n.* secuencias
football *n.* fútbol
footing *n.* a pie, marcha
footling *adj.* insignificante
for *prep.* para
foray *n.* incursión
forbear *v.* abstenerse
forbid *v.* prohibir
force *n.* fuerza
forceful *adj.* fuerte
forceps *n.* fórceps
forcible *adj.* forzoso
fore *adj.* anterior
forearm *n.* antebrazo
forebear *n.* ancestro
forecast *v.t* pronóstico
forefather *n.* antepasado
forefinger *n.* dedo índice
forehead *n.* frente
foregoing *adj.* precedente
foreign *adj.* extranjero
foreigner *n.* extranjero
foreknowledge *n.* precognición
foreleg *n.* pata delantera
foreman *n.* capataz
foremost *adj.* principal
forename *n.* nombre de pila
forensic *adj.* forense
foreplay *n.* preliminares del acto
    sexual
forerunner *n.* precursor
foresee *v.* prever
foresight *n.* previsión
forest *n.* bosque
forestall *v.* prevenir
forestry *n.* silvicultura
foretell *v.* predecir
forever *adv.* para siempre
foreword *n.* prefacio
forfeit *v.* perder

forge *v.t* falsificar
forgery *n.* falsificación
forget *v.* olvidar
forgetful *adj.* olvidadizo
forgive *v.* perdonar
forgo *v.* renunciar
fork *n.* tenedor
forlorn *adj.* desesperado, aban-
    donado
form *n.* forma, formulario
formal *adj.* formal
formality *n.* formalidad
format *n.* formato
formation *n.* formación
former *adj.* anterior
formerly *adv.* anteriormente
formidable *adj.* formidable
formula *n.* fórmula
formulate *v.* formular
forsake *v.* abandonar
forswear *v.* renegar
fort *n.* fuerte
forte *n.* fuerte
forth *adv.* en adelante
forthcoming *adj.* próximo
forthwith *adv.* inmediatamente
fortify *v.* fortalecer
fortitude *n.* fortaleza
fortnight *n.* quincena
fortress *n.* fortaleza
fortunate *adj.* afortunado
fortune *n.* fortuna
forty *adj.& n.* cuarenta
forum *n.* foro
forward *adv. &adj.* hacia delante
fossil *n.* fósil
foster *v.* acoger a un niño, fo-
    mentar
foul *adj.* sucio
foundation *n.* fundación
founder *n.* fundador
foundry *n.* fundación

fountain *n.* fuente
four *adj.& n.* cuatro
fourteen *adj.& n.* catorce
fourth *adj.& n.* cuarto
fowl *n.* ave
fox *n.* zorro
foyer *n.* vestíbulo
fraction *n.* fracción
fractious *adj.* quejumbroso
fracture *v.t* fracturar
fragile *adj.* frágil
fragment *n.* fragmento
fragrance *n.* fragancia
fragrant *adj.* fragante
frail *adj.* quebradizo
frame *n.* estructura,
  marco,montura
framework *n.* marco
franchise *n.* franquicia
frank *adj.* franco
frantic *adj.* frenético
fraternal *adj.* fraternal
fraternity *n.* fraternidad
fraud *n.* fraude
fraudulent *adj.* fraudulento
fraught *adj.* cargado de
fray *v.* deshilacharse
freak *n.* raro, monstruo, friki
freckle *n.* peca
free *adj.* libre
freebie *n.* regalo, algo gratuito
freedom *n.* libertad
freeze *v.* congelar
freezer *n.* congelador
freight *n.* carga
freighter *n.* carguero
French *adj.* francés
frenetic *adj.* frenético
frenzy *n.* frenesí
frequency *n.* frecuencia
frequent *adj.* frecuente
fresh *adj.* fresco

fret *v.t.* inquietarse
fretful *adj.* inquieto
friable *adj.* friable
friction *n.* fricción
Friday *n.* viernes
fridge *n.* frigorífico, nevera,
  refrigerador
friend *n.* amigo
fright *n.* susto
frighten *v.* asustar
frigid *adj.* frígido
frill *n.* volante
fringe *n.* flequillo
frisk *v.* cachear, retozar
fritter *v.* desperdiciar
frivolous *adj.* frívolo
frock *n.* vestido
frog *n.* rana
frolic *v.i.* juguetear
from *prep.* de
front *n.* parte delantera
frontbencher *n.* portavoz
frontier *n.* frontera
frost *n.* helada, escarcha
frosty *adj.* helado, escarchado
froth *n.* espuma
frown *v.i* fruncir el ceño
frowsty *adj.* sofocante
frugal *adj.* frugal
fruit *n.* fruta
fruitful *adj.* provechoso
frump *n.* antigualla
frustrate *v.* frustrar
fry *v.* freír
fudge *n.* dulce de azúcar
fuel *n.* combustible
fugitive *n.* fugitivo
fulcrum *n.* fulcro
fulfil *v.* satisfacer
fulfilment *n.* satisfacción, realización
full *adj.* lleno

fulsome *adj.* excesivo
fumble *v.* tocar
fume *n.* humo
fumigate *v.* fumigar
fun *n.* diversión
function *n.* función
functional *adj.* funcional
functionary *n.* funcionario
fund *n.* fondo, fuente
fundamental *adj.* fundamental
funeral *n.* funeral
fungus *n.* hongo
funky *adj.* funky, enrollado
funnel *n.* embudo
funny *adj.* gracioso, divertido
fur *n.* piel
furious *adj.* furioso
furl *v.* plegar
furlong *n.* octava parte de una milla
furnace *n.* horno
furnish *v.* amueblar
furnishing *n.* muebles
furniture *n.* mueble
furore *n.* furor
furrow *n.* surco
further *adv.* más, más lejos
furthermore *adv.* además
furthest *adj.& adv.* más lejano
fury *n.* furia
fuse *v.* fundir, fusionar
fusion *n.* fusión
fuss *n.* bulla, protesta
fussy *adj.* exigente
fusty *adj.* mohoso, anticuado
futile *adj.* vano
futility *n.* inutilidad
future *n.* futuro
futuristic *adj.* futurístico

G

gab *v.* cotorrear
gabble *v.t.* parlotear
gadget *n.* artilugio
gaffe *n.* metedura, gafe
gag *n.* chiste
gaga *adj.* majara
gaiety *n.* alegría
gaily *adv.* alegremente
gain *v.* ganar
gainful *adj.* remunerado
gait *n.* modo de andar
gala *n.* gala
galaxy *n.* galaxia
gale *n.* vendaval
gall *n.* descaro, hiel
gallant *adj.* galante, valiente
gallantry *n.* galantería
gallery *n.* galería, museo
gallon *n.* galón
gallop *n.* galope
gallows *n.* horca
galore *adj.* en abundancia
galvanize *v.i.* impulsar
gambit *n.* táctica
gamble *v.* apostar
gambler *n.* jugador
gambol *v.* retozar
game *n.* juego
gamely *adj.* animosamente
gammy *adj.* lisiado
gamut *n.* gama, espectro
gang *n.* pandilla
gangling *adj.* larguirucho
gangster *n.* gánster
gangway *n.* pasillo
gap *n.* hueco, intervalo
gape *v.* estar o quedar boquiabierto

garage *n.* garaje
garb *n.* vestimenta
garbage *n.* basura
garble *v.* tergiversar
garden *n.* jardín
gardener *n.* jardinero
gargle *v.* hacer gárgaras
garish *adj.* chillón
garland *n.* guirnalda
garlic *n.* ajo
garment *n.* prenda de vestir
garner *v.* recoger, reunir
garnet *n.* granate
garnish *v.* adornar, aderezar, decorar
garret *n.* buhardilla
garrulous *adj.* gárrulo
garter *n.* liga
gas *n.* gas
gasket *n.* junta
gasp *v.i* jadear
gastric *adj.* gástrico
gastronomy *n.* gastronomía
gate *n.* puerta, verja
gateau *n.* tarta
gather *v.* coger, reunir, entender
gaudy *adj.* chillón
gauge *n.* indicador
gaunt *adj.* descarnado, desolado
gauntlet *n.* guante
gauze *n.* gasa
gawky *adj.* torpe
gay *adj.* gay, alegre
gaze *v.* mirar con fijeza
gazebo *n.* cenador
gazette *n.* gaceta
gear *n.* herramientas, caja de cambios
geek *n.* obseso de la informática, ganso
gel *n.* gel
geld *v.* castrar

gem *n.* gema, joya
gender *n.* género
general *adj.* general
generalize *v.* generalizar
generate *v.* generar
generation *n.* generación
generator *n.* generador
generosity *n.* generosidad
generous *adj.* generoso
genesis *n.* génesis
genetic *adj.* genético
genial *adj.* simpático, cordial
genius *n.* genio
genteel *adj.* cortés
gentility *n.* gentileza
gentle *adj.* amable, dulce, suave
gentleman *n.* caballero
gentry *n.* alta burguesía
genuine *adj.* genuino
geographer *n.* geógrafo
geographical *adj.* geográfico
geography *n.* geografía
geologist *n.* geólogo
geology *n.* geología
geometric *adj.* geométrico
geometry *n.* geometría
germ *n.* germen, microbio
German *n.* alemán
germane *adj.* estar vinculado
germinate *v.* germinar
germination *n.* germinación
gerund *n.* gerundio
gestation *n.* gestación
gesture *n.* gesto
get *v.* obtener
geyser *n.* géiser
ghastly *adj.* horrible, pálido
ghost *n.* fantasma
giant *n.* gigante
gibber *v.* farfullar
gibe *v.* burlarse
giddy *adj.* vertiginoso

gift *n.* regalo
gifted *adj.* dotado
gigabyte *n.* gigabyte
gigantic *adj.* gigantesco
giggle *v.t.* sonreir, reir
gild *v.* dorar
gilt *adj.* dorado
gimmick *n.* truco
ginger *n.* jengibre
gingerly *adv.* cautelosamente
giraffe *n.* jirafa
girder *n.* viga
girdle *n.* faja
girl *n.* niña
girlish *adj.* de niña
giro *n.* giro
girth *n.* circunferencia
gist *n.* esencial
give *v.* dar
given *adj.* determinado, dado
glacial *adj.* glacial
glacier *n.* glaciar
glad *adj.* contento
gladden *v.* alegrar
glade *n.* claro
glamour *n.* glamour
glance *v.i.* mirada
gland *n.* glándula
glare *v.i* deslumbrar, resplandecer
glass *n.* cristal, vaso, copa
glaze *v.* glasear
glazier *n.* vidriero
gleam *v.* brillar
glean *v.* recoger, cosechar, deducir
glee *n.* alegría, regocijo
glide *v.* deslizarse
glider *n.* planeador
glimmer *v.* brillar con luz tenue
glimpse *n.* vistazo
glisten *v.* reducir, brillar
glitch *n.* problema, fallo
glitter *v.* destellar, brillar

gloat *v.* recrearse en, saborear
global *adj.* global
globalization *n.* globalización
globe *n.* globo, esfera
globetrotter *n.* trotamundos
gloom *n.* tinieblas, tristeza
gloomy *adj.* oscuro, triste, pesimista
glorification *n.* glorificación
glorify *v.* glorificar
glorious *adj.* glorioso
glory *n.* gloria
gloss *n.* brillo, esmalte
glossary *n.* glosario
glossy *adj.* lustroso
glove *n.* guante
glow *v.* brillar
glucose *n.* glucosa
glue *n.* pegamento
glum *adj.* abatido
glut *n.* superabundancia
glutton *n.* glotón
gluttony *n.* glotonería
glycerine *n.* glicerina
gnarled *adj.* nudoso
gnat *n.* mosquito
gnaw *v.* roer
go *v.t* ir
goad *v.* aguijonear
goal *n.* meta, gol
goalkeeper *n.* portero
goat *n.* cabra
gob *n.* escupitajo
gobble *v.* engullir
goblet *n.* copa
god *n.* dios
godchild *n.* ahijado
goddess *n.* diosa
godfather *n.* padrino
godly *adj.* piadoso
godmother *n.* madrina
goggles *n.* gafas, anteojos

going *n.* marcha, progreso
gold *n.* oro
golden *adj.* dorado
goldsmith *n.* orfebre
golf *n.* golf
gondola *n.* góndola
gong *n.* gong
good *adj.* bueno
goodbye *excl.* adiós
goodness *n.* bondad
goodwill *n.* buena voluntad
goose *n.* ganso
gooseberry *n.* grosella
gore *n.* sangre
gorgeous *adj.* precioso
gorilla *n.* gorila
gory *adj.* sangriento
gospel *n.* góspel
gossip *n.* cotilleo
gouge *v.* excavar
gourd *n.* calabaza
gourmand *n.* glotón
gourmet *n.* gourmet
gout *n.* gota
govern *v.* gobernar
governance *n.* gobernabilidad
governess *n.* institutriz
government *n.* gobierno
governor *n.* gobernador
gown *n.* traje, toga
grab *v.* coger, arrebatar
grace *n.* gracia
graceful *adj.* elegante
gracious *adj.* cortes, refinado
gradation *n.* gradación
grade *n.* grado, clase
gradient *n.* pendiente
gradual *adj.* gradual
graduate *n.* graduado, licenciado
graffiti *n.* grafiti
graft *n.* injerto
grain *n.* grano

gram *n.* gramo
grammar *n.* gramática
gramophone *n.* gramófono
granary *n.* granero
grand *adj.* magnifico
grandeur *n.* magnificencia
grandiose *adj.* grandioso
grandmother *n.* abuela
grange *n.* granja, casa de campo
granite *n.* granito
grant *v.* conceder
granule *n.* gránulo
grape *n.* uva
graph *n.* gráfica
graphic *adj.* gráfico
graphite *n.* grafito
grapple *v.t.* esforzarse en resolver
grasp *v.* agarrar, asir
grass *n.* hierba
grasshopper *n.* saltamontes
grate *v.t* rechinar, rallar
grateful *n.* agradecido
grater *n.* rallador
gratification *n.* gratificación
gratify *v.* gratificar
grating *n.* rejilla
gratis *adv. &adj.* gratis
gratitude *n.* gratitud
gratuitous *adj.* gratuito
gratuity *n.* gratificación
grave *n.* tumba
gravel *n.* grava
graveyard *n.* cementerio
gravitate *v.* gravitar
gravitation *n.* gravitación
gravity *n.* gravedad
gravy *n.* salsa, jugo
graze *v.* pastar
grease *n.* grasa
great *adj.* grande, magnífico, excelente

greatly *adv.* enormemente
greed *n.* codicia
greedy *adj.* avaricioso
green *adj. & n.* verde
greengrocer *n.* frutero, verdulero
greenery *n.* verdor, follaje
greet *v* saludar, recibir
greeting *n.* saludo, bienvenida
grenade *a.* granada
grey *n.* gris
greyhound *n.* galgo
grid *n.* reja, red
griddle *n.* plancha
grief *n.* dolor, pena
grievance *n.* agravio
grieve *v.* afligirse
grievous *adj.* penoso
grill *v.* asar a la parrilla
grim *adj.* siniestro
grime *n.* mugre
grin *v.* sonreír
grind *v.* moler
grinder *n.* triturador, molinillo
grip *v.* agarrar
gripe *v.* refunfuñar, renegar
grit *n.* gravilla
groan *v.* gemido
grocer *n.* tendero de ultramarinos
grocery *n.* ultramarinos
groggy *adj.* aturdido, grogui
groin *n.* ingle
groom *v.* acicalar
groove *n.* ranura, ritmo,
grope *v.* buscar a tientas
gross *adj.* grosero, enorme, asqueroso
grotesque *adj.* grotesco
grotto *n.* gruta
ground *n.* suelo, tierra
groundless *adj.* infundado
group *n.* grupo

grouping *n.* colocación
grout *n.* lechada
grovel *v.* humillarse
grow *v.i.* crecer
growl *v.* gruñir
growth *n.* crecimiento
grudge *n* resentimiento
grudging *adj.* reticente
gruel *n.* gacha
gruesome *adj.* horrible
grumble *v.* refunfuñar
grumpy *adj.* gruñón
grunt *v.i.* gruñir
guarantee *v.t* garantizar
guarantor *n.* fiador
guard *v.* guardia
guarded *adj.* cauteloso
guardian *n.* guardián
guava *n.* guayaba
gudgeon *n.* gorrón, ganga
guerilla *n.* guerrilla
guess *v.i* adivinar, suponer, acertar
guest *n.* invitado
guffaw *n.* carcajada
guidance *n.* dirección, consejos
guide *n.* guía
guidebook *n.* guía
guild *n.* gremio
guile *n.* astucia
guillotine *n.* guillotina
guilt *n.* culpabilidad
guilty *adj.* culpable
guise *n.* apariencia
guitar *n.* guitarra
gulf *n.* golfo, abismo
gull *n.* gaviota
gullet *n.* esófago
gullible *adj.* crédulo
gully *n.* barranco
gulp *v.* tragar saliva
gum *n.* encía, chicle

gun *n.* arma de fuego
gurgle *v.* gorgotear
gust *n.* ráfaga
gut *n.* intestino, tripa
gutsy *adj.* desafiante
gutter *n.* canalón
guy *n.* tío, tipo
guzzle *v.* tragar
gymnasium *n.* gimnasio
gymnast *n.* gimnasta
gymnastic *n.* patinazo
gynaecology *n.* ginecología
gypsy *n.* gitano
gyrate *v.* girar

H

habit *n.* habito
habitable *adj.* habitable
habitat *n.* hábitat
habitation *n.* habitación
habituate *v.t.* acostumbrarse
habitue *n.* asiduo
hack *v.* cortar, tajar
hackneyed *adj.* trillado
haemoglobin *n.* hemoglobina
haemorrhage *n.* hemorragia
haft *n.* mango
hag *n.* bruja
haggard *adj.* ojeroso
haggle *v.* regatear
hail *n.* granizo
hair *n.* pelo
haircut *n.* corte de pelo
hairstyle *n.* peinado
hairy *adj.* peludo
hajj *n.* peregrinación a la Meca
halal *adj.* sacrificado
hale *adj.* saludable

halitosis *n.* halitosis
hall *n.* sala, vestíbulo
hallmark *n.* marca, sello
hallow *v.* santificar
hallucinate *v.* alucinar
halogen *n.* halógeno
halt *v.* parar
halter *n.* cabestro, dogal
halting *adj.* titubeante, entrecortado
halve *v.* partir por la mitad
halyard *n.* driza
ham *n.* jamón
hamburger *n.* hamburguesa
hamlet *n.* aldea
hammer *n.* martillo
hammock *n.* hamaca
hamper *n.* cesto
hamster *n.* hámster
hamstring *n.* tendón
hand *n.* mano
handbag *n.* bolso
handcuff *n.* esposa
handbill *n.* folleto
handbook *n.* manual
handcuff *v.* poner esposas
handful *n.* puñado
handicap *n.* hándicap
handicapped *n.* incapacitado
handicraft *n.* artesanía
handiwork *n.* obra, trabajo
handkerchief *n.* pañuelo
handle *v.t* encargarse de, tocar
handout *n.* repartición, limosna
handshake *n.* apretón de manos
handsome *adj.* guapo
handy *adj.* practico
hang *v.i.* colgar
hangar *n.* hangar
hanger *n.* percha
hanging *n.* colgante, pendiente
hangover *n.* resaca

hank *n.* madeja
hanker *v.* añorar
haphazard *adj.* fortuito
hapless *adj.* desafortunado
happen *v.* suceder, ocurrir
happening *n.* suceso, acontecimiento
happiness *n.* felicidad
happy *adj.* feliz
harass *v.* acosar
harassment *n.* acoso
harbour *n.* puerto
hard *adj.* duro
hard drive *n.* disco duro
hardback *n.* encuadernado
harden *v.* endurecer
hardly *adv.* apenas
hardship *n.* penas
hardy *adj.* resistente
hare *n.* liebre
harelip *n.* labio leporino
harem *n.* harén
hark *v.* escuchar
harlequin *n.* arlequín
harm *n.* daño, mal
harmful *adj.* perjudicial
harmless *adj.* inofensivo
harmonious *adj.* armonioso
harmonium *n.* armonía
harmonize *v.* armonizar
harmony *n.* armonía
harness *n.* arnés
harp *n.* arpa
harpy *n.* arpía
harrow *n.* escarificador
harrowing *adj.* horroroso
harsh *adj.* cruel
harvest *n.* cosecha
haverster *n.* cosechadora
hassle *n.* molestar
hassock *n.* cojín
haste *n.* prisa

hasten *v.* darse prisa
hasty *adj.* apresurado
hat *n.* sombrero
hatch *n.* escotilla
hatchet *n.* hacha
hate *v.t.* odiar
hateful *adj.* odioso
haughty *adj.* arrogante
haulage *n.* transporte
haulier *n.* contratista de transportes
haunch *n.* anca, pierna
haunt *v.* aparecer
haunted *adj.* embrujado, atormentado
have *v.* tener
haven *n.* puerto, refugio
havoc *n.* estrago
hawk *n.* halcón
hawker *n.* vendedor ambulante
hawthorn *n.* espino
hay *n.* heno
hazard *n.* riesgo
hazardous *adj.* peligroso, arriesgado
haze *n.* neblina
hazy *adj.* brumoso, vago
he *pron.* el
head *n.* cabeza
headache *n.* dolor de cabeza
heading *n.* título
headlight *n.* faro
headline *n.* titular, encabezado
headmaster *n.* director de escuela
headphone *n.* auricular
headquarters *n.* sede central
headstrong *adj.* testarudo
heady *adj.* embriagador, fuerte
heal *v.* curar
health *n.* salud
healthy *adj.* saludable
heap *n.* montón

hear *v.* oír
hearing *n.* oído
hearse *n.* coche fúnebre
heart *n.* corazón
heartache *n.* angustia, pena
heartbreak *n.* desengaño, corazón roto
heartburn *n.* acidez, ardor de estómago
hearten *v.* alentar, animar
heartening *adj.* alentador
heartfelt *adj.* sincero, sentido
hearth *n.* hogar, chimenea
heartless *adj.* sin corazón, despiadado
hearty *adj.* abundante, cordial, sincero
heat *n.* calor
heater *n.* calentador
heath *n.* brezal
heathen *n.* pagano
heather *n.* brezo
heating *n.* calefacción
heave *v.* lanzar, jadear, vomitar
heaven *n.* cielo
heavenly *adj.* celestial, divino
heavy *adj.* pesado
heckle *v.* interrumpir
hectare *n.* hectárea
hectic *adj.* ajetreado
hector *v.* intimidar
hedge *n.* seto
hedonism *n.* hedonismo
heed *v.* tener en cuenta
heel *n.* talón
hefty *adj.* fornido
hegemony *n.* hegemonía
height *n.* altura
heighten *v.* elevar
heinous *adj.* atroz
heir *n.* heredero
helicopter *n.* helicóptero

heliport *n.* helipuerto
hell *n.* infierno
helm *n.* timón
helmet *n.* casco
help *v.* ayudar
helpful *adj.* útil
helping *n.* ración
helpless *adj.* indefenso, incapaz
hem *n.* dobladillo
hemisphere *n.* hemisferio
hen *n.* gallina
hence *adv.* por lo tanto
henceforth *adv.* de hoy en adelante
henchman *n.* secuaz
henna *n.* henna
henpecked *adj.* dominado por su mujer
hepatitis *adj.* hepatitis
herculean *adj.* hercúleo
herd *n.* rebaño
here *adv.* aquí
hereabouts *adv.* por aquí
hereafter *adv.* en lo sucesivo
hereby *adv.* por la presente
hereditary *adj.* hereditario
heredity *n.* herencia
heritage *n.* patrimonio
hermetic *adj.* hermético
hermit *n.* ermitaño
hermitage *n.* ermita
hernia *n.* hernia
hero *n.* héroe
heroic *adj.* heroico
heroine *n.* heroína
herpes *n.* herpes
herring *n.* arenque
hers *pron.* suyo, suya
herself *pron.* ella misma
hesitant *adj.* indeciso
hesitate *v.* dudar, vacilar
heterogeneous *adj.* heterogéneo

heterosexual *adj.* heterosexual
hew *v.* cortar con hacha
hexagon *n.* hexágono
heyday *n.* apogeo
hibernate *v.* invernar
hiccup *n.* hipo
hide *v.t* esconder
hideous *adj.* horrible
hierarchy *n.* jerarquía
high *adj.* alto
highlight *v.* destacar, resaltar
highly *adv.* sumamente
Highness *n.* alteza
highway *n.* autopista
hijack *v.* secuestrar
hike *n.* excursión
hilarious *adj.* graciosísimo
hilarity *n.* hilaridad
hill *n.* colina
hillock *n.* loma
hilt *n.* empuñadura
him *pron.* él, le, lo
himself *pron.* el mismo
hinder *v.* estorbar
hindrance *n.* estorbo, obstáculo
hindsight *n.* retrospectiva
hinge *n.* bisagra
hint *n.* indirecta
hip *n.* cadera
hire *v.t* contratar, alquilar, ar-
    rendar
hirsute *adj.* hirsuto
his *adj.* su, sus, de el
hiss *v.i* sisear
histogram *n.* histograma
historian *n.* historiador
historic *adj.* histórico
historical *adj.* histórico
history *n.* historiador
hit *v.* golpear, pegar
hitch *v.* hacer autostop, casarse,
    subir

hither *adv.* aquí
hitherto *adv.* hasta ahora
hive *n.* colmena
hoard *n.* tesoro
hoarding *n.* acaparamiento, valla
    publicitaria
hoarse *adj.* ronco
hoax *n.* engaño
hob *n.* placa
hobble *v.* cojear
hobby *n.* afición
hobgoblin *n.* duende
hockey *n.* hockey
hoist *v.* elevar
hold *v.t* sujetar, agarrar
holdall *n.* bolsa de viaje
hole *n.* agujero
holiday *n.* vacación
holistic *adj.* holístico
hollow *adj.* hueco
holly *n.* acebo
holmium *n.* holmio
holocaust *n.* holocausto
hologram *n.* holograma
holster *n.* pistolera
holy *adj.* sagrado
homage *n.* homenaje
home *n.* hogar, casa
homely *adj.* hogareño, acogedor
homicide *n.* homicidio
homogeneous *adj.* homogéneo
homoeopath *n.* homeópata
homeopathy *n.* homeopatía
homophobia *n.* homofobia
homosexual *n.* homosexual
honest *adj.* honesto
honesty *n.* honestidad
honey *n.* miel
honeycomb *n.* panal
honeymoon *n.* luna de miel
honk *n.* graznido, bocina
honorary *adj.* honorifico

honour *n.* honor
honourable *adj.* honorable
hood *n.* capucha
hoodwink *v.* engañar
hoof *n.* pezuña
hook *n.* gancho
hooked *adj.* enganchado, aguileño
hooligan *n.* vándalo, gamberro, hooligan
hoop *n.* aro
hoopla *n.* bombo y platillo
hoot *n.* bocina
hoover *n.* aspiradora
hop *v.* brincar
hop *n.* brinco
hope *n.* esperanza
hopefully *adv.* con esperanza
hopeless *adj.* desesperado
horde *n.* horda
horizon *n.* horizonte
horizontal *adj.* horizontal
hormone *n.* hormona
horn *n.* cuerno
hornet *n.* avispón
horoscope *n.* horóscopo
horrendous *adj.* horrendo
horrible *adj.* horrible
horrid *adj.* horroroso
horrific *adj.* horroroso
horrify *v.* horrorizar
horror *n.* horror
horse *n.* caballo
horsepower *n.* caballo
horticulture *n.* horticultura
hose *n.* manguera
hosiery *n.* calcetería
hospice *n.* hospicio
hospitable *adj.* hospitalario
hospital *n.* hospital
hospitality *n.* hospitalidad
host *n.* anfitrión

hostage *n.* rehén
hostel *n.* hostal
hostess *n.* anfitriona
hostile *adj.* hostil
hostility *n.* hostilidad
hot *adj.* caliente
hotchpotch *n.* amasijo
hotel *n.* hotel
hound *n.* perro de caza
hour *n.* hora
house *n.* casa
housewife *n.* ama de casa
housing *n.* alojamiento
hovel *n.* pocilga
hover *v.* flotar
how *adv.* como
however *adv.* sin embargo, no obstante
howl *n.* aullido
howler *n.* aullador
hub *n.* centro
hubbub *n.* barahúnda
huddle *v.* amontonarse
hue *n.* color, tono
huff *n.* rabieta
hug *v.* abrazar
huge *adj.* enorme
hulk *n.* barco viejo, armatoste
hull *n.* casco
hum *v.* tatarear, zumbar
human *adj.* humano
humane *adj.* humano
humanism *n.* humanismo
humanitarian *adj.* humanitario
humanity *n.* humanidad
humanize *v.* humanizar
humble *adj.* humilde
humid *adj.* húmedo
humidity *n.* humedad
humiliate *v.* humillar
humility *n.* humildad
hummock *n.* hamaca

humorist *n.* humorista
humorous *adj.* gracioso
humour *n.* humorista
hump *n.* joroba, giba, montículo
hunch *v.* encorvar
hundred *adj.& n.* cien
hunger *n.* hambre
hungry *adj.* hambriento
hunk *n.* trozo
hunt *v.* cazar
hunter *n.* cazador
hurdle *n.* valla, obstáculo
hurl *v.* lanzar
hurricane *n.* huracán
hurry *v.* apresurarse
hurt *v.* herir, dañar, doler
hurtle *v.* pasar volando
husband *n.* marido
husbandry *n* agricultura
hush *v.i* hacer callar
husk *n.* cáscara
husky *adj.* ronco
hustle *v.* empujar, apresurar
hut *n.* cabaña
hutch *n.* conejera
hybrid *n.* hibrido
hydrant *n.* boca de incendios, toma de agua
hydrate *v.* hidratar
hydraulic *adj.* hidráulico
hydrofoil *n.* aerodeslizador
hydrogen *n.* hidrógeno
hyena *n.* hiena
hygiene *n.* higiene
hymn *n.* himno
hype *n.* publicidad, propaganda
hyper *pref.* híper
hyperactive *adj.* hiperactivo
hyperbole *n.* hipérbola
hypertension *n.* hipertensión
hyphen *n.* guion
hypnosis *n.* hipnosis

hypnotism *n.* hipnotismo
hypnotize *v.* hipnotizar
hypocrisy *n.* hipocresía
hypocrite *n.* hipócrita
hypotension *n.* hipertensión
hypothesis *n.* hipótesis
hypothetical *adj.* hipotético
hysteria *n.* histeria
hysterical *adj.* histérico

I

I *pron.* Yo
ice *n.* hielo
iceberg *n.* iceberg
icecream *n.* helado
icicle *n.* carámbano
icing *n.* glaseado
icon *n.* icono
icy *adj.* helado
idea *n.* idea
ideal *n.* ideal
ideally *adv.* lo ideal
idealism *n.* idealismo
idealist *n.* idealista
idealistic *adj.* idealista
idealize *v.* idealizar
identical *adj.* idéntico
indentification *n.* identificación
identity *n.* identidad
identity *v.* identificar
ideology *n.* ideología
idiocy *n.* idiotez
idiom *n.* idioma
idiomatic *adj.* idiomático
idiosyncrasy *n.* idiosincrasia
idiot *n.* idiota
idiotic *adj.* idiota
idle *adj.* inactivo, parado, vago

idleness *n.* inactividad, ociosidad
idler *n.* ocioso
idol *n.* ídolo
idolatry *n.* idolatría
idolize *v.* idolatrar
idyll *n.* idilio
if *conj.* si
igloo *n.* iglú
igneous *adj.* ígneo
ignite *v.* encender
ignition *n.* encendido
ignoble *adj.* innoble
ignominy *n.* ignominia
ignominious *adj.* ignominioso
ignoramus *n.* ignorante, profano
ignorance *n.* ignorancia
ignorant *adj.* ignorante
ignore *v.* ignorar
ill *adj.* enfermo
illegal *adj.* ilegal
illegible *adj.* ilegible
illegibility *n.* ilegibilidad
illegitimate *adj.* ilegítimo
illicit *adj.* ilícito
illiteracy *n.* analfabetismo
illiterate *n.* analfabeto
illness *n.* enfermedad
illogical *adj.* ilógico
illuminate *v.* iluminar
illumination *n.* iluminación
illusion *v.t.* ilusión
illusory *adj.* ilusorio
illustrate *v* ilustrar
illustration *n.* ilustración
illustrious *adj.* ilustre
image *n.* imagen
imagery *n.* imágenes
imaginary *adj.* imaginario
imagination *n.* imaginación
imaginative *adj.* imaginativo
imagine *v.t.* imaginario
imbalance *n.* desequilibrio

imbibe *v.* ingerir
imbroglio *n.* embrollo
imbue *v.* imbuir
imitate *v.* imitar
imitation *n.* imitación
imitator *n.* imitador
immaculate *adj.* inmaculado
immanent *adj.* inmanente
immaterial *adj.* incorpóreo
immature *adj.* inmaduro
immaturity *n.* inmadurez
immeasurable *adj.* inmensurable
immediate *adj.* inmediato
immemorial *adj.* inmemorial
immense *adj.* inmenso
immensity *n.* inmensidad
immerse *v.* sumergir
immersion *n.* inmersión
immigrant *n.* inmigrante
immigrate *v.* inmigrar
immigration *n.* inmigración
imminent *adj.* inminente
immoderate *adj.* inmoderado
immodest *n.* inmodesto
immodesty *a.* inmodestia
immolate *v.* inmolar
immoral *adj.* inmoral
immorality *n.* inmoralidad
immortal *adj.* inmortal
immortality *n.* inmortalidad
immortalize *v.* inmortalizar
immovable *adv.* inamovible
immune *adj.* inmune
immunity *n.* inmunidad
immunize *v.* inmunizar
immunology *n.* inmunología
immure *v.* emparedar
immutable *adj.* inmutable
impact *n.* impacto
impair *v.* perjudicar
impalpable *adj.* impalpable
impart *v.* comunicar

impartial *adj.* imparcial
impartiality *n.* imparcialidad
impassable *adj.* infranqueable
impasse *n.* punto muerto
impassioned *adj.* apasionado
impassive *adj.* impasible
impatient *adj.* impaciente
impeach *v.* impugnar
impeachment *n.* impugnación
impeccable *adj.* impecable
impede *v.* estorbar
impediment *n.* impedimento
impel *v.* impeler
impending *adj.* inminente
impenetrable *adj.* impenetrable
imperative *adj.* imperativo
imperfect *adj.* imperfecto
imperfection *n.* imperfección
imperial *adj.* imperial
imperialism *n.* imperialismo
imperil *v.* arriesgar
impersonal *adj.* impersonal
impersonate *v.* imitar, hacerse
pasar por
impersonation *n.* suplantación
impertinence *n* impertinencia
impertinent *adj.* impertinente
impervious *adj.* impenetrable
impetuous *adj.* impetuoso
impetus *n.* ímpetu
impious *adj.* impío
implacable *adj.* implacable
implant *v.* implantar
implausible *adj.* inverosímil
implement *n.* implementar
implicate *v.* implicar
implication *n.* implicación
implicit *adj.* implícito
implode *v.* implorar
implore *v.t.* implorar
imply *v.* dar a entender
impolite *adj.* maleducado

import *v.* importar
importer *n.* importador
importance *n.* importancia
important *adj.* importante
impose *v.* imponer
imposing *adj.* imponente
imposition *n.* imposición
impossibility *n.* imposibilidad
impossible *adj.* imposible
imposter *n.* impostor
impotence *n.* impotencia
impotent *adj.* impotente
impound *v.* incautar
impoverish *v.* empobrecer
impracticable *adj.* impracticable
impractical *adj.* poco practico
impress *v.* impresionar
impression *n.* impresión
impressive *adj.* admirable
imprint *v.* imprimir
imprison *v.* encarcelar
improbable *adj.* improbable
improper *adj.* indecoroso
impropriety *n.* incorreción
improve *v.* mejorar
improvement *n.* mejora
improvident *adj.* imprevisor
improvise *v.* improvisar
imprudent *adj.* imprudente
impudent *adj.* insolente
impulse *n.* impulso
impulsive *adj.* impulsivo
impunity *n.* impunidad
impure *adj.* impuro
impurity *n.* impureza
impute *v.* imputar
in *prep.* en
inability *n.* incapacidad
inaccurate *adj.* erróneo
inaction *n.* inactividad
inactive *adj.* inactivo
inadequate *adj.* inadecuado

inadmissible *adj.* inadmisible
inadvertent *adj.* involuntario
inane *adj.* estúpido
inanimate *adj.* inanimado
inapplicable *adj.* inaplicable
innapropriate *adj.* inapropiado
inarticulate *adj.* inarticulado
inattentive *adj.* distraído
inaudible *adj.* inaudible
inaugural *adj.* inaugural
inaugurate *v.* inaugurar
inauspicious *adj.* adverso
inborn *adj.* innato
inbred *adj.* endogámico
incalculable *adj.* incalculable
incapable *adj.* incapaz
incapacity *n.* incapacidad
incarcerate *v.* encarcelar
incarnate *adj.* encarnar
incarnation *n.* encarnación
incense *n.* incienso
incentive *n.* incentivo
inception *n.* comienzo
incest *n.* incesto
inch *n.* pulgada
incidence *n.* incidencia
incident *n.* incidente
incidental *adj.* incidental
incisive *adj.* incisivo
incite *v.* incitar
inclination *n.* inclinación
incline *v.* inclinar
include *v.* incluir
inclusion *n.* inclusión
inclusive *adj.* inclusivo
incoherent *adj.* incoherente
income *n.* ingresos
incomparable *adj.* incomparable
incompatible *adj.* incompatible
incompetent *adj.* incompetente
incomplete *adj.* incompleto

inconclusive *adj.* inconcluyente
inconsiderate *adj.* inconsiderado
inconsistent *adj.* inconsistente
inconsolable *adj.* inconsolable
inconspicuous *adj.* insignificante, no llama la atención
inconvenience *n.* inconveniencia
incorporate *v.* incorporar
incorporation *n.* incorporación
incorrect *adj.* incorrecto
incorrigible *adj.* incorregible
incorruptible *adj.* incorruptible
increase *v.* incrementar, aumentar
incredible *adj.* increíble
increment *n.* incremento
incriminate *v.i.* incriminar
incubate *v.* incubar
inculcate *v.* inculcar
incumbent *adj.* titular
incur *v.* incurrir
incurable *adj.* incurable
incursion *n.* incursión
indebted *adj.* endeudado
indecency *n.* indecencia
indecent *adj.* indecente
indecision *n.* indecisión
indeed *adv.* ya lo creo
indefensible *adj.* indefensible
indefinite *adj.* indefinido
indemnity *n.* indemnización
indent *v.* mellarse
indenture *n.* escritura, contrato de prácticas
independence *n.* independencia
independent *adj.* independiente
indescribable *adj.* indescriptible
index *n.* índice
Indian *n.* Indio
indicate *v.* indicar
indication *n.* indicación
indicative *adj.* indicativo
indicator *n.* indicador

indict *v.* acusar
indictment *n.* acusación
indifference *n.* indiferencia
indifferent *adj.* indiferente
indigenous *adj.* indígena
indigestible *adj.* indigesto
indigestion *n.* indigestión
indignant *adj.* indignado
indignation *n.* indignación
indignity *n.* indignidad
indigo *n.* añil
indirect *adj.* indirecto
indiscipline *n.* indisciplina
indiscreet *adj.* indiscreto
indiscretion *n.* indiscreción
indiscriminate *adj.* indiscriminado
indispensable *adj.* indispensable
indisposed *adj.* indispuesto
indisputable *adj.* indiscutible
indistinct *adj.* indistinto
individual *adj.* individual
individualism *n.* individualismo
individuality *n.* individualidad
indivisible *adj.* indivisible
indolent *adj.* indolente
indomitable *adj.* indómito
indoor *adj.* interior
induce *v.* inducir
inducement *n.* incentivo
induct *v.* investir
induction *n.* iniciación
indulge *v.* consentir, mimar
indulgence *n.* indulgencia
indulgent *adj.* indulgente
industrial *adj.* industrial
industrious *adj.* trabajador
industry *n.* industria
ineffective *adj.* ineficaz
inefficient *adj.* ineficiente
ineligible *adj.* inelegible
inequality *n.* desigualdad

inert *adj.* inerte
inertia *n.* inercia
inescapable *adj.* ineludible
inevitable *adj.* inevitable
inexact *adj.* inexacto
inexcusable *adj.* inexcusable
inexhaustible *adj.* inagotable
inexorable *adj.* inexorable
inexpensive *adj.* barato
inexperience *n.* inexperiencia
inexplicable *adj.* inexplicable
inextricable *adj.* inextricable
infallible *adj.* infalible
infamous *adj.* infame
infamy *n.* infamia
infancy *n.* infancia
infant *n.* menor, niño
infanticide *n.* infanticidio
infantile *adj.* infantil, pueril
infantry *n.* infantería
infatuate *v.* encapricharse
infatuation *n.* infatuación
infect *v.* infectar
infection *n.* infección
infectious *adj.* infeccioso
infer *v.* inferir
inference *n.* inferencia
inferior *adj.* inferior
inferiority *n.* inferioridad
infernal *adj.* infernal
infertile *adj.* estéril
infest *v.* infestar
infidelity *n.* infidelidad
infighting *n.* luchas internas
infiltrate *v.* infiltrar
infinite *adj.* infinito
infinity *n.* infinito
infirm *adj.* endeble
infirmity *n.* dolencia
inflame *v.* inflamar, avivar, encender
inflammable *adj.* inflamable

inflammation *n.* inflamación
inflammatory *adj.* inflamatorio, incendiario
inflate *v.* inflar
inflation *n.* inflación
inflect *v.* declinar
inflexible *adj.* inflexible
inflict *v.* causar, inferir
influence *n.* influencia
influential *adj.* influyente
influenza *n.* gripe
influx *n.* afluencia
inform *v.* informar
informal *adj.* informal
information *n.* información
informative *adj.* informativo
informer *n.* informante
infrastructure *n.* infraestructura
infrequent *adj.* infrecuente
infringe *v.* incumplir
infringement *n.* violación
infuriate *v.* enfurecer
infuse *v.* infundir
infusion *n.* infusión
ingrained *adj.* arraigado
ingratitude *n.* ingratitud
ingredient *n.* ingrediente
inhabit *v.* habitar
inhabitable *adj.* habitable
inhabitant *n.* habitante
inhale *v.* inhalar
inhaler *n.* inhalador
inherent *adj.* inherente
inherit *v.* heredar
inheritance *n.* herencia
inhibit *v.* inhibir
inhibition *n.* inhibición
inhospitable *adj.* inhóspito
inhuman *adj.* inhumano
inimical *adj.* adverso
inimitable *adj.* inimitable
initial *adj.* inicial

initiate *v.* iniciar
initiative *n.* iniciativa
inject *v.* inyectar
injection *n.* inyección
injudicious *adj.* imprudente
injunction *n.* orden judicial
injure *v.* lesionar, herir
injurious *adj.* perjudicial
injury *n.* lesión
injustice *n.* injusticia
ink *n.* tinta
inkling *n.* atisbo
inland *adj.* interior
inmate *n.* interno, preso, paciente hospitalizado
inmost *adj.* más recóndito
inn *n.* taberna, hostal
innate *adj.* innato
inner *adj.* inferior
innermost *adj.* más recóndito
innings *n.* turno
innocence *n.* inocencia
innocent *adj.* inocente
innovate *v.* innovar
innovation *n.* innovación
innovator *n.* innovador
innumerable *adj.* innumerable
inoculate *v.* inocular
inoculation *n.* inoculación
inoperative *adj.* inoperante
inopportune *adj.* inoportuno
inpatient *n.* impaciente
input *n.* aportación
inquest *n.* investigación, pesquisa
inquire *v.* preguntar
inquiry *n.* pregunta, petición, investigación
inquisition *n.* inquisición
inquisitive *adj.* inquisitivo
insane *adj.* demente
insanity *n.* demencia
insatiable *adj.* insaciable

inscribe *v.* inscribir
inscription *n.* inscripción
insect *n.* insecto
insecticide *n.* insecticida
insecure *adj.* inseguro
insecurity *n.* inseguridad
insensible *adj.* insensible
inseparable *adj.* inseparable
insert *v.* insertar
insertion *n.* inserción
inside *n.* dentro
insight *n.* perspicacia
insignificance *n.* insignificancia
insignificant *adj.* insignificante
insincere *adj.* poco sincero
insincerity *n.* insinceridad
insinuate *v.* insinuar
insinuation *n.* insinuación
insipid *adj.* insípido
insist *v.* insistir
insistence *n.* insistencia
insistent *adj.* insistente
insolence *n.* insolencia
insolent *adj.* insolente
insoluble *adj.* insoluble
insolvency *n.* insolvencia
insolvent *adj.* insolvente
inspect *v.* inspeccionar
inspection *n.* inspección
inspector *n.* inspector
inspiration *n.* inspiración
inspire *v.* inspirar
instability *n.* inestabilidad
install *v.* instalar
installation *n.* instalación
instalment *n.* plazo, cuota
instance *n.* ejemplo
instant *adj.* instantáneo
instantaneous *adj.* instantáneo
instead *adv.* en vez de
instigate *v.* instigar
instil *v.* inculcar

instinct *n.* instinto
instinctive *adj.* instintivo
institute *n.* instituto
institution *n.* institución
instruct *v.* instruir, ordenar
instruction *n.* instrucción
instructor *n.* instructor
instrument *n.* instrumento
instrumental *adj.* instrumental
instrumentalist *n.* instrumentista
insubordinate *adj.* insubordinado
insubordination *n.* insubordinación
insufficient *adj.* insuficiente
insular *adj.* cerrado, estrecho
insulate *v.* aislar
insulation *n.* aislamiento
insulator *n.* aislante
insulin *n.* insulina
insult *v.t.* insultar
insupportable *adj.* insoportable
insurance *n.* seguro
insure *v.* asegurar
insurgent *n.* insurgente
insurmountable *adj.* insalvable
insurrection *n.* insurrección
intact *adj.* intacto
intake *n.* consumo
intangible *adj.* intangible
integral *adj.* integral
integrity *n.* integridad
intellect *n.* intelecto
intellectual *adj.* intelectual
intelligence *n.* inteligencia
intelligent *adj.* inteligente
intelligible *adj.* inteligible
intend *v.* pretender
intense *adj.* intenso
intensify *v.* intensificar
intensity *n.* intensidad
intensive *adj.* intensivo
intent *n.* intento

intention *n.* intención
intentional *adj.* intencional
interact *v.* interactuar
intercede *v.* interceder
intercept *v.* interceptar
interception *n.* intercepción
interchange *v.* intercambiar
intercom *n.* interfono, portero automático
interconnect *v.* interconectar
intercourse *n.* acto sexual
interdependent *adj.* interdependiente
interest *n.* interés
interesting *adj.* interesante
interface *n.* interfaz
interfere *v.* interferir, entrometerse
interference *n.* interferencia
interim *n.* intermedio, interino, provisional
interior *adj.* interior
interject *v.* lanzar, agregar
interlink *v.* encadenar
interlock *v.* entrelazar
interlocutor *n.* interlocutor
interloper *n.* intruso
interlude *n.* intervalo
intermediary *n.* intermediario
intermediate *adj.* intermedio
interminable *adj.* interminable
intermission *n.* intermedio
intermittent *adj.* intermitente
intern *v.* recluir
internal *adj.* interno
international *adj.* internacional
internet *n.* internet
interplay *n.* interacción
interpret *v.* interpretar
interpreter *n.* interprete
interracial *adj.* interracial
interrelate *v.* interrelacionar

interrogate *v.* interrogar
interrogative *adj.* interrogativo
interrupt *v.* interrumpir
interruption *n.* interrupción
intersect *v.* cruzarse
interstate *n.* interestatal
interval *n.* intervalo
intervene *v.* intervenir
intervention *n.* intervención
interview *n.* entrevista
intestine *n.* intestino
intimacy *n.* intimidad
intimate *adj.* intimo
intimidate *v.* intimidar
intimidation *n.* intimidación
into *prep.* en
intolerable *adj.* intolerable
intolerant *adj.* intolerante
intone *v.* entonar
intoxicate *v.* intoxicar
intoxication *n.* intoxicación
intractable *adj.* incorregible
intranet *n.* intranet
intransitive *adj.* intransitivo
intrepid *adj.* intrépido
intricate *adj.* complicado
intrigue *v.* intrigar
intrinsic *adj.* intrínseco
introduce *v.* presentar
introduction *n.* presentación
introductory *adj.* preliminar
introspective *adj.* introspectivo
introspection *n.* introspección
introvert *n.* introvertido
intrude *v.* importunar
intrusion *n.* intrusión
intrusive *adj.* intrusivo, entrometido
intuition *n.* intuición
intuitive *adj.* intuitivo
inundate *v.* inundar
invade *v.* invadir

invalid *n.* inválido
invalidate *v.* invalidar
invaluable *adj.* invalorable
invariable *adj.* invariable
invasion *n.* invasión
invective *adj.* ofensivo
invent *v.* inventar
invention *n.* invento
inventor *n.* inventor
inventory *n.* inventario
inverse *adj.* inverso
invert *v.* invertir
invest *v.t.* invertir
investigate *v.* investigar
investigation *n.* investigación
investment *n.* inversión
invigilate *adj.* supervisar un examen
invigilator *n.* encargado de supervisar un examen
invincible *adj.* invencible
inviolable *adj.* inviolable
invisible *adj.* invisible
invitation *n.* invitación
invite *v.* invitar
inviting *adj.* atractivo, atrayente, acogedor
invocation *n.* invocación
invoice *n.* factura
invoke *v.* invocar
involuntary *adj.* involuntario
involve *v.* implicar, involucrar, conllevar
invulnerable *adj.* invulnerable
inward *adj.* hacia adentro
irate *adj.* airado, furioso
ire *n.* ira
iris *n.* iris
irksome *adj.* fastidioso
iron *n.* hierro
ironical *adj.* irónico
irony *n.* ironía

irradiate *v.* irradiar
irrational *adj.* irracional
irreconcilable *adj.* irreconciliable
irredeemable *adj.* irremediable
irrefutable *adj.* irrefutable
irregular *adj.* irregular
irregularity *n.* irregularidad
irrelevant *adj.* irrelevante
irreplaceable *adj.* irremplazable
irresistible *adj.* irresistible
irresolute *adj.* irresoluto
irrespective *adv.* a pesar de, independientemente
irresponsible *adj.* irresponsable
irreversible *adj.* irreversible
irrevocable *adj.* irrevocable
irrigate *v.* irrigar
irrigation *n.* irrigación
irritable *adj.* irritable
irritant *n.* irritante, molestia
irritate *v.* irritar
irruption *n.* irrupción
Islam *n.* islam
island *n.* isla
isle *n.* isla
islet *n.* isleta, islote
isobar *n.* isobara
isolate *v.* aislar
isolation *n.* aislamiento
issue *n.* tema, asunto
it *pron.* lo, la, le
italic *adj.* cursiva
itch *v.i.* picar
itchy *adj.* picor, picazón
item *n.* artículo
iterate *v.* iterar
itinerary *n* itinerario
itself *pron.* el mismo
ivory *n.* marfil
ivy *n.* hiedra

J

jab *v.* pinchar
jabber *v.* farfullar
jack *n.* gato, enchufe
jackal *n.* chacal
jackass *n.* zopenco
jacket *n.* chaqueta
jackpot *n.* premio gordo
jacuzzi *n.* jacuzzi
jade *n.* jade
jaded *adj.* harto
jagged *adj.* irregular
jail *n.* cárcel
jailer *n.* carcelero
jam *v.t.* bloquear, trabar
jam *n.* mermelada
jamboree *n.* juerga
janitor *n.* conserje
january *n.* enero
jar *n.* tarro
jargon *n.* jerga
jasmine *n.* jazmín
jaundice *n.* ictericia
jaunt *n.* excursión
jaunty *adj.* garboso
javelin *n.* jabalina
jaw *n.* mandíbula
jay *n.* arrendajo
jazz *n.* jazz
jazzy *adj.* llamativo
jealous *adj.* envidioso
jealousy *n.* envidia
jeans *n.* vaqueros
jeep *n.* jeep
jeer *v.* burla
jelly *n.* gelatina
jellyfish *n.* medusa
jeopardize *v.* poner en peligro, arriesgar

jeopardy *n.* peligro, riesgo
jerk *n.* tirón
jerkin *n.* chaleco
jerrycan *n.* bidón
jersey *n.* jersey
jest *n.* broma
jester *n.* bufón
jet *n.* reactor
jet lag *n.* jet lago, desfase horario
jewel *n.* joya
jeweller *n.* joyero
jewellery *n.* alhajas
jibe *n.* burla
jig *n.* plantilla
jiggle *v.* sacudir
jigsaw *n.* rompecabezas
jingle *n.* cascabeleo
jinx *n.* gafe
jitters *n.* nervios
job *n.* trabajo
jockey *n.* jockey
jocose *adj.* jocoso
jocular *adj.* jocoso
jog *v.* empujar, sacudir levemente
joggle *v.* mover, sacudir
join *v.* juntar, unir
joiner *n.* ebanista
joint *n.* mutuo
joist *n.* viga
joke *n.* broma, chiste
joker *n.* bromista
jolly *adj.* alegre
jolt *v.t.* dar saltos
jostle *v.t.* empujar
jot *v.t.* jota, pizca
journal *n.* revista, publicación, periódico
journalism *n.* periodismo
journalist *n.* periodista
journey *n.* viaje
jovial *adj.* jovial
joviality *adv.* jovialidad

joy *n.* alegría
joyful *adj.* alegre
joyous *adj.* feliz
jubilant *adj.* exultante
jubilation *n.* jubilación
jubilee *n.* jubileo
judge *n.* juez
judgement *n.* juicio
judicial *adj.* judicial
judiciary *n.* judicatura
judicious *adj.* juicioso
judo *n.* judo
jug *n.* jarra
juggle *v.* hacer malabarismos
juggler *n.* malabarista
juice *n.* zumo
juicy *adj.* jugoso
july *n.* julio
jumble *n.* embrollo
jumbo *adj.* gigante
jump *v.i* saltar
jumper *n.* saltador
jumper *n.* jersey
junction *n.* cruce
juncture *n.* coyuntura
june *n.* junio
jungle *n.* jungla
junior *adj.* junior, menor,
junior *n.* subalterno
junk *n.* basura, chatarra, junto
jupiter *n.* Júpiter
jurisdiction *n.* jurisdicción
jurisprudence *n.* jurisprudencia
jurist *n.* jurista
juror *n.* jurado, miembro del
   jurado
jury *n.* jurado
just *adj.* justo
justice *n.* justicia
justifiable *adj.* justificable
justification *n.* justificación
justify *v.* justificar

jute *n.* yute
juvenile *adj.* juvenil

K

kaftan *n.* caftán
kaleidoscope *n.* calidoscopio
kangaroo *n.* canguro
karaoke *n.* karaoke
karate *n.* karate
karma *n.* karma
kebab *n.* kebab
keel *n.* quilla
keen *adj.* entusiasta
keenness *n.* entusiasmo
keep *v.* mantener, cumplir,
   guardar
keeper *n.* cuidador, guardián
keeping *n.* consonancia, cuidado
keepsake *n.* recuerdo
keg *n.* barril
kennel *n.* perrera
kerb *n.* bordillo
kerchief *n.* pañuelo
kernel *n.* almendra, grano
kerosene *n.* keroseno
ketchup *n.* kétchup
kettle *n.* hervidor
key *n.* llave
keyboard *n.* teclado
keyhole *n.* ojo de la cerradura
kick *v.* patear
kid *n.* niño, chaval
kidnap *v.* secuestrar
kidney *n.* riñón
kill *v.* matar
killing *n.* asesinato
kiln *n.* horno
kilo *n.* kilo

kilobyte *n.* kilobyte
kilometre *n.* kilometro
kilt *n.* falda escocesa
kimono *n.* quimono
kin *n.* parientes
kind *n.* tipo, clase, especie
kind *adj.* amable,bondadoso
kindergarten *n.* jardín de infancia, guardería
kindle *v.* encender
kindly *adv.* amablemente
kinetic *adj.* cinético
king *n.* rey
kingdom *n.* reino
kink *n.* enroscadura
kinship *n.* parentesco
kiss *v.t.* besar
kit *n.* paquete, kit
kitchen *n.* cocina
kite *n.* cometa
kith *n.* amigos
kitten *n.* gatito
kitty *n.* fondo común
knack *n.* don
knackered *adj.* agotado
knave *n.* truhan, sota
knead *v.* amasar
knee *n.* rodilla
kneel *v.* arrodillarse
knickers *n.* bragas
knife *n.* cuchillo
knight *n.* caballero
knighthood *n.* caballería
knit *v.* hacer punto
knob *n.* tirador
knock *v.* golpear, dar
knot *n.* nudo
knotty *adj.* enredado
know *v.* saber, conocer
knowing *adj.* astuto, sagaz
knowledge *n.* conocimiento
knuckle *n.* nudillo

kosher *adj.* Kosher
kudos *n.* prestigio
kung fu *n.* kung fu

L

label *n.* etiqueta
labial *adj.* labial
laboratory *n.* laboratorio
laborious *adj.* laborioso
labour *n.* trabajo
labourer *n.* peón
labyrinth *n.* laberinto
lace *n.* encaje, puntilla
lacerate *v.* lacerar
lachrymose *adj.* lacrimógeno
lack *n.* falta, carencia
lackey *n.* lacayo
lacklustre *adj.* deslucido
laconic *adj.* lacónico
lacquer *n.* laca
lacrosse *n.* lacrosse
lactate *v.* producir leche
lactose *n.* lactosa
lacuna *n.* laguna
lacy *adj.* vago
lad *n.* chico, chaval
ladder *n.* escalera
laden *adj.* cargado
ladle *n.* cucharón
lady *n.* señora, dama
ladybird *n.* mariquita
lag *v.* quedarse atrás
lager *n.* cerveza rubia
laggard *adj.* rezagado
lagging *n.* asilamiento
lagoon *n.* laguna
lair *n.* guarida
lake *n.* lago

lamb *n.* cordero
lambast *v.* arremeter contra
lame *adj.* pobre, débil, inútil
lament *n.* lamento
lamentable *adj.* lamentable
laminate *v.* laminar
lamp *n.* lámpara
lampoon *v.* satirizar
lance *n.* lanza
lancer *n.* lancero
lancet *n.* lanceta
land *n.* tierra
landing *n.* aterrizaje
landlady *n.* casera, dueña
landlord *n.* casero, dueño
landscape *n.* paisaje
lane *n.* camino, sendero, carril
language *n.* lenguaje
languid *adj.* lánguido
languish *v.* languidecer
lank *adj.* lacio
lanky *adj.* desgarbado
lantern *n.* farol
lap *n.* vuelta
lapse *n.* lapsus, fallo
lard *n.* manteca
larder *n.* despensa
large *adj.* grande
largesse *n.* gran escala
lark *n.* alondra
larva *n.* larva
larynx *n.* laringe
lasagne *n.* lasaña
lascivious *adj.* lascivo
laser *n.* laser
lash *v.* azotar
lashings *n.* latigazos
lass *n.* chica
last *adj.* último
lasting *adj.* duradero
latch *n.* pestillo
late *adj.* retrasado

lately *adv.* últimamente
latent *adj.* latente
lath *n.* listón
lathe *n.* torno
lather *n.* espuma
latitude *n.* latitud
latrine *n.* letrina
latte *n.* café con leche
latter *adj.* último
lattice *n.* entramado, enrejado
laud *v.* alabar, loar
laudable *adj.* loable
laugh *v.* reír
laughable *adj.* risible
laughter *n.* risa
launch *v.* lanzar
launder *v.* lavar, planchar
launderette *n.* lavandería
laundry *n.* lavandería
laurel *n.* laurel
laureate *n.* galardonado
lava *n.* lava
lavatory *n.* cuarto de baño
lavender *n.* lavanda
lavish *adj.* espléndido
law *n.* ley
lawful *adj.* legítimo, válido
lawless *adj.* desmandado, descontrolado
lawn *n.* césped
lawyer *n.* abogado
lax *adj.* poco estricto
laxative *n.* laxante
laxity *n.* relajación
lay *v.* poner, colocar
layer *n.* capa
layman *n.* laico
laze *v.* holgazanear
lazy *adj.* vago
leach *v.* filtrar
lead *n.* plomo
lead *v.* llevar, guiar

leaden *adj.* plomizo, pesado
leader *n.* líder
leadership *n.* liderazgo
leaf *n.* hoja
leaflet *n.* folleto, panfleto
league *n.* liga
leak *v.* gotear, perder
leakage *n.* escape, fuga
lean *v.* inclinar
leap *v.* saltar, brincar
learn *v.* aprender
learned *adj.* erudito
learner *n.* estudiante, alumno
learning *n.* aprendizaje, conocimientos
lease *n.* contrato de arrendamiento
leash *n.* correa
least *adj.& pron.* menos
leather *n.* cuero
leave *v.t.* salir, abandonar
lecture *n.* conferencia, charla, clase
lecturer *n.* conferenciante, profesor universitario
ledge *n.* cornisa
ledger *n.* libro mayor, libro de contabilidad
leech *n.* sanguijuela
leek *n.* puerro
left *n.* izquierda
leftist *n.* izquierdista
leg *n.* pierna
legacy *n.* legado
legal *adj.* legal
legality *n.* legalidad
legalize *v.* legalizar
legend *n.* leyenda
legendary *adj.* legendario
leggings *n.* leggings
legible *adj.* legible
legion *n.* legión

legislate *v.* legislar
legislation *n.* legislación
legislative *adj.* legislativo
legislator *n.* legislador
legislature *n.* legislatura
legitimacy *n.* legitimidad
legitimate *adj.* legitimo
leisure *n.* tiempo libre
leisurely *adj.* lento, pausado
lemon *n.* limón
lemonade *n.* limonada
lend *v.* prestar, dejar
length *n.* longitud
lengthy *adj.* largo, prolongado, larguísimo
leniency *n.* indulgencia
lenient *adj.* indulgente
lens *n.* lente, lupa
lentil *n.* lenteja
Leo *n.* leo
leopard *n.* leopardo
leper *n.* leproso
leprosy *n.* lepra
lesbian *n.* lesbiana
less *adj. & pron.* menos
lessee *n.* arrendatario
lessen *v.* aliviar, atenuar
lesser *adj.* menor
lesson *n.* lección
lessor *n.* arrendador
lest *conj.* no sea que
let *v.* dejar
lethal *adj.* letal
lethargic *adj.* letárgico
lethargy *n.* letargo
letter *n.* carta
level *n.* nivel
lever *n.* palanca
leverage *n.* apalancamiento
levity *n.* ligereza
levy *v.* recaudar
lewd *adj.* lascivo

lexical *adj.* léxico
lexicon *n.* léxico
liability *n.* responsabilidad
liable *adj.* responsable
liaise *v.* enlazar
liaison *n.* enlace, unión, coordinación
liar *n.* mentiroso
libel *n.* difamación
liberal *adj.* liberal
liberate *v.* liberar
liberation *n.* liberación
liberator *n.* libertador
liberty *n.* libertad
libido *n.* libido
libra *n.* libra
librarian *n.* bibliotecario
library *n.* biblioteca
licence *n.* licencia
licensee *n.* licenciatario
licentious *adj.* licencioso
lick *v.* lamer
lid *n.* tapa
lie *v.* mentir
liege *n.* vasallo
lien *n.* gravamen
lieu *n.* en vez de
lieutenant *n.* teniente
life *n.* vida
lifeless *adj.* inerte, sin vida, apagado
lifelong *adj.* de toda la vida
lift *v.t.* levantar
ligament *n.* ligamento
light *n.* luz
lighten *v.* aligerar
lighter *n.* mechero
lighting *n.* iluminación, alumbrado
lightly *adv.* suavemente, ligeramente
lightening *n.* aclaramiento

lignite *n.* lignito
like *prep.* como
likeable *adj.* agradable
likelihood *n.* probabilidad
likely *adj.* probable
liken *v.* comparar
likeness *n.* parecido, similitud
likewise *adv.* asimismo
liking *n.* afición
lilac *n.* lila
lily *n.* lirio
limb *n.* miembro, extremidad
limber *adj.* flexible
limbo *n.* limbo
lime *n.* lima
limelight *n.* candelero
limerick *n.* poema gracioso
limit *n.* limite
limitation *n.* limitación
limited *adj.* limitado
limousine *n.* limusina
limp *v.* cojear
line *n.* línea, raya
lineage *n.* linaje
linen *n.* ropa de cama
linger *v.* persistir, quedar, perdurar
lingerie *n.* lencería
lingo *n.* idioma, jerga
lingua *n.* lengua
lingual *n.* lingual
linguist *adj.* lingüista
linguistic *adj.* lingüístico
lining *n.* forro
link *n.* eslabón
linkage *n.* conexión
linseed *n.* linaza
lintel *n.* dintel
lion *n.* león
lip *n.* labio
liposuction *n.* liposucción
liquefy *v.* licuar

liquid *n.* líquido
liquidate *v.* liquidar
liquidation *n.* liquidación
liquor *n.* licor
lisp *n.* ceceo
lissom *adj.* grácil
list *n.* lista
listen *v.* escuchar
listener *n.* radioyente
listless *adj.* indiferente
literal *adj.* literal
literary *adj.* literario
literate *adj.* instruido
literature *n.* literatura
lithe *adj.* ágil
litigant *n.* litigante
litigate *v.* litigar
litigation *n.* litigación
litre *n.* litro
litter *n.* basura
little *adj.* pequeño
live *v.* vivir
livelihood *n.* sustento
lively *adj.* animado
liver *n.* hígado
livery *n.* librea
living *n.* vivo
lizard *n.* lagarto, lagartija
load *n.* carga, peso
loaf *n.* una barra
loan *n.* préstamo
loath *adj.* reacio, poco dispuesto
loathe *v.* odiar, detestar
loathsome *adj.* odioso, detestable, repugnante
lobby *n.* vestíbulo, lobby
lobe *n.* lóbulo
lobster *n.* langosta
local *adj.* local
locale *n.* escenario
locality *n.* localidad
localize *v.* localizar

locate *v.* localizar, ubicar
location *n.* localización
lock *n.* cerrojo, cerradura, candado
locker *n.* taquilla, archivo, consigna
locket *n.* relicario
locomotion *n.* locomoción
locomotive *n.* locomotora
locum *n.* suplente
locus *n.* lugar, punto
locust *n.* langosta
locution *n.* locución
lodge *n.* casa del guarda, portería, pabellón
lodger *n.* inquilino
lodging *n.* alojamiento
loft *n.* buhardilla, loft
lofty *adj.* noble
log *n.* tronco
logarithim *n.* logaritmo
logic *n.* lógica
logical *adj.* lógico
logistics *n.* logística
logo *n.* logo
loin *n.* lomo
loiter *v.* perder el tiempo, holgazanear
loll *v.* vagar
lollipop *n.* chupachups
lolly *n.* polo
lone *adj.* solitario
loneliness *n.* soledad
lonely *adj.* solo
loner *n.* solitario
lonesome *adj.* solo
long *adj.* largo
longevity *n.* longevidad
longing *n.* nostalgia
longitude *n.* longitud
loo *n.* baño
look *v.* mirar

look *n* mirada
lookalike *n.* doble
loom *n.* telar
loop *n.* curva, meandro
loose *adj.* suelto, holgado
loosen *v.* aflojar
loot *n.* botín
lop *v.* podar
lope *v.* trotar
lopsided *adj.* torcido
lord *n.* señor noble
lordly *adj.* altanero
lore *n.* tradición
lorry *n.* camión
lose *v.* perder
loss *n.* perdida
lot *pron.* mucho
lotion *n.* loción
lottery *n.* lotería
lotus *n.* loto
loud *adj.* fuerte, alto
lounge *v.* holgazanear
lounge *n.* salón
louse *n.* piojo
lousy *adj.* malo, asqueroso,
lout *n.* patán
louvre *n.* llama
lovable *adj.* adorable
love *n.* amor
lovely *adj.* bonito, precioso
lover *n.* amante
low *adj.* bajo
lower *adj.* inferior
lowly *adj.* humilde, modesto
loyal *adj.* leal
loyalist *n.* partidario
lozenge *n.* pastilla
lubricant *n.* lubricante
lubricate *v.* lubricar
lubrication *n.* lubricación
lucent *adj.* luciente
lucid *adj.* lúcido

lucidity *adv.* lucidez
luck *n.* suerte
luckless *adj.* desafortunado
lucky *adj.* afortunado
lucrative *adj.* lucrativo
lucre *n.* lucro
ludicrous *adj.* ridículo
luggage *n.* equipaje
lukewarm *adj.* tibio
lull *v.* arrullar, calmar
lullaby *n.* canción de cuna, nana
luminary *n.* luminaria
luminous *adj.* luminoso
lump *n.* bulto
lunacy *n.* locura
lunar *adj.* lunar
lunatic *n.* lunático
lunch *n.* comida, almuerzo
luncheon *n.* almuerzo
lung *n.* pulmón
lunge *n.* arremetida
lurch *n.* bandazo, tumbo, sacudida
lure *v.* atraer
lurid *adj.* escabroso
lurk *v.* merodear
luscious *adj.* cautivador
lush *adj.* exuberante
lust *n.* lujuria
lustful *adj.* lujurioso
lustre *n.* lustre
lustrous *adj.* brillante
lusty *adj.* sano, lozano
lute *n.* laúd
luxuriant *adj.* exuberante
luxurious *adj.* lujoso
luxury *n.* lujo
lychee *n.* lichi
lymph *n.* linfa
lynch *v.* linchar
lyre *n.* lira
lyric *n.* lírica

lyrical *adj.* lírico
lyricist *n.* letrista

M

macabre *adj.* macabro
machine *n.* maquina
machinery *n.* maquinaria
macho *adj.* macho
mackintosh *n.* Macintosh
mad *adj.* loco
madam *n.* señora
madcap *adj.* alocado
Mafia *n.* mafia
magazine *n.* revista
magenta *n.* magenta
magic *n.* magia
magician *n.* mago
magisterial *adj.* magistral
magistrate *n.* magistrado
magnanimous *adj.* magnánimo
magnate *n.* magnate
magnet *n.* imán
magnetic *adj.* magnético
magnetism *n.* magnetismo
magnificent *adj.* magnifico
magnify *v.* ampliar
magnitude *n.* magnitud
magpie *n.* urraca
mahogany *n.* caoba
mahout *n.* cuidador de elefantes
maid *n.* sirvienta, chica de
  servicio
maiden *n.* doncella
mail *n.* correo
mail order *n.* venta por correo
maim *v.* lisiar
main *adj.* principal
mainstay *n.* pilar, puntal

maintain *v.* mantener
maintenance *n.* mantenimiento
maisonette *n.* dúplex
majestic *adj.* majestuoso
majesty *n.* majestuosidad
major *adj.* mayor, principal
majority *n.* mayoría
make *v.* hacer, fabricar
make-up *n.* maquillaje
making *n.* producción, creación
maladjusted *adj.* inadaptado
malady *n.* mal, enfermedad
malaise *n.* malestar
malaria *n.* malaria
malcontent *n.* descontento
male *n.* masculino, macho
malediction *n.* maldición
malefactor *n.* malhechor
malformation *n.* malformación
malfunction *v.* fallar, funcionar
  mal
malice *n.* malicia
malicious *adj.* malicioso
malign *adj.* maligno
malignant *adj.* maligno
mall *n.* centro comercial
malleable *adj.* maleable
mallet *n.* mazo
malnutrition *n.* desnutrición
malpractice *n.* negligencia,
  malversación
malt *n.* malta
maltreat *v.* maltratar
mammal *n.* mamífero
mammary *adj.* mamario
mammon *n.* becerro de oro
mammoth *n.* colosal, enorme
man *n.* hombre
manage *v.* dirigir, gestionar,
  manejar
manageable *adj.* manejable
management *n.* dirección, administración

manager *n.* director, gerente
managerial *adj.* gerencial
mandate *n.* mandato
mandatory *adj.* obligatorio
mane *n.* crin, melena
manful *adj.* valiente
manganese *n.* manganeso
manger *n.* comedero
mangle *v.* destrozar
mango *n.* mango
manhandle *n.* pulso
manhole *n.* pozo, boca de acceso
manhood *n.* madurez
mania *n.* manía
maniac *n.* maniaco
manicure *n.* manicura
manifest *adj.* manifiesto
manifestation *n.* manifestación
manifesto *n.* manifiesto
manifold *adj.* colector
manipulate *v.* manipular
manipulation *n.* manipulación
mankind *n.* humanidad
manly *adj.* viril, varonil
manna *n.* maná
mannequin *n.* maniquí
manner *n.* forma, modo, manera
mannerism *n.* manierismo
manoeuvre *n.* maniobra
manor *n.* feudo
manpower *n.* mano de obra
mansion *n.* mansión
mantle *n.* manto
mantra *n.* mantra
manual *adj.* manual
manufacture *v.* fabricar, manu-
facturar
manufacturer *n.* fabricación
manumission *n.* manumisión
manure *n.* estiércol
manuscript *n.* manuscrito
many *adj.* muchos

map *n.* mapa
maple *n.* arce
mar *v.* estropear
marathon *n.* maratón
maraud *v.* saquear
marauder *n.* maleante
marble *n.* mármol
march *n.* marzo
march *v.* marchar
mare *n.* yegua
margarine *n.* margarina
margin *n.* margen
marginal *adj.* marginal
marigold *n.* caléndula
marina *n.* puerto deportivo
marinade *n.* adobo
marinate *v.* marinar
marine *adj.* marino, naval
mariner *n.* marinero
marionette *n.* marioneta
marital *adj.* matrimonial, conyugal
maritime *adj.* marítimo
mark *n.* marca
marker *n.* marcador
market *n.* mercado
marketing *n.* marketing
marking *n.* mancha, marca
marksman *n.* tirador
marl *n.* margarina
marmalade *n.* mermelada
maroon *n.* granate
marquee *n.* marquesina
marriage *n.* matrimonio
marriageable *adj.* casadero
marry *v.* casar
Mars *n.* marte
marsh *n* pantano
marshal *n.* mariscal
marshmallow *n.* malvavisco
marsupial *n.* marsupial
mart *n.* mercado

martial *adj.* marcial
martinet *n.* tirano
martyr *n.* mártir
martyrdom *n.* martirio
marvel *v.i* maravillarse
marvellous *adj.* maravilloso
Marxism *n.* marxismo
marzipan *n.* mazapán
mascara *n.* rímel
mascot *n.* mascota
masculine *adj.* masculino
mash *v.t* aplastar, machacar, triturar
mask *n.* máscara
masochism *n.* masoquismo
mason *n.* albañil, mampostero
masonry *n.* albañilería
masquerade *n.* mascarada
mass *n.* masa
massacre *n.* masacre
massage *n.* masaje
masseur *n.* masajista
massive *adj.* sólido, enorme
mast *n.* mástil
master *n.* señor, amo
mastermind *n.* cerebro
masterpiece *n.* obra maestra
mastery *n.* maestría
masticate *v.* masticar
masturbate *v.* masturbar
mat *n.* esterilla .
matador *n.* matador
match *n.* cerilla, partido
matchmaker *n.* celestina, casamentera
mate *n.* compañero, amigo, pareja
material *n.* material
materialism *n.* materialismo
materialize *v.* materializar
maternal *adj.* maternal
maternity *n.* maternidad
mathematical *adj.* matemático

mathematician *n.* matemático
mathematics *n.* matemáticas
matinee *n.* primera sesión
matriarch *n.* matriarca
matricide *n.* matricidio
matriculate *v.* matricular
matriculation *n.* matriculación
matrimonial *adj.* matrimonial
matrimony *n.* matrimonio
matrix *n.* matriz
matron *n.* matrona
matter *n.* materia
mattress *n.* colchón
mature *adj.* adulto
maturity *n.* madurez
maudlin *adj.* sensiblero
maul *v.* herir, magullar
maunder *v.* divagar
mausoleum *n.* mausoleo
maverick *n.* aventurero
maxim *n.* máxima
maximize *v.* maximizar
maximum *n.* máximo
May *n.* Mayo
may *v.* poder
maybe *adv.* quizás
mayhem *n.* tumulto, caos
mayonnaise *n.* mayonesa
mayor *n.* alcalde
maze *n.* laberinto
me *pron.* me
mead *n.* aguamiel, prado
meadow *n.* prado, pradera
meagre *adj.* precario
meal *n.* comida
mealy *adj.* harinoso, pálido
mean *v.* significar, querer decir
meander *v.* serpentear
meaning *n.* significado
means *n.* medio
meantime *adv.* mientras tanto
meanwhile *adv.* mientras tanto

measles *n.* sarampión
measly *adj.* mísero
measure *v.* medir
measure *a.* medida
measured *adj.* mesurado
measurement *n.* medición
meat *n.* carne
mechanic *n.* mecánico
mechanical *adj.* mecánico
mechanics *n.* mecánica
mechanism *n.* mecanismo
medal *n.* medalla
medallion *n.* medallón
medallist *n.* medallista
meddle *v.* entrometerse
media *n.* medios de comunicación
median *adj.* medio
mediate *v.* mediar
mediation *n.* mediación
medic *n.* médico
medical *adj.* médico
medication *n.* medicación
medicinal *adj.* medicinal
medicine *n.* medicina
medieval *adj.* medieval
mediocre *adj.* mediocre
mediocrity *n.* mediocridad
meditate *v.* meditar
meditation *n.* meditación
meditative *adj.* meditativo
mediterranean *adj.* Mediterráneo
medium *n.* mediano
medley *n.* mezcla, combinación
meek *adj.* dócil, sumiso
meet *v.* encontrarse
meeting *n.* reunión
mega *adj.* mega
megabyte *n.* megabyte
megahertz *n.* megahercio
megalith *n.* megalito
megalithic *adj.* megalítico
megaphone *n.* megáfono

megapixel *n.* megapíxel
melamine *n.* melamina
melancholia *n.* melancolia
melancholy *adj.* melancólico
melange *n.* mezcla
meld *n.* fusionar, unir
melee *n.* tumulto
meliorate *v.* mejorar
mellow *adj.* maduro, tenue, apacible
melodic *adj.* melódico
melodious *adj.* melodioso
melodrama *n.* melodrama
melodramatic *adj.* melodramáti-co
melody *n.* melodía
melon *n.* melón
melt *v.* derretir, fundir
member *n.* miembro, socio
membership *n.* afiliación
membrane *n.* membrana
memento *n.* recuerdo
memo *n.* memo
memoir *n.* memoria
memorable *adj.* memorable
memorandum *n.* memorándum
memorial *n.* monumento
memory *n.* memoria
menace *n.* amenaza
mend *v.* arreglar, coser, reparar
mendacious *adj.* mentiroso, falso
mendicant *adj.* mendigo
menial *adj.* sirviente
meningitis *n.* meningitis
menopause *n.* menopausia
menstrual *adj.* menstrual
menstruation *n.* menstruación
mental *adj.* mental
mentality *n.* mentalidad
mention *v.* mencionar
mentor *n.* mentor
menu *n.* menú

mercantile *adj.* mercantil
mercenary *adj.* mercenario
merchandise *n.* mercancía
merchant *n.* comerciante
merciful *adj.* compasivo
mercurial *adj.* volátil, voluble
mercury *n.* mercurio
mercy *n.* clemencia
mere *adj.* simple, mero
meretricious *adj.* rimbombante
merge *v.* fundirse, unirse
merger *n.* fusión, unión
meridian *n.* meridiano
merit *n.* merito
meritorious *adj.* meritorio
mermaid *n.* sirena
merry *adj.* alegre
mesh *n.* malla
mesmeric *adj.* fascinante
mesmerize *v.* fascinar
mess *n.* desorden
message *n.* mensaje
messenger *n.* mensajero
messiah *n.* mesías
messy *adj.* desordenado
metabolism *n.* metabolismo
metal *n.* metal
metallic *adj.* metálico
metallurgy *n.* metalurgia
metamorphosis *n.* metamorfosis
metaphor *n.* metáfora
metaphysical *adj.* metafísico
metaphysics *n.* metafísica
mete *v.* repartir
meteor *n.* meteorito
meteoric *adj.* meteórico
meteorology *n.* meteorología
meter *n.* contador
method *n.* método
methodical *adj.* metódico
methodology *n.* metodología
meticulous *adj.* meticuloso

metre *n.* metro
metric *adj.* métrico
metrical *adj.* métrico
metropolis *n.* metrópolis
metropolitan *adj.* metropolitano
mettle *n.* entereza
mettlesome *adj.* animoso
mew *v.* maullar
mews *n.* caballerizas
mezzanine *n.* entresuelo
miasma *n.* miasma
mica *n.* mica
microbiology *n.* microbiología
microchip *n.* microchip
microfilm *n.* microfilme
micrometer *n.* micrómetro
microphone *n.* micrófono
microprocessor *n.* microprocesador
microscope *n.* microscopio
microscopic *adj.* microscópico
microsurgery *n.* microcirugía
microwave *n.* microondas
mid *adj.* medio
midday *n.* mediodía
middle *adj.* medio
middleman *n.* intermediario
middling *adj.* mediano, regular
midget *n.* enano
midnight *n.* medianoche
midriff *n.* diafragma
midst *n* en medio de
midsummer *adj.* pleno verano
midway *adv.* medio camino
midwife *n.* matrona, comadrona
might *v.* poder
mighty *adj.* poderoso, fuerte
migraine *n.* migraña
migrant *n.* migrante
migrate *v.* emigrar
migration *n.* emigración
mild *adj.* afable, dulce

mile *n.* milla
mileage *n.* kilometraje
milestone *n.* hito
milieu *n.* entorno
militant *adj.* militante
militant *n.* militante
military *adj.* militar
militate *v.* militar
militia *n.* milicia
milk *n.* leche
milkshake *n.* batido
milky *adj.* lechoso
mill *n.* molino
millennium *n.* milenio
millet *n.* mijo
milligram *n.* miligramo
millimetre *n.* milímetro
milliner *n.* sombrerero
million *n.* millón
millionaire *n.* millonario
millipede *n.* milpiés
mime *n.* mímica
mime *v.* imitar
mimic *n.* imitador
mimicry *n.* imitación
minaret *n.* minarete
mince *v.* moler
mind *n.* mente
mindful *adj.* consciente de
mindless *adj.* irracional
mine *pron.* mio
mine *n.* mina
miner *n.* minero
mineral *n.* mineral
mineralogy *n.* mineralogía
minestrone *n.* minestrón
mingle *v.* mezclarse
mini *adj.* mini
miniature *adj.* miniatura
minibus *n.* minibús
minicab *n.* mini taxi
minim *n.* blanca

minimal *adj.* mínimo
minimize *v.* minimizar
minimum *n.* mínimo
minion *n.* subalterno
miniskirt *n.* minifalda
minister *n.* ministro
ministerial *adj.* ministerial
ministry *n.* sacerdocio
mink *n.* visón
minor *adj.* menor
minority *n.* minoría
minster *n.* catedral
mint *n.* menta
minus *prep.* menos
minuscule *adj.* minúsculo
minute *n.* minuto
minute *adj.* diminuto
minutely *adv.* minuciosamente
minx *n.* descarado
miracle *n.* milagro
miraculous *adj.* milagroso
mirage *n.* espejismo
mire *n.* lodo, fango
mirror *n.* espejo
mirth *n.* alborozo
mirthful *adj.* alborozado
misadventure *n.* desventura
misalliance *n.* mal casamiento
misapply *v.* emplear mal
misapprehend *v.* malinterpretar
misapprehension *n.* malentendido
misappropriate *v.* malversar
misappropriation *v.* malversación
misbehave *v.* portarse mal
misbehaviour *n.* mala conducta
misbelief *n.* incredulidad
miscalculate *v.* calcular mal
miscalculation *n.* error de cálculo
miscarriage *n.* aborto
miscarry *v.* abortar

miscellaneous *adj.* heterogéneo, variado
mischance *n.* infortunio, desgracia
mischief *n.* travesura
mischievous *adj.* travieso
misconceive *v.* interpretar erróneamente
misconception *n.* error, idea falsa
misconduct *n.* mala conducta
misconstrue *v.* malinterpretar
miscreant *n.* bellaco
misdeed *n.* fechoría
misdemeanour *n.* delito menor, jugarreta
misdirect *v.* desviar
miser *n.* avaro
miserable *adj.* abatido, triste
miserly *adj.* mezquino
misery *n.* miseria
misfire *v.* fallar
misfit *n.* inadaptado
misfortune *n.* desgracia
misgive *v.* hacer recelar
misgiving *n.* recelo
misguide *v.* engañar
mishandle *v.* maltratar
mishap *n.* accidente, percance
misinform *v.* malinformar
misinterpret *v.* malinterpretar
misjudge *v.* calcular mal
mislay *v.* perder, extraviar
mislead *v.* engañar
mismanagement *n.* mala gestión
mismatch *n.* desajuste
misnomer *n.* nombre inexacto
misplace *v.* perder, extraviar
misprint *n.* errata
misquote *v.* citar mal
misread *v.* leer mal
misrepresent *v.* tergiversar
misrule *n.* desgobierno

miss *v.* perder, echar de menos
miss *n.* señorita
missile *n.* misil
missing *adj.* desaparecido
mission *n.* misión
missionary *n.* misionario
missive *n.* misiva
misspell *v.* deletrear mal
mist *n.* niebla
mistake *n.* error
mistaken *adj.* equivocado
mistletoe *n.* muérdago
mistreat *v.* maltratar
mistress *n.* dueña, profesora, amada
mistrust *v.* desconfiar
misty *adj.* neblinoso
misunderstand *v.* malinterpretar
misunderstanding *n.* malentendido
misuse *v.* emplear mal
mite *n.* ácaro
mitigate *v.* mitigar
mitigation *n.* atenuante
mitre *n.* mitra
mitten *n.* mitón
mix *v.* mezclar
mixer *n.* mezcladora, batidora
mixture *n.* mezcla
moan *n.* gemido
moat *n.* foso
mob *n.* turba, mafia
mobile *adj.* móvil
mobility *n.* movilidad
mobilize *v.* movilizar
mocha *n.* moca
mock *v.* burlar, mofar
mockery *n.* burla, mofa
modality *n.* modalidad
mode *n.* modo, medio
model *n.* modelo
modem *n.* módem

moderate *adj.* moderado
moderation *n.* moderación
moderator *n.* moderador
modern *adj.* moderno
modernity *n.* modernidad
modernize *v.* modernizar
modernism *n.* modernismo
modest *adj.* modesto
modesty *n.* modestia
modicum *n.* un atisbo de
modification *n.* modificación
modify *v.t.* modificar
modish *adj.* a la moda
modulate *v.* modular
module *n.* módulo
moist *adj.* húmedo
moisten *v.* humedecer
moisture *n.* humedad
moisturize *v.* hidratar
molar *n.* molar
molasses *n.* melaza
mole *n.* topo
molecular *adj.* molecular
molecule *n.* molécula
molest *v.* abusar
molestation *n.* abuso
mollify *v.* calmar, aplacar
molten *adj.* fundido
moment *n.* momento
momentary *adj.* momentáneo
momentous *adj.* trascendental
momentum *n.* impulso, ímpetu
monarch *n.* monarca
monarchy *n.* monarquía
monastery *n.* monasterio
monastic *adj.* monástico
monasticism *n.* monacato
Monday *n.* lunes
monetarism *n.* monetarismo
monetary *adj.* monetario
money *n.* dinero
monger *n.* vendedor, chismoso

mongoose *n.* mangosta
mongrel *n.* chucho
monitor *n.* monitor
monitory *adj.* instructivo
monk *n.* monje
monkey *n.* mono
mono *n.* mono
monochrome *n.* monocromática
monocle *n.* monóculo
monocular *adj.* monocular
monody *n.* monodia
monogamy *n.* monogamia
monogram *n.* monograma
monograph *n.* monografía
monolith *n.* monolito
monologue *n.* monólogo
monophonic *adj.* monofónico
monopolist *n.* monopolista
monopolize *v.* monopolizar
monopoly *n.* monopolio
monorail *n.* monorraíl
monosyllable *n.* monosílabo
monotheism *n.* monoteísmo
monotheist *n.* monoteísta
monotonous *adj.* monótono
monotony *n.* monotonía
monsoon *n.* monzón
monster *n.* monstruo
monstrous *n.* monstruoso
montage *n.* montaje
month *n.* mes
monthly *adj.* mensual
monument *n.* monumento
monumental *adj.* monumental
moo *v.* mugir
mood *n.* humor
moody *adj.* malhumorado
moon *n.* luna
moonlight *n.* luz de luna
moor *n.* páramo, pantano
moorings *n.* amarradero
moot *adj.* discutible

mop *n.* fregona, mopa
mope *v.* estar deprimido
moped *n.* ciclomotor
moraine *n.* morena
moral *adj.* moral
morale *n.* moral
moralist *n.* moralista
morality *n.* moralidad
moralize *v.* moralizar
morass *n.* ciénaga
morbid *adj.* mórbido
morbidity *adv.* morbosidad
more *n.* mas
moreover *adv.* además
morganatic *adj.* morganático
morgue *n.* morgue
moribund *adj.* moribundo
morning *n.* mañana
moron *n.* imbécil, tarado
morose *adj.* taciturno
morphine *n.* morfina
morphology *n.* morfología
morrow *n.* mañana
morsel *n.* bocado
mortal *adj.* mortal
mortality *n.* mortalidad
mortar *n.* mortero
mortgage *n.* hipoteca
mortagagee *n.* acreedor hipotecario
mortgagor *n.* deudor hipotecario
mortify *v.* mortificar
mortuary *n.* depósito de cadáveres
mosaic *n.* mosaico
mosque *n.* mezquita
mosquito *n.* mosquito
moss *n.* musgo
most *n.* la mayoría
mote *n.* mota
motel *n.* motel
moth *n.* polilla

mother *n.* madre
motherboard *n.* placa base
motherhood *n.* maternidad
mother-in-law *n.* suegra
motherly *adj.* maternal
motif *n.* tema, motivo
motion *n.* movimiento
motionless *adj.* inmóvil
motivate *v.* motivar
motivation *n.* motivación
motive *n.* motivo, móvil
motley *adj.* variopinto
motor *n.* motor
motorcycle *n.* motocicleta
motorist *n.* automovilista, conductor
motorway *n.* autopista
mottle *n.* moteado
motto *n.* lema
mould *n.* matriz, molde
moulder *v.* desmoronar
moulding *n.* moldura
moult *v.* mudar
mound *n.* montículo
mount *v.* montar
mountain *n.* montaña
mountaineer *n.* montañero
mountaineering *n.* alpinismo
mountainous *adj.* montañoso
mourn *v.* llorar, lamentar
mourner *n.* doliente
mournful *adj.* lúgubre, triste, lastimero
mourning *n.* duelo, luto
mouse *n.* ratón
mousse *n.* mousse
moustache *n.* bigote
mouth *n.* boca
mouthful *n.* bocado, trago, bocanada
movable *adj.* movible
move *v.* mover

movement *n.* movimiento
mover *n.* movedor, autor
movies *n.* películas
moving *adj.* emotivo
mow *v.* segar, cortar el césped
mozzarella *n.* mozzarella
much *pron.* mucho
mucilage *n.* mucílago
muck *n.* estiércol
mucous *adj.* mucoso
mucus *n.* mucosidad
mud *n.* barro
muddle *v.* liar, desordenar
muesli *n.* muesli
muffin *n.* madalena
muffle *v.* amortiguar
muffler *n.* bufanda
mug *n.* taza, tarro, jarra
muggy *adj.* bochornoso
mulatto *n.* mulato
mulberry *n.* morera
mule *n.* mula
mulish *adj.* tozudo
mull *v.* calentar
mullah *n.* ulema
mullion *n.* parteluz
multicultural *adj.* multicultural
multifarious *adj.* variopinto
multiform *adj.* multiforme
multilateral *adj.* multilateral
multimedia *n.* multimedia
multiparous *adj.* multípara
multiple *adj.* múltiple
multiplex *n.* multíplice
multiplication *n.* multiplicación
multiplicity *n.* multiplicidad
multiply *v.* multiplicar
multitude *n.* multitud
mum *n.* mama
mumble *v.* farfullar
mummer *n.* máscara, momero
mummify *v.* momificar

mummy *n.* momia
mumps *n.* paperas
munch *v.* mascar
mundane *adj.* mundano
municipal *adj.* municipal
municipality *n.* municipio
munificent *adj.* munificente
muniment *n.* títulos
munitions *n.* municiones
mural *n.* mural
murder *n.* asesinato
murderer *n.* asesino
murk *n.* oscuridad
murky *adj.* turbio, opaco
murmur *v.* murmurar
muscle *n.* músculo
muscovite *n.* moscovita
muscular *adj.* muscular
muse *n.* musa
museum *n.* museo
mush *n.* papilla
mushroom *n.* champiñón
music *n.* música
musical *adj.* musical
musician *n.* músico
musk *n.* almizcle
musket *n.* mosquete
musketeer *n.* mosquetero
muslim *n.* musulmán
muslin *n.* muselina
mussel *n.* mejillón
must *v.* deber
mustang *n.* mustang
mustard *n.* mostaza
muster *v.* reunir
musty *adj.* mohoso
mutable *adj.* mutable
mutate *v.* mutar
mutation *n.* mutación
mute *adj.* mudo
mutilate *v.* mutilar
mutilation *n.* mutilación

mutinous *adj.* amotinado
mutiny *n.* motín
mutter *v.* refunfuñar
mutton *n.* carne de ovino
mutual *adj.* mutuo
muzzle *n.* hocico, bozal
muzzy *adj.* borroso
my *adj.* mi, mis
myalgia *n.* mialgia
myopia *n.* miopía
myopic *adj.* miope
myosis *n.* miosis
myriad *n.* miríada
myrrh *n.* mirra
myrtle *n.* mirto, doncella
myself *pron.* me, yo mismo
mysterious *adj.* misterioso
mystery *n.* miseria
mystic *n.* místico
mystical *adj.* místico
mysticism *n.* misticismo
mystify *v.* desconcertar
mystique *n.* aura de misterio
myth *n.* mito
mythical *adj.* mítico
mythological *adj.* mitológico
mythology *n.* mitología

N

nab *v.* coger, birlar
nabob *adj.* potentado
nacho *n.* nacho
nadir *n.* nadir
nag *v.t.* importunar, dar la lata
nail *n.* uña
naivety *n.* ingenuidad
naked *adj.* desnudo
name *n.* nombre

namely *n.* a saber
namesake *n.* homónimo
nanny *n.* niñera
nap *n.* siesta
nape *n.* nuca
napthalene *n.* naftalina
napkin *n.* servilleta
nappy *n.* pañal
narcissism *n.* narcisismo
narcissus *n.* narciso
narcotic *n.* narcótico
narrate *v.* narrar
narration *n.* narración
narrative *n.* narrativa
narrator *n.* narrador
narrow *adj.* estrecho
nasal *adj.* nasal
nascent *adj.* naciente
nasty *adj.* desagradable
natal *adj.* natal
natant *adj.* flotante
nation *n.* nación
national *adj.* nacional
nationalism *n.* nacionalismo
nationalist *n.* nacionalista
nationality *n.* nacionalidad
nationalization *n.* nacionalización
nationalize *v.* nacionalizar
native *n.* natal, materno
nativity *n.* natividad
natty *adj.* elefantón
natural *adj.* natural
naturalist *n.* naturalista
naturalize *v.* naturalizar
naturalization *n.* naturalización
naturally *adv.* naturalmente
nature *n.* naturaleza
naturism *n.* naturismo
naughty *adj.* travieso
nausea *n.* nausea
nauseate *v.* asquear

nauseous *adj.* nauseabundo
nautical *adj.* náutico
naval *adj.* naval
nave *n.* nave
navigable *adj.* navegable
navigate *v.* navegar
navigation *n.* navegación
navigator *n.* navegante
navy *n.* la marina
nay *adv.* no
near *adv.* cerca
nearby *adv.* cercano
near *v.i.* acercarse
nearest *adj.* seres queridos
nearly *adv.* casi
neat *adj.* aseado, pulcro
nebula *n.* nebulosa
nebulous *adj.* nebuloso
necessarily *adv.* necesariamente
necessary *adj.* necesario
necessitate *v.* necesitar
necessity *n.* necesidad
neck *n.* cuello
necklace *n.* collar
necklet *n.* gargantilla
necromancy *n.* necromancia
necropolis *n.* necrópolis
nectar *n.* néctar
nectarine *n.* nectarina
need *v.* necesitar
needful *adj.* necesario
needle *n.* aguja
needless *adj.* innecesario
needy *adj.* necesitado
nefarious *adj.* nefario
negate *v.* invalidar
negation *n.* negación
negative *adj.* negativo
negativity *n.* negatividad
neglect *v.* desatender
negligence *n.* negligencia
negligent *adj.* negligente

negligible *adj.* insignificante
negotiable *adj.* negociable
negotiate *v.* negociar
negotiation *n.* negociación
negotiator *n.* negociador
negress *n.* negra
negro *n.* negro
neigh *n.* relincho
neighbour *n.* vecino
neighbourhood *n.* vecindario
neighbourly *adj.* amable
neither *adj.* ninguna
nemesis *n.* némesis
neoclassical *adj.* neoclásico
neolithic *adj.* neolítico
neon *n.* neón
neophyte *n.* neófito
nephew *n.* sobrino
nepotism *n.* nepotismo
Neptune *n.* Neptuno
nerd *n.* ganso
Nerve *n.* nervio
nerveless *adj.* débil
nervous *adj.* nervioso
nervy *adj.* fresco, caradura
nescience *n.* nesciencia
nest *n.* nido
nestle *v.* acurrucarse
nestling *n.* polluelo
net *n.* red
nether *adj.* inferior
netting *n.* redes, mallas
nettle *n.* ortiga
network *n.* red, cadena
neural *adj.* neural
neurologist *n.* neurólogo
neurology *n.* neurología
neurosis *n.* neurosis
neurotic *adj.* neurótico
neuter *adj.* asexuado
neutral *adj.* neutral
neutralize *v.* neutralizar

neutron *n.* neutrón
never *adv.* nunca
nevertheless *adv.* sin embargo
new *adj.* nuevo
newly *adv.* recién
news *n.* noticias
next *adj.* próximo, siguiente
nexus *n.* nexo
nib *n.* plumín
nibble *v.* picar, picotear
nice *adj.* amable
nicety *n.* sutilezas
niche *n.* nicho
nick *n.* muesca
nickel *n.* níquel
nickname *n.* apodo
nicotine *n.* nicotina
niece *n.* sobrina
niggard *n.* tacaño
niggardly *adj.* tacaño
nigger *n.* negro
niggle *v.* quejarse
nigh *adv.* cerca
night *n.* noche
nightingale *n.* ruiseñor
nightmare *n.* pesadilla
nightie *n.* camisón
nihilism *n.* nihilismo
nil *n.* nada, cero
nimble *adj.* ágil
nimbus *n.* nimbo
nine *adj. & n.* nueve
nineteen *adj. & n.* diecinueve
nineteenth *adj. & n.* decimonoveno
ninetieth *adj. & n.* nonagésimo
ninth *adj. & n.* noveno
ninety *adj. & n.* noventa
nip *v.* pellizcar, mordisquear
nipple *n.* pezón
nippy *adj.* frio
nirvana *n.* nirvana

nitrogen *n.* nitrógeno
no *adj.* no
nobility *n.* nobleza
noble *adj.* noble
nobleman *n.* aristócrata
nobody *pron.* nadie
nocturnal *adj.* nocturno
nod *v.* asentir con la cabeza
node *n.* nódulo
noise *n.* ruido
noisy *adj.* ruidoso
nomad *n.* nómada
nomadic *adj.* nómada
nomenclature *n.* nomenclatura
nominal *adj.* nominal
nominate *v.* nominar
nomination *n.* nominación
nominee *n.* candidato
non-aligned *n.* no alineado
nonchalance *n.* desenfado
nonchalant *adj.* desenfadado
nonconformist *n.* inconformista
none *pron.* nadie, ninguno
nonentity *n.* nulidad
nonplussed *adj.* desconcertado
nonetheless *a.* no obstante
nonpareil *adj.* sin par
nonsense *n.* tontería
nonstop *adj.* directo, sin paradas
noodles *n.* fideos
nook *n.* rincón
noon *n.* mediodía
noose *n.* soga
nor *conj.&adv.* ni, no, tampoco
Nordic *adj.* nórdico
norm *n.* norma
normal *adj.* normal
normalcy *n.* normalidad
normalize *v.* normalizar
normative *adj.* normativo
north *n.* norte

northerly *adj.* norteño, del norte
northern *adj.* norteño, del norte
nose *n.* nariz
nostalgia *n.* nostalgia
nostril *n.* orificio nasal
nostrum *n.* panacea
nosy *adj.* entrometido
not *adv.* no
notable *adj.* notable
notary *n.* notario
notation *n.* notación
notch *n.* mella, muesca
note *n.* nota
notebook *n.* cuaderno, libreta
noted *adj.* célebre, famoso, destacado
noteworthy *adj.* notable
nothing *pron.* nada
notice *n.* informe, aviso
noticeable *adj.* evidente
noticeboard *n.* tablón de anuncios
notifiable *adj.* notificarle
notification *n.* notificación
notify *v.* notificar
notion *n.* noción
notional *adj.* nocional
notoriety *n.* notoriedad
notorious *prep.* notorio
nougat *n.* turrón
nought *n.* cero
noun *n.* nombre, sustantivo
nourish *v.* nutrir, alimentar
nourishment *n.* alimento
novel *n.* novela
novelette *n.* novela rosa
novelist *n.* novelista
novelty *n.* novedad
november *n.* noviembre
novice *n.* principiante, novato
now *adv.* ahora

nowhere *adv.* en ninguna parte, en ningún sitio
noxious *adj.* apestoso
nozzle *n.* cánula, boquilla
nuance *n.* matiz
nubile *a.* núbil
nuclear *adj.* nuclear
nucleus *n.* núcleo
nude *adj.* desnudo
nudge *v.* codear
nudist *n.* nudista
nudity *n.* desnudez
nudge *v.* codear
nugatory *adj.* fútil
nugget *n.* pepita
nuisance *n.* molestia
null *adj.* inútil, invalido
nullification *n.* anulación
nullify *v.* anular
numb *adj.* entumecido
number *n.* número
numberless *adj.* innumerable
numeral *n.* número
numerator *n.* numerador
numerical *adj.* numérico
numerous *adj.* numeroso
nun *n.* monja
nunnery *n.* convento
nuptial *adj.* nupcial
nurse *n.* enfermera
nursery *n.* guardería
nurture *v.* criar, educar
nut *n.* fruto seco
nutrient *n.* nutriente
nutrition *n.* nutrición
nutritious *adj.* nutritivo
nutritive *adj.* nutritivo
nutty *adj.* chiflado
nuzzle *v.* acariciar con el hocico
nylon *n.* nylon
nymph *n.* ninfa

O

oaf *n.* zoquete
oak *n.* roble
oar *n.* remo
oasis *n.* oasis
oat *n.* avena
oath *n.* juramento
oatmeal *n.* avena
obduracy *n.* inflexibilidad
obdurate *adj.* obstinado
obedience *n.* obediencia
obedient *adj.* obediente
obeisance *n.* reverencia
obesity *n.* obesidad
obese *adj.* obeso
obey *v.* obedecer
obfuscate *v.* ofuscar
obituary *n.* obituario
object *n.* objeto
objection *n.* objeción
objectionable *adj.* desagradable
objective *adj.* objetivo
objectively *adv.* objetivamente
oblation *n.* oblación
obligated *adj.* obligado
obligation *n.* obligación
obligatory *adj.* obligatorio
oblige *v.* obligar
obliging *adj.* obligado
oblique *adj.* oblicuo
obliterate *v.* borrar
obliteration *n.* obliteración
oblivion *n.* olvido
oblivious *adj.* inconsciente de
oblong *adj.* rectangular
obloquy *n.* calumnia
obnoxious *adj.* detestable
obscene *adj.* obsceno
obscenity *n.* obscenidad

obscure *adj.* oscuro
obscurity *n.* oscuridad
observance *n.* observancia
observant *adj.* observador
observation *n.* observación
observatory *n.* observatorio
observe *v.* observar
obsess *v.* obsesionar
obsession *n.* obsesión
obsolescent *adj.* obsolescente
obsolete *adj.* obsoleto
obstacle *n.* obstáculo
obstinacy *n* obstinancia
obstinate *adj.* obstinado
obstruct *v.* obstruir
obstruction *n.* obstrucción
obstructive *adj.* obstruccionista
obtain *v.* obtener
obtainable *adj.* asequible
obtrude *v.* imponer
obtuse *adj.* obtuso
obverse *n.* anverso
obviate *v.* obviar
obvious *adj.* obvio, lógico
occasion *n.* ocasión
occasional *adj.* ocasional
occasionally *adv.* ocasionalmente
occident *n.* occidente
occidental *adj.* occidental
occlude *v.* ocluir
occult *n.* oculto
occupancy *n.* ocupación
occupant *n.* ocupante, inquilino
occupation *n.* ocupación
occupational *adj.* ocupacional
occupy *v.* ocupar
occur *v.* ocurrir
occurrence *n.* ocurrencia
ocean *n.* océano
oceanic *adj.* oceánico
octagon *n.* octágono
octave *n.* octava

octavo *n.* octavo
October *n.* octubre
octogenarian *n.* octogenario
octopus *n.* pulpo
octroi *n.* fielato
ocular *adj.* ocular
odd *adj.* impar, desigual, extraño
oddity *n.* rareza
odds *n.* probabilidad, probabilidades
ode *n.* oda
odious *adj.* odioso
odium *n.* odio
odorous *adj.* oloroso
odour *n.* olor
odyssey *n.* odisea
of *prep.* de
off *adv.* desconectado, apagado,
offence *n.* ofensa
offend *v.* ofender
offender *n.* infractor
offensive *adj.* ofensivo
offer *v.* ofertar
offering *n.* ofrecimiento
office *n.* oficina
officer *n.* oficial
official *adj.* oficial
officially *adv.* oficialmente
officiate *v.* oficiar
officious *adj.* oficioso
offset *v.* compensar
offshoot *n.* retoño
offshore *adj.* extraterritorial, oceánico, submarino
offside *adj.* fuera de juego
offspring *n.* hijo, cría
oft *adv.* a menudo
often *adv.* a menudo
ogle *v.* comerse con los ojos
oil *n.* aceite, petróleo
oily *adj.* aceitoso
ointment *n.* pomada, ungüento

okay *adj.* bueno, conforme
old *adj.* viejo
oligarchy *n.* oligarquía
olive *n.* aceituna
olympic *adj.* olímpico
omelette *n.* tortilla
omen *n.* presagio
ominous *adj.* nefasto, siniestro
omission *n.* omisión
omit *v.* omitir
omnibus *n.* antología
omnipotence *n.* omnipotencia
omnipotent *adj.* omnipotente
omnipresence *n.* omnipresencia
omnipresent *adj.* omnipresente
omniscience *n.* omnisciencia
omniscient *adj.* omnisciente
on *prep.* en
once *adv.* una vez
one *n. & adj.* uno
oneness *n.* unidad, identidad
onerous *adj.* pesado
oneself *pron.* uno mismo
onion *n.* cebolla
onlooker *n.* espectador
only *adv.* sólo
onomatopoeia *n.* onomatopeya
onset *n.* llegada, inicio, principio
onslaught *n.* embestida
ontology *n.* ontología
onus *n.* carga, responsabilidad
onward *adv.* hacia delante
onyx *n.* ónice
ooze *v.i.* rezumar
opacity *n.* opacidad
opal *n.* ópalo
opaque *adj.* opaco
open *adj.* abierto
opening *n.* apertura, estreno, oportunidad
openly *adv.* abiertamente
opera *n.* opera

operate *v.* operar
operation *n.* operación
operational *adj.* operacional
operative *adj.* operativo
operator *n.* operador
opine *v.* opinar
opinion *n.* opinión
opium *n.* opio
opponent *n.* oponente, adversario
opportune *adj.* oportuno
opportunism *n.* oportunismo
opportunity *n.* oportunidad
oppose *v.* oponer
opposite *adj.* opuesto, contrario, de enfrente
opposition *n.* oposición
oppress *v.* oprimir
oppression *n.* opresión
oppressive *adj.* opresivo
oppressor *n.* opresor
opt *v.* optar
optic *adj.* óptico
optician *n.* óptico
optimism *n.* optimismo
optimist *n.* optimista
optimistic *adj.* optimista
optimize *v.* optimizar
optimum *adj.* óptimo
option *n.* opción
optional *adj.* opcional
opulence *n.* opulencia
opulent *adj.* opulento
or *conj.* o
oracle *n.* oráculo
oracular *adj.* de oráculo, misterioso
oral *adj.* oral
orally *adv.* verbalmente, oralmente
orange *n.* naranja
oration *n.* oración, discurso
orator *n.* orador

oratory *n.* oratorio
orb *n.* orbe
orbit *n.* órbita
orbital *adj.* orbital
orchard *n.* huerto
orchestra *n.* orquesta
orchestral *adj.* orquestal
orchid *n.* orquídea
ordeal *n.* prueba dura, sufrimiento
order *n.* orden, pedido
orderly *adj.* ordenado
ordinance *n.* ordenanza
ordinarily *adv.* generalmente
ordinary *adj.* corriente, común
ordnance *n.* artillería
ore *n.* mineral, mena
organ *n.* órgano
organic *adj.* orgánico
organism *n.* organismo
organization *n.* organización
organize *v.* organizar
orgasm *n.* orgasmo
orgy *n.* orgia
orient *n.* oriente
oriental *adj.* oriental
orientate *v.* orientar
origami *n.* papiroflexia
origin *n.* origen
original *adj.* original
originality *n.* originalidad
originate *v.* originarse, empezar
originator *n.* creador, autor
ornament *n.* adorno
ornamental *adj.* ornamental
ornamentation *n.* ornamentación
ornate *adj.* ornamentado
orphan *n.* huérfano
orphanage *n.* orfanato
orthodox *adj.* ortodoxo
orthodoxy *n.* ortodoxia
orthopaedics *n.* ortopedia

oscillate *v.* oscilar
oscillation *n.* oscilación
ossify *v.* osificarse
ostensible *adj.* ostensible
ostentation *n.* ostentación
osteopathy *n.* osteopatía
ostracize *v.* marginar
ostrich *n.* avestruz
other *adj. & pron.* otro
otherwise *adv.* si no
otiose *adj.* ocioso, superfluo
otter *n.* nutria
ottoman *n.* otomano
ounce *n.* onza
our *adj.* nuestro
ourselves *pron.* nosotros mismos
oust *v.* desbancar
out *adv.* fuera, afuera
outbid *v.* sobrepujar
outboard *n.* fueraborda
outbreak *n.* estallido
outburst *n.* arrebato, estallido
outcast *n.* marginado
outclass *v.* superar
outcome *n.* resultado
outcry *n.* protesta
outdated *adj.* anticuado
outdo *v.* superar
outdoor *adj.* al aire libre, exterior
outer *adj.* exterior
outfit *n.* conjunto
outgoing *adj.* sociable, extrovertido
outgrow *v.* superar, sobrepasar
outhouse *n.* excusado, dependencia
outing *n.* excursión, paseo
outlandish *adj.* estrafalario
outlast *v.* sobrevivir a, durar mas que
outlaw *n.* proscrito
outlay *n.* gastos, inversión

outlet *n.* salida, tienda al por menor
outline *n.* contorno
outlive *v.* sobrevivir
outlook *n.* punto de vista
outlying *adj.* alejado
outmoded *adj.* anticuado
outnumber *v.* superar en número
outpatient *n.* paciente externo
outpost *n.* avanzada
output *n.* producción
outrage *n.* atrocidad
outrageous *adj.* vergonzoso, atroz
outrider *n.* escolta
outright *adv.* rotundamente, terminantemente
outrun *v.* dejar atrás
outset *n.* principio, comienzo
outshine *v.* eclipsar
outside *n.* fuera
outsider *n.* forastero
outsize *adj.* impresionante, excesivo
outskirts *n.* alrededores, extrarradio
outsource *v.* externalizar
outspoken *adj.* directo, franco
outstanding *adj.* extraordinario
outstrip *v.* aventajar, sobrepasar
outward *adj.* exterior
outwardly *adv.* aparentemente
outweigh *v.* ser mayor que
outwit *v.* burlar
oval *adj.* ovalado
ovary *n.* ovario
ovate *adj.* ovado
ovation *n.* ovación
oven *n.* horno
over *prep.* sobre
overact *v.* sobreactuar
overall *adj.* total, global

overawe *v.* intimidar
overbalance *v.* perder el equilibrio
overbearing *adj.* autoritario, dominante
overblown *adj.* rimbombante
overboard *adv.* al mar, al agua
overburden *v.* sobrecargar
overcast *adj.* cauteloso
overcharge *v.* cobrar de mas
overcoat *n.* abrigo
overcome *v.* vencer, superar
overdo *v.* exagerar, excederse
overdose *n.* sobredosis
overdraft *n.* descubierto
overdraw *v.* estar al descubierto
overdrive *n.* a toda marcha
overdue *adj.* atrasado
overestimate *v.* sobrestimar
overflow *v.* inundar, desbordar
overgrown *adj.* abandonado
overhaul *v.* repasar
overhead *adv.* en lo alto
overhear *v.* oír por casualidad
overjoyed *adj.* encantado
overlap *v.* solapar
overleaf *adv.* al dorso
overload *v.* sobrecargar
overlook *v.* pasar por alto
overly *adv.* demasiado
overnight *adv.* por la noche
overpass *n.* paso elevado
overpower *v.* dominar
overrate *v.* supervalorar
overreach *v.* extralimitarse
overreact *v.* reaccionar exageradamente
override *v.* invalidar
overrule *v.* anular
overrun *v.* invadir
overseas *adv.* en el extranjero
oversee *v.* supervisar

overseer *n.* supervisor
overshadow *v.* ensombrecer
overshoot *v.* exceder
oversight *n.* descuido
overspill *n.* desbordamiento
overstep *v.* sobrepasar
overt *adj.* abierto
overtake *v.* alcanzar, pasar
overthrow *v.* derrocar, derribar
overtime *n* horas extras
overtone *n.* nota, resonancia
overture *n.* obertura
overturn *v.* volcar, voltear
overview *n.* resumen
overweening *adj.* presuntuoso
overwhelm *v.* abrumar
overwrought *adj.* sobrexcitado
ovulate *v.* ovular
owe *v.* deber
owing *adj.* deudor
owl *n.* búho
own *adj. & pron.* propio, suyo
owner *n.* dueño
ownership *n.* propiedad
ox *n.* buey
oxide *n.* óxido
oxygen *n.* oxigeno
oyster *n.* ostra
ozone *n* ozono

P

pace *n.* paso
pacemaker *n.* marcapasos
pacific *n.* pacifico
pacifist *n.* pacifista
pacify *v.* apaciguar
pack *n.* carga, fardo
package *n.* paquete

packet *n.* paquete
packing *n.* embalaje
pact *n.* pacto
pad *n.* almohadilla, hombrera
padding *n.* relleno
paddle *n.* zagual, paleta
paddock *n.* paddock, prado
padlock *n.* candado
paddy *n.* arrozal, irlandés
paediatrician *n.* pediatra
paediatrics *n.* pediatría
paedophile *n.* pederasta
pagan *n.* pagano
page *n.* página
pageant *n.* concurso, certamen
pageantry *n.* fausto
pagoda *n.* pagoda
pail *n.* balde, cubo
pain *n.* dolor
painful *adj.* doloroso
painkiller *n.* analgésico
painstaking *adj.* concienzudo
paint *n.* pintura
painter *n.* pintor
painting *n.* cuadro, pintura
pair *n.* par
paisley *n.* estampado
pal *n.* amigo
palace *n.* palacio
palatable *adj.* agradable
palatal *adj.* palatal
palate *n.* paladar
palatial *adj.* palaciego
pale *adj.* pálido
palette *n.* paleta
paling *n.* empalizada
pall *n.* paño mortuorio
pallet *n.* paleta
palm *n.* palmera, palma
palmist *n.* quiromántico
palmistry *n.* quiromancia
palpable *adj.* palpable

palpitate *v.* palpitar
palpitation *n.* palpitación
palsy *n.* parálisis
paltry *adj.* mísero
pamper *v.* mimar
pamphlet *n.* panfleto
pamphleteer *n.* panfletista
pan *n.* cacerola
panacea *n.* panacea
panache *n.* garbo, salero
pancake *n.* crepe
pancreas *n.* páncreas
panda *n.* panda
pandemonium *n.* pandemonio
pane *n.* cristal
panegyric *n.* panegírico
panel *n.* panel
pang *n.* punzada
panic *n.* pánico
panorama *n.* panorama
pant *v.* jadear
pantaloon *n.* pantalón
pantheism *n.* panteísmo
pantheist *adj.* panteísta
panther *n.* pantera
panties *n.* bragas
pantomime *n.* pantomima
pantry *n.* despensa
pants *n.* pantalones, calzoncillos,
bragas
papacy *n.* papado
papal *adj.* papal
paper *n.* papel
paperback *n.* libro de bolsillo
par *n.* par
parable *n.* parábola
parachute *n.* paracaídas
parachutist *n.* paracaidista
parade *n.* desfile
paradise *n.* paraíso
paradox *n.* paradoja
paradoxical *adj.* paradójico

paraffin *n.* parafina
paragon *n.* dechado
paragraph *n.* párrafo
parallel *n.* paralelo
parallelogram *n.* paralelogramo
paralyse *v.* paralizar
paralysis *n.* parálisis
paralytic *adj.* paralitico
paramedic *n.* paramédico
parameter *n.* parámetro
paramount *adj.* primordial
paramour *n.* amado
paraphernalia *n.* parafernalia
paraphrase *v.* paráfrasis
parasite *n.* parásito
parasol *n.* sombrilla
parcel *n.* paquete
parched *adj.* reseco
pardon *n.* perdón
pardonable *adj.* perdonable
pare *v.* pelar
parent *n.* padre
parentage *n.* parentesco
parental *adj.* parental
parenthesis *n.* paréntesis
pariah *n.* paria
parish *n.* parroquia
parity *n.* paridad
park *n.* parque
parky *adj.* frío, fresco
parlance *n.* lenguaje
parley *n.* negociación
parliament *n.* parlamento
parliamentary *adj.* parlamentario
parlour *n.* salón, sala
parochial *adj.* provinciano
parody *n.* parodia
parole *n.* libertad condicional
parricide *n.* parricidio
parrot *n.* loro
parry *v.* parar
parse *v.* analizar

parsimony *n.* mezquindad
parson *n.* cura
part *n.* parte
partake *v.* participar
partial *adj.* parcial
partiality *n.* parcialidad
participate *v.* participar
participant *n.* participante
participation *n.* participación
particle *n.* partícula
particular *adj.* preciso, especial
parting *n.* despedida
partisan *n.* partisano
partition *n.* partición, tabique, separación
partly *adv.* en parte
partner *n.* socio, pareja, compañero
partnership *n.* asociación
party *n.* fiesta
pass *v.* pasar
passable *adj.* pasable
passage *n.* paso, pasaje, callejón
passenger *n.* pasajero
passing *adj.* pasajero, fugaz
passion *n.* pasión
passionate *adj.* apasionado
passive *adj.* pasivo
passport *n.* pasaporte
past *adj.* pasado
pasta *n.* pasta
paste *n.* pasta, paté
pastel *n.* pastel
pasteurized *adj.* pasteurizado
pastime *n.* pasatiempo
pastor *n.* pastor
pastoral *adj.* pastoril
pastry *n.* masa, pastelito
pasture *n.* pastos
pasty *n.* empanadilla
pat *v.* dar palmaditas, acariciar con la mano

patch *n.* parche, mancha
patchy *adj.* disparejo
patent *n.* patente
paternal *adj.* paternal
paternity *n.* paternidad
path *n.* sendero, senda, camino
pathetic *adj.* patético
pathology *n.* patología
pathos *n.* patetismo
patience *n.* paciencia
patient *adj.* paciente
patient *n.* paciente
patio *n.* patio
patisserie *n.* pastelería
patriarch *n.* patriarca
patricide *n.* parricidio
patrimony *n.* patrimonio
patriot *n.* patriota
patriotic *adj.* patriótico
patriotism *n.* patriotismo
patrol *v.* patrullar
patron *n.* patrón, mecenas
patronage *n.* clientela
patronize *v.* patrocinar, tratar con
    condescendencia
pattern *n.* patrón, diseño, estam-
    pado
patty *n.* empanada
paucity *n.* escasez
paunch *n.* panza
pauper *n.* pobre, indigente
pause *n.* pausa
pave *v.* pavimentar
pavement *n.* acera
pavilion *n.* pabellón
paw *n.* pata
pawn *n.* peón
pawnbroker *n.* prestamista
pay *v.* pagar
payable *n.* pagadero
payee *n.* beneficiario
payment *n.* pago

pea *n.* guisante
peace *n.* paz
peaceable *adj.* pacífico
peaceful *adj.* pacífico
peach *n.* melocotón
peacock *n.* pavo real
peahen *n.* pava real
peak *n.* cima, cumbre, cúspide
peaky *adj.* pálido
peal *n.* repique, carillón
peanut *n.* cacahuete
pear *n.* pera
pearl *n.* perla
peasant *n.* campesino
peasantry *n.* del campo
pebble *n.* guijarro, piedra
pecan *n.* pacana
peck *v.i.* picotear, picar
peculiar *adj.* peculiar
pedagogue *n.* pedagogo
pedagogy *n.* pedagogía
pedal *n.* pedal
pedant *n.* pedante
pedantic *adj.* pedante
peddle *v.* vender
pedestal *n.* pedestal
pedestrian *n.* peatón
pedicure *n.* pedicura
pedigree *n.* pedigrí
pedlar *n.* buhonero
pedometer *n.* podómetro
peek *v.* atisbar, mirar rápidamente
peel *n.* piel, cáscara
peep *v.* piar
peer *n.* igual
peer *v.* mirar de cerca
peerage *n.* nobleza
peerless *adj.* incomparable
peg *n.* estaca, clavija
pejorative *adj.* peyorativo
pelican *n.* pelícano

pellet *n.* bolita, perdigón
pelmet *n.* galería, bastidor
pelt *v.* azotar, batir, ir a todo gas
pelvis *n.* pelvis
pen *n.* bolígrafo
penal *adj.* adj.
penalize *v.* penalizar, sancionar, castigar
penalty *n.* pena, castigo, multa, penalti
penance *n.* penitencia
penchant *n.* tendencia
pencil *n.* lápiz
pendant *n.* colgante
pendent *adj.* pendiente
pending *adj.* pendiente
pendulum *n.* péndulo
penetrate *v.* penetrar
penetration *n.* penetración
penguin *n.* pingüino
peninsula *n.* península
penis *n.* pene
penitent *adj.* penitente
penniless *adj.* pobre
penny *n.* penique
pension *n.* pensión
pensioner *n.* jubilado
pensive *adj.* pensativo
pentagon *n.* pentágono
penthouse *n.* ático, pent-house
penultimate *adj.* penúltimo
people *n.* gente
pepper *n.* pimienta
peppermint *n.* menta
peptic *adj.* péptico
per *prep.* por
perambulate *v.t.* deambular
perceive *v.* percibir
perceptible *adj.* perceptible
percentage *n.* porcentaje
perceptible *adj.* perceptible
perception *n.* percepción

perch *n.* percha
percipient *adj.* perceptor
percolate *v.* filtrarse
percolator *n.* filtrado
perdition *n.* perdición
perennial *adj.* perenne, vivaz
perfect *adj.* perfecto
perfection *n.* perfección
perfidious *adj.* pérfido
perforate *v.* perforar
perforce *adv.* forzosamente
perform *v.* actuar, trabajar
performance *n.* actuación, función, representación
performer *n.* artista
perfume *n.* perfume
perfume *v.* perfumar
perfunctory *adj.* somero, superficial
perhaps *adv.* quizás
peril *n.* peligro
perilous *adj.* peligroso
period *n.* periodo
periodic *adj.* periódico
periodical *adj.* periódico
periphery *n.* periferia
perish *v.* perecer
perishable *adj.* perecedero
perjure *v.* perjurar
perjury *n.* perjurio
perk *v.* filtrarse
perky *adj.* alegre
permanence *n.* permanencia
permanent *adj.* permanente
permeable *adj.* permeable
permissible *adj.* permisible
permission *n.* permiso
permissive *adj.* permisivo
permit *v.* permitir
permutation *n.* permutación
pernicious *adj.* pernicioso
perpendicular *adj.* perpendicular

perpetrate *v.* perpetrar
perpetual *adj.* perpetuo
perpetuate *v.t.* perpetuar
perplex *v.* desconcertar
perplexity *n.* perplejidad
perquisite *n.* gaje
perry *n.* sidra de pera
persecute *v.* perseguir
persecution *n.* persecución
perseverance *n.* perseverancia
persevere *v.i.* perseverar
persist *v.* persistir
persistence *n.* persistencia
persistent *adj.* persistente
person *n.* persona
persona *n.* persona
personage *n.* personaje
personal *adj.* personal
personality *n.* personalidad
personification *n.* personificación
personify *v.* personificar
personnel *n.* personal
perspective *n.* perspectiva
perspicuous *adj.* perspicuo
perspiration *n.* transpiración
perspire *v.t.* transpirar
persuade *v.* persuadir
persuasion *n.* persuasión
pertain *v.* pertenecer
pertinent *adj.* pertinente
perturb *v.* perturbar
perusal *n.* examen
peruse *v.* examinar
pervade *v.* dominar
perverse *adj.* perverso
perversion *n.* perversión
perversity *n.* obstinación
pervert *v.* pervertir
pessimism *n.* pesimismo
pessimist *n.* pesimista
pessimistic *adj.* pesimista

pest *n.* plaga
pester *v.* molestar
pesticide *n.* pesticida
pestilence *n.* pestilencia
pet *n.* mascota, animal de compañía
petal *n.* pétalo
petite *adj.* pequeño
petition *n.* petición
petitioner *n.* solicitante, demandante
petrify *v.* petrificar
petrol *n.* gasolina
petroleum *n.* petróleo
petticoat *n.* enagua
pettish *adj.* quisquilloso
petty *adj.* insignificante
petulance *n.* mal humor
petulant *adj.* irascible
phantom *n.* fantasma
pharmaceutical *adj.* farmacéutico
pharmacist *n.* farmacéutico
pharmacy *n.* farmacia
phase *n.* fase
phenomenal *adj.* espectacular
phenomenon *n.* fenómeno
phial *n.* ampolla
philanthropic *adj.* filantrópico
philanthropist *n.* filántropo
philanthropy *n.* filantropía
philately *n.* filatelia
philological *adj.* filológico
philologist *n.* filólogo
philology *n.* filología
philosopher *n.* filósofo
philosophical *adj.* filosófico
philosophy *n.* filosofía
phlegmatic *adj.* flemático
phobia *n.* fobia
phoenix *n.* fénix
phone *n.* teléfono

phonetic *adj.* fonético
phosphate *n.* fosfato
phosphorus *n.* fosforoso
photo *n.* foto
photocopy *n.* fotocopia
photograph *n.* fotografía
photographer *n.* fotógrafo
photographic *adj.* fotográfico
photography *n.* fotografía
photostat *n.* fotocopiadora
phrase *n.* frase
phraseology *n.* fraseología
physical *adj.* físico
physician *n.* médico
physics *n.* física
physiognomy *n.* fisionomía
physiotherapy *n.* fisioterapia
physique *n.* físico
pianist *n.* pianista
piano *n.* piano
piazza *n.* plaza
pick *v.* elegir, escoger
picket *n.* piquete
pickings *n.* ganancias
pickle *n.* samuera
picnic *n.* picnic
pictograph *n.* pictografía
pictorial *adj.* pictórico
picture *n.* cuadro, pintura
picturesque *adj.* pintoresco
pie *n.* pastel
piece *n.* pedazo, trozo
piecemeal *adv.* poco a poco
pier *n.* muelle
pierce *v.* perforar
piety *n.* piedad
pig *n.* cerdo
pigeon *n.* paloma
pigeonhole *n.* casillero
piggery *n.* granja porcina
pigment *n.* pigmento
pigmy *n.* pigmeo

pike *n.* pica
pile *n.* montón, pila
pilfer *v.* hurtar
pilgrim *n.* peregrino
pilgrimage *n.* peregrinación
pill *n.* pastilla, píldora
pillar *n.* pilar, columna
pillow *n.* almohada, cojín
pilot *n.* piloto
pimple *n.* grano
pin *n.* alfiler
pincer *n.* pinzas, tenazas
pinch *v.* pellizcar
pine *v.* sufrir
pineapple *n.* piña
pink *adj.* rosa
pinnacle *n.* pináculo
pinpoint *v.* señalar
pint *n.* pinta
pioneer *n.* pionero
pious *adj.* piadoso
pipe *n.* tubo, cañería
pipette *n.* pipeta
piquant *adj.* punzante
pique *n.* despecho
piracy *n.* piratería
pirate *n.* pirata
pistol *n.* pistola
piston *n.* pistón
pit *n.* hoyo, mina
pitch *n.* tono, terreno
pitcher *n.* jarra, lanzador
piteous *adj.* lastimero
pitfall *n.* escollo
pitiful *adj.* lastimero
pitiless *adj.* despiadado
pity *n.* pena
pivot *n.* pivote
pivotal *adj.* fundamental
pixel *n.* pixel
pizza *n.* pizza
placard *n.* letrero, pancarta

placate *v.* aplacar
place *n.* lugar
placement *n.* colocación
placid *adj.* plácido
plague *n.* plaga, peste
plain *adj.* sencillo
plaintiff *n.* demandante
plaintive *adj.* lastimero
plait *n.* trenza
plan *n.* plano
plane *n.* avión
planet *n.* planeta
planetary *adj.* planetario
plank *n.* tabla, tablón
plant *n.* planta
plantain *n.* plátano grande
plantation *n.* plantación
plaque *n.* placa
plaster *n.* yeso
plastic *n.* plástico
plate *n.* plato
plateau *n.* meseta
platelet *n.* plaqueta
platform *n.* plataforma
platinum *n.* platino
platonic *adj.* platónico
platoon *n.* sección
platter *n.* fuente
plaudits *n.* aplausos
plausible *adj.* verosímil
play *v.i.* jugar
playground *n.* área de juego
playwright *n.* dramaturgo
player *n.* jugador
plaza *n.* plaza
plea *n.* petición, ruego
plead *v.* defender, alegar
pleasant *adj.* agradable
pleasantry *n.* cumplido
please *v.* complacer
pleasure *n.* placer
pleat *n.* pliegue

plebeian *adj.* plebeyo
plebiscite *n.* plebiscito
pledge *n.* promesa
plenty *pron.* muchos
plethora *n.* plétora
pliable *adj.* maleable
pliant *adj.* maleable
pliers *n.* pinzas, alicates
plight *n.* situación difícil
plinth *n.* plinto, zócalo
plod *v.* andar con paso pesado
plot *n.* complot, argumento
plough *n.* arado
ploughman *n.* arador
ploy *n.* treta
pluck *v.* desplumar
plug *n.* tapón, enchufe
plum *n.* ciruela
plumage *n.* plumaje
plumb *v.* dilucidar
plumber *n.* fontanero
plume *n.* pluma
plummet *v.* caer en picado
plump *adj.* gordo, relleno
plunder *v.* saquear
plunge *v.* sumergir
plural *adj.* plural
plurality *n.* pluralidad
plus *prep.* más
plush *n.* felpa
ply *n.* chapa, lámina
pneumatic *adj.* neumático
pneumonia *n.* neumonía
poach *v.* escalfar, cazar furtivamente
pocket *n.* bolsillo
pod *n.* vaina
podcast *n.* podcast
podium *n.* podio
poem *n.* poema
poet *n.* poeta
poetry *n.* poesía

poignancy *n.* patetismo
poignant *adj.* conmovedor
point *n.* punto
pointing *n.* rejuntado
pointless *adj.* inútil
poise *n.* porte
poison *n.* veneno
poisonous *adj.* venenoso
poke *v.* husmear
poker *n.* atizador, póquer
poky *adj.* diminuto
polar *adj.* polar
pole *n.* poste, mástil
polemic *n.* polémico
police *n.* policía
policeman *n.* agente de policía
policy *n.* política
polish *n.* abrillantador
polite *adj.* educado
pliteness *n.* cortesía
politic *adj.* diplomático
political *adj.* político
politician *n.* político
politics *n.* política
polity *n.* sistema de gobierno
poll *n.* votación
pollen *n.* polen
pollster *n.* encuestador
pollute *v.* contaminar
pollution *n.* contaminación
polo *n.* polo
polyandry *n.* poliandria
polygamous *adj.* polígamo
polygamy *n.* poligamia
polyglot *adj.* poliglota
polygraph *n.* detector de mentiras
polytechnic *n.* politécnico
polytheism *n.* politeísmo
polytheistic *adj.* politeísta
pomegranate *n.* granada
pomp *n.* pompa
pomposity *n.* pomposidad

pompous *adj.* pomposo
pond *n.* estanque
ponder *v.* considerar
pontiff *n.* pontífice
pony *n.* poni
pool *n.* charca, billar
poor *adj.* pobre
poorly *adv.* mal
pop *v.* estallar, saltar
pope *n.* papa
poplar *n.* álamo
poplin *n.* popelina
populace *n.* el pueblo
popular *adj.* popular
popularity *n.* popularidad
popularize *v.* popularizar
populate *v.* poblar
population *n.* población
populous *adj.* populoso
porcelain *n.* porcelana
porch *n.* porche
porcupine *n.* puercoespín
pore *n.* poro
pork *n.* cerdo
pornography *n.* pornografía
porridge *n.* gachas de avena
port *n.* puerto
portable *adj.* portátil
portage *n.* porteo
portal *n.* portal
portend *v.* presagiar
portent *n.* presagio
porter *n.* maletero, porteador,
   portero
portfolio *n.* portafolio
portico *n.* pórtico
portion *n.* porción
portrait *n.* retrato
portraiture *n.* retrato
portray *v.* representar
portrayal *n.* representación
pose *v.* posar

posh *adj.* pija, elegante
posit *v.* plantear
position *n.* posición
positive *adj.* positivo
possess *v.* poseer, tener
possession *n.* posesión
possessive *adj.* posesivo
possibility *n.* posibilidad
possible *adj.* posible
post *n.* poste, correo, puesto
postage *n.* franqueo
postal *adj.* postal
postcard *n.* postal
postcode *n.* código postal
poster *n.* poster
posterior *adj.* posterior
posterity *n.* posteridad
postgraduate *n.* postgraduado
posthumous *adj.* póstumo
postman *n.* cartero
postmaster *n.* jefe de correos
postmortem *n.* autopsia
postoffice *n.* correos, oficina de correos
postpone *v.* aplazar
postponement *n.* aplazamiento
postscript *n.* postdata
posture *n.* postura
pot *n.* olla
potato *n.* patata
potency *n.* potencia
potent *adj.* fuerte
potential *adj.* potencial
pontentiality *n.* posibilidad
potter *v.* trajinar
pottery *n.* alfarería, cerámica
pouch *n.* bolsa, zurrón
poultry *n.* aves de corral
pounce *v.* saltar
pound *n.* libra
pour *v.* verter
poverty *n.* pobreza

powder *n.* polvo
power *n.* poder
powerful *adj.* poderoso
practicability *n.* factibilidad
practicable *adj.* factible
practical *adj.* práctico
practice *n.* practica
practise *v.* practicar
practitioner *n.* facultativo
pragmatic *adj.* pragmático
pragmatism *n.* pragmatismo
praise *v.t.* elogiar
praline *n.* praliné
pram *n.* cochecito
prank *n.* travesura
prattle *v.* parlotear
pray *v.* rezar
prayer *n.* oración
preach *v.* sermonear
preacher *n.* predicador
preamble *n.* preámbulo
precarious *adj.* precario
precaution *n.* precaución
precautionary *adj.* preventivo
precede *v.* preceder
precedence *n.* precedencia
precedent *n.* precedente
precept *n.* precepto
precint *n.* recinto
precious *adj.* precioso
precipitate *v.* precipitar
precis *n.* resumen
precise *adj.* preciso
precision *n.* precisión
precognition *n.* precognición
precondition *n.* requisito
precursor *n.* precursor
predator *n.* depredador
predecessor *n.* predecesor
predestination *n.* predestinación
predetermine *v.* predeterminar
predicament *n.* aprieto

predicate *n.* predicado
predict *v.* predecir
prediction *n.* predicción
predominance *n.* predominio
predominant *adj.* predominante
predominate *v.* predominar
pre-eminence *n.* preminencia
pre-eminent *adj.* preminente
pre-empt *v.* anticiparse
prefabricated *adj.* prefabricado
preface *n.* prefacio
prefect *n.* monitor
prefer *v.* preferir
preference *n.* preferencia
preferential *adj.* preferencial
preferment *n.* primacía
prefix *n.* prefijo
pregnancy *n.* embarazo
pregnant *adj.* embarazada
prehistoric *adj.* prehistórico
prejudge *v.* prejuzgar
prejudice *n.* prejuicio
prejudicial *adj.* perjudicial
prelate *n.* prelado
preliminary *adj.* preliminar
prelude *n.* preludio
premarital *adj.* prematrimonial
premature *adj.* prematuro
premeditate *v.* premeditar
premeditation *n.* premeditación
premier *adj.* primordial
premiere *n.* estreno
premise *n.* premisa
premises *n.* local
premium *n.* prima
premonition *n.* premonición
preoccupation *n.* preocupación
preoccupy *v.* preocupar
preparation *n.* preparación
preparatory *adj.* preparatorio
prepare *v.* preparar
preponderance *n.* preponderan-

cia
preponderate *v.* preponderar
preposition *n.* preposición
prepossessing *adj.* atractivo
preposterous *adj.* absurdo
prerequisite *n.* requisito
prerogative *n.* prerrogativa
presage *v.* presagiar
prescience *n.* presciencia
prescribe *v.* recetara
prescription *n.* receta
presence *n.* presencia
present *adj.* presente
present *n.* regalo
present *v.* presentar
presentation *n.* presentación
presently *adv.* actualmente
preservation *n.* preservación
preservative *n.* conservante
preserve *v.* conservar
preside *v.* presidir
president *n.* presidente
presidential *adj.* presidencial
press *v.* apretar, pulsar
pressure *n.* presión
pressurize *v.* presionar
prestige *n.* prestigio
prestigious *adj.* prestigioso
presume *v.* suponer
presumption *n.* presunción
presuppose *v.* presuponer
presupposition *n.* suposición
pretence *n.* pretexto
pretend *v.* fingir, pretender
pretension *n.* pretensión
pretentious *adj.* pretencioso
pretext *n.* pretexto
prettiness *n.* bonito
pretty *adj.* bonita
pretzel *n.* galleta salada
prevail *v.* prevalecer
prevalance *n.* preponderancia

prevalent *adj.* frecuente
prevent *v.* impedir, prevenir
prevention *n.* prevención
preventive *adj.* preventivo
preview *n.* preestreno
previous *adj.* previo, anterior
prey *n.* presa
price *n.* precio
priceless *adj.* invalorable
prick *v.* pinchar, picar
prickle *n.* espina
pride *n.* orgullo
priest *n.* cura
priesthood *n.* sacerdocio
prim *adj.* mojigato
primacy *n.* primacía
primal *adj.* primario
primarily *adv.* principalmente
primary *adj.* principal
primate *n.* primate
prime *adj.* principal
primer *n.* imprimación
primeval *adj.* primigenio
primitive *adj.* primitivo
prince *n.* príncipe
princely *adj.* principesco
princess *n.* princesa
principal *adj.* principal
principal *n.* director
principle *n.* principio
print *v.* imprimir
printout *n.* listado
printer *n.* impresora
prior *adj.* previo
priority *n.* prioridad
priory *n.* priorato
prism *n.* prisma
prison *n.* prisión
prisoner *n.* prisionero
pristine *adj.* inmaculado
privacy *n.* privacidad
private *adj.* privado

privation *n.* privación
privatize *v.* privatizar
privilege *n.* privilegio
privy *adj.* privado
prize *n.* precio
pro *n.* profesional
proactive *adj.* proactivo
probability *n.* probabilidad
probable *adj.* probable
probably *adv.* probablemente
probate *n.* probable
probation *n.* probación
probationer *n.* en libertad condicional
probe *n.* sonda
probity *n.* probidad
problem *n.* problema
problematic *adj.* problemático
procedure *n.* procedimiento
proceed *v.* proceder
proceedings *n.* medidas, actas
proceeds *n.* proceso
process *n.* proceso
procession *n.* procesión
proclaim *v.* proclamar
proclamation *n.* proclamación
proclivity *n.* proclividad
procrastinate *v.* aplazar las cosas
procrastination *n.* dilación
procreate *v.* procrear
procure *v.* procurar
procurement *n.* procuración
prod *v.* dar un codazo a
prodigal *adj.* pródigo
prodigious *adj.* prodigioso
prodigy *n.* prodigio
produce *v.* producir
producer *n.* productor
product *n.* producto
production *n.* producción
productive *adj.* productivo
productivity *n.* productividad

profane *adj.* profano
profess *v.* profanar
profession *n.* profesión
professional *adj.* profesional
professor *n.* profesor
proficiency *n.* competencia
proficient *adj.* competente
profile *n.* perfil
profit *n.* beneficio
profitable *adj.* beneficioso
profiteering *n.* especulación
profligacy *n.* despilfarro
profligate *adj.* despilfarrador
profound *adj.* profundo
profundity *n.* profundidad
profuse *adj.* profuso
profusion *n.* profusión
progeny *n.* progenie
prognosis *n.* pronóstico
prognosticate *v.* pronosticar
programme *n.* programa
progress *n.* progreso
progressive *adj.* progresivo
prohibit *v.* prohibir
prohibition *n.* prohibición
prohibitive *adj.* prohibitivo
project *n.* proyecto
projectile *n.* proyectil
projection *n.* proyección
projector *n.* proyector
prolapse *n.* prolapso
proliferate *v.* proliferar
proliferation *n.* proliferación
prolific *adj.* prolífico
prologue *n.* prólogo
prolong *v.* prolongar
prolongation *n.* prolongación
promenade *n.* paseo marítimo
prominence *n.* prominencia
prominent *adj.* prominente
promiscuous *adj.* promiscuo
promise *n.* promesa

promising *adj.* prometedor
promote *v.* ascender, promover, fomentar
promotion *n.* acenso
prompt *v.* provocar, dar, apuntar
prompter *n.* apuntador
promulgate *v.* promulgar
prone *adj.* propenso
pronoun *n.* pronombre
pronounce *v.* pronunciar
pronunciation *n.* pronunciación
proof *n.* prueba
prop *n.* apoyo, puntal
propaganda *n.* propaganda
propagate *v.* propagar
propagation *n.* propagación
propel *v.* propulsar
propeller *n.* hélice
proper *adj.* apropiado
property *n.* propiedad
prophecy *n.* profecía
prophesy *v.* vaticinar
prophet *n.* profeta
prophetic *adj.* profético
propitiate *v.* propiciar
proportion *n.* proporción
proportional *adj.* proporcional
proportionate *adj.* proporcional
proposal *n.* propuesta
propose *v.* proponer
proposition *n.* proposición
propound *v.* postular
proprietary *adj.* propietario
proprietor *n.* propietario
propriety *n.* corrección
prorogue *v.* prorrogar
prosaic *adj.* prosaico
prose *n.* prosa
prosecute *v.* procesar
prosecution *n.* acusación
prosecutor *n.* fiscal, fiscalía
prospect *n.* perspectiva

prospective *adj.* posible
prospectus *n.* prospecto
prosper *v.* prosperar
prosperity *n.* prosperidad
prosperous *adj.* próspero
prostate *n.* próstata
prostitute *n.* prostituta
prostitution *n.* prostitución
prostrate *adj.* postrado
prostration *n.* postración
protagonist *n.* protagonista
protect *v.* proteger
protection *n.* protección
protective *adj.* protector
protectorate *n.* protectorado
protein *n.* proteína
protest *n.* protesta
protestation *n.* declaración
protocol *n.* protocolo
prototype *n.* prototipo
protracted *adj.* prolongado
protractor *n.* transportador
protrude *v.* sobresalir
proud *adj.* orgulloso
prove *v.* demostrar
provenance *n.* procedencia
proverb *n.* proverbio
proverbial *adj.* proverbial
provide *v.* proveer
providence *n.* providencia
provident *adj.* previsor
providential *adj.* providencial
province *n.* provincia
provincial *adj.* provincial, provinciano
provision *n.* provisión
provisional *adj.* provisional
proviso *n.* condición
provocation *n.* provocación
provocative *adj.* provocador
provoke *v.* provocar
prowess *n.* destreza

proximate *adj.* próximo
proximity *n.* proximidad
proxy *n.* poder, apoderado, sustituto
prude *n.* mojigato
prudence *n.* prudencia
prudent *adj.* prudente
prudential *adj.* prudencial
prune *n.* pasa
pry *v.* curiosear
psalm *n.* salmo
pseudo *adj.* falso
pseudonym *n.* seudónimo
psyche *n.* psique
psychiatrist *n.* psiquiatra
psychiatry *n.* psiquiatría
psychic *adj.* psíquico, vidente
psychological *adj.* psicológico
psychologist *n.* psicólogo
psychology *n.* psicología
psychopath *n.* psicópata
psychosis *n.* psicosis
psychotherapy *n.* psicoterapia
pub *n.* pub
puberty *n.* pubertad
pubic *adj.* púbico
public *adj.* público
publication *n.* publicación
publicity *n.* publicidad
publicize *v.* anunciar
publish *v.* publicar
publisher *n.* editor
pudding *n.* postre dulce
puddle *n.* charco
puerile *adj.* pueril
puff *n.* soplo, racha, bocanada
puffy *adj.* esponjoso
pull *v.* tirar
pulley *n.* polea
pullover *n.* jersey
pulp *n.* pulpa
pulpit *n.* púlpito

pulsar *n.* púlsar
pulsate *v.* latir, palpitar
pulsation *n.* pulsación
pulse *n.* pulso
pummel *v.* aporrear
pump *n.* bomba, zapatos de salón
pumpkin *n.* calabaza
pun *n.* equívoco
punch *v.* picar, golpear
punctual *adj.* puntual
punctuality *n.* puntualidad
punctuate *v.* puntuar
punctuation *n.* puntuación
puncture *n.* pinchazo
pungency *n.* acritud
pungent *adj.* picante, mordaz
punish *v.* castigar
punishment *n.* castigo
punitive *adj.* punitivo
punter *n.* jugador
puny *adj.* enclenque
pup *n.* cría
pupil *n.* alumno
puppet *n.* marioneta
puppy *n.* cachorro
purblind *adj.* cegato, miope
purchase *v.* comprar
pure *adj.* puro
purgation *n.* purgación
purgative *adj.* purgante
purgatory *n.* purgatorio
purge *v.* purgar
purification *n.* purificación
purify *v.* purificar
purist *n.* purista
puritan *n.* puritano
puritanical *adj.* puritano
purity *n.* pureza
purple *n.* morado
purport *v.* pretender
purpose *n.* propósito
purposely *adv.* deliberadamente

purr *v.* ronronear
purse *n.* monedero
purser *n.* sobrecargo
pursuance *n.* cumplimiento
pursue *v.* perseguir
pursuit *n.* persecución
purvey *v.* proveer
purview *n.* ámbito
pus *n.* pus
push *v.* empujar
pushy *adj.* prepotente, avasallador
puss *n.* gatito
put *v.* poner
putative *adj.* supuesto
putrid *adj.* putrefacto
puzzle *v.t.* descifrar
pygmy *n.* pigmeo
pyjamas *n.* pijama
pyorrhoea *n.* piorrea
pyramid *n.* pirámide
pyre *n.* pira
pyromania *n.* piromanía
python *n.* pitón

Q

quack *n* graznido
quackery *n.* charlatanismo
quad *n.* cuatrillizo, quad
quadrangle *a.* cuadrángulo
quadrangular *n.* cuadrangular
quadrant *n.* cuadrante
quadrilateral *n.* cuadrilátero
quadruped *n.* cuadrúpedo
quadruple *adj.* cuádruple
quadruplet *n.* cuatrillizo
quaff *v.* zampar
quail *n.* codorniz

quaint *adj.* pintoresco
quaintly *adv.* de forma extraña
quake *v.* temblar
quaker *n.* cuáquero
qualification *n.* calificación
qualify *v.* calificar, clasificar, apacitar
qualitative *adj.* cualitativo
quality *n.* calidad
qualm *n.* escrúpulo
quandary *n.* disyuntiva
quango *n.* organización no gubernamental
quantify *v.* cuantificar
quantitative *adj.* cuantitativo
quantity *n.* cantidad
quantum *n.* cuántico, quantum
quarantine *n.* cuarentena
quark *n.* quark
quarrel *n.* riña
quarrelsome *adj.* pendenciero
quarry *n.* cantera
quart *n.* cuarto de galón
quarter *n.* cuarto
quarterly *adj.* trimestral
quartet *n.* cuarteto
quartz *n.* cuarzo
quash *v.* anular
quaver *v.* temblar
quay *n.* muelle
queasy *adj.* delicado
queen *n.* reina
queer *adj.* extraño, maricón
quell *v.* calmar
quench *v.* apagar
querulous *adj.* quejumbroso
query *n.* pregunta, duda
quest *n.* búsqueda
question *n.* pregunta
questionable *adj.* cuestionable
questionnaire *n.* cuestionario
queue *n.* cola

quibble *n.* subterfugio
quick *adj.* rápido
quicken *v.* apresurar
quickly *adv.* deprisa, rápidamente
quid *n.* libra
quiescent *adj.* inmóvil
quiet *adj.* callado
quieten *v.* calmarse
quietude *n.* quietud
quiff *n.* tupé
quilt *n.* edredón
quilted *adj.* acolchado
quin *n.* quintillizo
quince *n.* membrillo
quinine *n.* quinina
quintessence *n.* quintaesencia
quip *n.* pulla
quirk *n.* peculiaridad
quit *v.* abandonar
quite *adv.* bastante
quits *adj.* empatado
quiver *v.* estremecerse
quixotic *adj.* quijotesco
quiz *n.* concurso
quizzical *adj.* burlón
quorum *n.* quórum
quota *n.* cuota
quotation *n.* cita
quote *v.* presupuesto
quotient *n.* cociente

R

rabbit *n.* conejo
rabble *n.* chusma
rabid *adj.* rabioso
rabies *n.* rabia
race *n.* carrera

race *v.* competir
racial *adj.* racial, racista
racialism *n.* racismo
rack *n.* rejilla, estante
racket *n.* raqueta
racketeer *n.* mafioso
racy *adj.* picante, salado
radar *n.* radar
radial *adj.* radial
radiance *n.* brillantez
radiant *adj.* radiante
radiate *v.* irradiar
radiation *n.* radiación
radical *adj.* radical
radio *n.* radio
radioactive *adj.* radioactivo
radiography *n.* radiografía
radiology *n.* radiología
radish *n.* rábano
radium *n.* radio
radius *n.* radio
raffle *n.* rifa
raft *n.* balsa
rag *n.* trapo, harapo
rage *n.* rabia
ragged *adj.* irregular, andrajoso
raid *n.* incursión, ataque, redada
rail *n.* riel, raíl, carril
raling *n.* reja, verja
raillery *n.* burla
railway *n.* ferrocarril
rain *n* lluvia
rainbow *n.* arco iris
raincoat *n.* chubasquero
rainfall *n.* pluviosidad, precipitaciones
rainforest *n.* selva tropical
rainy *adj.* lluvioso
raise *v.* recaudar, elevar, aumentar
raisin *n.* pasa
rake *n.* rastrillo
rally *n.* reunión, mitin

ram *n.* carnero
ramble *v.* pasear
ramification *n.* ramificación
ramify *v.* ramificar
ramp *n.* rampa
rampage *v.* desbocarse
rampant *adj.* violento
rampart *n.* terraplén
ramshackle *adj.* destartalado
ranch *n.* rancho
rancid *adj.* rancio
rancour *n.* rencor
random *adj.* aleatorio
range *n.* cadena, cordillera, serie
ranger *n.* guardabosques
rank *n.* rango
rank *v.* clasificar
rankle *v.* doler
ransack *v.* saquear
ransom *n.* rescate
rant *v.* divagar
rap *v.* golpear con los nudillos
rapacious *adj.* rapaz, codicioso
rape *v.* violar
rapid *adj.* rápido
rapidity *n.* rapidez
rapier *n.* florete, estoque
rapist *n.* violador
rapport *n.* armonía
rapprochment *n.* acercamiento
rapt *adj.* extasiado
rapture *n.* éxtasis
rare *adj.* raro
raring *adj.* ávido
rascal *n.* pillo
rash *adj.* precipitado
rasp *n.* escofina
raspberry *n.* frambuesa
rat *n.* rata
ratchet *n.* trinquete
rate *n.* precio, tipo, grado
rather *adv.* más que, en lugar, bastante

ratify *v.* ratificar
rating *n.* tasación
ratio *n.* ratio, razón
ration *n.* ración
rational *adj.* racional
rationale *n.* razón
rationalism *n.* racionalismo
rationalize *v.* racionalizar
rattle *v.* sonar
raucous *adj.* estridente
ravage *v.t.* destrozar
rave *v.* desvariar
raven *n.* cuervo
ravenous *adj.* hambriento
ravine *n.* barranco
raw *adj.* crudo
ray *n.* rayo
raze *v.* arrasar
razor *n.* navaja, cuchilla de afeitar
reach *v.* alcanzar
react *v.* reaccionar
reaction *n.* reacción
reactionary *adj.* reaccionario
reactor *n.* reactor
read *v.* leer
reader *n.* lector
readily *adv.* fácilmente
reading *n.* lectura
readjust *v.* reajustar
ready *adj.* listo
reaffirm *v.* reafirmar
real *adj.* real
realism *n.* realismo
realistic *adj.* realista
reality *n.* realidad
realization *n.* realización, comprensión
realize *v.* darse cuenta
really *adv.* realmente
realm *n.* reino
ream *n.* resma

reap *v.* segar
reaper *n.* segadora
reappear *v.* reaparecer
reappraisal *n.* revaluación
rear *n.* parte trasera
rearrange *v.* reorganizar
reason *n.* razón
reasonable *adj.* razonable
reassess *v.* revaluar
reassure *v.* tranquilizar
rebate *n.* rembolso
rebel *v.* rebelarse
rebellion *n.* rebelión
rebellious *adj.* rebelde
rebirth *n.* renacimiento
rebound *v.* rebotar
rebuff *v.* rechazar
rebuild *v.* reconstruir
rebuke *v.t.* reprender
recall *v.* recordar
recap *v.* resumir
recapitulate *v.* recapitular
recapture *v.* reconquistar
recede *v.* retroceder
receipt *n.* recibo
receive *v.* recibir
receiver *n.* auricular, receptor, destinatario
recent *adj.* reciente
recently *adv.* recientemente
receptable *n.* receptáculo
reception *n.* recepción
receptionist *n.* recepcionista
receptive *adj.* receptivo
recess *n.* hueco, nicho
recession *n.* recesión
recessive *adj.* recesivo
recharge *v.* recargar
recipe *n.* receta
recipient *n.* destinatario
reciprocal *adj.* reciproco
reciprocate *v.* corresponder

recital *n.* recital
recite *v.* recitar
reckless *adj.* temerario
reckon *v.t.* contar
reclaim *v.* recuperar
reclamation *n.* reclamación
recline *v.* reclinarse
recluse *n.* recluso
recognition *n.* reconocimiento
recognize *v.i.* reconocer
recoil *v.* retroceder
recollect *v.* recordar
recollection *n.* recolección
recommend *v.* recomendar
recommendation *n.* recomendación
recompense *v.* recompensar
reconcile *v.* reconciliar
reconciliation *n.* reconciliación
reconditior *v.* reacondicionar
reconsider *v.* reconsiderar
reconstitute *v.* reconstituir
reconstruct *v.* reconstruir
record *n.* registro, disco
recorder *n.* grabadora
recount *v.* contar
recoup *v.* recobrar
recourse *n.* recurso
recover *v.* recuperar
recovery *n.* recuperación
recreate *v.* recrear
recreation *n.* recreación
recrimination *n.* recriminación
recruit *v.* reclutar
rectangle *n.* rectángulo
rectangular *adj.* rectangular
rectification *n.* rectificación
rectify *v.* rectificar
rectitude *n.* rectitud
rectum *n.* recto
recumbent *adj.* recostado
recuperate *v.* recuperarse

recur *v.* repetirse
recurrence *n.* recurrencia
recurrent *adj.* recurrente
recycle *v.* reciclar
red *adj.* rojo
reddish *adj.* rojizo
redeem *v.* redimir
redemption *n.* redención
redeploy *v.* redistribuir
redolent *adj.* rememorativo
redouble *v.* redoblar
redoubtable *adj.* imponente
redress *v.* reajustar
reduce *v.* reducir
reduction *n.* reducción
reductive *adj.* reductor
redundancy *n.* desempleo
redundant *adj.* superfluo
reef *n.* arrecife
reek *v.* oler
reel *n.* carrete, bobina
refer *v.* referir
referee *n.* árbitro
reference *n.* referencia
referendum *n.* referéndum
refill *v.* rellenar
refine *v.* refinar
refinement *n.* refinamiento
refinery *n.* refinería
refit *v.* reparar
reflect *v.* reflejar
reflection *n.* reflexión
reflective *adj.* reflector
reflex *n.* reflejo
reflexive *adj.* reflexivo
reflexology *n.* reflexología
reform *v.* reformar
reformation *n.* reformación
reformer *n.* reformador
refraction *n.* refracción
refrain *v.t.* abstenerse
refresh *v.* refrescar

refreshment *n.* refresco
refrigerate *v.* refrigerar
refrigeration *n.* refrigeración
refrigerator *n.* refrigerador
refuge *n.* refugio
refugee *n.* refugiado
refulgence *n.* fulgor
refulgent *adj.* refulgente
refund *v.* reembolsar
refund *n.* reembolso
refurbish *v.* restaurar
refusal *n.* negativa
refuse *v.* negarse, rehusar
refuse *n.* basura
refutation *n.* refutación
refute *v.* refutar
regain *v.* recuperar
regal *adj.* regio, real
regard *v.* considerar
regarding *prep.* respecto a
regardless *adv.* a pesar de todo
regenerate *v.* regenerar
regeneration *n.* regeneración
regent *n.* regente
reggae *n.* reggae
regicide *n.* regicidio
regime *n.* régimen
regiment *n.* regimiento
region *n.* región
regional *adj.* regional
register *n.* registro
registrar *n.* secretario registro civil
registration *n.* inscripción
registry *n.* registro
regress *v.* revertir
regret *n.* remordimiento
regrettable *adj.* lamentable
regular *adj.* corriente
regularity *n.* regularidad
regularize *v.* regularizar
regulate *v.* regular

regulation *n.* reglamento
regulator *n.* regulador
rehabilitate *v.* rehabilitar
rehabilitation *n.* rehabilitación
rehearsal *n.* ensayo
rehearse *v.* ensayar
reign *v.* reinar
reimburse *v.* reembolsar
rein *n.* rienda
reincarnate *v.* reencarnar
reinforce *v.* reforzar
reinforcement *n.* refuerzo
reinstate *v.* restituir
reinstatement *n.* restablecimiento
reiterate *v.* reiterar
reiteration *n.* reiteración
reject *v.* rechazar
rejection *n.* rechazo
rejoice *v.* regocijarse
rejoin *v.* reincorporarse
rejoinder *n.* réplica
rejuvenate *v.* rejuvenecer
rejuvenation *n.* rejuvenecimiento
relapse *v.* recaída, reincidencia
relate *v.* relacionar
relation *n.* relación
relationship *n.* relación
relative *adj.* pariente, familiar
relativity *n.* relatividad
relax *v.* relajarse
relaxation *n.* relajación
relay *n.* relevo
release *v.* liberar
relegate *v.* relegar
relent *v.* ceder
relentless *adj.* implacable
relevance *n.* relevancia
relevant *adj.* relevante
reliable *adj.* fidedigno
reliance *n.* dependencia
relic *n.* reliquia
relief *n.* alivio

relieve *v.* aliviar
religion *n.* religión
religious *adj.* religioso
relinquish *v.* renunciar a, abandonar
relish *v.* saborear
relocate *v.* reubicar
reluctance *n.* reticencia .
reluctant *adj.* reticente
rely *v.* confiar en
remain *v.* quedar, sobrar
remainder *n.* restos
remains *n.* restos, desperdicios
remand *v.* detener
remark *v.* comentar
remarkable *adj.* extraordinario
remedial *adj.* curativo
remedy *n.* remedio
remember *v.* recordar
remembrance *n.* recuerdo
remind *v.* recordar
reminder *n.* recordatorio
reminiscence *n.* reminiscencia
reminiscent *adj.* reminiscente
remiss *adj.* descuidado
remission *n.* remisión
remit *n.* remisión
remittance *n.* remesa, envío
remnant *n.* resto
remonstrate *v.* protestar
remorse *n.* remordimiento
remote *adj.* remoto
removable *adj.* amovible
removal *n.* mudanza
remove *v.* quitar, destituir
remunerate *v.* remunerar
remuneration *n.* remuneración
remunerative *adj.* remunerado
renaissance *n.* renacimiento
render *v.* prestar
rendezvous *n.* cita
renegade *n.* renegado

renew *v.* renovar, reanudar, cambiar
renewal *n.* renovación, reanudación
renounce *v.t.* renunciar
renovate *v.* renovar
renovation *n.* renovación
renown *n.* renombre
renowned *adj.* renombrado
rent *n.* alquiler
rental *n.* alquiler
renunciation *n.* renuncia
reoccur *v.* volver a ocurrir
reorganize *v.* reorganizar
repair *v.* reparar
repartee *n.* repertorio
repatriate *v.* repatriar
repatriation *n.* repatriación
repay *v.* reembolsar
repayment *n.* reembolso
repeal *v.* revocar
repeat *v.* repetir
repel *v.* repugnar
repellent *adj.* repelente
repent *v.* arrepentirse
repentance *n.* arrepentimiento
repentant *adj.* arrepentido
repercussion *n.* repercusión
repetition *n.* repetición
replace *v.* reemplazar
replacement *n.* reemplazo
replay *v.* repetir
replenish *v.* rellenar, reponer
replete *adj.* repleto
replica *n.* réplica, copia
replicate *v.* repetir, duplicar
reply *v.* responder, contestar
report *v.* informar, denunciar
reportage *n.* reportaje
reporter *n.* periodista
repose *n.* reposo
repository *n.* depósito

repossess *v.* recuperar
reprehensible *adj.* reprensible
represent *v.* representar
representation *n.* representación
representative *adj.* representante
repress *v.* reprimir
repression *n.* represión
reprieve *v.* indultar
reprimand *v.* reprender
reprint *v.* reimprimir
reprisal *n.* represalia
reproach *v.* reproche
reprobate *n.* réprobo
reproduce *v.* reproducir
reproduction *n.* reproducción
reproductive *adj.* reproductor
reproof *n.* reprobación
reprove *v.* reprender
reptile *n.* reptil
republic *n.* república
republican *adj.* republicano
repudiate *v.* repudiar
repudiation *n.* repudiación
repugnance *n.* repugnancia
repugnant *adj.* repugnante
repulse *v.* repeler
repulsion *n.* repulsión
repulsive *adj.* repulsivo
reputation *n.* reputación
repute *n.* reputación
request *n.* petición, solicitud
requiem *n.* réquiem
require *v.* necesitar, exigir
requirement *n.* requisito
requisite *adj.* imprescindible
requiste *n.* requisito
requisition *n.* requisición
requite *v.t.* recompensar
rescind *v.* rescindir
rescue *v.* rescatar
research *n.* investigación
resemblance *n.* parecido

resemble *v.* parecerse
resent *v.* resentirse
resentment *n.* resentimiento
reservation *n.* reserva
reserve *v.* reservar
reservoir *n.* embalse
reshuffle *v.* remodelación
reside *v.* residir
residence *n.* residencia
resident *n.* residente
residential *adj.* residencial
residual *adj.* residual
residue *n.* residuo
resign *v.* renunciar
resignation *n.* renuncia
resilient *adj.* resistente
resist *v.* resistir
resistance *n.* resistencia
resistant *adj.* resistente
resolute *adj.* resuelto
resolution *n.* resolución
resolve *v.* resolver
resonance *n.* resonancia
resonant *adj.* resonante
resonate *v.* resonar
resort *n.* centro de turismo, recurso
resound *v.* resonar
resource *n.* recurso
resourceful *adj.* habilidoso
respect *n.* respeto
respectable *adj.* respetable
respectful *adj.* respetuoso
respective *adj.* respectivo
respiration *n.* respiración
respirator *n.* respirador
respire *v.* respirar
respite *n.* respiro
resplendent *adj.* resplandeciente
respond *v.* responder
respondent *n.* encuestado, demandado

response *n.* respuesta
responsibility *n.* responsabilidad
responsible *adj.* responsable
responsive *adj.* receptivo
rest *v.* descansar
restaurant *n.* restaurante
restaurateur *n.* restaurador
restful *adj.* descansado
restitution *n.* restitución
restive *adj.* inquieto
restoration *adj.* restaurado
restore *v.* restaurar
restrain *v.* refrenar
restraint *n.* restricción
restrict *n.* limitación
restriction *n.* restricción
restrictive *adj.* restrictivo
result *n.* resultado
resultant *adj.* resultante
resume *v.* reanudar
resumption *n.* reanudación
resurgence *a.* resurgimiento
resurgent *adj.* resurgente
resurrect *v.* resucitar
retail *n.* minorista
retailer *n.* minorista
retain *v.i.* retener
retainer *n.* anticipo, criado
retaliate *v.* contraatacar
retaliation *n.* represalias
retard *v.* retardar
retardation *n.* retraso
retarded *adj.* retrasado
retch *v.* dar arcadas
retention *n.* retención
retentive *adj.* retentivo
rethink *v.* reconsiderar
reticent *adj.* reticente
retina *n.* retinar
retinue *n.* séquito, comitiva
retire *v.* retirarse
retirement *n.* jubilación, retiro

retiring *adj.* saliente, retraído
retort *v.* contestar
retouch *v.* retocar
retrace *v.t.* deshacer
retract *v.* retirar
retread *v.* repisar
retreat *v.t.* retirarse, replegarse
retrench *v.* reducir
retrenchment *n.* recorte
retrial *n.* nuevo juicio
retribution *n.* retribución
retrieve *v.* recobrar
retriever *n.* perro cobrador,
　retriever
retro *adj.* retro
retroactive *adj.* retroactivo
retrograde *adj.* retrogrado
retrospect *n.* retrospección
retrospective *adj.* retrospectiva
return *v.* volver
return *n.* retorno, vuelta
reunion *n.* reunión
reunite *v.* reunir
reuse *v.* reusar
revamp *v.* renovar
reveal *v.* revelar
revel *v.* deleitarse
revelation *n.* revelación
revenge *n.* venganza
revenue *n.* ganancia
reverberate *v.* retumbar
revere *v.* reverenciar
reverence *n.* reverencia
reverend *adj.* reverendo
reverent *adj.* reverente
reverential *adj.* reverencial
reverie *n.* ensueño
reversal *n.* inversión
reverse *v.* invertir
reversible *adj.* reversible
revert *v.* volver a
review *n.* reseña, critica

revile *v.* injuriar
revise *v.* revisar
revision *n.* revisión
revival *n.* renacimiento
revivalism *n.* evangelismo
revive *v.* revivir
revocable *adj.* revocable
revocation *n.* revocación
revoke *v.* revocar
revolt *v.* revelarse
revolution *n.* revolución
revolutionary *adj.* revolucionario
revolutionize *v.* revolucionar
revolve *v.* girar
revolver *n.* revólver
revulsion *n.* repulsión
reward *n.* recompensa
rewind *v.* rebobinar, retroceder
rhapsody *n.* rapsodia
rhetoric *n.* retórica
rhetorical *adj.* retórico
rheumatic *adj.* reumático
rheumatism *n.* reumatismo
rhinoceros *n.* rinoceronte
rhodium *n.* rodio
rhombus *n.* rombo
rhyme *n.* rima
rhythm *n.* ritmo
rhythmic *adj.* rítmico
rib *n.* costilla
ribbon *n.* cinta
rice *n.* arroz
rich *adj.* rico
richly *adv.* ricamente
richness *n.* riqueza
rick *n.* pajar
rickets *n.* raquitismo
rickety *adj.* destartalado
rickshaw *n.* calesa oriental
rid *v.* deshacerse
riddance *n.* liberación
riddle *n.* acertijo

riddled *adj.* acribillado
ride *v.* montar
rider *n.* jinete, ciclista, motorista
ridge *n.* cresta
ridicule *n.* ridículo
ridiculous *adj.* ridículo
rife *adj.* lleno, plegado
rifle *n.* rifle
rifle *v.* desvalijar
rift *n.* grieta, ruptura
rig *v.* amañar
rigging *n.* aparejo
right *adj.* correcto, exacto
right *n* correcto, exacto
righteous *adj.* honrado, justo
rightful *adj.* legítimo
rigid *adj.* rígido
rigmarole *n.* galimatías
rigorous *adj.* riguroso
rigour *n.* rigor
rim *n.* borde
ring *n.* anillo, llamada
ring *v.* llamar
ringlet *n.* tirabuzón
ringworm *n.* tiña
rink *n.* pista
rinse *v.* enjuagar
riot *n.* motín, disturbio
rip *v.* rasgar
ripe *adj.* maduro
ripen *v.* madurar
riposte *n.* réplica
ripple *n.* onda, rizo
rise *v.* elevarse, subir
risible *adj.* irrisorio
rising *n.* creciente
risk *n.* riesgo
risky *adj.* arriesgado
rite *n.* rito
ritual *n.* ritual
rival *n.* rival
rivalry *n.* rivalidad

riven *n.* hendido
river *n.* rio
rivet *n.* remache
rivulet *n.* riachuelo
road *n.* carretera
roadworks *n.* obras viales
roadworthy *adj.* en condiciones de circular
roadster *n.* roadster
roam *v.* vagar
roar *n.* rugido
roar *v.* rugir
roast *v.* asar, tostar
rob *v.* robar
robber *n.* ladrón
robbery *n.* robo
robe *n.* bata
robot *n.* robot
robust *adj.* robusto
rock *n.* roca
rocket *n.* cohete
rocky *adj.* rocoso
rod *n.* vara
rodent *n.* roedor
rodeo *n.* rodeo
roe *n.* corzo
rogue *n.* pillo
roguery *n.* pillería
roguish *adj.* pícaro
roister *v.* parrandear
role *n.* papel, rol
roll *v.i.* enrollar
roll *n.* rollo
roll-call *n.* pasada de lista, nómina
roller *n.* rodillo
rollercoaster *n.* montaña rusa
romance *n.* romanticismo
romantic *adj.* romántico
romp *v.* retozo
roof *n.* techo
roofing *n.* techumbre

rook *n.* grafa, torre (ajedrez)
rookery *n.* colonia de grajos
room *n.* habitación
roomy *adj.* espacioso
roost *n.* percha
rooster *n.* gallo
root *n.* raíz
rooted *adj.* arraigado
rope *n.* cuerda
rosary *n.* rosario
rose *n.* rosa
rosette *n.* roseta
roster *n.* alineación
rostrum *n.* tribuna
rosy *adj.* rosado, optimista
rot *v.* pudrirse
rota *n.* lista
rotary *adj.* rotatorio
rotate *v.* rotar
rotation *n.* rotación
rote *n.* memorización
rotor *n.* rotor
rotten *adj.* podrido
rouge *n.* colorete
rough *adj.* áspero, bruto
roulette *n.* ruleta
round *adj.* redondo
roundabout *n.* rotonda
rounded *adj.* redondeado
roundly *adv.* rotundamente
rouse *v.* suscitar
rout *n.* derrota
route *n.* ruta
routine *n.* rutina
rove *v.* vagar
rover *n.* trotamundos
roving *adj.* errante
row *n.* línea, bronca
rowdy *adj.* ruidoso
royal *n.* real
royalist *n.* monárquico
royalty *n.* familia real

rub *n.* frotamiento, roce
rub *v.* frotar
rubber *n.* caucho, goma
rubbish *n.* basura
rubble *n.* escombros
rubric *n.* rúbrica
ruby *n.* rubí
rucksack *n.* mochila
ruckus *n.* jaleo
rudder *n.* timón
rude *adj.* grosero
rudiment *n.* rudimento
rudimentary *adj.* rudimentario
rue *v.* arrepentirse
rueful *adj.* arrepentido
ruffian *n.* rufián
ruffle *v.* despeinar
rug *n.* alfombra
rugby *n.* rugbi
rugged *adj.* accidentado
ruin *n.* ruin
ruinous *adj.* ruinoso
rule *n.* norma
rule *v.* gobernar
ruler *n.* soberano, regla
ruling *n.* dirigente
rum *n.* ron
rumble *v.* retumbar
rumbustious *adj.* agitador
ruminant *n.* rumiante
ruminate *v.* rumia
rumination *n.* reflexión
rummage *v.* revolver
rummy *n.* rummy
rumour *n.* rumor
rumple *v.* arrugar
rumpus *n.* lío
run *n.* carrera
run *v.* correr
runaway *adj.* desbocado, fugitivo, incontrolado
rundown *adj.* debilitado

runway *n.* pista
rung *n.* escalón
runnel *n.* arroyo pequeño
runner *n.* corredor
runny *adj.* derretido
rupture *v.t.* quebrarse
rural *adj.* rural
ruse *n.* ardid
rush *v.* apresurar
rusk *n.* bizcocho tostado
rust *n.* herrumbre
rustic *adj.* rustico
rusticity *n.* rusticidad
rustle *v.* susurrar, crujir, hurtar
rusty *adj.* oxidado
rut *n.* carril
ruthless *adj.* despiadado
rye *n.* centeno

S

sabbath *n.* sábado
sabotage *v.* sabotaje
sabre *n.* sable
saccharin *n.* sacarina
saccharine *adj.* azucarado
sachet *n.* bolsita
sack *n.* saco
sack *v.* despedir, saquear
sacrament *n.* sacramento
sacred *adj.* sagrado
sacrifice *n.* sacrificio
sacrifice *v.* sacrificar
sacrificial *adj.* sacrificatorio
sacrilege *n.* sacrilegio
sacrilegious *adj.* sacrílego
sacrosanct *adj.* sacrosanto
sad *adj.* triste
sadden *v.* entristecer

saddle *n.* montura
saddler *n.* talabartero
sadism *n.* sadismo
sadist *n.* sádico
safari *n.* safari
safe *adj.* seguro
safe *n.* caja fuerte
safeguard *n.* protección
safety *n.* seguridad
saffron *n.* azafrán
sag *v.* caerse
saga *n.* saga
sagacious *adj.* sagaz
sagacity *n.* sagacidad
sage *n.* salvia
sage *adj.* sabio
sail *n.* vela
sail *v.* navegar
sailor *n.* marinero
saint *n.* santo
saintly *adj.* santo
sake *n.* bien, causa
salable *adj.* vendible
salad *n.* ensalada
salary *n.* salario
sale *n.* venta
salesman *n.* vendedor
salient *adj.* destacado
saline *adj.* salino
salinity *n.* salinidad
saliva *n.* saliva
sallow *adj.* cetrino
sally *n.* salida
salmon *n.* salmón
salon *n.* salón
saloon *n.* taberna
salsa *n.* salsa
salt *n.* sal
salty *adj.* salado
salutary *adj.* saludable
salutation *n.* saludo
salute *n.* saludo

salvage *v.* salvamento
salvation *n.* salvación
salver *n.* bandeja
salvo *n.* salva
samaritan *n.* samaritano
same *adj.* mismo
sample *n.* muestra
sampler *n.* muestrario
sanatorium *n.* sanatorio
sanctification *n.* santificación
sanctify *v.* santificar
sanctimonious *adj.* beato
sanction *v.* sancionar
sanctity *n.* santidad
sanctuary *n.* santuario
sanctum *n.* sagrario
sand *n.* arena
sandal *n.* sandalia
sandalwood *n.* sándalo
sander *n.* lijadora
sandpaper *n.* papel de lija
sandwich *n.* sándwich
sandy *adj.* arenoso
sane *adj.* cuerdo
sangfroid *n.* sangre fría
sanguinary *adj.* sanguinario
sanguine *adj.* optimista
sanitarium *n.* sanatorio
sanitary *adj.* sanitario
sanitation *n.* saneamiento
sanitize *v.* desinfectar
sanity *n.* cordura
sap *n.* savia
sapling *n.* árbol nuevo o joven
sapphire *n.* zafiro
sarcasm *n.* sarcasmo
sarcastic *adj.* sarcástico
sarcophagus *n.* sarcófago
sardonic *adj.* sardónico
sari *n.* sari
sartorial *adj.* sartorial
sash *n.* faja

satan *n.* satanás
satanic *adj.* satánico
satanism *n.* satanismo
satchel *n.* bolsa
sated *adj.* saturado
satellite *n.* satélite
satiable *adj.* saciable
satiate *v.* saciar
satiety *n.* saciedad
satin *n.* raso
satire *n.* sátira
satirical *adj.* satírico
satirist *n.* satírico
satirize *v.* satirizar
satisfaction *n.* satisfacción
satisfactory *adj.* satisfactorio
satisfy *v.* satisfacer
saturate *v.* saturar
saturation *n.* saturación
Saturday *n.* sábado
saturnine *adj.* saturnino
sauce *n.* salsa
saucer *n.* platillo
saucy *adj.* descarado
sauna *n.* sauna
saunter *v.* deambular
sausage *n.* salchicha
savage *adj.* salvaje
savagery *n.* ferocidad
save *v.* salvar
savings *n.* ahorros
saviour *n.* saborear
savour *v.t.* saborear
savoury *adj.* sabroso, salado
saw *n.* sierra
saw *v.* serrar
sawdust *n.* serrín
saxophone *n.* saxófono
say *n.* decir, dicho
saying *n.* dicho, refrán
scab *n.* costra
scabbard *n.* vaina

scabies *n.* sarna
scabrous *adj.* escabroso
scaffold *n.* cadalso
scaffolding *n.* andamio
scald *v.* escaldar
scale *n.* escala, báscula
scallop *n.* vieira
scalp *n.* cabellera
scam *n.* estafa
scamp *n.* travieso
scamper *v.t.* irse corriendo
scan *v.* escanear
scanner *n.* escáner
scandal *n.* escandalo
scandalize *v.* escandalizar
scant *adj.* escaso
scanty *adj.* escaso
scapegoat *n.* cabeza de turco
scar *n.* cicatriz
scarce *adj.* escaso
scarcely *adv.* apenas
scare *v.* asustar
scarecrow *n.* espantapájaros
scarf *n.* bufanda
scarlet *n.* escarlata
scarp *n.* escarpa
scary *adj.* aterrador
scathing *adj.* mordaz
scatter *v.* esparcir
scavenge *v.* hurgar
scenario *n.* escenario
scene *n.* escena
scenery *n.* decorado
scenic *adj.* pintoresco
scent *n.* olor
sceptic *n.* escéptico
sceptical *adj.* escéptico
sceptre *n.* cetro
schedule *n.* horario, calendario
schematic *adj.* esquemático
scheme *n.* plan
schism *n.* cisma

schizophrenia *n.* esquizofrenia
scholar *n.* escolar
scholarly *adj.* académico
scholarship *n.* beca
scholastic *adj.* educacional
school *n.* escuela
sciatica *n.* ciática
science *n.* ciencia
scientific *adj.* científico
scientist *n.* científico
scintillating *adj.* ingenioso
scissors *n.* tijeras
scoff *v.i.* engullir
scold *v.* regañar
scoop *n.* cucharon
scooter *n.* motocicleta
scope *n.* ámbito
scorch *v.* chamuscar
score *n.* puntuación
score *v.* marcar
scorer *n.* marcador
scorn *n.* desprecio
scornful *adj.* despreciativo
scorpion *n.* escorpión
Scot *n.* escocés
scot-free *adv.* salir ileso
scoundrel *n.* canalla
scour *v.* restregar
scourge *n.* azote
scout *n.* explorador
scowl *n.* ceño
scrabble *v.* escarbar
scraggy *adj.* descarnado
scramble *v.* mezclar, trepar
scrap *n.* pizca
scrape *v.* rasguñar
scrappy *adj.* rudimentario
scratch *v.t.* rascar, arañar
scrawl *v.* hacer garabatos
scrawny *adj.* esquelético
scream *v.* gritar
screech *n.* chirrido

screed *n.* texto largo
screen *n.* pantalla
screw *n.* tornillo
screwdriver *n.* destornillador
scribble *v.* garabatear
scribe *n.* escriba
scrimmage *n.* escaramuza
scrimp *v.* escatimar
script *n.* guion
scripture *n.* escritura
scroll *n.* rollo
scrooge *n.* rácano
scrub *v.* restregar
scruffy *adj.* desaliñado
scrunch *v.* apretujar, crujir
scruple *n.* escrúpulo
scrupulous *adj.* escrupuloso
scrutinize *v.* escudriñar
scrutiny *n.* escrutinio
scud *v.* moverse rápido
scuff *v.* desgastar
scuffle *n.* refriega
scult *v.* esculpir
sculptor *n.* escultor
sculptural *adj.* escultural
sculpture *n.* escultura
scum *n.* escoria
scurrilous *adj.* injurioso
scythe *n.* guadaña
sea *n.* mar
seagull *n.* gaviota
seal *n.* foca
sealant *n.* sellante
seam *n.* costura
seamless *adj.* sin costura
seamy *adj.* sórdido
sear *v.* quemar
search *v.* buscar
seaside *n.* orilla del mar
season *n.* estación
seasonable *adj.* estacional
seasonal *adj.* estacional

seasoning *n.* condimento
seat *n.* asiento
seating *n.* asientos
secede *v.* separarse
secession *n.* secesión
seclude *v.* recluir
secluded *adj.* recluido
seclusion *n.* retiro
second *adj.* segundo
secondary *adj.* secundario
secrecy *n.* secreto
secret *adj.* secreto
secretariat *n.* secretariado
secretary *n.* secretaria
secrete *v.* ocultar
secretion *n.* secreción
secretive *adj.* reservado
sect *n.* sectario
sectarian *adj.* sectario
section *n.* sección
sector *n.* sector
secular *adj.* secular
secure *adj.* seguro
security *n.* seguridad
sedan *n.* sedán
sedate *adj.* tranquilo
sedation *n.* sedación
sedative *n.* sedante
sedentary *adj.* sedentario
sediment *n.* sedimento
sedition *n.* sedición
seditious *adj.* sedicioso
seduce *v.* seducir
seduction *n.* seducción
seductive *adj.* seductor
sedulous *adj.* diligente
see *v.* ver
seed *n.* semilla
seedy *adj.* desaseado
seek *v.i.* buscar
seem *v.* parecer
seemly *adj.* apropiado

seep *v.* filtrarse
seer *n.* vidente
see-saw *n.* balancín
segment *n.* segmento
segregate *v.* segregar
segregation *n.* segregación
seismic *adj.* sísmico
seize *v.* agarrar
seizure *n.* ataque
seldom *adv.* rara vez
select *v.* seleccionar
selection *n.* selección
selective *adj.* selectivo
self *n.* mismo
selfish *adj.* egoísta
selfless *adj.* desinteresado
selfmade *adj.* artífice de su éxito
sell *v.* vender
seller *n.* vendedor
selvedge *n.* orillo
semantic *adj.* semántico
semblance *n.* semblante
semen *n.* semen
semester *n.* semestre
semicircle *n.* semicírculo
semicolon *n.* punto y coma
seminal *adj.* influyente
seminar *n.* seminario
semitic *adj.* semítico
senate *n.* senado
senator *n.* senador
senatorial *adj.* senatorial
send *v.* mandar, enviar
senile *adj.* senil
senility *n.* senilidad
senior *adj.* senior
seniority *n.* antigüedad
sensation *n.* sensación
sensational *adj.* sensacionalista
sensationalize *v.* desnacionalizar
sense *n.* sentido
senseless *adj.* insensato

sensibility *n.* sensibilidad
sensible *adj.* sensato
sensitive *adj.* sensible
sensitize *v.* sensibilizar
sensor *n.* sensor
sensory *adj.* sensorial
sensual *adj.* sensual
sensuality *n.* sensualidad
sensuous *adj.* sensual
sentence *n.* sentencia
sententious *adj.* sentencioso
sentient *adj.* sensible
sentiment *n.* sentimiento
sentimental *adj.* sentimental
sentinel *n.* centinela
sentry *n.* centinela
separable *adj.* separado
separate *v.* separar
separation *n.* separación
separatist *n.* separatista
sepsis *n.* sepsis
September *n.* Septiembre
septic *adj.* séptico
sepulchral *adj.* sepulcral
sepulchre *n.* sepulcro
sepulture *n.* sepultura
sequel *n.* secuela
sequence *n.* secuencia
sequential *adj.* secuencial
sequester *v.* recluir
serene *adj.* sereno
serenity *n.* serenidad
serf *n.* siervo
serge *n.* sarga
sergeant *n.* sargento
serial *adj.* consecutivo
serialize *v.* seriar
series *n.* series
serious *adj.* serio
sermon *n.* sermón
sermonize *v.* sermonear
serpent *n.* serpiente

serpentine *adj.* serpentino
serrated *adj.* dentellado
servant *n.* sirviente
serve *v.* servir
server *n.* servidor
service *n.* servicio
serviceable *adj.* utilizable
serviette *n.* servilleta
servile *adj.* servil
servility *n.* servilismo
serving *n.* porción, ración
sesame *n.* sésamo
session *n.* sesión
set *v.* establecer
set *n* colección, aparato,
settee *n.* sofá
setter *n.* regulador
setting *n.* colocación, marco
settle *v.* liquidar, acordar, colonizar
settlement *n.* liquidación, acuerdo, pueblo
settler *n.* colono
seven *adj. & n.* siete
seventeen *adj. & n.* diecisiete
seventeenth *adj. & n.* decimoséptimo
seventh *adj. & n.* séptimo
seventieth *adj. & n.* septuagésimo
seventy *adj. & n.* setenta
sever *v.* cortar
several *adj. & pron.* varios,
algunos
severance *n.* ruptura
severe *adj.* severo
severity *n.* severidad
sew *v.* coser
sewage *n.* alcantarillado
sewer *n.* alcantarilla
sewerage *n.* alcantarillado
sex *n.* sexo
sexism *n.* sexismo

sexton *n.* sacristán
sextuplet *n.* sextillo
sexual *adj.* sexual
sexuality *n.* sexualidad
sexy *adj.* sexy
shabby *adj.* raído
shack *n.* choza
shackle *n.* grillete
shade *n.* sombra
shade *v.* dar sombra
shadow *n.* sombra
shadow *n.* sombra
shadowy *adj.* oscuro
shady *adj.* sombreado
shaft *n.* astil
shag *n.* cormorán
shake *v.* sacudir
shaky *adj.* trémulo
shall *v.* modal futuro
shallow *adj.* superficial
sham *n.* fraude
shamble *v.* arrastrar los pies al andar
shambles *n.* confusión
shame *n.* vergüenza
shameful *adj.* vergonzoso
shameless *adj.* descarado
shampoo *n.* champú
shank *n.* mango
shanty *n.* chabola
shape *n.* forma
shapeless *adj.* sin forma
shapely *adj.* bien formado
shard *n.* casco
share *n.* parte
shark *n.* tiburón
sharp *adj.* afilado
sharpen *v.* afilar
- **sharpener** *n.* afilador
shatter *v.t.* destrozar
shattering *adj.* aplastante
shave *v.* afeitar

shaven *adj.* afeitado
shaving *n.* afeitado
shawl *n.* chal
she *pron.* ella
sheaf *n.* gavilla
shear *v.* esquilar
sheath *n.* vaina
shed *n.* cobertizo
sheen *n.* brillo
sheep *n.* oveja
sheepish *adj.* tímido
sheer *adj.* puro
sheet *n.* sábana, hoja
shelf *n.* estante
shell *n.* concha
shelter *n.* refugio
shelve *v.* aplazar
shepherd *n.* pastor
shield *n.* escudo
shift *v.* cambiar, mover
shiftless *adj.* vago
shifty *adj.* sospechoso
shimmer *v.* relucir
shin *n.* espinilla
shine *v.* brillar
shingle *n.* herpes
shiny *adj.* brillante
ship *n.* barco
shipment *n.* envio
shipping *n.* embarque
shipwreck *n.* naufragio
shipyard *n.* astillero
shire *n.* condado
shirk *v.* eludir
shirker *n.* haragán
shirt *n.* camisa
shiver *v.* temblar
shoal *n.* banco
shock *n.* choque
shock *v.* conmocionar
shocking *adj.* impactante
shoddy *adj.* pacotilla

shoe *n.* zapato
shoestring *n.* cordón, presupuesto limitado
shoot *v.* disparar
shooting *n.* tiroteo
shop *n.* tienda
shopkeeper *n.* tendero
shoplifting *n.* hurto en tiendas
shopping *n.* ir de compras
shore *n.* orilla
short *adj.* corto
shortage *n.* escasez
shortcoming *n.* defecto
shortcut *n.* atajo
shorten *v.* acortar
shortfall *n.* déficit
shortly *adv.* brevemente
should *v.* deber
shoulder *n.* hombro
shout *v.i.* gritar
shove *v.* empujar
shovel *n.* excavadora
show *v.* espectáculo
showcase *n.* escaparate
showdown *n.* enfrentamiento
shower *n.* ducha
showy *adj.* lluvioso
shrapnel *n.* metralla
shred *n.* triza
shrew *n.* musaraña, arpía
shrewd *adj.* astuto
shriek *v.* chillar
shrill *adj.* agudo
shrine *n.* sepulcro
shrink *v.* encoger
shrinkage *n.* encogimiento
shrivel *v.* marchitarse
shroud *n.* sudario
shrub *n.* arbusto
shrug *v.* encoger los hombros
shudder *v.* estremecerse
shuffle *v.t.* barajar

shun *v.t.* esquivar
shunt *v.* maniobrar
shut *v.* cerrar
shutter *n.* contraventana, obturador
shuttle *n.* lanzadera
shuttlecock *n.* volante
shy *adj.* tímido
sibilant *adj.* sibilante
sibling *n.* hermano
sick *adj.* enfermo
sickle *n.* hoz
sickly *adj.* enfermizo
sickness *n.* enfermedad
side *n.* lado
sideline *n.* línea lateral
siege *n.* cerco
siesta *n.* siesta
sieve *n.* coladera
sift *v.* cribar
sigh *v.i.* suspirar
sight *n.* vista
sighting *n.* observación
sightseeing *n.* visitas turísticas
sign *n.* seña
signal *n.* señal
signatory *n.* signatario
signature *n.* firma
significance *n.* significancia
significant *n.* significativo
signification *n.* significación
signify *v.* significar
silence *n.* silencio
silencer *n.* silenciador
silent *adj.* silencioso
silhouette *n.* silueta
silicon *n.* silicona
silk *n.* seda
silken *adj.* satinado
silkworm *n.* gusano de seda
silky *adj.* sedoso
sill *n.* alféizar

silly *adj.* tonto
silt *n.* sedimento
silver *n.* plata
similar *adj.* parecido
similarity *n.* similitud
simile *n.* símil
simmer *v.* hervir a fuego lento
simper *v.* sonreír
simple *adj.* sencillo
simpleton *n.* simplón
simplicity *n.* sencillez
simplification *n.* simplificación
simplify *v.* simplificar
simulate *v.* simular
simultaneous *adj.* simultaneo
sin *n.* pecado
since *prep.* desde
sincere *adj.* sincero
sincerity *n.* sinceridad
sinecure *n.* sinecura
sinful *adj.* pecaminoso
sing *v.* cantar
singe *v.* chamuscar
singer *a.* cantante
single *adj.* soltero
singlet *n.* camiseta
singleton *n.* solterón
singular *adj.* singular
singularity *n.* singularidad
singularly *adv.* particularmente
sinister *adj.* siniestro
sink *v.* hundir
sink *n.* fregadero
sinner *n.* pecador
sinuous *adj.* sinuoso
sinus *n.* seno
sip *v.* sorber
siphon *n.* sifón
sir *n.* señor
siren *n.* sirena
sissy *n.* mariquita
sister *n.* hermana

sisterhood *n.* hermandad
sisterly *adj.* fraternal
sit *v.* sentarse
site *n.* sitio, solar
sitting *n.* sesión, turno
situate *v.* situar
situation *n., a* situación
six *adj.& n.* seis
sixteen *adj. & n.* dieciséis
sixteenth *adj. & n.* decimo sexto
sixth *adj. & n.* sexto
sixtieth *adj. & n.* sexagésimo
sixty *adj. & n.* sesenta
size *n.* talla
sizeable *adj.* considerable
sizzle *v.* crepitar
skate *n.* patín
skateboard *n.* skateboard
skein *n.* madeja
skeleton *n.* esqueleto
sketch *n.* esbozo, dibujo
sketchy *adj.* incompleto
skew *v.* sesgar
skewer *n.* brocheta
ski *n.* esquí
skid *v.* deslizarse
skilful *adj.* experto
skill *n.* destreza
skilled *adj.* experto, capaz
skim *v.* rasar, hojear
skimp *adj.* escaso
skin *n.* piel
skinny *adj.* flaco
skip *v.* omitir, saltar
skipper *n.* capitán
skirmish *n.* escaramuza
skirt *n.* falda
skirting *n.* rodapié
skit *n.* parodia
skittish *adj.* voluble
skittle *n.* bolo
skull *n.* cráneo

sky *n.* cielo
skylight *n.* tragaluz
skyscraper *n.* rascacielos
slab *n.* losa, tajada
slack *adj.* flojo
slacken *v.* aflojar
slag *n.* escoria
slake *v.t.* saciar
slam *v.* cerrar de golpe
slander *n.* calumnia
slanderous *adj.* difamatorio
slang *n.* argot
slant *v.* inclinar
slap *v.t.* abofetear
slash *v.* cortar, reducir
slat *n.* listón
slate *n.* pizarra
slattern *n.* abandonada
slatternly *adj.* desaliñado
slaughter *n.* matanza
slave *n.* esclavo
slavery *n.* esclavitud
slavish *adj.* servil
slay *v.* matar
sleaze *n.* sordidez
sleazy *adj.* de mala fama
sledge *n.* trineo
sledgehammer *n.* mazo
sleek *adj.* pulcro
sleep *n.* dormir
sleeper *n.* durmiente
sleepy *adj.* soñoliento
sleet *n.* nevisca
sleeve *n.* manga
sleigh *n.* trineo
sleight *n.* escamoteo
slender *adj.* escaso
sleuth *n.* sabueso
slice *n.* rebanada, rodaja
slick *adj.* hábil
slide *v.* deslizar
slight *adj.* delgado

slightly *adv.* ligeramente
slim *adj.* esbelto
slime *n.* limo
slimy *adj.* limoso
sling *n.* cabestrillo
slink *v.* escabullirse
slip *v.* resbalón
slipper *n.* zapatilla
slippery *adj.* resbaladizo
slit *v.t.* raja
slither *v.* deslizarse
slob *n.* patán
slobber *v.* babear
slogan *n.* eslogan
slope *v.* inclinarse
sloppy *adj.* descuidado
slot *n.* ranura
sloth *n.* pereza
slothful *adj.* perezoso
slouch *v.* gandulear
slough *n.* cenagal
slovenly *adj.* desaliñado
slow *adj.* lento
slowly *adv.* lentamente
slowness *n.* lentitud
sludge *n.* lodo
slug *n.* babosa
sluggard *n.* perezoso
sluggish *adj.* lento
sluice *n.* esclusa
slum *n.* tugurio
slumber *v.* dormir
slump *v.* hundirse
slur *v.* calumniar
slurp *v.* sorber
slush *n.* nieve medio derretida
slushy *adj.* fangoso
slut *n.* marrana
sly *adj.* astuto
smack *n.* manotada
small *adj.* pequeño
smallpox *n.* viruela

smart *adj.* listo
smarten *v.* arreglarse
smash *v.* aplastar
smashing *adj.* fantástico
smattering *n.* nociones
smear *v.* untar
smell *n.* olor
smelly *adj.* maloliente
smidgen *n.* pizca
smile *v.* sonreír
smirk *v.* sonrisa falsa
smith *n.* herrero
smock *n.* bata, delantal
smog *n.* niebla tóxica
smoke *n.* humo
smoky *adj.* lleno de humo
smooch *v.* besuquearse
smooth *adj.* liso
smoothie *n.* bebida de frutas
smother *v.* sofocar
smoulder *v.* arder sin llama
smudge *v.* manchar
smug *adj.* petulante
smuggle *v.* pasar de contrabando
smuggler *n.* contrabandista
snack *n.* tentempié
snag *n.* dificultad
snail *n.* caracol
snake *n.* serpiente
snap *v.* chasquear
snapper *n.* chasquido, golpe
snappy *adj.* ágil
snare *n.* trampa
snarl *v.t.* gruñir
snarl *n.* gruñido
snatch *v.* arrebatar
snazzy *adj.* elegante
sneak *v.* sacar
sneaker *n.* zapatilla de deporte
sneer *n.* mueca
sneeze *v.i.* estornudar
snide *adj.* malicioso

sniff *v.* husmear
sniffle *v.* gimotear
snigger *n.* risa disimulada
snip *v.* tijeretear
snipe *v.* criticar
snippet *n.* retazo
snob *n.* esnob
snobbery *n.* esnobismo
snobbish *adj.* esnob
snooker *n.* billar
snooze *n.* cabezada
snore *n.* ronquido
snort *n.* bufido
snout *n.* hocico
snow *n.* nieve
snowball *n.* bola de nieve
snowy *adj.* nevado
snub *v.* desairar
snuff *v.* cortar
snuffle *v.* resoplar
snug *adj.* abrigado
snuggle *v.* arrimarse
so *adv.* tan
soak *v.* empapar
soap *n.* jabón
soapy *adj.* jabonoso
soar *v.i.* remontarse
sob *v.* sollozar
sober *adj.* sobrio
sobriety *n.* sobriedad
soccer *n.* futbol
sociability *n.* sociabilidad
sociable *adj.* sociable
social *adj.* social
socialism *n.* socialismo
socialist *n. & adj.* socialista
socialize *v.* socializar
society *n.* sociedad
sociology *n.* sociología
sock *n.* calcetín
socket *n.* enchufe
sod *n.* césped, terrón

soda *n.* soda, gaseosa
sodden *adj.* anegado
sodomy *n.* sodomía
sofa *n.* sofá
soft *adj.* suave
soften *v.* suavizar
soggy *adj.* empapado
soil *n.* tierra, suelo
sojourn *n.* estancia
solace *n.* consuelo
solar *adj.* solar
solder *n.* soldar
soldier *n.* soldado
sole *n.* único
solely *adv.* únicamente
solemn *adj.* solemne
solemnity *n.* solemnidad
solemnize *v.* solemnizar
solicit *v.* solicitar
solicitation *n.* requerimiento
solicitor *n.* notario
solicitious *adj.* solícito
solicitude *n.* solicitud
solid *adj.* sólido
solidarity *n.* solidaridad
soliloquy *n.* monólogo
solitaire *n.* solitario
solitary *adj.* solitario
solitude *n.* soledad
solo *n.* solo
soloist *n.* solista
solubility *n.* solubilidad
soluble *adj.* soluble
solution *n.* solución
solve *v.* resolver
solvency *n.* solvencia
solvent *n.* solvente
sombre *adj.* sombrío
some *adj.* algo, algunos
somebody *pron.* alguien
somehow *adv.* de algún modo
someone *pron.* alguien

somersault *n.* salto mortal
something *pron.* algo
somewhat *adv.* algo
somewhere *adv.* en algún lugar
somnambulism *n.* sonambulismo
somnambulist *n.* sonámbulo
somnolence *n.* somnolencia
somnolent *adj.* soñoliento
son *n.* hijo
song *n.* canción
songster *n.* cantante
sonic *adj.* sónico
sonnet *n.* soneto
sonority *n.* sonoridad
soon *adv.* pronto
soot *n.* hollín
soothe *v.* aliviar
sophism *n.* sofisma
sophist *n.* sofista
sophisticate *n.* sofisticado
sophisticated *adj.* sofisticado
sophistication *n.* sofisticación
soporific *adj.* soporífero
sopping *adj.* empapado
soppy *adj.* romanticón
sorbet *n.* sorbete
sorcerer *n.* hechicero
sorcery *n.* hechicería
sordid *adj.* asqueroso
sore *adj.* doloroso
sorely *adv.* profundamente
sorrow *n.* pena
sorry *adj.* arrepentido
sort *n.* clase, género
sortie *n.* salida
sough *v.* susurrar
soul *n.* alma
soulful *adj.* conmovedor
soulless *adj.* desalmado
soulmate *n.* alma gemela
sound *n.* sonido
soundproof *adj.* insonorizado

soup *n.* sopa
sour *adj.* agrío
source *n.* fuente
souse *v.* marinar
south *n.* sur
southerly *adj.* del sur
southern *adj.* del sur
souvenir *n.* recuerdo
sovereign *n.* soberano
sovereignty *n.* soberanía
sow *n.* cerda
spa *n.* balneario
space *n.* espacioso
spacious *adj.* espacioso
spade *n.* pala
spam *n.* correo basura
span *n.* período, espacio
Spaniard *n.* español
spaniel *n.* spaniel
Spanish *n.* español
spank *v.* zurrar
spanking *adj.* paliza
spanner *n.* llave inglesa
spare *adj.* desocupado
sparing *adj.* parco
spark *n.* chispa
sparkle *v.* relucir, brillar
sparkling *n.* espumoso
sparrow *n.* gorrión
sparse *adj.* esparcido
spasm *n.* espasmo
spasmodic *adj.* espasmódico
spastic *adj.* espástico
spat *n.* disputa
spate *n.* racha, serie
spatial *adj.* espacial
spatter *v.* salpicar, rociar
spawn *v.* engendrar
spay *v.* esterilizar
speak *v.* hablar
speaker *n.* orador
spear *n.* lanza

spearhead *n.* punta de lanza
spearmint *n.* menta verde
special *adj.* especial
specialist *n.* especialista
speciality *n.* especialidad
specialization *n.* especialización
specialize *v.* especializarse
species *n.* especies
specific *adj.* especifico
specification *n.* especificación
specify *v.* especificar
specimen *n.* espécimen
specious *adj.* engañoso
speck *n.* grano
speckle *n.* mota
spectacle *n.* espectáculo
spectacular *adj.* espectacular
spectator *n.* espectador
spectral *adj.* espectral
spectre *n.* espectro
spectrum *n.* espectro
speculate *v.* especular
speculation *n.* especulación
speech *n.* discurso, habla
speechless *adj.* sin habla, mudo
speed *n.* velocidad
speedway *n.* circuito
speedy *adj.* veloz
spell *v.t.* deletrear
spellbound *adj.* hechizado
spelling *n.* ortografía
spend *v.* gastar
spendthrift *n.* derrochador
sperm *n.* esperma
sphere *n.* esfera
spherical *n.* esférico
spice *n.* especia
spicy *adj.* picante
spider *n.* araña
spike *n.* punta
spiky *adj.* puntiagudo
spill *v.* derramar

spillage *n.* vertido
spin *v.* girar
spinach *n.* espinaca
spinal *adj.* espinal
spindle *n.* huso
spindly *adj.* flacucho
spine *n.* columna
spineless *adj.* débil
spinner *n.* hilador
spinster *n.* solterona
spiral *adj.* espiral
spire *n.* chapitel
spirit *n.* espíritu
spirited *adj.* enérgico
spiritual *adj.* espiritual
spiritualism *n.* espiritualismo
spiritualist *n.* espiritual
spirituality *n.* espiritualidad
spit *n.* asador, espetón
spite *n.* rencor
spiteful *adj.* rencoroso
spittle *n.* baba
spittoon *n.* escupidera
splash *v.* chapotear
splatter *v.* salpicar
splay *v.* abrirse
spleen *n.* bazo
splendid *adj.* esplendido
splendour *n.* esplendor
splenetic *adj.* iracundo
splice *v.* empalmar
splint *n.* tabilla
splinter *n.* astilla
split *v.* partir, rajar
splutter *v.* balbucear
spoil *v.* estropear, mimar
spoiler *n.* aguafiestas
spoke *n.* rayo, radio
spokesman *n.* portavoz
sponge *n.* esponja
sponsor *n.* patrocinador
sponsorship *n.* patrocinio

spontaneity *n.* espontaneidad
spontaneous *adj.* espontáneo
spool *n.* carrete
spoon *n.* cuchara
spoonful *n.* cucharada
spoor *n.* rastro
sporadic *adj.* esporádico
spore *n.* espora
sport *n.* deporte
sporting *adj.* deportivo
sportive *adj.* deportivo
sportsman *n.* deportista
spot *n.* punto, lugar
spotless *adj.* nítido
spousal *n.* conyugal
spouse *n.* esposa
spout *n.* pico
sprain *v.t.* torcer
sprat *n.* espadín
sprawl *v.* tumbarse
spray *n.* espray
spread *v.* extender, untar
spreadsheet *n.* hoja de calculo
spree *n.* juerga
sprig *n.* mata
sprightly *adj.* ágil
spring *v.* brotar, nacer
sprinkle *v.i.* rociar
sprinkler *n.* aspersor
sprinkling *n.* salpicaduras
sprint *v.* correr a toda velocidad
sprinter *n.* corredor
sprout *v.* brotar
spry *adj.* activo
spume *n.* espuma
spur *n.* espuela
spurious *adj.* espurio
spurn *v.* desdeñar
spurt *v.* esforzarse
sputum *n.* esputo
spy *n.* espía
squabble *n.* riña**

squad *n.* escuadra
squadron *n.* escuadrón
squalid *adj.* escuálido
squall *n.* chubasco
squander *v.* derrochar
square *n.* cuadrado, plaza
squash *v.* aplastar
squat *v.i.* ponerse en cuclillas
squawk *v.* graznar
squeak *n.* crujido
squeal *n.* grito
squeeze *v.* apretar
squib *n.* petardo
squid *n.* pulpo
squint *v.* bizquear
squire *n.* escudero
squirm *v.* retorcerse
squirrel *n.* ardilla
squirt *v.* salir a chorros
stab *v.* puñalada
stability *n.* estabilidad
stabilization *n.* estabilización
stabilize *v.* estabilizar
stable *adj.* estable
stable *n.* establo
stack *n.* montón
stadium *n.* estadio
staff *n.* personal
stag *n.* ciervo
stage *n.* escenario
stagecoach *n.* diligencia
stagger *v.* asombrar
staggering *adj.* asombroso
stagnant *adj.* estancado
stagnate *v.* estancarse
stagnation *n.* estancamiento
staid *adj.* formal
stain *v.t.* manchar
stair *n.* escalón
staircase *n.* escalera
stake *n.* estaca
stale *adj.* duro, pasado

stalemate *n.* tablas
staleness *n.* ranciedad
stalk *n.* tallo
stalker *n.* acosador
stall *n.* puesto
stallion *n.* semental
stalwart *adj.* incondicional
stamen *n.* estambre
stamina *n.* estamina
stammer *v.* tartamudear
stamp *n.* sello
stamp *v.* sellar
stampede *n.* estampida
stance *n.* postura
stanchion *n.* puntal
stand *v.* estar de pie
standard *n.* estándar
standardization *n.* estandarización
standardize *v.* estandarizar
standing *n.* de pie
standpoint *n.* punto de vista
standstill *n.* parada
stanza *n.* estrofa
staple *n.* grapa
staple *v.* grapar
stapler *n.* grapadora
star *n.* estrella
starch *n.* almidón
starchy *adj.* feculento
stare *v.* mirar fijo
stark *adj.* escueto
starlet *n.* actriz principiante
startling *n.* estornino
starry *adj.* estrellado
start *v.* empezar
starter *n.* entrante
startle *v.* asustar
starvation *n.* hambre
starve *v.* pasar hambre
stash *v.* introducir
state *n.* estado

stateless *adj.* apátrida
stately *adj.* imponente
statement *n.* declaración
statesman *n.* estadista
static *adj.* estático
statically *adv.* estáticamente
station *n.* estación
stationary *adj.* estacionario
stationer *n.* dependiente de papelería
stationery *n.* papelería
statistical *adj.* estadístico
statistician *n.* estadista
statistics *n.* estadística
statuary *n.* estatuaria
statue *n.* estatua
statuesque *adj.* escultural
statuette *n.* estatuilla
stature *n.* estatura
status *n.* estatus
statute *n.* estatuto
statutory *adj.* estatutario
staunch *adj.* acérrimo
stave *n.* evitar
stay *v.* quedarse
stead *n.* el lugar de otro, ventaja
steadfast *adj.* resuelto
steadiness *n.* firmeza
steady *adj.* constante, firme
steak *n.* filete
steal *v.* robar
stealth *n.* a escondidas
stealthily *adv.* sigilosamente
stealthy *adj.* cauteloso
steam *n.* vapor
steamer *n.* barco de vapor
steed *n.* corcel
steel *n.* acero
steep *adj.* empinado
steeple *n.* torre, aguja
steeplechase *n.* carrera de obstáculos

steer *v.* conducir, dirigir
stellar *adj.* estelar
stem *n.* tallo
stench *n.* hedor
stencil *n.* cliché
stenographer *n.* taquígrafa
stenography *n.* taquigrafía
stentorian *adj.* estentóreo
step *n.* paso
steppe *n.* estepa
stereo *n.* estéreo
stereophonic *adj.* estereofónico
stereoscopic *adj.* estereoscópico
stereotype *n.* estereotipo
sterile *adj.* estéril
sterility *n.* esterilidad
sterilization *n.* esterilización
sterilize *v.* esterilizar
sterling *n.* esterlina
stern *adj.* severo
sternum *n.* esternón
steroid *n.* esteroide
stertorous *adj.* estertoroso
stethoscope *n.* estetoscopio
stew *n.* estofado
steward *n.* camarero, administrador
stick *n.* palo
sticker *n.* pegatina
stickleback *n.* espinoso
stickler *n.* puntilloso
sticky *adj.* pegajoso
stiff *adj.* rígido
stiffen *v.* fortalecer
stifle *v.* sofocar
stigma *n.* estigma
stigmatize *v.* estigmatizar
stile *n.* montante
stiletto *n.* tacón de aguja
still *adj.* inmóvil
stillborn *n.* nacido muerto
stillness *n.* quietud

stilt *n.* zanco
stilted *adj.* forzado
stimulant *n.* estimulante
stimulate *v.* estimular
stimulus *n.* estimulo
sting *n.* picadura
stingy *adj.* tacaño
stink *v.* apestar
stint *n.* tarea
stipend *n.* estipendio
stipple *v.* puntear
stipulate *v.* estipular
stipulation *n.* estipulación
stir *v.* remover
stirrup *n.* estribo
stitch *n.* punto
stitch *v.* coser, suturar
stock *n.* existencias
stockbroker *n.* agente de bolsa
stockade *n.* empalizada
stocking *n.* media
stockist *n.* distribuidor
stocky *adj.* robusto
stoic *n.* estoico
stoke *v.* avivar el fuego
stoker *n.* fogonero
stole *n.* estola
stolid *adj.* impasible
stomach *n.* estomago
stomp *v.* pisando fuerte
stone *n.* piedra
stony *adj.* pedregoso
stooge *n.* títere
stool *n.* taburete
stoop *v.* inclinarse
stop *v.* parar
stoppage *n.* interrupción
stopper *n.* tapón
storage *n.* almacenaje
store *n.* tienda
storey *n.* piso
stork *n.* cigüeña

storm *n.* tormenta
stormy *adj.* tempestuoso
story *n.* historia, relato
stout *adj.* macizo
stove *n.* cocina, estufa
stow *v.* meter, poner
straddle *v.* combinar, extenderse
straggle *v.* rezagarse
straggler *n.* rezagado
straight *adj.* recto, derecho
straighten *v.* enderezar
straightforward *adj.* sencillo
straightway *adv.* en seguida
strain *v.* torcer, cansar
strain *n.* tensión, torcedura
strained *adj.* torcido, tenso
strait *n.* estrecho
straiten *v.i.* estrechando
strand *v.* encallar
strange *adj.* extraño, raro
stranger *n.* desconocido
strangle *v.* estrangular
strangulation *n.* estrangulación
strap *n.* correa
strapping *adj.* fornido
stratagem *n.* estratagema
strategic *adj.* estratégico
strategist *n.* estratega
strategy *n.* estrategia
stratify *v.* estratificar
stratum *n.* estrato
straw *n.* paja, pajita
strawberry *n.* fresa
stray *v.* extraviarse
streak *n.* racha, raya, trazo
streaky *adj.* rayado
stream *n.* riachuelo
streamer *n.* serpentina
streamlet *n.* arroyuelo
street *n.* calle
strength *n.* fuerza
strengthen *v.* fortalecer

strenuous *adj.* extenuante
stress *n.* estrés
stress *v.t.* estresar
stretch *v.* estirar
stretch *n.* estiramiento
stretcher *n.* camilla
strew *v.* esparcir
striation *n.* estriación, estría
stricken *adj.* afectado
strict *adj.* estricto
strictly *adv.* estrictamente
stricture *n.* constricción
stride *v.* dar zancadas
strident *adj.* estridente
strife *n.* conflicto
strike *v.* huelga, ataque
striker *n.* huelguista, delantero
striking *adj.* impactante
string *n.* cuerda, cadena, hilo
stringency *n.* severidad
stringent *adj.* riguroso
stringy *adj.* fibroso
strip *v.t.* desnudar
stripe *n.* raya
stripling *n.* mozuelo
stripper *n.* artista de striptease
strive *v.* esforzarse
strobe *n.* estroboscopio
stroke *n.* golpe, caricia
stroll *v.* dar un paseo
strong *adj.* fuerte
stronghold *n.* fortaleza
strop *n.* estrobo
stroppy *adj.* insolente
structural *adj.* estructural
structure *n.* estructura
strudel *n.* estrúdel
struggle *v.* luchar
strum *v.* rasgar
strumpet *n.* prostituta
strut *n.* puntal
stuart *adj.* Estuardo

stub *n.* talón
stubble *n.* barba de pocos días
stubborn *adj.* testarudo
stucco *n.* estuco
stud *n.* taco
stud *v.* incrustar
student *n.* estudiante
studio *n.* estudio
studious *adj.* estudioso
study *n.* estudio
study *v.* estudiar
stuff *n.* materia, material
stuffing *n.* relleno
stuffy *adj.* mal ventilado
stultify *v.* anquilosar
stumble *v.* tropezar
stump *n.* muñón
stun *v.* aturdir
stunner *n.* marvilla, bella
stunning *adj.* despampanante
stunt *v.* atrofiar
stupefy *v.* dejar estupefacto
stupendous *adj.* estupendo
stupid *adj.* estúpido
stupidity *n.* estupidez
stupor *n.* estupor
sturdy *adj.* robusto
stutter *v.* tartamudear
sty *n.* pocilga
stygian *adj.* estigio
style *n.* estilo
stylish *adj.* elegante
stylist *n.* estilista
stylistic *adj.* estilístico
stylized *adj.* estilizado
stylus *n.* aguja
stymie *v.* obstaculizar
styptic *adj.* astringente
suave *adj.* cortés
subaltern *n.* subalterno
subconscious *adj.* subconsciente
subcontract *v.* subcontrato

subdue *v.* dominar
subedit *v.* corregir
subject *n.* tema, súbdito
subjection *n.* sujeción
subjective *adj.* subjetivo
subjudice *adj.* pendiente
resolución judicial
subjugate *v.* subyugar
subjugation *n.* subyugación
subjunctive *adj.* subjuntivo
sublet *v.t.* subarrendar
sublimate *v.* sublimar
sublime *adj.* sublime
subliminal *adj.* subliminal
submarine *n.* submarino
submerge *v.* sumergir
submersible *adj.* sumergible
submission *n.* sumisión
submissive *adj.* sumiso
submit *v.* presentar
subordinate *adj.* subordinado
subordination *n.* subordinación
suborn *v.* cohechar
subscribe *v.* suscribir
subscript *adj.* subíndice
subscription *n.* suscripción
subsequent *adj.* subsecuente
subservience *n.* sumisión
subservient *adj.* servil
subside *v.* disminuir
subsidiary *adj.* subsidiaria
subsidize *v.* subvencionar
subsidy *n.* subsidio
subsist *v.* subvención
subsistence *n.* subsistencia
subsonic *adj.* subsónico
substance *n.* sustancial
substantial *adj.* sustancial
substantially *adv.* sustancialmente
substantiate *v.* comprobar
substantiation *n.* confirmación

substantive *adj.* sustantivo
substitute *n.* sustituto
substitution *n.* sustitución
subsume *v.* subsumir
subterfuge *n.* subterfugio
subterranean *adj.* subterráneo
subtitle *n.* subtítulo
subtle *adj.* sutil
subtlety *n.* sutileza
subtotal *n.* subtotal
subtract *v.* restar
subtraction *n.* resta
subtropical *adj.* subtropical
suburb *n.* suburbio
suburban *adj.* suburbano
suburbia *n.* periferia
subversion *n.* subversión
subversive *adj.* subversivo
subvert *v.i.* trastornar
subway *n.* metro
succeed *v.* tener éxito
success *n.* éxito
successful *adj.* exitoso
succession *n.* sucesión
successive *adj.* sucesivo
successor *n.* sucesor
succint *adj.* sucinto
succour *n.* socorro
succulent *adj.* suculento
succumb *v.* sucumbir
such *adj.* tal, tan
suck *v.* chupar
sucker *n.* ventosa, bobo
suckle *v.* amamantar
suckling *n.* lactancia
suction *n.* succión
sudden *adj.* repentino
suddenly *adv.* de repente
sudoku *n.* sudoku
sue *v.t.* demandar
suede *n.* ante
suffer *v.i.* sufrir

sufferance *n.* sufrimiento
suffice *v.* ser suficiente
sufficiency *n.* suficiencia
sufficient *adj.* suficiente
suffix *n.* sufijo
suffocate *v.* asfixiarse
suffocation *n.* asfixia
suffrage *n.* sufragio
suffuse *v.* teñir, invadir
sugar *n.* azúcar
suggest *v.* sugerir
suggestible *adj.* sugestionable
suggestion *n.* sugerencia
suggestive *adj.* sugerente
suicidal *adj.* suicida
suicide *n.* suicidio
suit *n.* traje
suitability *n.* idoneidad
suitable *adj.* adecuado
suite *n.* suite
suitor *n.* pretendiente
sulk *v.* tener mohíno
sullen *adj.* malhumorado
sully *v.* mancillar
sulphur *n.* azufre
sultana *n.* sultana
sultry *adj.* sofocante, seductor
sum *n.* sumario
summarily *adv.* sumariamente
summarize *v.* resumir
summary *n.* sumario
summer *n.* verano
summit *n.* cumbre
summon *v.* convocar
summons *n.* llamamiento
sumptuous *adj.* suntuoso
sun *n.* sol
sun *v.* tomar el sol
sundae *n.* helado
Sunday *n.* domingo
sunder *v.* desgarrar
sundry *adj.* diversos

sunken *adj.* hundido
sunny *adj.* soleado
super *adj.* súper
superb *adj.* magnífico
supercharger *n.* sobrealimentado
supercilious *adj.* desdeñoso
superficial *adj.* superficial
superficiality *n.* superficialidad
superfine *adj.* extrafino
superfluity *n.* superfluidad
superfluous *adj.* superfluo
susperhuman *adj.* sobrehumano
superimpose *v.* sobreponer
superintend *v.* supervisar
superintendence *n.* superintendencia
superintendent *n.* superintendente
superior *adj.* superior
superiority *n.* superioridad
superlative *adj.* superlativo
supermarket *n.* supermercado
supernatural *adj.* supernatural
superpower *n.* superpotencia
superscript *adj.* sobreescrito
supersede *v.* suplantar
supersonic *adj.* supersónico
superstition *n.* superstición
superstitious *adj.* supersticioso
superstore *n.* hipermercado
supervene *v.* sobrevenir
supervise *v.* supervisar
supervision *n.* supervisión
supervisor *n.* supervisor
supper *n.* cena
supplant *v.* sustituir
supple *adj.* flexible
supplement *n.* suplemento
supplementary *adj.* suplementario
suppliant *n.* suplicante
supplicate *v.* suplicar

supplier *n.* distribuidor
supply *v.* suministrar
support *v.* apoyar
support *n.* apoyo
suppose *v.* suponer
supposition *n.* suposición
suppository *n.* supositorio
suppress *v.* suprimir
suppression *n.* represión
suppurate *v.* supurar
supremacy *n.* supremacía
supreme *adj.* supremo
surcharge *n.* sobrecarga
sure *adj.* seguro
surely *adv.* seguramente
surety *n.* garantía
surf *n.* surf
surface *n.* superficie
surfeit *n.* exceso de
surge *n.* oleada
surgeon *n.* cirujano
surgery *n.* cirugía
surly *adj.* malhumorado
surmise *v.t.* conjeturar
surmount *v.* superar
surname *n.* apellido
surpass *v.* exceder
surplus *n.* superávit
surprise *n.* sorpresa
surreal *adj.* surreal
surrealism *n.* surrealismo
surrender *v.* rendirse
surrender *n.* rendición
surreptitious *adj.* subrepticio
surrogate *n.* sustituto
surround *v.* cercar
surroundings *n.* alrededores
surtax *n.* recargo
surveillance *n.* vigilancia
survey *v.t.* inspeccionar
surveyor *n.* inspector
survival *n.* supervivencia

survive *v.* sobrevivir
susceptible *adj.* susceptible
suspect *v.* sospechar
suspect *n* sospechoso
suspend *v.* suspender
suspense *n.* suspense
suspension *n.* suspensión
suspicion *n.* sospechar
suspicious *adj.* receloso
sustain *v.* sostener
sustainable *adj.* sostenible
sustenance *n.* sustento
suture *n.* sutura
svelte *adj.* esbelto
swab *n.* hisopo
swaddle *v.* envolver
swag *n.* botín
swagger *v.* pavonearse
swallow *v.* tragar
swamp *n.* pantano
swan *n.* cisne
swank *v.* fanfarronear
swanky *n.* fanfarrón
swap *v.* intercambiar
swarm *n.* enjambre
swarthy *adj.* moreno
swashbuckling *adj.* héroe
swat *v.* aplastar
swathe *n.* parte
sway *v.* mecerse
swear *v.* sudar
sweat *n.* sudor
sweater *n.* suéter
sweep *v.* barrer
sweeper *n.* barredor
sweet *adj.* dulce
sweet *n.* dulce
sweeten *v.* endulzar
sweetheart *n.* cariño
sweetmeat *n.* dulce
sweetener *n.* edulcorante
sweetness *n.* dulzura

swell *v.* hinchar
swell *n.* marejada
swelling *n.* hinchazón
swelter *v.* sofocarse de calor
swerve *v.* desviar
swift *adj.* veloz
swill *v.* lavar
swim *v.* nadar
swimmer *n.* nadador
swindle *v.* estafa
swindler *n.* estafador
swine *n.* cerdo
swing *n.* columpio
swing *v.* columpiar
swingeing *adj.* durísimo
swipe *v.* golpear fuerte
swirl *v.* arremolinarse
swish *adj.* suizo
switch *n.* interruptor
swivel *v.* girar
swoon *v.* desmayarse
swoop *v.* calarse
sword *n.* espada
sybarite *n.* sibarita
sycamore *n.* sicomoro
sycophancy *n.* adulación
sycophant *n.* adulador
syllabic *adj.* silábico
syllable *n.* silaba
syllabus *n.* programa
syllogism *n.* silogismo
sylph *n.* sílfide
sylvan *adj.* silvestre
symbiosis *n.* simbiosis
symbol *n.* símbolo
symbolic *adj.* simbólico
symbolism *n.* simbolismo
symbolize *v.* simbolizar
symmetrical *adj.* simétrico
symmetry *n.* simetría
sympathetic *adj.* compasivo
sympathize *v.* compadecerse

sympathy *n.* compasión
symphony *n.* sinfonía
symposium *n.* simposio
symptom *n.* síntoma
symptomatic *adj.* sintomático
synchronize *v.* sincronizar
synchronous *adj.* sincronizado
syndicate *n.* sindicato
syndrome *n.* síndrome
synergy *n.* sinergia
synonym *n.* sinónimo
synonymous *adj.* sinónimo
synopsis *n.* sinopsis
syntax *n.* sintaxis
synthesis *n.* síntesis
synthesize *v.* sintetizar
synthetic *adj.* sintético
syringe *n.* jeringa
syrup *n.* sirope
system *n.* sistema
systematic *adj.* sistemático
systematize *v.* sistematizar
systemic *adj.* sistémico

T

tab *n.* pestaña
table *n.* mesa
tableau *n.* retablo
tablet *n.* tableta
tabloid *n.* tabloide
taboo *n.* tabú
tabular *adj.* tabular
tabulate *v.* tabular
tabulation *n.* tabulación
tabulator *v.* tabulador
tachometer *n.* tacómetro
tacit *adj.* tácito
taciturn *adj.* taciturno

tack *n.* tachuela
tackle *v.t.* enfrentar
tacky *adj.* hortera
tact *n.* tacto
tactful *adj.* diplomático
tactic *n.* táctica
tactician *n.* táctico
tactical *adj.* táctico
tactile *adj.* táctil
tag *n.* etiqueta
tail *n.* cola
tailor *n.* sastre
taint *v.* contaminar, enturbiar
take *v.* tomar, llevar
takeaway *n.* comida para llevar
takings *n.* ingresos
talc *n.* talco
tale *n.* cuento
talent *n.* talento
talented *adj.* talentoso
talisman *n.* talismán
talk *v.* hablar
talkative *adj.* hablador
tall *adj.* alto
tallow *n.* sebo
tally *n.* cuenta
talon *n.* garra
tamarind *n.* tamarindo
tambourine *n.* pandereta
tame *adj.* manso
tamely *adv.* dócilmente
tamp *v.* apisonar
tamper *v.* entrometerse
tampon *n.* tampón
tan *n.* bronceado
tandem *n.* tándem
tang *n.* sabor fuerte
tangent *n.* tangente
tangerine *n.* mandarina
tangible *adj.* tangible
tangle *v.t.* enredo
tank *n.* depósito, tanque

tanker *n.* buque cisterna
tanner *n.* curtidor
tannery *n.* curtiduría
tantalize *v.* atormentar
tantamount *adj.* equivalente
tantrum *n.* rabieta
tap *n.* grifo
tapas *n.* tapas
tape *n.* cinta
tape *v.i.* grabar
taper *v.* cirio
tapestry *n.* tapiz
tappet *n.* empujador
tar *n.* alquitrán
tardy *adj.* tardío
target *n.* blanco
tariff *n.* tarifa
tarn *n.* lago de montaña
tarnish *v.* empañar
tarot *n.* tarot
tarpaulin *n.* alquitranado
tart *n.* tarta
tartar *n.* sarro
task *n.* tarea
tassel *n.* borla
taste *n.* sabor
taste *v.* probar, saber a
tasteful *adj.* de buen gusto
tasteless *adj.* insípido
tasty *adj.* sabroso
tatter *n.* andrajo
tattle *n.* chismorreo
tattoo *n.* tatuaje
tatty *adj.* raído
taunt *n.* burla
taut *adj.* tirante
tavern *n.* taberna
tawdry *adj.* cursi
tax *n.* impuesto
taxable *adj.* imponible
taxation *n.* impuestos
taxi *n.* taxi

taxi *v.* rodar, carretear
taxonomy *n.* taxonomía
tea *n.* té
teach *v.* enseñar
teacher *n.* profesor
teak *n.* teca
team *n.* equipo
tear *v.* rasgar
tear *n.* lagrima
tearful *adj.* lloroso
tease *v.* bromear
teat *n.* tetina
technical *adj.* técnico
technicality *n.* tecnicidad
technician *n.* técnico
technique *n.* técnica
technological *adj.* tecnológico
technologist *n.* tecnólogo
technology *n.* tecnología
tedious *adj.* tedioso
tedium *n.* tedio
teem *v.* abundar
teenager *n.* adolescente
teens *adj.* adolescencia
teeter *v.* balancearse
teethe *v.* echar los dientes
teetotal *adj.* abstemio
teetotaller *n.* abstemio
telecast *v.t.* televisar
telegram *n.* telegrama
telegraph *n.* telégrafo
telegraphic *adj.* telegráfico
telegraphy *n.* telegrafía
telepathic *adj.* telepático
telepathist *n.* telepate
telepathy *n.* telepatía
telephone *n.* teléfono
teleprinter *n.* teletipo
telescope *n.* telescopio
teletext *n.* teletexto
televise *v.* televisar
television *n.* televisión

tell *v.* contar, decir
teller *n.* cajero
telling *adj.* revelador
telltale *adj.* indicativo
temerity *n.* temeridad
temper *n.* genio
temperament *n.* temperamento
temperamental *adj.* temperamental
temperance *n.* moderación
temperate *adj.* moderado
temperature *n.* temperatura
tempest *n.* tempestad
tempestuous *adj.* tempestuoso
template *n.* plantilla
temple *n.* templo, sien
tempo *n.* ritmo
temporal *adj.* temporal
temporary *adj.* provisional
temporize *v.* temporizar
tempt *v.* tentar
temptation *n.* tentación
tempter *n.* tentador
ten *adj. & adv.* diez
tenable *adj.* sostenible
tenacious *adj.* tenaz
tenacity *n.* tenacidad
tenancy *n.* alquiler
tenant *n.* inquilino
tend *v.* tender a
tendency *n.* tendencia
tendentious *adj.* tendencioso
tender *adj.* tierno
tender *n.* oferta
tendon *n.* tendón
tenement *n.* vecindario
tenet *n.* principio
tennis *n.* tenis
tenor *n.* tenor
tense *adj.* tenso
tensile *adj.* tenso
tension *n.* tensión

tent *n.* tienda de campaña
tentacle *n.* tentáculo
tentative *adj.* experimental
tenterhook *n.* sobre ascuas
tenth *adj. & n.* décimo
tenuous *adj.* tenue
tenure *n.* posesión
tepid *adj.* tibio
term *n.* limite, término
termagant *n.* arpía
terminal *adj.* terminal
terminate *v.* terminar
termination *n.* terminación
terminological *adj.* terminológico
terminology *n.* terminología
terminus *n.* término
termite *n.* termita
terrace *n.* terraza
terracotta *n.* terracota
terrain *n.* terreno
terrestrial *adj.* terrestre
terrible *adj.* terrible
terrier *n.* terrier
terrific *adj.* genial
terrify *v.* aterrorizar
territorial *adj.* territorial
territory *n.* territorio
terror *n.* terror
terrorism *n.* terrorismo
terrorist *n.* terrorista
terrorize *v.* aterrorizar
terry *n.* tela de toalla
terse *adj.* conciso
tertiary *adj.* terciario
test *n.* prueba
testament *n.* testamento
testate *adj.* testado
testicle *n.* testículo
testify *v.* testificar
testimonial *n.* testimonial
testimony *n.* testimonio
testis *n.* testículo

testosterone *n.* testosterona
testy *adj.* hosco
tetchy *adj.* irritable
tether *v.t.* amarrar
text *n.* texto
textbook *n.* libro de texto
textual *adj.* textual
textile *n* textil
textual *adj.* textual
texture *n.* textura
thank *v.* agradecer
thankful *adj.* agradecido
thankless *adj.* ingrato
that *pron. & adj.* eso-esa
thatch *n.* paja
thaw *v.* derretir
the *adj.* el,la,los,las
theatre *n.* teatro
theatrical *adj.* teatral
theft *n.* robo
their *adj.* su
theism *n.* teísmo
them *pron.* los, las, les
thematic *adj.* temático
theme *n.* temario
themselves *pron.* ellos mismos
then *adv.* entonces
thence *adv.* desde allí
theocracy *n.* teocracia
theodolite *n.* teodolito
theologian *n.* teólogo
theology *n.* teología
theorem *n.* teorema
theoretical *adj.* teórico
theorist *n.* teórico
theorize *v.* teorizar
theory *n.* teoría
theosophy *n.* teosofía
therapeutic *adj.* terapéutico
therapist *n.* terapeuta
therapy *n.* terapia
there *adv.* allí, ahí

thermal *adj.* termal
thermodynamics *n.* termodinámico
thermometer *n.* termómetro
thermos *n.* termo
thermostat *n.* termostato
thesis *n.* tesis
they *pron.* ellos
thick *adj.* grueso
thicken *v.* espesarse
thicket *n.* matorral
thief *n.* ladrón
thigh *n.* muslo
thimble *n.* dedal
thin *adj.* fino
thing *n.* cosa
think *v.* pensar
thinker *n.* pensador
third *adj.* tercero
thirst *n.* sed
thirsty *adj.* sediento
thirteen *adj. & n.* trece
thirteen *adj. & n.* trece
thirteenth *adj. & n.* decimo
tercero
thirtieth *adj. & n.* decimo tercero
thirtieth *adj. & n.* decimo tercero
thirty *adj. & n.* treinta
thirty *adj. & n.* treinta
this *pron.& adj.* esto, esta, este
thistle *n.* cardo
thither *adv.* hacia allá
thong *n.* correa
thorn *n.* espina
thorny *adj.* espinoso
thorough *adj.* minucioso
thoroughfare *n.* vía publica
though *conj.* aunque
thoughtful *adj.* pensativo
thoughtless *adj.* desconsiderado
thousand *adj. & n.* mil
thrall *n.* esclavitud

thrash *v.* apalear, golpear, derrotar
thread *n.* hilo
threat *n.* amenaza
threaten *v.* amenazar
three *adj. & n.* tres
thresh *v.* trillar
threshold *n.* umbral
thrice *adv.* tres veces
thrift *n.* económica
thrifty *adj.* económico
thrill *n.* emoción
thriller *n.* suspense
thrive *v.* prosperar
throat *n.* garganta
throaty *adj.* ronco
throb *v.* latir
throes *n.* agonía
throne *n.* trono
throng *n.* multitud
throttle *n.* acelerador
through *prep. &adv.* a través
throughout *prep.* por todas
partes, por todo
throw *v.* tirar
thrush *n.* empuje
thrust *v.* empujar
thud *n.* sordo
thug *n.* criminal, bruto
thumb *n.* pulgar
thunder *n.* trueno
thunderous *adj.* atronador
Thursday *n.* Jueves
thus *adv.* así
thwart *v.* frustrar
thyroid *n.* tiroides
tiara *n.* diadema
tick *n.* garrapata
ticket *n.* billete
ticking *n.* tic-tac
tickle *v.* hacer cosquillas

ticklish *adj.* que tiene cosquillas
tidal *adj.* de marea
tiddly *n.* alegre
tide *n.* marea
tidings *n.* noticias
tidiness *n.* limpieza
tidy *adj.* ordenado
tie *v.* atar
tie *n.* corbata
tied *adj.* atado
tier *n.* grada
tiger *n.* tigre
tight *adj.* ajustado
tighten *v.* ajustar
tile *n.* azulejo
till *prep.* hasta
tiller *n.* caña del timón
tilt *v.* inclinar
timber *n.* madera
time *n.* hora
timely *adj.* oportuno
timid *adj.* tímido
timidity *n.* timidez
timorous *adj.* timorato
tin *n.* lata
tincture *n.* tintura
tinder *n.* yesca
tinge *n.* matiz
tingle *n.* picotazo
tinker *v.* manosear
tinkle *v.* tintinear
tinsel *n.* oropel
tint *n.* tinte
tiny *adj.* pequeño
tip *n.* propina
tipple *v.* empinar el codo
tipster *n.* pronosticador
tipsy *n.* entonado
tiptoe *v.* de puntillas
tirade *n.* diatriba
tire *v.* cansar
tired *adj.* cansado

tireless *adj.* descansado
tiresome *adj.* aburrido
tissue *n.* pañuelo
titanic *adj.* titánico
titbit *n.* golosina
tithe *n.* diezmo
titillate *v.* estimular
titivate *v.* emperejilar
title *n.* título
titled *adj.* titulado
titular *adj.* titular
to *prep.* hacia
toad *n.* sapo
toast *n.* tostada
toaster *n.* tostadora
tobacco *n.* tabaco
today *adv.* hoy
toddle *v.* hacer pinitos
toddler *n.* niño que empieza a andar
toe *n.* dedo del pie
toffee *n.* caramelo
tog *n.* tog
toga *n.* toga
together *adv.* juntos
toggle *n.* botón de trenca
toil *v.i.* esforzarse
toilet *n.* aseo
toiletries *n.* artículo de aseo
toils *n.* trabajos duros
token *n.* muestra, cupón
tolerable *adj.* soportable
tolerance *n.* tolerancia
tolerant *adj.* tolerante
tolerate *v.* tolerar
toleration *n.* tolerancia
toll *n.* peaje
tomato *n.* tomate
tomb *n.* tumba
tomboy *n.* poco femenina
tome *n.* tomo
tomfoolery *n.* payasadas

tomorrow *adv.* mañana
ton *n.* tonelada
tone *n.* tono
toner *n.* tóner
tongs *n.* tenazas
tongue *n.* lengua
tonic *n.* tónico
tonight *adv.* esta noche
tonnage *n.* tonelaje
tonne *n.* tonelada
tonsil *n.* angina
tonsure *n.* tonsura
too *adv.* también
tool *n.* herramienta
tooth *n.* diente
toothache *n.* dolor de muelas
toothless *adj.* desdentado
toothpaste *n.* pasta de dientes
toothpick *n.* palillo
top *n.* cumbre, tapa
topaz *n.* topacio
topiary *n.* topiario
topic *n.* tópico
topical *adj.* actual
topless *adj.* topless
topographer *n.* topógrafo
topographical *adj.* topográfico
topography *n.* topografía
topping *n.* aderezo para postres
topple *v.* volcar
tor *n.* peñasco
torch *n.* linterna
toreador *n.* toreador
torment *n.* tormento
tormentor *n.* torturador
tornado *n.* tornado
torpedo *n.* torpedo
torpid *adj.* aletargado
torrent *n.* torrente
torrential *adj.* torrencial
torrid *adj.* tórrido
torsion *n.* torsión

torso *n.* torso
tort *n.* agravio
tortoise *n.* tortuga
tortuous *adj.* tortuoso
torture *n.* tortura
toss *v.* echar
tot *n.* pequeñito
total *adj.* total
total *n.* total
totalitarian *adj.* totalitario
totality *n.* totalidad
tote *v.* llevar
totter *v.* tambalearse
touch *v.* tocar
touching *adj.* tocado
touchy *adj.* susceptible
tough *adj.* duro
toughen *v.* endurecer
toughness *n.* resistencia
tour *n.* viaje
tourism *n.* turismo
tourist *n.* turista
tournament *n.* torneo
tousle *v.* despeinarse
tout *v.* solicitar clientes
tow *v.* remolcar
towards *prep.* hacia
towel *n.* toalla
towelling *n.* tela de toalla
tower *n.* torre
town *n.* ciudad
township *n.* municipio
toxic *adj.* tóxico
toxicology *n.* toxicología
toxin *n.* toxina
toy *n.* juguete
trace *v.t.* trazar
traceable *adj.* rastreado
tracing *n.* calco
track *n.* huella, pista
tracksuit *n.* chándal
tract *n.* extensión

tractable *adj.* tratable
traction *n.* tracción
tractor *n.* tractor
trade *n.* negocio
trademark *n.* marca de fábrica
trader *n.* comerciante
tradesman *n.* tendero
tradition *n.* tradición
traditional *adj.* tradicional
traditionalist *n.* tradicionalista
traduce *v.* traducir
traffic *n.* trafico
trafficker *n.* traficante
trafficking *n.* traficar
tragedian *n.* actor dramático
tragedy *n.* tragedia
tragic *adj.* trágico
trail *n.* rastro
trailer *n.* remolque
train *n.* tren
train *v.* entrenar
trainee *n.* aprendiz
trainer *n.* entrenador
training *n.* entrenamiento
traipse *v.* patear
trait *n.* rasgo
traitor *n.* traidor
trajectory *n.* trayectoria
tram *n.* tranvía
trammel *n.* atadura
tramp *v.* recorrer a pie
trample *v.* pisotear
trampoline *n.* trampolín
trance *n.* trance
tranquil *adj.* tranquilo
tranquility *n.* tranquilidad
tranquillize *v.* tranquilizar
transact *v.* tramitar
transaction *n.* transacción
transatlantic *adj.* transatlántico
transceiver *n.* transmisor
transcend *v.* transcender

transcendent *adj.* transcendente
transcendental *adj.* trascendental
transcontinental *adj.* transcontinental
transcribe *v.* transcribir
transcript *n.* transcripción
transcription *n.* transcripción
transfer *v.* transferir
transferable *adj.* transferible
transfiguration *n.* transfiguración
transfigure *v.* transfigurar
transform *v.* transformar
transformation *n.* transformación
transformer *n.* transformador
transfuse *v.* transfundir
transfusion *n.* transfusión
transgress *v.* transgredir
transgression *n.* transgresión
transient *adj.* transitorio
transistor *n.* transistor
transit *n.* transito
transition *n.* transición
transitive *adj.* transitivo
transitory *adj.* transitorio
translate *v.* traducir
translation *n.* traducción
transliterate *v.* transliterar
translucent *adj.* translucido
transmigration *n.* transmigración
transmission *n.* transmisión
transmit *v.* transmitir
transmitter *n.* transmisor
transmute *v.* transmutar
transparency *n.* transparencia
transparent *adj.* transparente
transpire *v.* transpirar
transplant *v.* trasplante
transport *v.* transporte
transportation *n.* transportación
transporter *n.* transportador
transpose *v.* trasponer

transsexual *n.* transexual
transverse *adj.* transversal
transvestite *n.* travesti
trap *n.* trampa
trapeze *n.* trapecio
trash *n.* basura
trauma *n.* trauma
travel *v.* viaje
traveller *n.* viajero
travelogue *n.* diario de viaje
traverse *v.* atravesar
travesty *n.* parodia
trawler *n.* barco rastreador
tray *n.* bandeja
treacherous *adj.* traidor
treachery *n.* traición
treacle *n.* melaza
tread *v.* pisada
treadle *n.* pedal
treadmill *n.* rueda de molino
treason *n.* traición
treasure *n.* tesoro
treasurer *n.* tesorero
treasury *n.* tesorería
treat *v.* regalo
treatise *n.* tratado
treatment *n.* tratamiento
treaty *n.* tratado
treble *adj.* triple
tree *n.* árbol
trek *n.* caminata
trellis *n.* enrejado
tremble *v.* temblar
tremendous *adj.* tremendo
tremor *n.* temblor
tremulous *adj.* tembloroso
trench *n.* trinchera
trenchant *adj.* mordaz
trend *n.* tendencia
trendy *adj.* moderno
trepidation *n.* agitación
trespass *v.* traspasar

tress *n.* mechón
trestle *n.* caballete
trial *n.* pleito, prueba
triangle *n.* triangulo
triangular *adj.* triangular
triathlon *n.* triatlón
tribal *adj.* tribal
tribe *n.* tribu
tribulation *n.* tribulación
tribunal *n.* tribunal
tributary *n.* tributario
tribute *n.* tributo
trice *n.* periquete
triceps *n.* tríceps
trick *n.* truco
trickery *n.* engaño
trickle *v.* gotear
trickster *n.* estafador
tricky *adj.* peliagudo
tricolour *n.* tricolor
tricycle *n.* triciclo
trident *n.* tridente
trier *n.* juez
trifle *n.* nimiedad
trigger *n.* gatillo
trigonometry *n.* trigonometría
trill *n.* trino
trillion *adj & n.* trillón
trilogy *n.* trilogía
trim *v.* arreglar
trimmer *n.* que recorta
trimming *n.* recorte
trinity *n.* trinidad
trinket *n.* chuchería
trio *n.* trío
trip *v.* viaje
tripartite *adj.* tripartita
triple *n.* triple
triplet *n.* trilizo
triplicate *adj.* triplicado
tripod *n.* trípode
triptych *n.* tríptico

trite *adj.* trillado
triumph *n.* triunfo
triumphal *adj.* triunfal
triumphant *adj.* triunfante
trivet *n.* salvamanteles
trivia *n.* trivialidades
trivial *adj.* trivial
troll *n.* trol
trolley *n.* carro
troop *n.* banda
trooper *n.* soldado de caballería
trophy *n.* trofeo
tropic *n.* trópico
tropical *adj.* tropical
trot *v.* trote
trotter *n.* pata
trouble *n.* problema
troubleshooter *n.* conciliador
troublesome *adj.* molesto
trough *n.* abrevadero
trounce *v.* derrotar
troupe *n.* grupo
trousers *n.* pantalones
trousseau *n.* ajuar
trout *n.* trucha
trowel *n.* paleta
troy *n.* Troya
truant *n.* hacer novillos
truce *n.* tregua
truck *n.* camión
trucker *n.* camionero
truculent *adj.* agresivo
trudge *v.* andar con dificultad
true *adj.* verdadero
truffle *n.* trufa
trug *n.* cesto
truism *n.* obviedad
trump *n.* triunfo
trumpet *n.* trompeta
truncate *v.* truncar
truncheon *n.* porra

trundle *v.* rodar
trunk *n.* tronco
truss *n.* brequero
trust *n.* confianza
trustee *n.* fideicomisario
trustful *adj.* confiado
trustworthy *adj.* digno de confianza
trusty *adj.* leal
truth *n.* verdad
truthful *adj.* sincero
try *v.* intentar
trying *adj.* difícil
tryst *n.* cita
tsunami *n.* maremoto
tub *n.* cubo
tube *n.* tubo
tubercle *n.* tumor
tuberculosis *n.* tuberculosis
tubular *adj.* tubular
tuck *v.* poner
Tuesday *n.* Martes
tug *v.* remolcador
tuition *n.* enseñanza
tulip *n.* tulipán
tumble *v.* tropezar
tumbler *n.* vaso
tumescent *adj.* tumescente
tumour *n.* tumor
tumult *n.* tumulto
tumultuous *adj.* tumultuoso
tun *n.* cuba
tune *n.* melodía
tuner *n.* afinador
tunic *n.* túnica
tunnel *n.* túnel
turban *n.* turbante
turbid *adj.* turbio
turbine *n.* turbina
turbocharger *n.* turbocompresor
turbulence *n.* turbulencia
turbulent *adj.* turbulento

turf *n.* turba
turgid *adj.* pesado
turkey *n.* pavo
turmeric *n.* cúrcuma
turmoil *n.* alboroto
turn *v.* girar
turner *n.* tornero
turning *n.* vuelta
turnip *n.* nabo
turnout *n.* participación
turnover *n.* volumen de negocio
turpentine *n.* trementina
turquoise *n.* turquesa
turtle *n.* tortuga
tusk *n.* colmillo
tussle *n.* lucha
tutelage *n.* tutela
tutor *n.* tutor
tutorial *n.* seminario
tuxedo *n.* esmoquin
tweak *v.* pellizcar
twee *adj.* cursi
tweed *n.* tweed
tweet *v.* piar, tuitear
tweeter *n.* gorjeo
tweezers *n.* pinzas de depilar
twelfth *adj.&n.* duodécimo
twelve *adj.&n.* doce
twentieth *adj.&n.* vigésimo
twenty *adj.&n.* veinte
twice *adv.* dos veces
twiddle *v.* juguetear
twig *n.* ramita
twilight *n.* crepúsculo
twin *n.* gemelo
twine *n.* bramante
twinge *n.* punzada
twinkle *v.* centelleo
twirl *v.* giro
twist *v.* torsión
twitch *v.* crisparse, contraerse
twitter *v.* gorjear

two *adj.&n.* dos
twofold *adj.* duplicado
tycoon *n.* magnate
type *n.* tipo
typesetter *n.* cajista
typhoid *n.* tifoideo
typhoon *n.* tifón
typhus *n.* tifus
typical *adj.* típico
typify *v.* tipificar
typist *n.* mecanógrafo
tyrannize *v.* tiranizar
tyranny *n.* tiranía
tyrant *n.* tirano
tyre *n.* neumático

U

ubiquitous *adj.* ubicuo
udder *n.* ubre
ugliness *n.* fealdad
ugly *adj.* feo
ulcer *n.* ulcera
ulterior *adj.* oculto
ultimate *adj.* último
ultimately *adv.* por último
ultimatum *n.* ultimátum
ultra *pref.* ultra
ultramarine *n.* ultramarino
ultrasonic *adj.* ultrasónico
ultrasound *n.* ultrasonido
umber *n.* sombra
umbilical *adj.* umbilical
umbrella *n.* paraguas
umpire *n.* árbitro
unable *adj.* ser incapaz
unanimity *a.* unanimidad
unaccountable *adj.* incontable
unadulterated *adj.* inalterado

unalloyed *adj.* puro
unanimous *adj.* unánime
unarmed *adj.* desarmado
unassailable *adj.* inexpugnable
unassuming *adj.* modesto
unattended *adj.* desatendido
unavoidable *adj.* inevitable
unaware *adj.* inconsciente
unbalanced *adj.* desequilibrado
unbelievable *adj.* increíble
unbend *v.* suavizarse
unborn *adj.* sin nacer
unbriddled *adj.* desenfrenado
unburden *v.* desahogarse
uncalled *adj.* inmerecido
uncanny *adj.* extraño, extraordinario
uncertain *adj.* incierto
uncharitable *adj.* poco caritativo
uncle *n.* tío
unclean *adj.* poco limpio
uncomfortable *adj.* incomodo
uncommon *adj.* poco común
uncompromising *adj.* inflexible
unconditional *adj.* incondicional
unconscious *adj.* inconsciente
uncouth *adj.* grosero
uncover *v.* destapar
unctuous *adj.* untuoso
undeceive *v.* desengañar
undecided *adj.* indeciso
undeniable *adj.* innegable
under *prep.* debajo
underarm *adj.* axila
undercover *adj.* infiltrado
undercurrent *n.* trasfondo
undercut *v.* reducir
underdog *n.* desvalido, perdedor esperado
underestimate *v.* subestimar
undergo *v.* sufrir
undergraduate *n.* universitario

underground *adj.* subterráneo
underhand *adj.* solapado
underlay *n.* calzo
underline *v.t.* subrayar
underling *n.* subordinado
undermine *v.* socavar
underneath *prep.* debajo de
underpants *n.* calzoncillos
underpass *n.* paso inferior
underprivileged *adj.* desfavorecido
underrate *v.* menospreciar
underscore *v.* destacar
undersigned *n.* abajo firmante
understand *v.t.* comprender
understanding *n.* comprensión
understate *v.* infravalorar
undertake *v.* acometer
undertaker *n.* sepulturero
underwear *n.* ropa interior
underworld *n.* inframundo
underwrite *v.* asegurar
undesirable *adj.* indeseable
undo *v.* deshacer
undoing *n.* perdición
undone *adj.* inacabado
undress *v.* desvestir
undue *adj.* excesivo
undulate *v.* ondear
undying *adj.* imperecedero
unearth *v.* desenterrar
uneasy *adj.* incómodo
unemployable *adj.* inapelable
unemployed *adj.* desempleado
unending *adj.* interminable
unequalled *adj.* inigualado
uneven *adj.* irregular
unexceptionable *adj.* inocuo
unexceptional *adj.* normal
unexpected *adj.* inesperado
unfailling *adj.* indefectible
unfair *adj.* injusto

unfaithful *adj.* infiel
unfit *adj.* inadecuado
unfold *v.* desdoblar
unforeseen *adj.* imprevisto
unforgettable *adj.* inolvidable
unfortunate *adj.* desafortunado
unfounded *adj.* infundado
unfurl *v.* desplegar
ungainly *adj.* desgarbado
ungovernable *adj.* ingobernable
ungrateful *adj.* desagradecido
unguarded *adj.* indefenso
unhappy *adj.* infeliz
unhealthy *adj.* malsano
unheard *adj.* insólito
unholy *adj.* pecaminoso
unification *n.* unificación
uniform *adj.* uniforme
unify *v.* unificar
unilateral *adj.* unilateral
unimpeachable *adj.* irreprochable
uninhabited *adj.* deshabitado
union *n.* unión
unionist *n.* sindicalista
unique *adj.* único
unisex *adj.* unisex
unison *n.* unísono
unit *n.* unidad
unite *v.* unir
unity *n.* unidad
universal *adj.* universal
universality *adv.* universalidad
universe *n.* universo
university *n.* universidad
unjust *adj.* injusto
unkempt *adj.* desarreglado
unkind *adj.* desagradable
unknown *adj.* desconocido
unleash *v.* desencadenar
unless *conj.* a menos que
unlike *prep.* diferente, distinto de

unlikely *adj.* improbable
unlimited *adj.* ilimitado
unload *v.* descargar
unmanned *adj.* no tripulado
unmask *v.* desenmascarar
unmentionable *adj.* inmencionable
unmistakable *adj.* inconfundible
unmitigated *adj.* absoluto
unmoved *adj.* impasible
unnatural *adj.* antinatural
unnecessary *adj.* innecesario
unnerve *v.* desconcertar
unorthodox *adj.* poco ortodoxo
unpack *v.* desempaquetar
unpleasant *adj.* desagradable
unpopular *adj.* impopular
unprecedented *adj.* sin precedentes
unprepared *adj.* improvisado
unprincipled *adj.* sin principios
unprofessional *adj.* poco profesional
unqualified *adj.* no calificado
unreasonable *adj.* irrazonable
unreliable *n* informal
unreserved *adj.* incondicional
unrest *n.* malestar
unrivalled *adj.* incomparable
unruly *adj.* rebelde
unscathed *adj.* ileso
unscrupulous *adj.* inescrupuloso
unseat *v.* desmontar
unselfish *adj.* desinteresado
unsettle *v.* perturbar
unshakeable *adj.* inamovible
unskilled *adj.* no cualificado
unsocial *adj.* antisocial
unsolicited *adj.* no deseado
unstable *adj.* inestable
unsung *adj.* olvidado
unthinkable *adj.* impensable

untidy *adj.* desordenado
until *prep.* hasta
untimely *adj.* prematuro
untold *adj.* indecible
untouchable *adj.* intocable
untoward *adj.* adverso
unusual *adj.* inusual
unutterable *adj.* inenarrable
unveil *v.* desvelar
unwarranted *adj.* injustificado
unwell *adj.* indispuesto
unwilling *adj.* poco dispuesto
unwind *v.* desenrollar, relajarse
unwise *adj.* insensato
unworldly *adj.* ajeno al mundo
unworthy *adj.* indigno
up *adv.* arriba
upbeat *adj.* optimista
upbraid *adj.* reprender
upcoming *adj.* próximo
update *v.* actualizar
upgrade *v.* actualizar, mejorar
upheaval *n.* agitación
uphold *v.* defender
upholster *v.* tapicero
upholstery *n.* tapicería
uplift *v.* elevar
upload *v.* cargar
upper *adj.* superior
upright *adj.* vertical
uprising *n.* levantamiento
uproar *n.* alboroto
uproarious *adj.* escandaloso
uproot *v.* desarraigar
upset *v.* disgustado
upshot *n.* advenedizo
upstart *n.* advenedizo
upsurge *n.* aumento
upturn *n.* auge
upward *adv.* hacia arriba
urban *adj.* urbano
urbane *adj.* cortés

urbanity *n.* urbanidad
urchin *n.* erizo
urge *v.* urgir
urgent *adj.* urgente
urinal *n.* orinal
urinary *adj.* urinario
urinate *v.* orinar
urine *n.* orina
urn *n.* urna
usable *adj.* utilizable
usage *n.* uso
use *v.t.* usar
useful *adj.* útil
useless *adj.* inútil
user *n.* usuario
usher *n.* acomodador
usual *adj.* usual
usually *adv.* normalmente
usurp *v.* usurpar
usurpation *n.* usurpación
usury *n.* usura
utensil *n.* utensilio
uterus *n.* útero
utilitarian *adj.* utilitario
utility *n.* utilidad
utilization *n.* utilización
utilize *v.* utilizar
utmost *adj.* máximo
utopia *n.* utópia
utopian *adj.* utópico
utter *adj.* total
utterance *n.* afirmación
uttermost *adj.* máximo

V

vacancy *n.* vacante
vacant *adj.* libre
vacate *v.* vaciar

vacation *n.* vacaciones
vaccinate *v.* vacunar
vaccination *n.* vacunación
vaccine *n.* vacuna
vacillate *v.* vacilar
vacillation *n.* vacilación
vacuous *adj.* vacío
vacuum *n.* vacío
vagabond *n.* vagabundo
vagary *n.* capricho
vagina *n.* vagina
vagrant *n.* vagabundo
vague *adj.* vago
vagueness *n.* vaguedad
vain *adj.* vanidoso
vainglorious *adj.* vanaglorioso
vainly *adv.* vanidosamente
valance *n.* cenefa
vale *n.* vale
valediction *n.* despedida
valency *n.* valencia
Valentine *n.* Valentín
valet *n.* ayuda de cámara
valetudinarian *n.* valetudinario
valiant *adj.* valiente
valid *adj.* válido
validate *v.* validar
validity *n.* validez
valise *n.* valija
valley *n.* valle
valour *n.* valentía
valuable *adj.* valioso
valuation *n.* valuación
value *n.* valor
valve *n.* válvula
vamp *n.* empeine
vampire *n.* vampiro
van *n.* furgoneta
vandal *n.* vándalo
vandalize *v.* vandalizar
vane *n.* veleta
vanguard *n.* vanguardia

vanish *v.* desvanecerse
vanity *n.* vanidad
vanquish *v.* vencer
vantage *n.* ventaja
vapid *adj.* insípido
vaporize *v.* vaporizar
vapour *n.* vapor
variable *adj.* variable
variance *n.* desacuerdo
variant *n.* variante
variation *n.* variación
varicose *adj.* variz
varied *adj.* variado
variegated *adj.* abigarrado
variety *n.* variedad
various *adj.* varios
varnish *n.* barniz
vary *v.* variar
vascular *adj.* vascular
vase *n.* jarrón
vasectomy *n.* vasectomía
vassal *n.* vasallo
vast *adj.* vasto
vaudeville *n.* vodevil
vault *n.* bóveda
vaunted *adj.* pregonado
veal *n.* ternera
vector *n.* vector
veer *n.* viraje
vegan *n.* vegetariano estricto
vegetable *n.* verdura
vegetarian *n.* vegetariano
vegetate *v.* vegetar
vegetation *n.* vegetación
vegetative *adj.* vegetativo
vehement *adj.* vehemente
vehicle *n.* vehículo
vehicular *adj.* vehicular
veil *n.* velo
vein *n.* vena
velocity *n.* velocidad
velour *n.* velvetón

velvet *n.* terciopelo
velvety *adj.* aterciopelado
venal *adj.* venal
venality *n.* venalidad
vend *v.* vender
vendetta *n.* vendetta
vendor *n.* vendedor
veneer *n.* chapa
venerable *adj.* venerable
venerate *v.* venerar
veneration *n.* veneración
venetian *adj.* veneciano
vengeance *n.* venganza
vengeful *adj.* vengativo
venial *adj.* venial
venom *n.* veneno
venomous *adj.* venenoso
venous *adj.* venoso
vent *n.* respiradero
ventilate *v.* ventilar
ventilation *n.* ventilación
ventilator *n.* ventilador
venture *n.* aventura
venturesome *adj.* atrevido
venue *n.* lugar
veracious *adj.* veraz
veracity *n.* veracidad
verandah *n.* veranda
verb *n.* verbo
verbal *adj.* verbal
verbally *adv.* verbalmente
verbalize *v.* verbalizar
verbatim *adv.* textualmente
verbiage *n.* verborrea
verbose *adj.* verboso
verbosity *n.* verborrea
verdant *adj.* verdeante
verdict *n.* veredicto
verge *n.* borde
verification *n.* verificación
verify *v.* verificar
verily *adv.* verdaderamente

verisimilitude *n.* verosimilitud
veritable *adj.* auténtico
verity *n.* verdad
vermillion *n.* bermellón
vermin *n.* bichos
vernacular *n.* vernáculo
vernal *adj.* vernal
versatile *adj.* versátil
versatility *n.* versatilidad
verse *n.* verso
versed *adj.* versado
versification *n.* versificación
versify *v.* versificar
version *n.* versión
verso *n.* reverso
versus *prep.* contra
vertebra *n.* vertebrado
vertebrate *n.* vertebra
vertex *n.* vértice
vertical *adj.* vertical
vertiginous *adj.* vertiginoso
vertigo *n.* vértigo
verve *n.* brío
very *adv.* muy
vesicle *n.* vesícula
vessel *n.* vasija
vest *n.* camiseta/chaleco
vestibule *n.* vestíbulo
vestige *n.* vestigio
vestment *n.* vestidura
vestry *n.* sacristía
veteran *n.* veterano
veterinary *adj.* veterinario
veto *n.* veto
vex *v.* irritar
vexation *n.* vejación
via *prep.* por vía de
viable *adj.* viable
viaduct *n.* viaducto
vial *n.* vial
viands *n.* vituallas
vibe *n.* vibración

vibrant *adj.* vibrante
vibraphone *n.* vibráfono
vibrate *v.* vibrar
vibration *n.* vibración
vibrator *n.* vibrador
vicar *n.* párroco
vicarious *adj.* indirecto
vice *n.* vice
viceroy *n.* virrey
vice-versa *adv.* viceversa
vicinity *n.* proximidad
vicious *adj.* violento
vicissitude *n.* vicisitud
victim *n.* victima
victimize *n.* victimizar
victor *n.* vencedor
victorious *adj.* victorioso
victory *n.* victoria
victualler *n.* vendedor de bebidas
    alcohólicas
victuals *n.* vituallas
video *n.* video
vie *v.* competir con
view *n.* vista
vigil *n.* vigilia
vigilance *n.* vigilancia
vigilant *adj.* vigilante
vignette *n.* viñeta
vigorous *adj.* vigoroso
vigour *n.* vigor
viking *n.* vikingo
vile *adj.* infame
vilify *v.* vilipendiar
villa *n.* chalet
village *n.* pueblo
villager *n.* aldeano
villain *n.* malvado
vindicate *v.* vindicar
vindication *n.* vindicación
vine *n.* vid
vinegar *n.* vinagre
vintage *n.* vendimia

vintner *n.* vinatero
vinyl *n.* vinilo
violate *v.* violar
violation *n.* violación
violence *n.* violencia
violent *adj.* violento
violet *n.* violeta
violin *n.* violín
violinist *n.* violinista
virago *n.* virago
viral *adj.* vírico
virgin *n.* virgen
virginity *n.* virginidad
virile *adj.* viril
virility *n.* virilidad
virtual *adj.* virtual
virtue *n.* virtud
virtuous *adj.* virtuoso
virulence *n.* virulencia
virulent *adj.* virulento
virus *n.* virus
visa *n.* visado
visage *n.* rostro
viscid *adj.* viscoso
viscose *n.* viscosa
viscount *n.* vizconde
viscountess *n.* vizcondesa
viscous *adj.* viscoso
visibility *n.* visibilidad
visible *adj.* visible
vision *n.* visión
visionary *adj.* visionario
visit *v.* visitar
visitation *n.* visita
visitor *n.* visitante
visor *n.* visera
vista *n.* vista
visual *adj.* visual
visualize *v.* visualizar
vital *adj.* vital
vitality *n.* vitalidad
vitalize *v.* reavivar

vitamin *n.* vitamina
vitiate *v.* viciar
viticulture *n.* viticultura
vitreous *adj.* vítreo
vitrify *v.* vitrificar
vitriol *n.* vitriolo
vituperation *n.* vituperio
vivacious *adj.* vivaz
vivacity *n.* vivacidad
vivarium *n.* vivero
vivid *adj.* vivo
vivify *v.* vivificar
vixen *n.* zorra
vocabulary *n.* vocabulario
vocal *adj.* vocal
vocalist *n.* vocalista
vocalize *v.* vocalizar
vocation *n.* vocación
vociferous *adj.* vocinglero
vogue *n.* moda
voice *n.* voz
voicemail *n.* mensaje de voz
void *adj.* nulo
voile *n.* voluptuoso
volatile *adj.* volátil
volcanic *adj.* volcánico
volcano *n.* volcán
volition *n.* volición
volley *n.* descarga
volt *n.* voltio
voltage *n.* voltaje
voluble *adj.* voluble
volume *n.* volumen
voluminous *adj.* voluminoso
voluntarily *adv.* voluntariamente
voluntary *adj.* voluntario
volunteer *n.* voluntario
voluptuary *n.* voluptuoso
voluptuous *adj.* voluptuoso
vomit *v.* vomitar
voodoo *n.* vudú
voracious *adj.* voraz

vortex *n.* vórtice
votary *n.* devoto
vote *n.* voto
voter *n.* votante
votive *adj.* votivo
vouch *v.* garantizar
voucher *n.* vale
vouchsafe *v.* conceder
vow *n.* voto
vowel *n.* vocal
voyage *n.* viaje
voyager *n.* viajero
vulcanize *v.* vulcanizar
vulgar *adj.* vulgar
vulgarian *n.* vulgaridad
vulgarity *n.* vulgaridad
vulnerable *adj.* vulnerable
vulpine *adj.* sagaz
vulture *n.* buitre

W

wacky *adj.* chiflado
wad *n.* fajo
waddle *v.* balancearse
wade *v.* vadear
wader *n.* ave zancuda
wadi *n.* uadi
wafer *n.* barquillo
waffle *v.* meter paja
waft *v.* flotar
wag *v.* menear
wage *n.* sueldo
wager *n. & v.* apuesta, apostar
waggle *v.* vagón
wagon *n.* carro
wagtail *n.* lavandera
waif *n.* sin hogar

wail *n.* gemido
wain *n.* carreta
wainscot *n.* revestimiento
waist *n.* cintura
waistband *n.* faja
waistcoat *n.* chaleco
wait *v.* esperar
waiter *n.* camarero
waitress *n.* camarera
waive *v.* renunciar
wake *v.* despertar
wakeful *adj.* desvelado
waken *v.* despertar
walk *v.* andar
wall *n.* pared
wallaby *n.* ualabí
wallet *n.* bolsillo
wallop *v.* zurrar
wallow *v.* revolcarse
wally *n.* imbécil
walnut *n.* nuez
walrus *n.* morsa
waltz *n.* vals
wan *adj.* pálido
wand *n.* varita
wander *v.* deambular
wane *v.* menguar
wangle *v.* agenciarse algo
want *v.* querer
wanting *adj.* deficiente
wanton *adj.* juguetón
war *n.* guerra
warble *v.* trinar
warbler *n.* curruca
ward *n.* sala
warden *n.* director
warder *n.* guardián
wardrobe *n.* armario
ware *n.* utensilios
warehouse *n.* fabrica
warfare *n.* guerra
warlike *adj.* bélico

warm *adj.* caliente
warmth *n.* calor
warn *v.* avisar
warning *n.* aviso, advertencia
warp *v.* alabear
warrant *n.* orden judicial
warrantor *n.* garante
warranty *n.* garantía
warren *n.* madriguera
warrior *n.* guerrero
wart *n.* verruga
wary *adj.* cauteloso
wash *v.* lavar
washable *adj.* lavable
washer *n.* lavadora
washing *n.* colada
wasp *n.* avispa
waspish *adj.* mordaz
wassail *n.* borrachera
wastage *n.* desgaste
waste *v.* malgastar
wasteful *adj.* derrochador
watch *v.* ver/observar
watchful *adj.* vigilante
watchword *n.* lema
water *n.* agua
waterfall *n.* cascada
watermark *n.* marca de agua,
  filigrana
watermelon *n.* sandía
waterproof *adj.* impermeable
watertight *adj.* hermético
watery *adj.* desvaído
watt *n.* vatio
wattle *n.* quincha, barba
wave *v.* ondear
waver *v.* oscilar
wavy *adj.* ondulado
wax *n.* cera
way *n.* manera, camino
waylay *v.* acechar
wayward *adj.* voluntarioso

we *pron.* nosotros
weak *adj.* débil
weaken *v.* debilitarse
weakling *n.* delicada
weakness *n.* debilidad
weal *n.* verdugón
wealth *n.* riqueza
wealthy *adj.* rico
wean *v.* destetar
weapon *n.* arma
wear *v.* llevar, ponerse
wearisome *adj.* tedioso
weary *adj.* harto
weasel *n.* comadreja
weather *n.* tiempo
weave *v.* tejer
weaver *n.* tejedor
web *n.* red, telaraña
webby *adj.* membranoso
webpage *n.* página web
website *n.* sitio web
wed *v.* casar
wedding *n.* boda
wedge *n.* cuña
wedlock *n.* matrimonio
Wednesday *n.* Miércoles
weed *n.* maleza
week *n.* semana
weekday *n.* día de la semana
weekly *adj.* semanal
weep *v.* llorar
weepy *adj.* llorón
weevil *n.* gorgojo
weigh *v.* pesar
weight *n.* peso
weighting *n.* suplemento
weightlifting *n.* levantamiento de pesas
weighty *adj.* pesado
weir *n.* presa
weird *adj.* raro
welcome *n.* bienvenida

weld *v.* soldar
welfare *n.* bienestar
well *adv.* bien
well *n.* pozo
wellington *n.* bota de agua
welt *n.* verdugón
welter *n.* fárrago
wen *n.* quiste sebáceo, monstruosidad
wench *n.* moza
wend *v.* retomar el camino
west *n.* oeste
westerly *adv.* viento del oeste
western *adj.* occidente
westerner *n.* occidental
westernize *v.* occidentalizar
wet *adj.* mojado
wetness *n.* humedad
whack *v.* golpear
whale *n.* ballena
whaler *n.* ballenero
whaling *n.* caza de ballenas
wharf *n.* muelle
wharfage *n.* amarraje
what *pron. & adj.* que
whatever *pron.* cualquier
wheat *n.* trigo
wheaten *adj.* trigueño
wheedle *v.* sonsacar
wheel *n.* rueda
wheeze *v.* resollar
whelk *n.* buccino
whelm *v.* abrumar
whelp *n.* cachorro
when *adv.* cuando
whence *adv.* de dónde
whenever *conj.* cuando
where *adv.* donde
whereabout *adv.* paradero
whereas *n.* mientras
whet *v.* estimular
whether *conj.* si

whey *n.* suero
which *pron. & adj.* cual/cuales
whichever *pron.* cualquier
whiff *n.* bocanada
while *n.* momento
whilst *conj.* mientras
whim *n.* capricho
whimper *v.* lloriquear
whimsical *adj.* caprichoso
whimsy *n.* banal
whine *n.* gemido
whinge *v.* quejarse
whinny *n.* relincho
whip *n.* látigo
whir *n.* zumbido
whirl *v.* dar vueltas
whirligig *n.* molinete
whirlpool *n.* remolino
whirlwind *n.* torbellino
whirr *v.* rechinar
whisk *v.* batir
whisker *n.* bigotes de un animal
whisky *n.* whisky
whisper *v.* susurrar
whist *n.* juego de naipes
whistle *n.* silbato
whit *n.* pizca
white *adj.* blanco
whitewash *n.* cal
whither *adv.* más blanca
whiting *n.* pescadilla
whittle *v.* tallar, mermar, minar
whiz *v.* silbar, aparecer
who *pron.* quien
whoever *pron.* cualquiera
whole *adj.* todo/entero
whole-hearted *adj.* sincero
wholesale *n.* venta al por mayor
wholesaler *n.* mayorista
wholesome *adj.* sano
wholly *adv.* totalmente
whom *pron.* que/a quien

whoop *n.* chillido
whopper *n.* enorme, trola
whore *n.* puta
whose *adj. & pron.* de quién
why *adv.* por qué
wick *n.* mecha
wicked *adj.* malvado
wicker *n.* mimbre
wicket *n.* palos
wide *adj.* ancho
widen *v.* ensanchar
widespread *adj.* extendido
widow *n.* viuda
widower *n.* viudo
width *n.* anchura
wield *v.* manejar
wife *n.* esposa
wig *n.* peluca
wiggle *v.* menear
wight *n.* persona
wigwam *n.* tienda de indios
wild *adj.* salvaje
wilderness *n.* desierto
wile *n.* treta
wilful *adj.* obstinado
will *n.* voluntad, testamento
willing *adj.* dispuesto
willingness *adj.* buena voluntad
willow *n.* sauce
wily *adj.* astuto
wimple *n.* griñón
win *v.* ganar
wince *v.* estremecerse
winch *n.* torno
wind *n.* viento
windbag *n.* charlatán, fuelle
winder *n.* devanadera
windlass *n.* molinete
windmill *n.* molino de viento
window *n.* ventana
windy *adj.* con viento
wine *n.* vino

winery *n.* bodega
wing *n.* ala
wink *v.* guiño
winkle *n.* bígaro
winner *n.* ganador
winning *adj.* ganador
winnow *v.* aventar
winsome *adj.* encantador
winter *n.* invierno
wintry *adj.* invernal
wipe *v.* pasar un trapo
wire *n.* alambre
wireless *adj.* inalámbrico
wiring *n.* alambrado
wisdom *n.* sabiduría
wise *adj.* sabio
wish *v.* desear
wishful *adj.* quimera
wisp *n.* mechón
wisteria *n.* glicinia
wistful *adj.* nostálgico
wit *n.* gracia
witch *n.* bruja
witchcraft *n.* brujería
witchery *n.* hechicería
with *prep.* con
withal *adv.* además
withdraw *v.* retirar
withdrawal *n.* retirada
withe *n.* mimbre
wither *v.* marchitarse
withhold *v.* retener
within *prep.* dentro
without *prep.* sin
withstand *v.* resistir
witless *adj.* estúpido
witness *n.* testigo
witter *v.* parlotear
witticism *n.* ingenio
witty *adj.* ingenioso
wizard *n.* hechicero
wizened *adj.* marchito

woad *n.* hierba pastel
wobble *v.* tambalearse
woe *n.* desgracia
woeful *adj.* desgraciado
wok *n.* sartén china
wold *n.* terreno ondulado
wolf *n.* lobo
woman *n.* mujer
womanhood *n.* femineidad
womanize *v.* ser mujeriego
womb *n.* útero
wonder *v.* maravillar
wonderful *adj.* maravilloso
wondrous *adj.* asombroso
wonky *adj.* torcido
wont *n.* costumbre
wonted *adj.* acostumbrado
woo *v.* cortejar
wood *n.* madera
wooded *adj.* arbolado
wooden *adj.* de madera
woodland *n.* bosque
woof *n.* ladrido
woofer *n.* bafle
wool *n.* lana
woollen *adj.* de lana
woolly *adj.* confuso, lanudo
woozy *adj.* atontado
word *n.* palabra
wording *n.* redacción
wordy *adj.* verboso
work *n.* trabajo
workable *adj.* factible
workaday *adj.* rutinario
worker *n.* trabajador
working *n.* trabajo
workman *n.* obrero
workmanship *n.* habilidad
workshop *n.* taller
world *n.* mundo
worldly *adj.* terrenal
worm *n.* gusano

wormwood *n.* ajenjo
worried *adj.* preocupado
worrisome *adj.* preocupante
worry *v.* preocupar
worse *adj.* peor
worsen *v.* empeorar
worship *n.* culto
worshipper *n.* devoto
worst *adj.* el peor
worsted *n.* estambre
worth *adj.* que vale
worthless *adj.* sin valor
worthwhile *adj.* valioso
worthy *adj.* digno
would *v.* modal
wouldbe *adj.* aspirante
wound *n.* herida
wrack *n.* ruina
wraith *n.* espectro
wrangle *n.* disputa
wrap *v.* envolver
wrapper *n.* envoltorio
wrath *n.* cólera
wreak *v.* sembrar
wreath *n.* corona
wreathe *v.* ceñir
wreck *n.* restos
wreckage *n.* escombros
wrecker *n.* demolición
wren *n.* carrizo
wrench *v.* desgarrar
wrest *v.* arrancar
wrestle *v.* luchar
wrestler *n.* luchador
wretch *n.* miseria
wretched *adj.* miserable
wrick *v.* torcerse
wriggle *v.* serpentear
wring *v.* torcer
wrinkle *n.* arruga
wrinkle *n.* arruga
wrist *n.* muñeca

writ *n.* mandato judicial
write *v.* escribir
writer *n.* escritor
writhe *v.* retorcerse
writing *n.* escritura
wrong *adj.* incorrecto
wrongful *adj.* injusto
wry *adj.* irónico

X

xenon *n.* xenón
xenophobia *n.* xenofobia
xerox *n.* Xerox
Xmas *n.* Navidades
x-ray *n.* radiografía
xylophagous *adj.* xilófago
xylophone *n.* xilófono

Y

yacht *n.* yate
yachting *n.* balandrismo
yatchsman *n.* balandrista
yak *n.* yak
yam *n.* ñame
yap *v.* aullar
yard *n.* patio
yarn *n.* hilo
yashmak *n.* velo
yaw *v.* virar
yawn *v.* bostezar
year *n.* año
yearly *adv.* anual
yearn *v.* añorar
yearning *n.* añoranza

yeast *n.* levadura
yell *n.* grito
yellow *adj.* amarillo
yelp *n.* aullido
Yen *n.* Yen
yeoman *n.* alabardero
yes *excl.* si
yesterday *adv.* ayer
yet *adv.* todavía
yeti *n.* yeti
yew *n.* tejo
yield *v.* producir
yob *n.* gamberro
yodel *v.* cantar al estilo tirolés
yoga *n.* yoga
yogi *n.* yogui
yogurt *n.* yogur
yoke *n.* yunta
yokel *n.* pueblerino
yolk *n.* yema
yonder *adj.* aquellos
yonks *n.* eternidad
yore *n.* antaño
you *pron.* tú, usted
young *adj.* joven
youngster *n.* jovencito
your *adj.* tu/vuestro
yourself *pron.* tú mismo
youth *n.* juventud
youthful *adj.* juvenil
yowl *n.* alarido
yummy *adj.* delicioso

Z

zany *adj.* tonto
zap *v.* liquidar
zeal *n.* entusiasmo
zealot *n.* fanático
zealous *adj.* entusiasta
zebra *n.* cebra
zebra crossing *n.* paso de peatones
zenith *n.* cénit
zephyr *n.* céfiro
zero *adj.* cero
zest *n.* vivacidad
zigzag *n.* zigzag
zinc *n.* zinc
zing *n.* silbido
zip *n.* cremallera
zircon *n.* circonita
zither *n.* cítara
zodiac *n.* zodiaco
zombie *n.* zombi
zonal *adj.* zonal
zone *n.* zona
zoo *n.* zoo
zoological *adj.* zoológico
zoologist *n.* zoólogo
zoology *n.* zoología
zoom *v.* enfocar

SPANISH - ENGLISH

A

a *prep.* at
a bordo *adv.* aboard
a escondidas *n.* stealth
a flote *adj.* afloat
a horcajadas *prep.* astride
a la deriva *adj.* adrift
a la moda *adj.* modish
a lo largo de *prep.* along
a menos que *conj.* unless
a menudo *adv.* oft
a menudo *adv.* often
a pesar de *prep.* despite
a pesar de *prep.* notwithstanding
a pesar de todo *adv.* regardless
a pie *n.* footing
a toda marcha *n.* overdrive
a través *adv.* across
a través *prep.* through
a un lado *adv.* aside
abad *n.* abbot
abadía *n.* abbey
abajo firmante *n.* undersigned
abajo *adv.* down
abandonada *n.* slattern
abandonado *adj.* overgrown
abandonar *v.t.* abandon, quit
abarcar *v.* encompass
abastecer *v.* cater
abatido *adj.* glum
abatido *adj.* miserable
abatimiento *n.* dejection
abatir *v.* deject
abdicación *n.* abdication
abdicar *v.i.* abdicate
abdomen *n.* abdomen
abdominal *a.* abdominal
abedul *n.* birch
abeja *n.* bee
aberración *n.* aberration

aberrante *adj.* aberrant
abertura *n.* aperture
abeto *n.* fir
abiertamente *adv.* openly
abierto *adj.* open
abigarrado *adj.* variegated
abismal *adj.* abysmal
abismo *n.* abyss
ablandarse *v.* relent
abnegación *n.* denial
ablución *n.* ablutions
abofetear *v.t.* slap
abogado *n.* lawyer
abogar por *v.* advocate
abolición *v.* abolition
abolir *v.t* abolish
abolladura *n.* dent
abollar *v.* crumple
abominable *adj.* abominable
abominar *v.* abominate
abono *n.* compost
abordar *v.* accost
aborigen *adj.* aboriginal
aborrecer *v.* abhor
aborrecible *adj.* abhorent
abortar *v.i* abort
abortivo *adj.* abortive
aborto *n.* abortion
abrasión *n.* abrasion
abrasivo *adj.* abrasive
abrazadera *n.* brace, clamp
abrazar *v.* embrace, hug
abrazo *n.* hug
abrevadero *n.* trough
abreviación *n.* abbreviation
abreviar *v.t.* abbreviate
abrigado *adj.* snug
abrigo *n.* coat
abrillantador *n.* polish
abrirse *v.* splay
abrochar *v.* fasten
abrumar *v.* overwhelm

absceso *n.* abscess
absolución *n.* absolution
absoluto *adj.* absolute
absolver *v.* absolve
absorber *v.* absorb
abstemio *adj.* teetotal
abstemio *n.* teetotaller
abstenerse *v.* abstain
abstinencia *n.* abstinence
abstracto *adj.* abstract
abstruso *adj.* abstruse
absurdo *adj.* absurd
absurdo *n.* absurdity
abuela *n.* grandmother
abundancia *n.* abundance
abundante *adj.* hearty
abundar *v.* abound
abundar *adj.* abundant
aburrido *adj.* tiresome, dull
abusar *v.* abuse, molest
abusivo *adj.* abusive
abuso *n.* molestation
acabar *v.* accomplish
academia *n.* academy
académico *adj.* academic
acantonamiento *n.* cantonment
acaparamiento *n.* hoarding
acariciar *v.* caress, fondle
ácaro *n.* mite
acatar *v.* comply
acceder *v.* accede
accesible *adj.* accessible
accesión *n.* accession
acceso *n.* access
accesorio *n.* accessory
accidentado *adj.* rugged
accidental *adj.* accidental
accidente *n.* accident
acción *n.* action
acebo *n.* holly
acechar *v.* waylay
aceite de ricino *a.* castor oil

aceite *n.* oil
aceitoso *adj.* oily
aceituna *n.* olive
acelerador *n.* accelerator
acelerar *v.* accelerate
acenso *n.* promotion
acento *n.* accent
acentuar *v.* accentuate
aceptable *adj.* acceptable
aceptación *n.* acceptance
aceptar *v.* accept
acera *n.* pavement
acerbo *adj.* acerbic
acercamiento *n.* rapprochment
acercarse *v.t.* approach
acero *n.* steel
acérrimo *adj.* staunch
acertado *adj.* accurate
acertijo *n.* riddle
acetato *n.* acetate
acetona *n.* acetone
achaque *n.* ailment
acicalar *v.* groom
acidez *n.* acidity
ácido *n.* acid
aclamar *v.* acclaim
aclaración *n.* clarification
aclaramiento *n.* lightening
aclarar *v.* clarify
aclimatar *v.* acclimatise
acné *n.* acne
acobardarse *v.* flinch
acogedor *adj.* cozy, homely
acoger *v.* receive, greet
acolchado *adj.* quilted
acólito *n.* acolyte
acometer *v.* undertake
acomodación *n.* accommodation
acomodador *n.* usher
acomodar *v.* accommodate
acompañar *v.* accompany
acondicionador *n.* conditioner

acongojado *adj.* mournful
aconsejable *adj.* advisable
aconsejar *v.* advise, counsel
acordado *adv.* according
acordar *v.* accord, agree
acorde *n.* chord
acortar *v.* shorten
acosador *n.* stalker
acosar *v.* harass
acoso *n.* harassment
acostumbrado *adj.* accustomed
acostumbrar *v,t* accustom
acostumbrarse *v.* habituate
acre *adj.* acrid
acreditado *adj.* accredited
acreditar *v.* accredit
acreedor *n.* creditor
acreedor hipotecario *n.* mortagagee
acribillado *adj.* riddled
acrílico *adj.* acrylic
acrimonia *n.* acrimony
acróbata *n.* acrobat
acrobático *adj.* acrobatic
actinio *n.* actinium
actitud *n.* attitude
activar *v.* activate
actividad *n.* activity
activista *n.* activist
activo *adj.* active, spry
acto *v.* act
acto sexual *n.* intercourse
actor *n.* actor
actor dramático *n.* tragedian
actriz *a.* actress
actriz principiante *n.* starlet
actuación *n.* performance
actual *adj.* actual, current
actualizar *v.* update
actualmente *adv.* actually
actuar *v.* perform
actuario *n.* actuary

acuario *n.* aquarium
acuático *adj.* aquatic
acuerdo *n.* agreement
acumulación *n.* accumulation
acumular *v.* accumulate
acumulativo *adj.* cumulative
acuñación *n.* coinage
acuoso *adj.* aqueous
acupuntura *n.* acupuncture
acurrucarse *v.* cower, nestle
acusación *n.* indictment, prosecution, accusation
acusado *n.* accused
acusar *v.* accuse, indict, charge
acústico *adj.* acoustic
adaptación *n.* adaptation
adaptar *v.* adapt
adecuado *adj.* suitable
adecuado *n.* fitting
además *adv.* furthermore
además *adv.* moreover
adepto *adj.* adept
aderezar *v.* garnish
aderezo para postres *n.* topping
adherencia *n.* adherence
adherir *v.* adhere
adherirse *v.* cohere
adhesivo *n.* adhesive
adicción *n.* addiction
adicional *adj.* additional
adictivo *adj.* addicted
adicto *n.* addict
adiós *n.* goodbye
adiós *interj.* farewell
adiós *excl.* goodbye
aditivo *n.* additive
adivinanza *n.* conundrum
adivinar *v.t.* guess
adjetivo *n.* adjective
adjuntar *v.* adjoin, bind
adjunto *n.* adjunct, deputy
administración *n.* administration, management

administrador *adj.* administrator
administrar *v.* administer, manage
administrativo *adj.* administrative
administrativo *n.* clerk
admirable *adj.* admirable
admiración *n.* admiration
admirar *v.* admire
admisible *adj.* admissible
admisión *n.* admission
admitir *v.* admit
adobe *n.* adobe
adobo *n.* marinade
adolescencia *n.* adolescence
adolescencia *adj.* teens
adolescente *adj.* adolescent
adolescente *n.* teenager
adopción *n.* adoption
adoptar *v.* adopt
adoptivo *adj.* adoptive
adoquín *n.* cobble
adorable *adj.* adorable
adoración *n.* adoration
adorar *v.t.* adore
adornar *v.* adorn, embellish
aderezar *v.* garnish
adorno *n.* ornament
adquirir *v.* acquire, purchase
adquisición *n.* acquisition
aducir *v.* adduce
adulación *n.* adulation
adulador *n.* sycophant
adular, halagar *v.* flatter
adulteración *n.* adulteration
adulterar *v.* adulterate
adulterio *n.* adultery
adulto *n.* adult
adulto *adj.* mature
advenedizo *n.* upstart,upshot
advenimiento *n.* advent
adverbio *n.* adverb

adversario *n.* adversary
adversidad *n.* adversity
adverso *adj.* adverse
advertencia *n.* warning
advertido *adj.* cautionary
adyacente *adj.* adjacent
aerobático *n.* aerobatics
aerobics *n.* aerobics
aerodeslizador *n.* hydrofoil
aeródromo *n.* aerodrome
aeroespacial *n.* aerospace
aeronáutica *n.* aeronautics
aerosol *n.* aerosol
afable *adj.* affable, mild
afectación *n.* affectation
afectado *adj.* affected, stricken
afectar *v.* affect
afecto *n.* affection
afectuoso *adj.* affectionate
afeitado *adj.* shaven
afeitado *n.* shaving
afeitar *v.* shave
afeminado *adj.* effeminate
aferrar *v.* cling
afición *n.* hobby
aficionado *n.* amateur
afilado *adj.* sharp
afilador *n.* sharpener
afilar *v.* sharpen
afiliación *n.* affiliation
afiliar *v.* affiliate
afín *adj.* cognate
afinador *n.* tuner
afinidad *n.* affinity
afirmación *n.* affirmation
afirmar *v.* affirm, assert
afirmativo *adj.* affirmative
aflicción *n.* affliction
afligir *v.* afflict
afligirse *v.* grieve
aflojar *v.* loosen, slacken

afluencia *n.* influx
aforismo *n.* aphorism
afortunado *adj.* lucky, fortunate
afrenta *n.* affront
africano *adj.* african
afuera *adv.* out
agacharse *v.* crouch
agarrar *v.t* grip, seize
ágata *n.* agate
agencia *n.* agency, bureau
agenciarse *v.* wangle
agenda *n.* agenda
agente *n.* agent
agente de policía *n.* constable
policía *n.* policeman
ágil *adj.* agile
agilidad *n.* agility
agitación *n.* agitation, upheaval
agitador *adj.* rumbustious
agitar *v.* agitate
aglomeración *n.* conglomeration
aglomerarse *v.* agglomerate
agnóstico *n.* agnostic
agonía *n.* agony
agonizar *v.* agonize
Agosto *n* August
agotador *adj.* demanding
agotar *v.* deplete, exhaust
agradable *adj.* pleasant, agreeable
agradecer *v.* thank
agradecido *n.* grateful
agradecido *adj.* thankful
agrandar *v.* enlarge
agrario *adj.* agrarian
agravación *n.* aggravation
agravar *v.* aggravate
agravio *n.* grievance
agregado *n.* attache
agresión *n.* aggression
agresivo *adj.* aggressive
agresor *n.* aggressor

agrícola *adj.* agricultural
agricultura *n.* agriculture
agrío *adj.* sour
agua *n.* water
aguacate *n.* avocado
aguacero *n.* downpour
aguafiestas *n.* spoiler
aguantar *v.t* bear, endure
agudo *adj.* acute
aguijonear *v.* goad
águila *n.* eagle
águila real *n.* golden eagle
aguileño *adj.* hooked
aguja *n.* needle
agujerear *v.* bore
agujero *n.* hole
ahí *adv.* there
ahijado *n.* godchild
ahogar *v.* drown
ahondar *v.* delve
ahora *adv.* now
ahorros *n.* savings
aire *n.* air
aislamiento *n.* insulation, isolation
aislante *n.* insulator
aislar *v.* insulate, isolate
ajedrez *n.* chess
ajenjo *n.* wormwood
ajeno al mundo *adj.* unworldly
ajetreado *adj.* hectic
ajo *n.* garlic
ajuar *n.* trousseau
ajustado *adj.* tight
ajustar *v.* adjust, tighten
al aire libre *adj.* outdoor
al dorso *adv.* overleaf
al lado de *prep.* beside
al mar, al agua *adv.* overboard
ala *n.* wing
alabar *v.* laud
alabardero *n.* yeoman

alabear *v.* warp
alambrado *n.* wiring
alambre *n.* wire
álamo *n.* poplar
alardear *v.* brag
alargar *v.* elongate
alarido *n.* yowl
alarma *n* alarm
albacea *n.* executor
albahaca *n.* basil
albañil *n.* mason
albañilería *n.* masonry
albaricoque *n.* apricot
alboroto *n.* turmoil, uproar
alborozado *adj.* mirthful
alborozo *n.* mirth
álbum *n* album
albúmina *n.* albumen
albumen *n.* albumen
alcachofa *n.* artichoke
alcalde *n.* mayor
álcali *n.* alkali
alcanfor *n.* camphor
alcantarilla *n.* sewer
alcantarillado *n.* sewage
alcanzar *v.* reach, overtake
alcohol *n.* alcohol
alcohólico *adj.* alchoholic
aldea *n.* hamlet
aldeano *n.* villager
aleatorio *adj.* random
aleccionar *v.* chasten
alegación *n.* allegation
alegoría *n.* allegory
alegrar *v.* gladden
alegre *adj.* cheerful, jolly,
alegremente *adv.* gaily
alegría *n.* joy
alejado *adj.* outlying
alemán *n.* German
alentador *adj.* heartening
alérgeno *n.* allergen

alergia *n.* allergy
alérgico *adj.* allergic
alerta *n.* alert
aleta *n.* fin
aletargado *adj.* torpid
alfa *n.* alpha
alfabético *adj.* alphabetical
alfabeto *n.* alphabet
alfarería *n.* pottery
alféizar *n.* sill
alfiler *n.* pin
alfombra *n.* rug
algebra *n.* algebra
algo *pron.* something
algo *adv.* somewhat
algo se esta tramando *adv.* afoot
algo *adj.* some
algo *pron.* anything
algodón *n.* cotton
alguacil *n.* bailiff
alguien *pron.* anyone
alguien *pron.* somebody, some-one
algún *adj.* any
alguna vez *adv.* ever
alhajas *n.* jewellery
aliado *adj.* allied
aliado *n.* ally
alianza *n.* alliance
alias *adv.* alias
alias *n.* alias
alicates *n.* pliers
aligerar *v.* lighten
alijo *n.* cache
alimentar *v.* feed
alimento *n.* nourishment
alimentos *n.* alimony
alineación *n.* alignment
alinear *v.* align
alistar *v.* enlist
aliteración *n.* alliteration
aliterar *v.* alliterate

aliviar *v.* alleviate, relieve
alivio *n.* relief
allí *adv.* there
alma *n.* soul
alma gemela *n.* soulmate
almacenaje *n.* storage
almanaque *n.* almanac
almendra *n.* almond
almidón *n.* starch
almirante *n.* admiral
almizcle *n.* musk
almohada *n.* pillow
almohadilla *n.* pad
almuerzo *n.* brunch
alocado *adj.* madcap
alojamiento *n.* accommodation, lodging
alondra *n.* lark
alpinismo *n.* mountaineering
alpino *adj.* alpine
alquiler *n.* rent, tenancy
alquimia *n.* alchemy
alquitrán *n.* tar
alquitranado *n.* tarpaulin
alrededor *adv.* around
alrededores *n.* surroundings
alta burguesía *n.* gentry
altanero *adj.* lordly
altar *n.* altar
altercado *n.* altercation
alternarse *v.* alternate
alternativo *adj.* alternative
alteza *n.* Highness
altitud *n.* altitude
alto *adj.* tall, high
alto (ruido) *adj.* loud
alto el fuego *n.* ceasefire
altruismo *n.* altruism
altura *n.* height
alucinar *v.* hallucinate
aludir *v.i.* allude
alumbrado *n.* lighting

aluminio *n.* aluminium
alumno *n.* pupil
alumno graduado *n.* alumnus
alusión *n.* allusion
ama de casa *n.* housewife
amable *adj.* nice
amablemente *adv.* kindly
amado *adj.* beloved
amado *n.* paramour
amalgama *n.* amalgam
amalgamación *n.* amalgamation
amalgamar *v.* amalgamate
amamantar *v.* suckle
amanecer *n.* dawn
amanerado *adj.* effete
amante *n.* lover
amañar *v.* rig
amargar *v.* embitter
amargo *adj.* bitter
amarillo *adj.* yellow
amarradero *n.* berth, moorings
amarraje *n.* wharfage
amarrar *v.t.* belay,tether, bind
amasar *v.* knead
amasijo *n.* hotchpotch
amatorio *adj.* amatory
amazonas *n.* amazon
ámbar *n.* amber
ambición *n.* ambition
ambicioso *adj.* ambitious
ambiental *adj.* ambient
ambigüedad *n.* ambiguity
ambiguo *adj.* ambiguous
ámbito *n.* scope, ambit
ambivalente *adj.* ambivalent
ambos *adj. & pron.* both
ambrosia *n.* ambrosia
ambulancia *n.* ambulance
amenaza *n.* menace, threat
amenazar *v.* threaten
amigo *n.* friend, pal
amigos *n.* kith

amilanar *v.* daunt
aminorar *v.* decelerate
amistoso *adj.* amicable
amnesia *n.* amnesia
amnistía *n.* amnesty
amonestar *v.* admonish
amontonar *v.* amass
amontonarse *v.* huddle
amor *n.* love
amoral *adj.* amoral
amorfo *adj.* amorphous
amoroso *adj.* amorous, lovable
amortiguar *v.* muffle
amotinado *adj.* mutinous
amovible *adj.* removable
amperio *n.* ampere
ampliar *v.* magnify
amplificación *n.* amplification
amplificador *n.* amplifier
amplificar *v.* amplify
amplio *adj.* ample, broad
amplitud *n.* amplitude
ampolla *n.* blister
amueblar *v.* furnish
amuleto *n.* amulet
anacardo *n.* cashew
anacronismo *n.* anachronism
anal *adj.* anal
anales *n.* annals
analfabetismo *n.* illiteracy
analfabeto *n.* illiterate
analgésico *n.* painkiller
análisis *n.* analysis
analista *n.* analyst
analítico *adj.* analytical
analizar *v.* analyse
analogía *n.* analogy
analógico *adj.* analogue
análogo *adj.* analogous
anarquía *n.* anarchy
anarquismo *n.* anarchism
anarquista *n.* anarchist

anatomía *n.* anatomy
anca *n.* haunch
ancestral *adj.* ancestral
ancestro *n.* ancestor
ancho *adj.* wide
anchura *n.* width
anciano *n.* elderly
ancipadamente *adv.* beforehand
ancla *n.* anchor
anclaje *n.* anchorage
andamio *n.* scaffolding
andar *v.* walk
andar a zancadas *v.* stride
andar con dificultad *v.* trudge
andrajo *n.* tatter
andrajoso *adj.* ragged
androide *n.* android
anécdota *n.* anecdote
anegado *adj.* sodden
anemia *n.* anaemia
anestesia *n.* anaesthesia
anestésica *adj.* anaesthetic
anexión *n.* annexation
anexo *n.* annex
anfibio *n.* amphibian
anfiteatro *n.* amphitheatre
anfitrión *n.* host
anfitriona *n.* hostess
angel *n.* angel
angina *n.* angina, tonsil
angular *adj.* angular
ángulo *n.* angle
angustia *n.* anguish, distress
anillo *n.* ring
animación *n.* animation
animado *adj.* animated, lively
animal *n.* animal
animar *v. t.* cheer, encourage
animosamente *adv.* gamely
animosidad *n.* animosity
animoso *adj.* mettlesome
aniquilación *n.* annihilation

aniquilar *v.* annihilate
anís *n.* aniseed
aniversario *n.* anniversary
ano *n.* anus
anochecer *n.* dusk
anodino *adj.* lifeless
ánodo *n.* anode
anomalía *n.* anomaly
anómalo *adj.* anomalous
anonadar *v.* boggle
anonimato *n.* anonymity
anónimo *adj.* anonymous
anorexia *n.* anorexia
anormal *adj.* abnormal
anotar *v.* annotate
anquilosar *v.* stultify
ansiado *adj.* agog
ansiar *v. t* crave
ansiedad *n.* anxiety
antagonismo *n.* antagonism
antagonista *n.* antagonist
antaño *n.* yore
Antártico *adj.* antarctic
ante *n.* suede
antebrazo *n.* forearm
antecedente *n.* antecedent
anteceder *v.* antedate
antena *n.* aerial, antenna
anteojeras *n.* blinkers
antepasado *n.* forefather
anterior *adj.* former, fore
anteriormente *adv.* formerly
antes *adv.* before
anti *n.* anti
antiácido *n.* antacid
antibiótico *n.* antibiotic
anticipación *n.* anticipation
anticipar *v.* anticipate
anticiparse *v.* pre-empt
anticipo *n.* retainer
anticoncepción *n.* contraception
anticonceptivo *n.* contraceptive

anticuado *adj.* antiquated
anticuario *n.* antiquarian
anticuerpo *n.* antibody
antídoto *n.* antidote
antigualla *n.* frump
antigüedad *n.* antique, antiquity
antiguo *adj.* ancient
antílope *n.* antelope
antinatural *adj.* unnatural
antioxidante *n.* antioxidant
antipatía *n.* antipathy
antiperspirante *n.* antiperspirant
antiséptico *adj.* antiseptic
antisocial *adj.* antisocial
antítesis *n.* antithesis
antología *n.* anthology, omnibus
antónimo *n.* antonym
ántrax *n.* anthrax
antropología *n.* anthropology
anual *adj.* annual
anual *adv.* yearly
anulación *n.* nullification
anular *v.* annul, nullify
anunciar *v.* advertise, announce
anuncio *n.* advertisement
anverso *n.* obverse
añadidura *n.* appendage
añadir *v.t.* add
añejo *adj.* stale
añil *n.* indigo
año *n.* year
añoranza *n.* yearning
añorar *v.* yearn
apaciguar *v.* pacify, appease
apagado *adj.* off
apagar *v.t.* extinguish
apalancamiento *n.* leverage
apalear *v.* thrash
aparador *n.* cupboard
aparato *n.* appliance, device, apparatus
aparecer *v.* appear, emerge

aparejar *v.* rig
aparejo *n.* rigging
aparente *adj.* apparent
aparentemente *adv.* outwardly
aparición *n.* appearance
apariencia *n.* guise
apartamento *n.* apartment
apartar *v.* avert
aparte *adv.* apart
apartheid *n.* apartheid
apasionado *adj.* passionate
apatía *n.* apathy
apátrida *adj.* stateless
apego *n.* attachment
apelar *v.i.* appeal
apellido *n.* surname
apenas *adv.* barely, hardly
apéndice *n.* appendix
apendicitis *n.* appendicitis
aperitivo *n.* appetizer
apertura *n.* opening
apestar *v.* stink
apestoso *adj.* noxious
apetito *n.* appetite
ápice *n* apex
apisonar *v.* tamp
aplacar *v.* placate, mollify
aplanar *v.t.* flatten
aplastante *adj.* shattering
aplastar *v.* smash, squash
aplaudir *v.* applaud, clap
aplauso *n.* applause
aplausos *n.* plaudits
aplazamiento *n.* postponement
aplazar *v.* postpone
aplazar cosas *v.* procrastinate
aplicable *adj.* applicable
aplicación *n.* application
aplomo *n.* aplomb
apocalipsis *n.* apocalypse
apoderado *n.* proxy
apodo *n.* nickname

apogeo *n.* acme, heyday
apoplético *adj.* apoplectic
aporrear *v.* pummel
aportación *n.* input
apósito *n.* dressing
apostar *v.* bet, gamble
apóstata *n.* apostate
apóstol *n.* apostle
apostrofe *n.* apostrophe
apoyar *v.* support
apoyo *n.* support, backing
apreciación *n.* appreciation
apreciar *v.* appreciate
aprender *v.* learn
aprendiz *n.* apprentice, trainee
aprensión *n.* apprehension
aprensivo *adj.* apprehensive
apresurado *adj.* hasty
apresurar *v.* quicken, rush
apresurarse *v.* hurry
apretar *v.* press, squeeze
apretón manos *n.* handshake
aprieto *n.* predicament
aprobación *n.* approval
aprobar *v.* approve, endorse
apropiación *n.* appropriation
apropiado *adj.* appropriate
aprovechar *v.* avail
aproximado *adj.* approximate
aptitud *n.* aptitude
apuesta *n.* wager
apostar *v.* wager
apuntador *n.* prompter
apuntar *v.t.* aim
aquejar *v.* ail
aquellos *pro.* yonder
aquí *adv.* here
Árabe *n.* Arab
Arábico *n.* Arabic
Arábigo *n.* Arabian
arado *n.* plough
arador *n.* ploughman

araña *n.* spider
araña de luces *n.* chandelier
arbitraje *n.* arbitration
arbitrar *v.* arbitrate
arbitrario *adj.* arbitrary
árbitro *n.* referee, umpire
árbol *n.* tree
árbol nuevo *n.* sapling
arbolado *adj.* wooded
arbusto *n.* bush, shrub
arca *n.* ark, chest
arcada *n.* arcade
arcaico *adj.* archaic
arcángel *n.* archangel
arce *n.* maple
archivos *n.* archives
arcilla *n.* clay
arco *n.* arc, arch
arco iris *n.* rainbow
arder *v.* burn
arder sin llama *v.* smoulder
ardid *n.* ruse
ardiente *adj.* ardent, fervent
ardilla *n.* squirrel
ardor *n.* ardour
ardor de estomago *n.* heartburn
área *n.* area
área de juego *n.* playground
arena *n.* sand
arenoso *adj.* sandy
arenque *n.* herring
argot *n.* slang
argucia *n.* chicanery
argumentativo *adj.* argumentative
argumento *n.* argument
árido *adj.* arid, barren
aristocracia *n.* aristocracy
aristócrata *n.* aristocrat
aritmética *n.* arithmetic
aritmético *adj.* arithmetical
arlequín *n.* harlequin

arma *n.* weapon
arma de fuego *n.* gun
armada *n.* armada
armadura *n.* armour
Armagedón *n.* Armageddon
armamento *n.* armament
armario *n.* closet, wardrobe
armazón *n.* carcass
armería *n.* armoury
armisticio *n.* armistice
armonía *n.* harmony
armonioso *adj.* harmonious
armonizar *v.* harmonize
arnés *n.* harness
aro *n.* hoop
aroma *n.* aroma
aromaterapia *n.* aromatherapy
arpa *n.* harp
arpía *n.* harpy
arquear *v.* bow
arqueología *n.* archaeology
arquero *n.* archer
arquilla *n.* cist
arquitecto *n.* architect
arquitectura *n.* architecture
arraigado *adj.* ingrained, rooted
arrancar *v.* wrest
arranque *n.* outburst
arrasar *v.* raze
arrastrar *v. t* drag, crawl
arrastrar los pies *v.* shamble
arrebatar *v.* snatch
arrebato *n.* outburst
arrecife *n.* reef
arreglado *adj.* neat
arreglar *v.* arrange, trim, mend
arreglo *n.* arrangement
arremeter contra *v.* lambast
arremetida *n.* lunge
arremolinarse *v.* swirl
arrendador *n.* lessor
arrendajo *n.* jay

arrendatario *n.* lessee
arrepentido *adj.* repentant, roeful
arrepentimiento *n.* repentance
arrepentirse *v.* repent, rue
arrestar *v.* arrest
arriba *adv.* above, up
arriesgado *adj.* risky
arriesgar *v.* imperil
arrimarse *v.* snuggle
arrodillarse *v.* kneel
arrogancia *n.* arrogance
arrogante *adj.* arrogant
arrojar *v.* throw, fling
arroyo *n.* brook
arroyo pequeño *n.* runnel
arroyuelo *n.* streamlet
arroz *n.* rice
arruga *n.* wrinkle, crease
arsenal *n.* arsenal
arsénico *n.* arsenic
arte *n.* art
artefacto *n.* artefact
arteria *n.* artery
artesanía *n.* handicraft
artesano *n.* artisan
Ártico *n.* Arctic
articulado *adj.* articulate
artículo *n.* article, item
artículo de aseo *n.* toiletries
artificial *adj.* artificial
artificio *n.* artifice
artillería *n.* artillery
artilugio *n.* gadget
artista *n.* artist, performer
artista de striptease *n.* stripper
artístico *adj.* artistic
artritis *n.* arthritis
arzobispo *n.* archbishop
as *n.* ace
asador *n.* carvery
asalto *n.* assault
asamblea *n.* assembly

asar a la parrilla *v.* grill
asar *v.* roast
asbesto *n.* asbestos
ascendente *adj.* ascendant
ascender *v.* ascend, promote
ascenso *n.* ascent
ascensor *n.* elevator
ascético *adj.* ascetic
asco *n.* revulsion
asediado *adj.* beleaguered
asediar *v.* beset
asegurar *v.* ensure
asentamiento *n.* settlement
asentimiento *n.* assent
asentir con la cabeza *v.* nod
aseo *n.* toilet
aséptico *adj.* aseptic
asequible *adj.* obtainable
asesinar *v.* assassinate
asesinato *n.* murder, assassination, killing
asesino *n.* murderer, assassin
asesor *n.* consultant
asexuado *adj.* neuter
asexual *adj.* asexual
asfixia *n.* suffocation
asfixiar *v.* asphyxiate, suffocate
así *adv.* thus
asir *v.* grasp
asiático *adj.* Asian
asiduo *adj.* assiduous
asiduo *n.* habitue
asiento *n.* seat
asientos *n.* seating
asignación *n.* assignation
asignar *v.* assign, allot
asilamiento *n.* lagging
asilo *n.* asylum
asimilación *n.* assimilation
asimilar *v.* assimilate
asimismo *adv.* likewise
asistencia *n.* assistance, attendance

asistente *n.* assistant
asistir *v.* assist
asma *n.* asthma
asno *n.* ass
asociación *n.* association, partner-ship
asociarse *v.* associate
asombrar *v.* amaze, astonish
asombro *n.* amazement, astonish-ment, awe
asombroso *adj.* staggering, wondrous
asonancia *n.* assonance
aspecto *n.* aspect
aspereza *n.* asperity
áspero *adj.* rough
aspersor *n.* sprinkler
aspiración *n.* aspiration
aspiradora *n.* hoover
aspirante *n.* candidate
aspirante *adj.* candidate
aspirar *v.* aspire
asquear *v.* nauseate
asqueroso *adj.* disgusting, filthy
asterisco *n.* asterisk
asteroide *n.* asteroid
astigmatismo *n.* astigmatism
astil *n.* shaft
astilla *n.* splinter
astillero *n.* shipyard
astral *adj.* astral
astringente *adj.* styptic
astrológica *n.* astrology
astrologo *n.* astrologer
astronauta *n.* astronaut
astronomía *n.* astronomy
astrónomo *n.* astronomer
astucia *n.* guile
astuto *adj.* astute, canny, sly
asumir *v.* assume
asunto *v.* concern
asustar *v* frighten, scare

atacar *v.* attack, assail
atado *adj.* tied
atajo *n.* shortcut
ataque *n.* seizure
atar *v.* tie, attach, bind
ataúd *n.* coffin
atávico *adj.* atavistic
atavío *n.* apparel
ateísmo *n.* atheism
atención *n.* attention
atender *v.* attend
atento *adj.* attentive
atenuante *n.* mitigation
atenuar *v.* lessen
ateo *n.* atheist
aterciopelado *adj.* velvety
aterrador *adj.* scary
aterrizaje *n.* landing
aterrorizar *v.* terrify, terrorize
atestiguar *v.* attest
ático *n.* attic, penthouse
atigrado *adj.* brindle
atildado *adj.* dapper
atisbo *n.* inkling
atizador *n.* poker
atlas *n.* atlas
atleta *n.* athlete
atlético *adj.* athletic
atmosfera *n.* atmosphere
atolón *n.* atoll
atómico *adj.* atomic
átomo *n.* atom
atontado *adj.* woozy
atormentado *adj.* haunted
atormentar *v.* tantalize
atracción *n.* attraction
atractivo *adj.* attractive
atraer *v.* attract, lure
atrapar *v. t.* entrap
atrasado *adj.* backward
atrasos *n.* arrears, backlog
atravesado *adj.* cantankerous

atravesar *v.* traverse
atrayente *adj.* inviting
atreverse *v.* dare
atrevido *adj.* bold, cheeky
atrevimiento *n.* boldness
atribuir *v.t.* attribute, ascribe
atrio *n.* atrium
atrocidad *n.* atrocity, outrage
atrofiar *v.* stunt
atronador *adj.* thunderous
atronar *v.* blare
atroz *adj.* atrocious
atuendo *n.* attire
aturdido *adj.* addled
aturdir *v.* daze, stun
audible *adj.* audible
audición *n.* audition
audiencia *n.* audience
audio *n.* audio
auditoría *n.* audit
auditorio *n.* auditorium
auge *n.* upturn
augurio *n.* portent
aullador *n.* howler
aullar *v.* yap
aullido *n.* howl, yelp
aumentar *v.t.* increase
aumento *n.* increase, rise
aunque *conj.* although, though
aura *n.* aura
auricular *n.* headphone
ausencia *n.* absence
ausente *adj.* absent
ausente *n.* absentee
austero *adj.* austere
Australiano *n.* Australian
autenticidad *n.* authenticity
autentico *adj.* authentic
autismo *n.* autism
autobiografía *n.* autobiography
autobús *n.* bus
autocar *n.* coach

autocracia *n.* autocracy
autócrata *n.* autocrat
autocrático *adj.* autocratic
autógrafo *n.* autograph
automático *adj.* automatic
automóvil *n.* automobile
automovilista *n.* motorist
autónomo *adj.* autonomous
autopista *n.* highway, motorway
autopsia *n.* autopsy
autor *n.* author
autoridad *n.* authority
autoritario *adj.* authoritative
autorización *n.* clearance
autorizar *v.* authorize
auxiliar *adj.* auxiliary
avalancha *n.* avalanche, spate
avance *n.* advance
avanzada *n.* outpost
avanzar *v.* advance
avaricia *n.* avarice
avaricioso *adj.* greedy
avaro *adj.* miser
avasallador *adj.* pushy
ave *n.* fowl
ave zancuda *n.* wader
avena *n.* oat
avenida *n.* avenue
aventajado *adj.* advantageous
aventajar *v.t.* advantage
aventar *v.* winnow
aventura *n.* adventure, affair
aventurero *adj.* adventurous
avergonzado *adj.* ashamed
aversión *n.* aversion
aves de corral *n.* poultry
avestruz *n.* ostrich
aviación *n.* aviation
aviador *n.* aviator
aviario *n.* aviary
ávidamente *adv.* avidly
ávido *adj.* avid, raring

avión *n.* plane, aeroplane
avisar *v.* warn, acquaint
aviso *n.* warning, notice
avispa *n.* wasp
avispón *n.* hornet
avivar el fuego *v.* stoke
axila *adj.* underarm
ayer *adv.* yesterday
ayuda *n.* aid
ayuda de cámara *n.* valet
ayudar *v.* help
azafrán *n.* saffron
azotar *v.* lash, flog, pelt
azote *n.* scourge
azúcar *n.* sugar
azucarado *adj.* saccharine
azufre *n.* sulphur
azul *adj.* blue
azul verdoso *n.* cyan
azulejo *n.* tile

B

baba *n.* spittle
babear *v.* slobber
babel *n.* babel
babero *n.* bib
babosa *n.* slug
bacón *n.* bacon
bacteria *n.* bacteria
bádminton *n.* badminton
bafle *n.* woofer
bahía *n.* bay
bailar *v.* dance
bailarín *n.* dancer
bajar *v.* come down
bajo *adj.* low
bala *n.* bullet
balada *n.* ballad

balancearse *v.* teeter, waddle
balancín *n.* see-saw
balandrismo *n.* yachting
balandrista *n.* yatchsman
balar *v. i* bleat
balbucear *v.* splutter
balcón *n.* balcony
balde *n.* pail
ballena *n.* whale
ballenero *n.* whaler
ballet *n.* ballet
balneario *n.* spa
balsa *n.* raft
bálsamo *n.* balm, balsam
baluarte *n.* bastion
bambú *n.* bamboo
banal *adj.* banal
banal *n.* whimsy
bancarrota *n.* bankruptcy
banco *n.* bank
banco (de asiento) *n.* bench
banda *n.* troop, band
bandazo *n.* lurch
bandeja *n.* tray
bandera *n.* flag
bandido *n.* bandit
banjo *n.* banjo
banquero *n.* banker
banquete *n.* banquet, feast
bañarse *v.* bathe
baño *n.* bath, loo
bar *n.* bar
barahúnda *n.* hubbub
barajar *v.* shuffle
barandilla *n.* rail
barato *adj.* cheap
barba *n.* beard
barba de pocos días *n.* stubble
barbacoa *n.* barbecue
bárbaro *n.* barbarian
bárbaro *adj.* barbaric
barbecho *adj.* fallow

barbero *n.* barber
barbilla *n.* chin
barbullar *v.* babble
barcaza *n.* barge
barco *n.* boat, ship
barco de vapor *n.* steamer
barco rastreador *n.* trawler
barco viejo *n.* hulk
bardo *n.* bard
barniz *n.* varnish
barómetro *n.* barometer
barón *n.* baron
barquillo *n.* wafer
barra de pan *n.* baguette
barracuda *n.* barracuda
barranco *n.* gully, ravine
barredor *n.* sweeper
barrer *v.* sweep
barrera *n.* barrier
barricada *n.* barricade
barril *n.* cask, barrel, keg
barro *n.* mud
barullo *n.* din
báscula *n.* scale
base *n.* base, basis
base de datos *n.* database
básico *n.* basic
basílica *n.* basilica
bastante *adv.* quite
bastardo *adj.* bastard
bastidor *n.* pelmet
basura *n.* garbage, litter, rubbish, trash, junk
basurero *n.* dump
bata *n.* robe
batalla *n.* battle
batallón *n.* battalion
bateador *n.* batter
batido *n.* milkshake
batik *n.* batik
batir *v.* whisk
batista *n.* cambric

batuta *n.* baton
bautismo *n.* baptism
bautista *n.* baptist
bautizar *v.* baptize
baya *n.* berry
bayoneta *n.* bayonet
bazar *n.* bazaar
bazo *n.* spleen
bazuca *n.* bazooka
Beagle *n.* beagle
beatitud *n.* beatitude
beato *adj.* sanctimonious
bebe *n.* baby
beber *v. t* drink
bebida de frutas *n.* smoothie
beca *n.* scholarship
becerro *n.* calf
becerro de oro *n.* mammon
beis *n.* beige
bélico *adj.* warlike
belicoso *adj.* bellicose
beligerante *adj.* belligerent
bellaco *n.* cad, miscreant
belleza *n.* beauty
bellota *n.* acorn
bendecido *adj.* blessed
bendecir *v.* bless
bendición *n.* blessing
benefactor *n.* benefactor
beneficiado *adj.* incumbent
beneficiario *n.* payee
beneficio *n.* benefit
beneficioso *adj.* beneficial, profitable
benéfico *adj.* beneficent
benevolencia *n.* benevolence
benévolo *adj* benevolent
bengala *n.* flare
benigno *adj.* benign
berenjena *n.* aubergine
bergamota *n.* bergamot
bermellón *n.* vermillion

besar *v.t.* kiss
bestia *n.* beast
bestial *adj.* beastly
besuquearse *v.* smooch
bi- *comb.* bi
biblia *n.* Bible
bibliófilo *n.* bibliophile
bibliografía *n.* bibliography
biblioteca *n.* library
bibliotecario *n.* librarian
bicentenario *n.* bicentenary
bíceps *n.* biceps
bicho *n.* bug
bichos *n.* vermin
bicicleta *n.* bicycle
bidé *n.* bidet
bidón *n.* jerrycan
bien *adv.* well
bien formado *adj.* shapely
bien *n.* sake
bienal *adj.* biennial
bienestar *n.* welfare
bienvenida *n.* welcome
bifocal *adj.* bifocal
bigamia *n.* bigamy
bígaro *n.* winkle
bigote *n.* moustache
bigotes *n.* whisker
bikini *n.* bikini
bilateral *adj.* bilateral
bilingüe *adj.* bilingual
bilis *n.* bile
billar *n.* billiards
billete *n.* ticket
billón *n.* billion
binario *adj.* binary
binocular *adj.* binocular
biodegradable *adj.* biodegradable
biodiversidad *n.* biodiversity
biografía *n.* biography
biología *n.* biology
biólogo *n.* biologist

biopsia *n.* biopsy
bioquímica *n.* biochemistry
biplaza descapotable *n.* roadster
bis *n.* encore
bisagra *n.* hinge
bisecar *v.* bisect
bisel *n.* bevel
bisexual *adj.* bisexual
bisonte *n.* bison
bit *n.* bit
bizcocho tostado *n.* rusk
bizquear *v.* squint
blanca *n.* minim
blanco *n.* target
blanco *adj.* white
blandir *v.* brandish
blanquear *v.t.* bleach
blog *n.* blog
bloque *n.* bloc, block
bloqueo *n.* blockade
blusa *n.* blouse
boca *n.* mouth
boca de incendios *n.* hydrant
bocado *n.* mouthful
bocanada *n.* whiff
bochornoso *adj.* clammy, muggy
bocina *n.* hoot
bocinazo *n.* honk
boda *n.* wedding
bodega *n.* winery
boicotear *v.* boycott
bol *n.* bowl
bola de navidad *n.* bauble
bola de nieve *n.* snowball
bolardo *n.* bollard
boletín *n.* bulletin
bolígrafo *n.* pen
bolita *n.* pellet
bollo *n.* bun
bolo *n.* skittle
bolsa *n.* satchel
bolsa de viaje *n.* holdall

bolsillo *n.* pocket, wallet
bolsita *n.* sachet
bolso *n.* handbag
bomba *n.* bomb, pump
bombachos *n.* bloomers
bombardear *v.* bombard
bombardeo *n.* bombardment
bombardeo aéreo *n.* blitz
bombardero *n.* bomber
bombo publicitario *n.* hype
bombo y platillo *n.* hoopla
bonanza *n.* bonanza
bondad *n.* goodness
bondadoso *adj.* kind
bonita *adj.* pretty
bonito *n.* prettiness
bonito *adj.* lovely
boom *n.* boom
borbotear *v.* burble
bordado *n.* embroidery
borde *n.* brink, rim, verge
bordillo *n.* kerb
borla *n.* tassel
borrachera *n.* wassail
borracho *adj.* drunk
borrador *n.* draft
borrar *v.* erase, obliterate
borrón *n.* blot
borroso *adj.* muzzy
bosque *n.* forest, woodland
bostezar *v.* yawn
bota *n.* boot
bota de agua *n.* wellington
botánica *n.* botany
bote *n.* can
botella *n.* bottle
botín *n.* booty, loot, swag
botón *n.* button
botón de trenca *n.* toggle
boutique *n.* boutique
bóveda *n.* vault
boxeador *n.* boxer

boxeo *n* boxing
boya *n.* buoy
bozal *n.* muzzle
bragas *n.* knickers, panties
braille *n.* braille
bramante *n.* twine
bramar *v.* bellow
brandy *n.* brandy
bravuconear *v.* bluster
braza *n.* fathom
brazalete *n.* bangle
brazo *n.* arm
brequero *n.* truss
breve *adj.* brief
brevedad *n.* brevity
brevemente *adv.* shortly
brezal *n.* heath
brezo *n.* heather
brida *n.* bridle
brigada *n.* brigade
brigadier *n.* brigadier
brillante *adj.* bright, brilliant, shiny
brillantez *n.* brilliance
brillar *v.* glow, shine
brillar con luz tenue *v.* glimmer
brillo *n.* sheen, gloss
brincar *v.* hop
brinço *n.* hop
brío *n.* verve
brisa *n.* breeze
británico *adj.* British
brocado *n.* brocade
brocheta *n.* skewer
brócoli *n.* broccoli
broma *n.* jest
bromas *n.* banter
bromear *v.* tease
bromista *n.* joker
bronca *n.* row
bronce *n.* bronze
bronceado *n.* tan

bronquial *adj.* bronchial
brotar *v.* sprout, spring
brote *n.* bud
bruja *n.* witch, hag
brujería *n.* witchcraft, witchery
brújula *n.* compass
brumoso *adj.* hazy
brusco *adj.* abrupt, brusque
brutal *adj.* brutal
bruto *adj.* brute, rough,
buen ánimo *n.* fettle
buen gusto *adj.* tasteful
buena voluntad *n.* goodwill, willingness
bueno *adj.* good, fine, okay
buey *n.* bullock, ox
búfalo *n.* buffalo
bufanda *n.* scarf
buffet *n.* buffet
bufido *n.* snort
bufón *n.* buffoon, jester
bufonerías *n.* antic
buhardilla *n.* garret, loft
búho *n.* owl
buhonero *n.* pedlar
buitre *n.* vulture
bulbo *n.* bulb
bulevar *n.* boulevard
bulimia *n.* bulimia
bulla *n.* fuss
bulldog *n.* bulldog
bullicioso *adj.* boisterous
bullir *v.* bustle
bulo *n.* canard
bulto *n.* bulge, lump
bungalow *n.* bungalow
búnker *n.* bunker
buque cisterna *n.* tanker
burbujear *v.* fizz
burdel *n.* brothel
burla *v.* jeer
burla *n.* jibe, mockery

burlar *v.* mock, outwit
burlarse *v.* gibe
burlón *adj.* quizzical
burocracia *n.* bureaucracy
burócrata *n.* bureaucrat
burro *n.* donkey
buscar *v.t.* seek, search
buscar a tientas *v.* grope
búsqueda *n.* quest
busto *n.* bust
buzón *n.* letter box
byte *n.* byte

C

cabalgar *v.* bestride
cabalgata *n.* cavalcade
caballería *n.* cavalry, knighthood
caballerizas *n.* mews
caballero *n.* gentleman, knight
caballerosidad *n.* chivalry
caballete *n.* trestle
caballo *n.* horse
caballo (potencia) *n.* horsepower
cabaña *n.* hut
cabaret *n.* cabaret
cabellera *n.* scalp
cabestrillo *n.* sling
cabestro *n.* halter
cabeza *n.* head
cabeza de turco *n.* scapegoat
cabezada *n.* snooze
cabina de mando *n.* cockpit
cabina *n.* booth
cable *n.* cable
cabo *n.* corporal
cabra *n.* goat
cabrestante *n.* capstan
cabriolar *v.* cavort

cacahuete *n.* peanut
cacao *n.* cocoa
cacareo *n.* cackle
cacerola *n.* pan
cachear *v.* frisk
cachemir *n.* cashmere
cachorro *n.* puppy, cub, whelp
cacique *n.* chieftain
cactus *n.* cactus
cada uno *adj.* each
cadalso *n.* scaffold
cadáver *n.* cadaver, corpse
cadena *n.* chain, range
cadena tobillo *n.* anklet
cadera *n.* hip
cadete *n.* cadet
cadmio *n.* cadmium
caducar *v.* expire
caduco *adj.* defunct
caer *v.* fall, drop
caer en picado *v.* plummet
café *n.* coffee, cafe
café con leche *n.* latte
cafetería *n.* cafeteria
caftán *n.* kaftan
caimán *n.* alligator
caja *n.* box
caja de cambios *n.* gear
caja fuerte *n.* safe
cajero *n.* cashier, teller
cajista *n.* compositor, typesetter
cajón *n.* drawer
cal *n.* whitewash
cala *n.* cove, creek
calabaza *n.* pumpkin
calambre *n.* cramp
calamidad *n.* calamity
calarse *v.* swoop
calcetería *n.* hosiery
calcetín *n.* sock
calcio *n.* calcium
calco *n.* tracing

calculadora *n.* calculator
calcular *v. t* calculate
calcular mal *v.* miscalculate,
  misjudge
cálculo *n.* calculation
caldera *n.* boiler
caldero *n.* cauldron
caldo *n.* broth
calefacción *n.* heating
calendario *n.* calendar
caléndula *n.* marigold
calentador *n.* heater
calentar *v.* mull
calesa oriental *n.* rickshaw
calesa *n.* buggy
calibrar *v.* calibrate
calibre *n.* calibre
calidad *n.* quality
calidoscopio *n.* kaleidoscope
caliente *adj.* hot, warm
calificación *n.* qualification
calificar *v.* qualify
caligrafía *n.* calligraphy
cáliz *n.* chalice
callado *adj.* quiet
calle *n.* street
callejuela *n.* alley
calmado *adj.* calm
calmar *v.* calm, quell
calor *n.* heat, warmth
caloría *n.* calorie
calumnia *n.* calumny, slander
calumniar *v.* slur
calvo *adj.* bald
calzada *n.* causeway
calzo *n.* underlay
calzoncillos *n.* underpants
cama *n.* bed
cámara *n.* camera, chamber
camarada *n.* comrade
camaradería *n.* camaraderie
camarera *n.* waitress

camarero *n.* waiter
camarote *n.* cabin
cambiar *v.* change, shift
camello *n.* camel
cameo *n.* cameo
camilla *n.* stretcher
caminar lentamente *v.* plod
caminata *n.* trek
camino *n.* lane
camión *n.* lorry, truck
camionero *n.* trucker
camisa *n.* shirt
camiseta *n.* singlet
camisón *n.* nightie
campamento *n.* camp
campana *n.* bell
campaña *n.* campaign
campeón *n.* champion
campesino *n.* peasant
campo *n.* field
campus *n.* campus
canal *n.* channel, canal
canalla *n.* scoundrel
canalón *n.* gutter
cancelación *n.* cancellation
cancelar *v.* cancel
cáncer *n.* cancer
canciller *n.* chancellor
cancillería *n.* Chancery
canción *n.* song
canción de cuna *n.* lullaby
candado *n.* padlock
candela *n.* candela
candidato *n.* candidate, nominee, applicant
canela *n.* cinnamon
cangrejo *n.* crab
canguro *n.* kangaroo
caníbal *n.* cannibal
canino *adj.* canine
cannabis *n.* cannabis
canoa *n.* canoe

canon *n.* canon
cansado *adj.* tired
cansar *v.* tire
cantante *adj.* singer
cantar *v.* sing
cantera *n.* quarry
cantidad *n.* amount, quantity
cantina *n.* canteen
canto *n.* chant
cantón *n.* canton
cánula *n.* nozzle
caña *n.* cane
caña del timón *n.* tiller
cañón *n.* cannon, canyon
caoba *n.* mahogany
caos *n.* chaos
caótico *adj.* chaotic
capa *n.* cape, cloak, layer, coating
capacidad *n.* capacity, capability
capacitar *v.* qualify
capataz *n.* foreman
capaz *adj.* able, capable
capellán *n.* chaplain
capilla *n.* chapel
capital *n.* capital
capitalismo *n.* capitalism
capitalista *n. &adj.* capitalist
capitalizar *v.* capitalize
capitán *n.* captain, skipper
capitanía *n.* captaincy
capitulación *n.* capitation
capitular *v.* capitulate
capítulo *n.* chapter
capota *n.* bonnet
capricho *n.* caprice, fancy
caprichoso *adj.* capricious, whimsical
capsula *n.* capsule
captor *n.* captor
capturar *v.* capture
capucha *n.* hood
capullo *n.* cocoon

cara *n.* face
caracol *n.* snail
carácter *n.* personality, character
característica *n.* characteristic, feature
caradura *adj.* cheeky
carámbano *n.* icicle
caramelo *n.* caramel, toffee
caravana *n.* caravan
carbohidrato *n.* carbohydrate
carbón *n.* coal
carbón de leña *n.* charcoal
carbonatado *adj.* carbonated
carbonizar *v.* char
carbono *n.* carbon
carcajada *n.* guffaw
carcasa *n.* carcass
cárcel *n.* jail
carcelero *n.* jailer
cardamomo *n.* cardamom
cardenal *n.* cardinal, bruise
cardíaco *adj.* cardiac
cardiógrafo *n.* cardiograph
cardiología *n.* cardiology
cardo *n.* thistle
carenado *n.* fairing
carencia *n.* lack
carga *n.* burden, freight, pack, load
cargado *adj.* laden
cargador *n.* charger
cargamento *n.* cargo
cargar *v.* upload
carguero *n.* freighter
caricatura *n* caricature
caridad *n.* charity
cariño *n.* sweetheart
cariñoso *adj.* fond
carisma *n.* charisma
carismático *adj.* charismatic
caritativo *adj.* charitable
carmesí *n.* crimson

carmín *n.* carmine
carnal *adj.* carnal
carnaval *n.* carnival
carne *n.* meat, flesh
carne de ovino *n.* mutton
carnero *n.* ram
carnicería *n.* butchery
carnicero *n.* butcher
carnívoro *n.* carnivore
caro *adj.* expensive
carpeta *n.* file
carpiano *adj.* carpal
carpintería *n.* carpentry
carpintero *n.* carpenter
carrera *n.* career, run
carrera *n.* race
carreta *n.* cart
carrete *n.* reel, spool
carretera *n.* road
carril *n.* rut
carrito *n.* caddy
carrizo *n.* trolley, wren
carro de guerra *n.* chariot
carruaje *n.* carriage
carta *n.* letter
carta de navegación *n.* chart
cartel *n.* cartel
cartero *n.* postman
cartílago *n.* cartilage
cartón *n.* cardboard
cartucho *n.* cartridge
casa *n.* house
casa del guarda *n.* lodge
casadero *adj.* marriageable
casamentera *adj.* matchmaker
casanova *adj.* casanova
casar *v.* marry, wed
cascabeleo *n.* jingle
cascada *n.* waterfall
cáscara *n.* husk
casco *n.* helmet
casera *n.* landlady

casero *n.* landlord
casi *adv.* almost, nearly
casillero *n.* pigeonhole
casino *n.* casino
casita de campo *n.* cottage
caso *n.* case
caspa *n.* dandruff
casta *n.* caste
castaña *n.* chestnut
castidad *n.* chastity
castigar *v.* punish, castigate
castigo *n.* punishment
castillo *n.* castle
castillo en francés *n.* chateau
casto *adj.* chaste
castor *n.* beaver
castrar *v.* castrate, emasculate,
  geld
casualidad *n.* casualty
cataclismo *n.* cataclysm
catalítico *adj.* catalyst
catalizar *v.* catalyse
catalogo *n.* catalogue
catarata *n.* cataract
catarsis *n.* catharsis
catástrofe *n.* catastrophe
catedral *n.* cathedral, minster
categoría *n.* category
categórico *adj.* categorical
catequesis *n.* catechism
católico *adj.* catholic
catorce *adj.& n.* fourteen
caucásico *adj.* caucasian
caucho *n.* rubber
causa *n.* cause, sake
causal *adj.* causal
causar *v.* inflict
cáustico *adj.* caustic
cautela *n.* caution
cautelosamente *adv.* gingerly
cauteloso *adj.* guarded, stealthy,
  wary

cautivador *adj.* luscious
cautivar *v.* captivate, enchant,
  enrapture
cautiverio *n.* bondage
cautividad *n.* captivity
cautivo *n.* captive
cauto *adj.* cautious
cavar *v.* dig
caverna *n.* cavern
cavernoso *adj.* cavernous
cavidad *n.* cavity
cavilar *v.* cogitate
caza de ballenas *n.* whaling
cazador *n.* hunter
cazar *v.* hunt
cazar furtivamente *v.* poach
cazuela *n.* casserole
cebada *n.* barley
cebo *n.* bait
cebolla *n.* onion
cebra *n.* zebra
ceceo *n.* lisp
ceder *v.* cede, relent
cedro *n.* cedar
céfiro *n.* zephyr
cegato *adj.* purblind
ceguera *n.* blindness
ceja *n.* brow
celda *n.* cell
celebración *n.* celebration
celebrante *n.* celebrant
celebrar *v.* celebrate
celebridad *n.* celebrity
celestial *adj.* heavenly
celestina *adj.* matchmaker
celibato *n.* celibacy
célibe *adj.* celibate
celidonia *n.* celandine
celta *adj.* Celtic
celular *adj.* cellular
celulitis *n.* cellulite
celuloide *n.* celluloid

celulosa *n.* cellulose
cementerio *n.* cemetery
cemento *n.* cement
cena *n.* dinner, supper
cenador *n.* arbour, gazebo
cenagal *n.* slough
cenar *v.* dine
cenefa *n.* valance
cénit *n.* zenith
ceniza *n.* ash
censor *n.* censor, census
censura *n.* censorship
censurado *adj.* censorious
censurar *v.* censure
centelleo *v.* twinkle
centenario *n.* centenary
centeno *n.* rye
centígrado *n.* centigrade
centígrados *n.* celsius
centímetro *n.* centimetre
céntimo *n.* cent
centinela *n.* sentinel, sentry
central *adj.* central
centralizar *v.* centralize
centro *n.* center, centre
centro comercial *n.* mall
centro de atención *n.* limelight
centro de turismo *n.* resort
centro núcleo *n.* core
ceñir *v.* wreathe
ceño *n.* scowl
cepillo *n.* brush
cera *n.* wax
cerámica *n.* ceramic, pottery
cerca *n.* fence
cerca *adv.* near, nigh
cercano *adv.* nearby
cercano *adj.* close
cercar *v.* surround
cerco *n.* siege
cerda *n.* bristle, sow
cerdo *n.* pig, pork, swine

cereal *n.* cereal
cerebral *adj.* cerebral
cerebro *n.* brain
ceremonia *n.* ceremony
ceremonial *adj.* ceremonial
ceremonioso *adj.* ceremonious
cerilla *n.* match
cero *n.* nought
cero *adj.* zero
cerrado *adj.* insular
cerrar *v.* shut
cerrar de golpe *v.* slam
cerrojo *n.* lock
certidumbre *n.* certitude
certificado *n.* certificate
certificar *v.* certify
cerveza *n.* beer, ale
cerveza rubia *n.* lager
cervical *adj.* cervical
cesar *v.* cease
cesárea *n.* caeserean
cese *n.* cessation
cesión *n.* cession
césped *n.* lawn
cesta *n.* basket
cesto *n.* hamper, trug
cetrino *adj.* sallow
cetro *n.* sceptre
chabola *n.* shanty
chacal *n.* jackal
chal *n.* shawl
chaleco *n.* waistcoat, vest
chalet *n.* villa, chalet
chambelán *n.* chamberlain
champan *n.* champagne
champiñón *n.* mushroom
champú *n.* shampoo
chamuscar *v.* scorch, char
chándal *n.* tracksuit
chantaje *n.* blackmail
chapa *n.* badge, ply
chaparrón *n.* downpour

chapitel *n.* spire
chapotear *v.* splash, dabble
chaqueta *n.* jacket, blazer
chaqueta sin mangas *n.* jerkin
charca *n.* pool
charco *n.* puddle
charlar *v. i.* chat
charlar *v.* chatter
charlatán *n.* charlatan
charlatanismo *n.* quackery
chasis *n.* chasis
chasquear *v.* snap
chasquido *n.* click, snapper
chatarra *n.* banger, junk
chef *n.* chef
cheque *n.* cheque
chic *adj.* chic
chica *n.* lass
chica de bandera *n.* stunner
chichón *n.* bump
chicle *n.* gum
chico *n.* lad
chiflado *adj.* nutty, wacky
chillar *v.* bawl, shriek
chillido *n.* whoop
chillón *adj.* garish, gaudy
chimenea *n.* chimney
chimpancé *n.* chimpanzee
chiripa *n.* fluke
chirrido *n.* screech
chismorreo *n.* tattle
chispa *n.* spark
chiste *n.* joke, gag
chistoso *adj.* facetious
chocante *adj.* shocking
chocar *v.* clash, collide
chocolate *n.* chocolate
chofer *n.* chauffeur
choque *n.* shock, brunt
chovinismo *n.* chauvinism
chovinista *n. &adj.* chauvinist
choza *n.* shack

chubasco *n.* squall
chubasquero *n.* raincoat
chuchería *n.* trinket
chucho *n.* mongrel
chuleta *n.* chop, cutlet
chulo *adj.* cocky
chupachups *n.* lollipop
chupar *v.* suck
chusma *n.* rabble
chutney (conserva agridulce) *n.* chutney
cianuro *n.* cyanide
ciática *n.* sciatica
ciber *comb.* cyber
ciberespacio *n.* cyberspace
cicatriz *n.* scar
cíclico *adj.* cyclic
ciclista *n.* cyclist
ciclo *n.* cycle
ciclomotor *n.* moped
ciclón *n.* cyclone
ciego *adj.* blind
cielo *n.* heaven, sky
ciempiés *n.* centipede
cien *adj.& n.* hundred
ciénaga *n.* bog, morass
ciencia *n.* science
científico *adj.* scientific
científico *n.* scientist
cierre *n.* closure
ciertamente *adv.* certainly
ciervo *n.* deer, buck, stag
cifrar *v.* encrypt
cigarro *n.* cigarette
cigüeña *n.* stork
cilantro *n.* coriander
cilindro *n.* cylinder
cima *n.* peak
cincel *n.* chisel
cinco *adj. & n.* five
cincuenta *adj. & n.* fifty
cine *n* cinema

cinético *adj.* kinetic
cínico *n.* cynic
cinta *n.* tape, ribbon
cintura *n.* waist
cinturón *n.* belt
ciprés *n.* cypress
circo *n.* circus
circonita *n.* zircon
circuito *n.* circuit
circuito de carreras *n.* speedway
circulación *n.* circulation
circular *adj.* circular
circular *v.* circulate
circulo *n.* circle
circuncidar *v.* circumcise
circunferencia *n.* circumference
circunscribir *v.* circumscribe
circunspecto *adj.* circumspect
circunstancia *n.* circumstance
circunvalación *n.* bypass
cirio *v.* taper
ciruela *n.* plum
cirugía *n.* surgery
cirujano *n.* surgeon
cisma *n.* schism
cisne *n.* swan
cisterna *n.* cistern
cístico *adj.* cystic
cita *n.* quotation, rendezvous, date
citar *v.* cite
citar mal *v.* misquote
cítara *n.* zither
cítrico *adj.* citric
cítricos *n.* citrus
ciudad *n.* city, town
ciudadanía *n.* citizenship
ciudadano *n.* citizen
ciudadela *n.* citadel
cívica *n.* civics
cívico *adj.* civic
civil *n.* civilian
civilización *n.* civilization

civilizar *v.* civilize
clamor *n.* clamour
clan *n.* clan
clandestino *adj.* clandestine
claramente *adv.* clearly
claridad *n.* clarity
clarín *n.* bugle, clarion
claro *adj.* clear
claro *n.* glade
clase *n.* class, sort
clásico *adj.* classic, classical
clasificación *n.* classification
clasificar *v.* classify
claustro *n.* cloister
claustrofobia *n.* claustrophobia
cláusula *n.* clause
clavija *n.* peg
clavo *n.* clove
clemencia *n.* clemency, mercy
clemente *adj.* clement
clementina *n.* clementine
clerical *adj.* clerical
clérigo *n.* cleric
clero *n.* clergy
cliché *n.* stencil
cliente *n.* client, customer
clientela *n.* clientele, patronage
clima *n.* climate
clímax *n.* climax
clínica *n.* clinic
clip *n.* clip
clon *n.* clone
cloro *n.* chlorine
cloroformo *n.* chloroform
club *n.* club
coacción *n.* constraint
coaccionar *v.* coerce
coágulo *n.* clot
coalición *n.* coalition
coartada *n.* alibi
cobalto *n.* cobalt
cobarde *n.* coward

cobarde *adj.* craven
cobardía *n.* cowardice
cobertizo *n.* shed
cobra *n.* cobra
cobrar *v.* charge
cobrar de mas *v.* overcharge
cobre *n.* copper
cocaína *n.* cocaine
coche *n.* car
coche cama *n.* sleeper
coche de caballos *n.* coach
coche fúnebre *n.* hearse
cochecito de niño *n.* pram
cociente *n.* quotient
cocina *n.* cooker, cuisine, kitchen
cocina, estufa *n.* stove
cocinar *v.* cook
cocinero *n.* cook
coco *n.* coconut
cocodrilo *n.* crocodile
coctel *n.* cocktail
codear *v.* nudge
codicia *n.* greed
codiciar *v.* covet
codificar *v.* encode
código *n.* code
código postal *n.* postcode
codo *n.* elbow
codorniz *n.* quail
coeducación *n.* co-education
coeficiente *n.* coefficient
coetáneo *adj.* coeval
coexistencia *n.* coexistence
coexistir *v.* coexist
cofia *n.* coil
cofre *n.* casket, coffer
coger *v.* catch, grab
cohabitar *v.* cohabit
cohechar *v.* suborn
coherente *adj.* coherent
cohesión *n.* cohesion
cohesivo *adj.* cohesive

cohete *n.* rocket
coincidencia *n.* coincidence
coincidir *v.* coincide
cojear *v.* hobble, limp
cojín *n.* cushion
cojo *adj.* lame, gimp
col *n.* cabbage
cola *n.* queue
cola (animal) *n.* tail
colaboración *n.* collaboration
colaborar *v.* collaborate
colada *n.* washing
coladera *n.* sieve
colapsar *v.* collapse
colateral *n.* collateral
colchón *n.* mattress
colección *n.* collection
coleccionista *n.* collector
colectivo *adj.* collective
colector *adj.* manifold
colegiado *adj.* chartered
colegio universitario *n.* college
cólera *n.* cholera, wrath
colgante *n.* hanging
colgar *v,t.* hang, dangle
cólico *n.* colic
coliflor *n.* cauliflower
colina *n.* hill
colirio *n.* eyewash
colisión *n.* collision
collage *n.* collage
collar *n.* necklace
collarín *n.* collar
colmena *n.* hive
colmenar *n.* apiary
colmillo *n.* fang, tusk
colocación *n.* placement, setting
colocar *v.* lay
colon *n.* colon
colonia *n.* cologne, colony
colonia de grajos *n.* rookery
colonial *adj.* colonial

colonizar *v.* settle
colono *n.* settler
coloquial *adj.* colloquial
color *n.* colour
color de tono *n.* hue
colorete *n.* blusher, rouge
colorido *n.* colouring
colosal *adj.* colossal
coloso *n.* colossus
columna *n.* column
columna vertebral *n.* backbone, spine
columpiar *v.* swing
columpio *n.* swing
colusión *n.* collusion
coma *n.* coma, comma
comadreja *n.* weasel
comadrona *n.* midwife
comandante *n.* commander
comando *n.* commando
combate *n.* combat
combatiente *n* fighter, combatant
combinación *n.* combination
combinar *v.* combine
combustible *n.* fuel
combustión *n.* combustion
comedero *n.* feeder
comedia *n* comedy
comedido *adj.* measured
comensal *n.* diner
comentar *v.* remark
comentario *n.* comment
comentarista *n.* commentator
comenzar *v.* begin, commence
comer *v.* eat
comercial *adj.* commercial
comerciante *n.* merchant, trader
comercio *n.* commerce
comerse con los ojos *v.* ogle
comestible *adj.* edible
cometa *n.* comet
cometa (juguete) *n.* kite

cometer *v.* commit
comible *adj.* eatable
cómico *n.* comedian
cómico *adj.* comic
comida *n.* food, meal
comida para llevar *n.* takeaway
comida *n.* lunch
comienzo *n.* beginning, start
comino *n.* cumin
comisión *n.* commission
comisionado *n.* commissioner
comisura *n.* commissure
comité *n.* committee
Commonwealth *n.* Commonwealth
como *adv.* as, how
como *prep.* like
cómoda *n.* commode
cómodo *adj.* confortable
compacto *adj.* compact
compadecer *v.* commiserate
compadecerse *v.* sympathize
compañerismo *n.* fellowship
compañero *n.* colleague, companion, fellow
compañía *n.* company
comparación *n.* comparison
comparar *v.* compare, liken
comparativo *adj.* comparative
compartimiento *n.* compartment
compasión *n.* compassion
compasivo *adj.* sympathetic
compatible *adj.* compatible
compatriota *n.* compatriot
compeler *v.* compel
compendio *n.* compendium
compendioso *adj.* compendious
compensación *n.* compensation
compensar *v.* compensate
competencia *n.* competence
competente *adj.* competent
competición *n.* competition

competidor *n.* competitor
competir *v.* compete, race
competitivo *adj.* competitive
complacer *v.* please
complejidad *n.* complexity
complejo *adj.* complex
complementario *adj.* complementary
complemento *n.* complement
completo *adj.* complete
complicación *n.* complication
complicado *adj.* complicated
complicar *v.* complicate
cómplice *n.* accomplice
complicidad *n.* complicity
complot *n.* plot
componente *n.* component
componer *v.* compose
comportamiento *n.* behaviour
comportarse *v.* behave
composición *n.* composition
compositor *n.* composer
compostura *n.* composure
comprador *n.* buyer
comprar *v.* buy, purchase
comprender *v.t.* understand
comprensible *adj.* comprehensible
comprensión *n.* comprehension
compresión *n.* compression
comprimir *v.* compress
comprobar *v.* substantiate
compromiso *n.* commitment
compromiso (wedding) *n.* engagement
compuesto *adj.* composite
compuesto de *n.* compound
compulsión *n.* compulsion
compulsivo *adj.* compulsive
compunción *n.* compunction
computación *n.* computation
computar *v.* compute

computerizar *v.* computerize
comulgante *n.* communicant
común *adj.* common
comuna *n.* commune
comunal *adj.* communal
comunicable *adj.* communicable
comunicación *n.* communication
comunicado *n.* announcement
comunicar *v.* communicate
comunidad *n.* community
comunión *n.* communion
comunismo *n.* communism
con *prep.* with
con desconfianza *adv.* askance
con esperanza *adv.* hopefully
con suerte *adv.* lucky
concatenación *n.* concatenation
cóncavo *adj.* concave
concebir *v. t* conceive
conceder *v.* grant
conceder el voto *v.* enfranchise
concejal *n.* councillor
concentración *n.* concentration
concentrar *v.* concentrate
concepción *n.* conception
concepto *n.* concept
concertado *adj.* concerted
concesión *n.* concession
concha *n.* shell, conch
conciencia *n.* conscience
concienzudo *adj.* painstaking
concierto *n.* concert
conciliador *n.* troubleshooter
conciliar *v.* conciliate
concilio *n.* council
conciso *adj.* concise, terse
concluir *v.* conclude
conclusión *n.* conclusion
conclusivo *adj.* conclusive
concomitante *adj.* concomitant
concordancia *n.* concordance
concordia *n.* concord

concubina *n.* concubine
concurrente *adj.* concurrent
concurrir *v.* concur
concurso *n.* contest, competition
concusión *n.* concussion
condado *n.* shire, county
conde *n.* earl
condenación *n.* condemnation
condenar *v.* condemn
condenar al ostracismo *v.* ostracize
condensador *n.* capacitor
condensar *v.* condense
condición *n.* condition
condición femenina *n.* womanhood
condicional *adj.* conditional
condimento *n.* seasoning
condolencia *n.* condolence
condón *n.* condom
conducir *v.* drive, steer
conducta *n.* conduct
conducto *n.* duct
conductor *n.* driver
conectar *v.* connect
conejera *n.* hutch
conejo *n.* rabbit
conexión *n.* connection
confabularse *v.* connive
confederación *n.* confederation
confederado *adj.* confederate
conferencia *n.* conference, lecture
conferenciante *n.* lecturer
conferir *v.* bestow, confer
confesar *v.* confess, avow
confesión *n.* confession
confiado *adj.* trustful
confianza *n.* confidence, trust
confiar *v.* confide, entrust
confiar en *v.* rely
confidencial *adj.* confidential
confidente *n.* confidant

configuración *n.* configuration
confirmación *n.* confirmation
confirmar *v.* confirm
confiscación *n.* confiscation
confiscar *v.* confiscate
confitería *n.* confectionery
confitero *n.* confectioner
conflicto *n.* conflict, strife
confluencia *n.* confluence
confluente *adj.* confluent
conformar *v.* conform
conformarse *v.* acquiesce
conforme *adj.* compliant
conformidad *n.* compliance
confort *n.* comfort
confortable *adj.* comfortable
confortar *v.* comfort
confrontación *n.* confrontation
confrontar *v.* confront
confundir *v.* confuse
confusión *n.* confusion
confuso *adj.* woolly
congelador *n.* freezer
congelar *v.* defrost, freeze
congénito *adj.* congenital
congestión *n.* congestion
congestionado *adj.* congested
conglomerado *n.* conglomerate
congregar *v.* congregate
congreso *n.* congress
congruente *adj.* congruent
cónico *adj.* conical
conjetura *n.* conjecture
conjeturar *v.t.* surmise
conjugar *v.* conjugate
conjunción *n.* conjunction
conjuntivitis *n.* conjunctivitis
conjunto *n.* aggregate, outfit
conjurar *v.* conjure
conmemoración *n.* commemoration
conmemorar *v.* commemorate

conmoción *n.* commotion
conmocionar *v.* shock
conmovedor *adj.* poignant, soulful, moving
conmutar *v.* commute
cono *n.* cone
conocer *v.* acknowledge
conocido *adj.* noted
conocimiento *n.* knowledge
conquista *n.* conquest
conquistar *v.* conquer
consagrar *v.* consecrate
consciente *adj.* conscious
consciente de *adj.* mindful
consecuencia *n.* consequence
consecutivamente *adv.* consecutively
consecutivo *adj.* consecutive, serial
consejero *n.* counsellor
consejo *n.* advice, counsel
consenso *n.* consensus
consentimiento *n.* consent
consentir *v.t.* consent, indulge
conserje *n.* caretaker, janitor
conservación *n.* conservation
conservador *adj.* conservative
conservante *n.* preservative
conservar *v. t* preserve
conservatorio *n.* conservatory
considerable *adj.* considerable
consideración *n.* consideration
considerado *adj.* considerate
considerar *v.* consider, deem
consigna *n.* locker
consignar *v.* consign
consiguiente *adj.* consequent
consistencia *n.* consistency
consistente *adj.* consistent
consolación *n.* consolation
consolar *v. t.* console
consolidación *n.* consolidation

consolidar *v.* consolidate
consonancia *n.* keeping
consonante *n.* consonant
consorcio *n.* consortium
consorte *n.* consort
conspicuo *adj.* conspicuous
conspiración *n.* conspiracy
conspirador *n.* conspirator
conspirar *v.* conspire
constante *adj.* constant, steady
constar *v.* consist
constelación *n.* constellation
consternación *n.* consternation, dismay
constitución *n.* constitution
constitucional *adj.* constitutional
constituir *v.* constitute
constitutivo *adj.* constituent
constreñir *v.* constrain
constricción *n.* stricture
construcción *n.* construction
constructivo *adj.* constructive
construir *v.* build, construct
consuelo *n.* solace
cónsul *n.* consul
consulado *n.* consulate
consular *adj.* consular
consulta *n.* query
consultar *v.* consult
consumar *v.* consummate
consumidor *n.* consumer
consumir *v.* consume
consumo *n.* consumption
contabilidad *n.* accountancy
contable *n.* accountant
contacto *n.* contact
contador *n.* meter
contagio *n.* contagion
contagioso *adj.* contagious
contaminación *n.* pollution
contaminar *v.* contaminate, pollute

contar *v.t.* count, tell,
contemplación *n.* contemplation
contemplar *v.* contemplate
contemporáneo *adj.* contemporary
contención *n.* contention
contencioso *adj.* contentious
contendiente *n.* contestant
contenedor *n.* container
contener *v.t.* contain
contenido *n.* content
contento *adj.* content, glad
contestar *v.* retort
contexto *n.* context
contienda *n.* contest
contiguo *adj.* contiguous
continental *adj.* continental
continente *n.* continent
contingencia *n.* contingency
continuación *n.* continuation
continuado *adj.* continuous
continuar *v.* continue
continuidad *n.* continuity
continuo *adj.* continual
contorno *n.* contour, outline
contra *prep.* contra, versus
contrabajo *n.* bass
contrabandista *n.* smuggler
contrabando *n.* contraband
contracción *n.* contraction
contractual *adj.* contractual
contradecir *v.* contradict
contradicción *n.* contradiction
contrariado *adj.* disgruntled
contrario *adj.* averse, contrary
contrarrestar *v.* counteract
contraste *n.* contrast
contratar *v.t* hire, contract
contratista *n.* contractor
contrato *n.* contract
contrato alquiler *n.* lease
contravenir *v.* contravene

contraventana *n.* shutter
contribución *n.* contribution
contribuir *v.* contribute
control *n.* control
controversia *n.* controversy
contusión *n.* contusion
conurbación *n.* conurbation
convencer *v.* convince, coax
convención *n.* convention
conveniencia *n.* convenience
conveniente *adj.* convenient
convenio *n.* covenant
convenir *v.* befit
convento *n.* convent
converger *v.* converge
conversación *n.* conversation
conversión *n.* conversion
converso *n.* convert
convertir *v.* convert
convertirse *v.* become
convicción *n.* conviction
convicto *n.* convict
convincente *adj.* cogent
convocación *n.* convocation
convocar *v.* summon
convoy *n.* convoy
convulsión *n.* convulsion
convulsionar *n.* convulse
conyugal *adj.* marital
concienzudo *adj.* earnest
coñac *n.* brandy
cooperación *n.* cooperation
cooperar *v.* cooperate
cooperativo *adj.* cooperative
coordinación *n.* coordination
coordinar *v. t* coordinate
copa *n.* goblet
copia *n.* copy, replica
copiar *v.* copy
copioso *adj.* copious
copista *n.* copier
copo *n.* flake

copular *v.* copulate
coral *adj.* choral
coral *n.* coral
corazón *n.* heart
corazón roto *n.* heartbreak
corbata *n.* tie, cravat
corcel *n.* steed
corchete *n.* bracket
corcho *n.* cork
cordero *n.* lamb
cordial *adj.* cordial
cordialidad *n.* amity
cordillera *n.* range
cordón *n.* shoestring
cordura *n.* sanity
cornea *n.* cornea
corneta *n.* cornet
cornisa *n.* ledge
cornudo *adj.* horned
coro *n.* choir, chorus
corona *n.* crown, wreath
coronación *n.* coronation
coronar *v.* crown
coronel *n.* colonel
corpiño *n.* bodice
corporación *n.* corporation
corporativo *adj.* corporate
corpulento *adj.* corpulent
correa *n.* leash, strap
corrección *n.* correction
correctivo *adj.* corrective
correcto *adj.* correct, right
correcto *n* right
corredor *n.* runner, sprinter
corredor de bolsa *n.* stockbroker
corregir *v.* correct, subedit
correlación *n.* correlation
correlacionar *v.* correlate
correo *n.* mail
correo electrónico *n.* email
correo no deseado *n.* spam
correr *v.* run

correr ràpido *v.* sprint
corredor bolsa *n.* broker
corresponder *v.* correspond, reciprocate
corriente *n.* current
corriente *adj.* regular, ordinary
corroborar *v.* corroborate
corroer *v.* corrode
corromper *v.* corrupt
corrosión *n.* corrosion
corrosivo *adj.* corrosive
corrupción *n.* corruption
corrupto *adj.* corrupt
corta fuegos *n.* firewall
corta vidrios *n.* cutter
cortante *adj.* biting, curt
cortar *v.* cut, sever
cortar cn hacha *v.* hew
corte de pelo *n.* haircut
cortejar *v.* woo
cortés *adj.* courteous
cortesana *n.* courtesan
cortesano *n.* courtier
cortesía *n.* courtesy
corteza *n.* bark
corteza comida *n.* crust
cortina *n.* curtain
cortisona *n.* cortisone
corto *adj.* short
corzo *n.* roe
cosa *n.* thing
cosa enorme *n.* whopper
cosecha *n.* crop, harvest
cosechadora *n.* haverster
coser *v.* sew, stitch
cosmético *adj.* cosmetic
cosmético *n.* cosmetic
cósmico *adj.* cosmic
cosmología *n.* cosmology
cosmopolita *adj.* cosmopolitan
cosmos *n.* cosmos
costa *n.* coast

costear *v.t.* cost, afford
costilla *n.* rib
costoso *adj.* costly
costra *n.* scab
costumbre *n.* custom
costura *n.* seam
cotilleo *n.* gossip
cotorrear *v.* gab
coyuntura *n.* conjuncture
cráneo *n.* skull
creación *n.* creation
creador *n.* creator
crear *v.* create
creativo *adj.* creative
crecer *v.i.* grow
crecer más que *v.* outgrow
creciente *n.* crescent, rising
crecimiento *n.* growth
credenciales *n.* credentials
crédito *n.* credit
credo *n.* creed
credulidad *n.* credulity
crédulo *adj.* gullible
creencia *n.* belief
creer *v.* believe
creíble *adj.* credible
cremallera *n.* zip
crematorio *n.* crematorium
crepe *n.* pancake
crepitar *v.* sizzle
crepúsculo *n.* twilight
cresta *n.* crest, ridge
cría *n.* pup
criar *v.* breed, nurture
criatura *n.* creature
cribar *v.* sift
crimen *n.* crime
criminal *n.* criminal
criminología *n.* criminology
crin *n.* mane
cripta *n.* crypt
crisis *n.* crisis

cristal *n.* crystal
cristianismo *n.* christianity
cristiano *adj.* christian
Cristo *n.* Christ
criterio *n.* criterion
crítica *n.* criticism, critique
criticar *v.* criticize, snipe
crítico *n.* critic
crítico *adj.* critical
croar *n.* croak
croissant *n.* croissant
cromo *n.* chrome
crónica *n.* chronicle
crónico *adj.* chronic
cronógrafo *n.* chronograph
cronología *n.* chronology
cruce *n.* junction
crucero *n.* cruiser
crucial *adj.* crucial
crudo *adj.* raw
cruel *adj.* cruel, harsh
crueldad *n.* cruelty
crujido *n.* creak, squeak
crujiente *adj.* crisp
crujir *v.* crackle, creak
cruz *n.* cross
cruzada *n.* crusade, cruise
cruzarse *v.* intersect
cuaderno *n.* notebook
cuadrado *n.* square
cuadrangular *adj.* quadrangular
cuadrángulo *a.* quadrangle
cuadrante *n.* quadrant
cuadrilátero *n.* quadrilateral
cuadro *n.* painting, picture
cuadrúpedo *n.* quadruped
cuádruple *adj.* quadruple
cuajada *n.* curd
cual *pron. & adj.* which
cuales *pron. & adj.* which
cualitativo *adj.* qualitative

cualquier *pron.* whatever, whichever
cualquiera *pron.* whoever
cuando *adv.* when
cuando *conj.* whenever
cuántico *n.* quantum
cuantía *n.* quantum
cuantificar *v.* quantify
cuantitativo *adj.* quantitative
cuáquero *n.* quaker
cuarenta *adj.& n.* forty
cuarentena *n.* quarantine
cuartel *n.* barrack
cuarteto *n.* quartet
cuarto *adj.& n.* fourth
cuarto *n.* quarter
cuarto de baño *n.* lavatory
cuarto de galón *n.* quart
cuarzo *n.* quartz
cuatrillizo *n.* quadruplet
cuatro *adj.& n.* four
cuba *n.* tun
cúbico *adj.* cubical
cubículo *n.* cubicle
cubierta *n.* deck, cover
cubierto *adj.* covert
cubo *n.* bucket, bin
cubrir *v.* cover
cucaracha *n.* cockroach
cuchara *n.* spoon
cucharada *n.* spoonful
cucharon *n.* scoop, ladl
cuchillo *n.* knife
cuco *n.* cuckoo
cuello *n.* neck
cuenta *n.* account, bil
cuento *n.* tale
cuerda *n.* rope, string
cuerdo *adj.* sane
cuerno *n.* antler, horn
cuero *n.* leather
cuerpo *n.* body, corps

cuervo *n.* crow, raven
cuestionable *adj.* questionable
cuestionario *n.* form
cueva *n.* cave
cuidado *n.* care
cuidador *n.* carer, keeper
cuidador de elefantes *n.* mahout
cuidadoso *adj.* careful
culinario *adj.* culinary
culminar *v.* culminate
culo *n.* ass
culpabilidad *n.* guilt
culpable *adj.* guilty
culpar *v.* blame
cultivable *adj.* arable
cultivado *adj.* literate
cultivar *v.* cultivate
culto *n.* cultm worship
cultura *n.* culture
cultural *adj.* cultural
cumbre *n.* summit, top
cumplido *n.* compliment
cumplimiento *n.* pursuance
cuna *n.* cot, cradle, crib
cuña *n.* wedge
cuota *n.* quota
cupé *n.* coupe
cupón *n.* coupon
cúpula *n.* dome
cura *n.* priest
curable *adj.* curable
curar *v. t.* cure, heal
curativo *adj.* curative
cúrcuma *n.* turmeric
curiosear *v.* pry
curiosidad *n.* curiosity
curioso *adj.* curious, quaint
currículo *n.* curriculum
curriculum *n.* curriculum
curruca *n.* warbler
curry *n.* curry
cursi *adj.* tawdry, twee

cursiva *adj.* italic
cursivo *adj.* cursive
curso *n.* course
cursor *n.* cursor
curtidor *n.* tanner
curtiduría *n.* tannery
curva *n.* curve, loop
custodia *n.* custody
cutis *n.* complexion

D

dado *n.* dice
dado *adj.* given
daga *n.* dagger
dama *n.* dame
damisela *n.* damsel
daño *n.* damage, harm
dar *v.t.* give, deal
dar a entender *v.* imply
dar arcadas *v.* retch
dar de alta *v.* discharge
dar derecho a *v.* entitle
dar la lata *v.* nag
dar palmaditas *v.* pat
dar parte *v.* debrief
dar saltos *v.* jolt
dar sombra *v.* shade
dar un golpe *v.* whack
dar un codazo *v.* prod
dar un paseo *v.* stroll
dar vueltas *v.* whirl, revolve
dardo *n.* dart
darse cuenta *v.* realize
darse prisa *v.* hasten
dato *n.* datum
datos *n.* data
de *prep.* of, from
de aficionado *adj.* amateurish

de alguna modo *adv.* somehow
de dónde *adv.* whence
de encargo *adj.* bespoke
de frente *adv.* abreast
de lado *adv.* edgewise
de nuevo *adv.* afresh, anew
de pie *n.* standing
de quién *pron.* whose
de repente *adv.* suddenly
deambular *v.i.* wander, stroll
debacle *n.* debacle
debajo *adv.* beneath
debajo *prep.* under, below
debajo de *prep.* underneath
debate *n.* debate, discussion
debatir *v.* debate, discuss
deber *n.* duty
deber *v.* should, must
débil *adj.* weak, faint
debilidad *n.* weakness
debilitado *adj.* rundown
debilitar *v.* debilitate
débilmente *adv.* duly
débito *n.* debit
debut *n.* debut
debutante *n.* debutante
década *n.* decade
decadente *adj.* decadent
decaer *v.i.* decline
decano *n.* dean
decantar *v.* decant
decapitar *v.* behead
decencia *n.* decency
decente *adj.* decent
decepción *n.* deception
decepcionar *v.* disappoint
dechado *n.* paragon
decibelio *n.* decibel
decidido *adj.* decided
decidir *v.* decide
decimal *adj.* decimal
décimo *adj. & n.* tenth

decimo sexto *adj. & n.* sixteenth
decimo tercero *adj. & n.* thirteenth
decimo tercero *adj. & n.* thirtieth
decimo tercero *adj. & n.* thirtieth
decimonoveno *adj. & n.* nineteenth
decimoséptimo *adj. & n.* seventeenth
decir *n.* say
decisión *n.* decision
decisivo *adj.* decisive
declamar *v.* declaim
declaración *n.* statement, declaration, affidavit
declarar *v.t.* declare
declinar *v.* inflect
declive *n.* declivity
decolorar *v.* discolour
decoración *n.* decor, decoration
decorado *n.* scenery
decorar *v.* decorate
decorativo *adj.* decorative
decoro *n.* decorum
decoroso *adj.* decorous
decrépito *adj.* decrepit
decreto *n.* decree
dedal *n.* thimble
dedicación *n.* dedication
dedicar *v.* dedicate, devote
dedo *n.* finger
dedo del pie *n.* toe
dedo índice *n.* forefinger
deducción *n.* deduction
deducir *v.* deduce, deduct
defecar *v.* defecate
defecto *n.* defect, flaw
defectuoso *adj.* defective, faulty
defender *v.* defend, uphold
defendible *adj.* defensible
defensa *n.* defence
defensivo *adj.* defensive

deferencia *n.* deference
deficiencia *n.* deficiency
deficiente *adj.* deficient
déficit *n.* deficit, shortfall
definición *n.* definition
definir *v.* define
definitivo *adj.* definite
deflación *n.* deflation
deforestar *v.* deforest
deformar *v.* deform, distort
deformidad *n.* deformity
defunción *n.* demise
degenerar *v.* degenerate
degradar *v.* degrade, demean
deidad *n.* deity
deificar *v.* deify
deja vu *n.* deja vu
dejar *v.* let
dejar atrás *v.* outrun
delantal *n.* apron
delante de *adv.* ahead
delantero *n.* striker
delegación *n.* delegation
delegado *n.* delegate
delegar *v.* depute
deleitar *v. t.* delight
deleitarse *v.r* revel
deleite *n.* delectation
deletrear *v.* spell
deletrear mal *v.* misspell
delgado *adj.* slight
deliberación *n.* deliberation
deliberadamente *adv.* purposely
deliberado *adj.* deliberate
delicadeza *n.* delicacy
delicado *adj.* delicate, dainty
delicioso *adj.* delicious, yummy
delimitación *n.* demarcation
delincuente *adj.* delinquent
delinear *v.* delineate
delirante *adj.* delirious
delirio *n.* delirium

delito menor *n.* misdemeanour
delta *n.* delta
demanda *n.* demand
demandado *n.* defendant
demandante *n.* claimant
demandar *v.t.* demand, sue
demasiado *adv.* overly
demencia *n.* dementia
demente *adj.* insane, demented
democracia *n.* democracy
democrático *adj.* democratic
demografía *n.* demography
demoler *v.* demolish
demolición *n.* wrecker
demonio *n.* demon,
demonstración *n.* demonstration
demonstrar *v.* demonstrate
denigrar *v.* denigrate
denominación *n.* denomination
denominador *n.* denominator
denotar *v. t* denote
densidad *n.* density
denso *adj.* dense
dentadura postiza *n.* denture
dental *adj.* dental
dentellado *adj.* serrated
dentista *n.* dentist
dentro *n.* inside
dentro *prep.* within
denudar *v.* denude
denuncia *n.* denunciation
denunciar *v.* report, denounce
departamento *n.* department
departir *v.* converse
dependencia *n.* dependency
depender *v.* depend
dependiente *n.* dependant
dependiente *adj.* dependent
depilatorio *adj.* depilatory
deplorable *adj.* damnable
deponer *v.* depose
deportar *v. t* deport

deporte *n.* sport
deportista *n.* sportsman
deportivo *adj.* sportive
depósito *n.* deposit, depot
depravar *v.* deprave
depreciación *n.* depreciation
depreciar *v.* depreciate
depredador *n.* predator
depresión *n.* depression
deprimir *v.* depress
deprisa *adv.* quickly
derecho de retención *n.* lien
derivar *v.* derive
derivativo *adj.* derivative
derogar *v.* abrogate
derramamiento de sangre *n.*
  bloodshed
derramar *v.* spill
derramarse *v.* overflow
derretido *adj.* runny
derretir *v.* melt
derribar *v.* overthrow
derrocar *v.* overthrow
derrochador *n.* spendthrift
derrochador *adj.* wasteful
derrochar *v.* squander
derrota *n.* rout
derrotar *v.* defeat
derrotista *n.* defeatist
desacato *n.* disrespect
desacreditado *adj.* disreputable
desacreditar *v.* discredit
desactivar *v.* defuse
desacuerdo *n.* disagreement
desafecto *adj.* disaffected
desafiante *adj.* gutsy
desafiar *v.* defy
desafilado *adj.* blunt
desafío *n.* challenge
desafortunado *adj.* unfortunate,
  luckless
desagradable *adj.* disagreeable

desagradar *v.* dislike, displease
desagradecido *adj.* ungrateful
desagrado *n.* displeasure
desahogarse *v.* unburden
desahuciar *v.* evict
desairar *v.* snub
desajuste *n.* mismatch
desalentado *adj.* despondent
desalentar *v.* discourage
desaliñado *adj.* scruffy, blowzy
desalmado *adj.* soulless
desalojo *n.* eviction
desandar *v.t.* retrace
desanimado *adj.* dispirited
desanimar *v.* dishearten
desaparecer *v.* disappear
desaparecido *adj.* missing
desapasionado *adj.* dispassionate
desaprobación *n.* disapproval
desarmado *adj.* unarmed
desarmar *v.* disarm
desarme *n.* disarmament
desarraigar *v.* uproot
desarreglado *adj.* deranged
desarreglar *v.* disarrange
desarrollar *v.* develop
desarrollo *n.* development
desaseado *adj.* seedy
desastre *n.* disaster
desastroso *adj.* disastrous
desatender *v.* neglect
desatendido *adj.* unattended
desayuno *n.* breakfast
desbancar *v.* oust
desbocado *adj.* runaway
desbocarse *v.* overflow, rampage
desbordamiento *n.* overspill
descafeinado *adj.* decaffeinated
descalificación *n.* disqualification
descalificar *v.* disqualify
descansado *adj.* restful, tireless
descansar *v.* rest

descarado *adj.* brazen, cheeky
descarga *n.* barrage, volley
descargar *v.* download
descarnado *adj.* scraggy, gaunt
descaro *n.* gall
descarriado *adj.* errant
descarrilar *v. t.* derail
descender *v.* descend
descendencia *n.* offspring
descendiente *n.* descendant
descenso *n.* descent
descentralizar *v.* decentralize
descifrar *v.t.* decipher
desclasificar *v.* declassify
descodificar *v.* decode
descomponerse *v.r.* decay
descomposición *n.* decomposition
descomprimir *v.* decompress
desconcertado *adv.* aback
desconcertado *adj.* bemused
desconcertar *v.* disconcert
desconectado *adj.* off
desconectar *v.* disconnect
desconfianza *n.* distrust
desconfiar *v.* mistrust
descongestionante *n.* decongestant
desconocer *v.* disclaim
desconocido *n.* stranger
desconocido *adj.* unknown
desconsiderado *adj.* thoughtless
desconsolado *adj.* disconsolate
descontaminar *v.* decontaminate
descontento *n.* discontent, dissatisfaction
descontrolado *adj.* lawless
descortés *adj.* discourteous
describir *v.* describe
descripción *n.* description
descubierto *n.* overdraft
descubrimiento *n.* discovery
descubrir *v.* discover

descuento *n.* discount
descuidado *adj.* careless, remiss
descuidar *v. t* disregard
descuido *n.* oversight
desde *prep.* since
desde allí *adv.* thence
desde lejos *adv.* afar
desdén *n.* disdain
desdentado *adj.* toothless
desdeñar *v.* spurn
desdeñoso *adj.* dismissive
desdibujar *v.* blur
desdoblar *v.* unfold
deseable *adj.* desirable
desear *v.* wish
desechable *adj.* disposable
desechar *v.* discard
desembarcar *v.* disembark
desembolsar *v.* disburse
desempaquetar *v.* unpack
desempleado *adj.* unemployed
desempleo *n.* redundancy
desencadenar *v.* unleash
desenfadado *adj.* nonchalant
desenfado *n.* nonchalance
desenfrenado *adj.* unbriddled
desengañar *v.* undeceive
desengaño *n.* heartbreak
desenmascarar *v.* unmask
desenredar *v.* disentangle
desenrollar *v.* unwind
desenterrar *v.* unearth
desenvuelto *adj.* brash
deseo *n.* desire
deseoso *adj.* desirous
desequilibrado *adj.* unbalanced
desequilibrio *n.* imbalance
desertar *v.* desert
desesperación *n.* despair
desesperado *adj.* desperate
desestabilizar *v.* destabilize

desfase horario *n.* jet lag
desfavorecido *adj.* underprivileged
desfile *n.* parade
desgarbado *adj.* lanky, ungainly
desgarrar *v.* sunder, wrench
desgastar *v.* scuff
desgaste *n.* wastage
desgobierno *n.* misrule
desgracia *n.* misfortune, woe
desgraciadamente *conj.* alas
desgraciado *adj.* woeful
deshabitado *adj.* uninhabited
deshacer *v.t.* retrace, undo
desheredar *v.* disinherit
deshidratar *v.* dehydrate
deshilachar *v.t.* fray
deshonesto *adj.* dishonest
deshonor *n.* dishonour
deshonra *n.* disrepute
deshumanizar *v.* dehumanize
desierto *n.* wilderness
designar *v.* designate
desigual *adj.* bumpy
desigualdad *n.* inequality
desilusión *v.* disillusion
desilusionar *v.* disenchant
desinfectar *v.* disinfect, sanitize
desinflar *v.* deflate
desintegrar *v.* disintegrate
desinteresado *adj.* selfless, unselfish
desintoxicar *v.* detoxify
desistir *v.* desist
desleal *adj.* disloyal, faithless
deslizar *v.* slide
deslizarse *v.* creep, glide, skid, slither
deslucido *adj.* lacklustre
deslumbrar *v. t.* dazzle, glare
desmandado *adj.* lawless
desmayarse *v.* swoon

desmayo *n.* blackout
desmentido *n.* denial
desmentir *v.* belie
desmigajar *v.* crumble
desmitificar *v.* demystify
desmontar *v.* dismantle, unseat
desmoralizar *v.* demoralize
desmoronar *v.* moulder
desmovilizar *v.* demobilize
desnacionalizar *v.* denationalize
desnudar *v.t.* strip, undress
desnudez *n.* nudity
desnudo *adj.* naked, bare
desnutrición *n.* malnutrition
desobedecer *v.* disobey
desobediente *adj.* disobedient
desocupado *adj.* spare
desodorante *n.* deodorant
desolado *adj.* desolate, gaunt
desorden *n.* mess, disarray
desordenado *adj.* disorganized,
  messy, untidy
desorientar *v.* disorientate
despampanante *adj.* stunning
despecho *n.* pique
despectivo *adj.* derogatory
despedida *n.* parting
despedir *v.* dismiss, sack
despeinar *v.* ruffle
despeinarse *v.* tousle
despejado *adj.* clear
despenalizar *v.* decriminalize
despensa *n.* pantry, larder
desperdiciar *v.* fritter
despertar *v.* awake, wake
despiadado *adj.* pitiless, ruthless
despilfarrador *adj.* profligate
despilfarro *n.* profligacy
desplazar *v. t* displace
desplegar *v.* deploy, unfurl
desplumar *v.* pluck
despojar *v.* divest

desposeer *v.* bereaved, dispossess
déspota *n.* despot
despreciable *adj.* despicable
despreciar *v.* despise
despreciativo *adj.* contemptuous,
  scornful
desprecio *n.* scorn
despreocupado *adj.* blithe,
  carefree
despreocupado (con la ropa)
  adj. casual
desproporcionado *adj.* dispro-
  portionate
desprovisto *adj.* devoid, bereft
después *adv.* after
desregular *v.* deregulate
destacado *adj.* salient
destacar *v.* highlight
destapar *v.* uncover
destartalado *adj.* ramshackle
destellar *v.* flash, glitter
desteñir *v.* fade
desterrar *v.* banish
destetar *v.* wean
destierro *n.* banishment
destilar *v.* distil
destilería *n.* distillery
destinación *n.* destination
destinatario *n.* addressee, recipient
destino *n.* destiny, fate
destornillador *n.* screwdriver
destreza *n.* dexterity, skill
destronar *v.* dethrone
destrozar *v.t.* ravage, shatter
destrucción *n.* destruction
destructor *n.* destroyer
destruir *v.* destroy
desvaído *adj.* watery
desvalido *adj.* underdog
desvalijar *v.* rifle
desvanecer *v.* vanish

desvelado *adj.* wakeful
desvelar *v.* unveil
desvencijado *adj.* rickety
desventaja *n.* disadvantage
desventura *n.* misadventure
desvestir *v.* undress
desviación *n.* diversion
desviado *adj.* deviant
desviar *v. t* divert, deflect
desviarse bruscamente *v.* swerve
desvío *n.* detour
detalle *n.* detail
detectar *v.* detect
detective *n.* detective
detector de mentiras *n.* polygraph
detención *n.* detention
detener *v. t* detain
detenido *n.* detainee
detergente *n.* detergent
deteriorarse *v.* deteriorate
deterioro *n.* disrepair
determinación *n.* determination
determinado *adj.* given
determinante *adj.* determinant
determinar *v. t* determine
detestable *adj.* obnoxious
detestar *v.* detest
detonar *v.* detonate
detraer *v.* detract
detrás *adv.* behind
detrimento *n.* detriment
detrito *n.* detritus
deuda *n.* debt
deudor *adj.* indebted
deudor *n.* debtor
deudor hipotecario *n.* mortgagor
devaluar *v.* devalue
devanadera *n.* winder
devastar *v.* devastate
devoción *n.* devotion
devolución *n.* devolution

devolver *v.* refund
devorar *v.* devour
devoto *n.* devotee, votary
día *n.* day
día de la semana *n.* weekday
diabetes *n.* diabetes
diablo *n.* devil
diadema *n.* tiara
diafragma *n.* midriff
diagnosticar *v.* diagnose
diagnostico *n.* diagnosis
diagrama *n.* diagram
dialecto *n.* dialect
diálisis *n.* dialysis
diálogo *n.* dialogue
diamante *n.* diamond
diámetro *n.* diameter
diana *n.* dashboard
diario *adj.* daily
diario *n.* diary
diario de viaje *n.* travelogue
diarrea *n.* diarrhoea
diáspora *n.* diaspora
diatriba *n.* tirade
dibujar *v.* draw
dibujo *n.* drawing, sketch
dibujo animado *n.* cartoon
dicción *n.* diction
diccionario *n.* dictionary
dicha *n.* bliss
dicho *n.* saying, say
diciembre *n.* december
dictado *n.* dictation
dictador *n.* dictator
dictar *v.* dictate
didáctico *adj.* didactic
diecinueve *adj. & n.* nineteen
dieciocho *adj. & n.* eighteen
dieciséis *adj. & n.* sixteen
diecisiete *adj. & n.* seventeen
diente *n.* tooth
diente de león *n.* dandelion

diesel *n.* diesel
diestro *adj.* skilled
dieta *n.* diet
dietista *n.* dietitian
diez *adj. & adv.* ten
diezmar *v.* decimate
diezmo *n.* tithe
difamación *n.* defamation
difamar *v.* defame
difamatorio *adj.* slanderous
diferencia *n.* difference
diferenciado *adj.* discrete
diferente *adj.* different
diferir *v.* differ, defer
difícil *adj.* difficult
dificultad *n.* difficulty
difundir *v.* diffuse
difunto *adj.* deceased
digerir *v.* digest
digestión *n.* digestion
digital *adj.* digital
dígito *n.* digit
dignarse *v.* condescend, deign
dignatario *n.* dignitary
dignidad *n.* dignity
dignificar *v.* dignify
digno *adj.* dignified, worthy
digno de confianza *adj.* trustworthy
dilación *n.* procrastination
dilatarse *v.* dilate, dilute
dilema *n.* dilemma
diligencia *n.* stagecoach
diligente *adj.* diligent
dilucidar *v. t* elucidate
dimensión *n.* dimension
diminuto *adj.* minute, poky
dinámica *n.* dynamics
dinámico *adj.* dynamic
dinamita *n.* dynamite
dinamo *n.* dynamo
dinastía *n.* dynasty

dinero *n.* money
dinero en efectivo *n.* cash
dinosaurio *n.* dinosaur
dintel *n.* lintel
dios *n.* god
diosa *n.* goddess
diploma *n.* diploma
diplomacia *n.* diplomacy
diplomático *n.* diplomat
diplomático *adj.* diplomatic, tactful
dipsomanía *n.* dipsomania
dirección *n.* management, direction
directamente *adv.* directly
directo *adj.* direct, nonstop
director *n.* director, manager
directorio *n.* directory
directriz *n.* directive
dirigente *n.* ruling
dirigir *v.* manage
discapacidad *n.* disability
discapacitado *adj.* disabled
disciplina *n.* discipline
discípulo *n.* disciple
disco *n.* disc
disco duro *n.* hard drive
discordante *adj.* discordant
discordia *n.* discord
discrepancia *n.* discrepancy
discrepar *v.* dissent
discreto *adj.* discreet
discriminar *v.* discriminate
disculpa *n.* apology
disculpar *v.* apologize
discursión *n.* discussion
discutible *adj.* debatable, moot
discutir *v.* argue
diseccionar *v.* dissect
disentería *n.* dysentery
diseño *n.* design
disertación *n.* dissertation

disfraz *n.* costume
disfrazar *v.* disguise
disfrutar *v.* enjoy
disfuncional *adj.* dysfunctional
disgustado *adj.* upset
disgusto *n.* disgust
disidente *n.* dissident
disimular *v.* dissimulate
disipación *n.* debauchery
disipar *v.* dissipate
dislexia *n.* dyslexia
dislocar *v.* dislocate
disminución *n.* diminution
disminuir *v.t..* decrease, diminish, subside
disminuirse *v.i.* dwindle
disolver *v. t* dissolve
disparar *v.* shoot
disparejo *adj.* patchy
disparidad *n.* disparity
dispensario *n.* dispensary
dispepsia *n.* dyspepsia
dispersar *v.* disperse
disponer *v. t* dispose
disponer de *v.i.* dispose of
disponible *adj.* available
disposición *n.* disposal, beck
dispositivo *n.* device
dispuesto *adj.* willing
disputa *n.* dispute
disputar *v. i* dispute
distancia *n.* distance
distante *adj.* distant
distinción *n.* distinction
distinguido *adj.* courtly
distinguir *v. t* distinguish
distinto *adj.* distinct
distracción *n.* distraction
distraer *v.* distract
distraído *adj.* inattentive
distribuidor *n.* distributor, supplier

distribuir *v.* distribute
distrito electoral *n.* constituency
disuadir *v.* dissuade, deter
disuasivo *adj.* deterrent
disyuntiva *n.* quandary
divagar *v.* digress
diván *n.* chaise
divergir *v.* diverge
diversidad *n.* diversity
diversión *n.* amusement
diverso *adj.* diverse
divertido *adj.* funny
dividendo *n.* dividend
dividir *v.* divide
divinidad *n.* divinity
divino *adj.* divine
división *n.* division
divorce *v.* divorce
divorciado *n.* divorcee
divorcio *n.* divorce
divulgar *v.* divulge
dobladillo *n.* hem
doblar *v.* bend
doble *adj.* double
doble *n.* lookalike
doce *adj.&n.* twelve
docena *n.* dozen
dócil *adj.* docile, meek
dócilmente *adv.* tamely
doctor *n.* doctor
doctorado *n.* doctorate
doctrina *n.* doctrine
documental *n.* documentary
documento *n.* document
dogma *n.* dogma
dogmático *adj.* dogmatic
dólar *n.* dollar
dolencia *n.* infirmity
doler *v.* rankle
doliente *adj.* mourner
dolor *n.* ache, pain, grief
dolor de cabeza *n.* headache

dolor de muelas *n.* toothache
doloroso *adj.* painful, sore
doméstico *adj.* domestic
domicilio *n.* domicile
dominante *adj.* dominant
dominar *v.* dominate
domingo *n.* Sunday
dominio *n.* domain
don *n.* knack
donante *n.* donor
donar *v.* donate
doncella *n.* maiden
donde *adv.* where
dorado *adj.* golden
dorar *v.* gild
dormido *adj.* asleep
dormir *n.* sleep
dormitar *v. i* doze
dormitorio *n.* bedroom
dos *adj.&n.* two
dos veces *adv.* twice
dosel *n.* canopy
dosis *n.* dose
dossier *n.* dossier
dotado *adj.* gifted
dotar de *v.* endow
dote *n.* dowry
dragón *n.* dragon
drama *n.* drama
dramático *adj.* dramatic
dramaturgo *n.* playwright
drástico *adj.* drastic
drenar *v. t* drain
driza *n.* halyard
droga *n.* drug
dual *adj.* dual
ducha *n.* shower
duda *n.* doubt
dudar *v.* hesitate
dudoso *adj.* dubious
duelo *n.* duel
duende *n.* hobgoblin

dueña *n.* mistress
dueño *n.* owner
dulce *adj.* sweet
dulce *n.* sweet
dulce de azúcar *n.* fudge
dulzura *n.* sweetness
dúo *n.* duet
duodécimo *adj.&n.* twelfth
dúplex *n.* duplex, maisonette
duplicado *adj.* duplicate
duplicar *v.* replicate
duplicidad *n.* duplicity
durable *adj.* durable
duración *n.* duration
duradero *adj.* lasting
durante *adv.* during
duro *adj.* hard, tough

E

ebanista *n.* joiner
ébano *n.* ebony
echar *v.* toss
echar a perder *v.* bungle
echar de menos *v.* miss
echar los dientes *v.* teethe
eclipsar *v.* outshine
eclipse *n.* eclipse
eco *n.* echo
ecología *n.* ecology
economía *n.* economy
económico *adj.* economical
ecuación *n.* equation
ecuador *n.* equator
ecuestre *adj.* equestrian
edad *n.* age
edecán *n.* aide
edición *n.* edition
edicto *n.* edict

edificación anexa *n.* outhouse
edificio *n.* building, edifice
editar *v.* edit
editor *n.* editor, publisher
editorial *adj.* editorial
edredón *n.* duvet, quit
educación *n.* education
educacional *adj.* educational
educado *adj.* polite
educar *v.* educate
edulcorante *n.* sweetener
efectivo *adj.* effective
efecto *n.* effect
eficacia *n.* efficacy
eficiencia *n.* efficiency
eficiente *adj.* efficient
efigie *n.* effigy
ego *n.* ego
egoísta *adj.* selfish
egotismo *n.* egotism
eje *n.* axis, axle
ejecución *n.* execution
ejecutar *v.* execute
ejecutivo *n.* executive
ejemplo *n.* example
ejercer *v.* exert
ejercicio *n.* exercise
ejército *n.* army
el *art.* he
el mismo *pron.* himself
el peor *adj.* worst
el,la,los,las *art.* the
elástico *adj.* elastic
elección *n.* choice
elecciones *n.* elections
electo *adj.* elective
electorado *n.* electorate
electricidad *n.* electricity
electricista *n.* electrician
eléctrico *adj.* electric
electrificar *v.* electrify
electrocutar *v.* electrocute

electrónico *adj.* electronic
elefante *n.* elephant
elefantón *adj.* natty
elegancia *n.* elegance
elegante *adj.* elegant, graceful
elegir *v.t.* elect, choose
elemental *adj.* elementary
elemento *n.* element
elementos fijos *n.* fixture
elevar *v.t.* elevate
elevarse *v.r.* rise
elfo *n.* elf
eliminación *n.* deletion
eliminar *v.* eliminate
elipse *n.* ellipse
elite *n.* elite
ella *pron.* she
ella misma *pron.* herself
ellos *pron.* they
ellos mismos *pron.* themselves
elocución *n.* elocution
elocuencia *n.* eloquence
elogiar *v.t.* praise
elogio *n.* compliment
eludir *v.* elude, shirk
emancipar *v. t* emancipate
embadurnar *v.* daub
embajada *n.* embassy
embajador *n.* ambassador
embalaje *n.* packing
embalsamar *v.* embalm
embalse *n.* reservoir
embarazada *adj.* pregnant
embarazo *n.* pregnancy
embarazoso *adj.* cumbersome
embarcar *v. t* embark
embargo *n.* embargo
embarque *n.* shipping
embelesar *v.* enthral
embellecer *v.* beautify
embestida *n.* onslaught
emblema *n.* emblem

emboscada *n.* ambush
embriagador *adj.* heady
embrión *n.* embryo
embrollo *n.* jumble
embrujado *adj.* haunted
embudo *n.* funnel
embustero *adj.* deceitful
emergencia *n.* emergency
emigrar *v.* emigrate
eminencia *n.* eminence
eminente *adj.* eminent
emisario *n.* emissary
emitir *v. t* broadcast
emoción *n.* emotion, thrill
emocional *adj.* emotional
emoliente *adj.* emollient
emolumento *n.* emolument
emotivo *adj.* emotional
empalagoso *adj.* cloying
empalizada *n.* stockade, paling
empalmar *v.* splice
empanada *n.* patty
empanadilla *n.* pasty
empañar *v.* tarnish
empapado *adj.* soaked
empapar *v.* soak, drench
emparedar *v.* immure
empatado *adj.* quits
empatar *v. t* equalize
empatía *n.* empathy
empeine *n.* vamp
empeñar *v.* engage
empeorar *v.* worsen
empequeñecer *v.* belittle
emperador *n.* emperor
emperatriz *n.* empress
emperejilar *v.* titivate
empezar *v.* start
empinado *adj.* steep
empleado *n.* employee
empleador *n.* employer
emplear mal *v.* misapply, misuse, misdirect

empobrecer *v.* impoverish
empresa *n.* enterprise
empresario *n.* entrepreneur
empujar *v.t.* push
empuje *n.* thrush
empuñadura *n.* hilt
emular *v. t* emulate
en *prep.* in, on, at, into
en adelante *adv.* forth
en algún lugar *adv.* somewhere
en alto *adv.* aloft
en contra de *prep.* against
en cualquier sitio *adv.* anywhere
en desuso *adv.* abeyance
en el extranjero *adv.* abroad, overseas
en forma *adj.* fit
en libertad *n.* probationer
en lo alto *adv.* overhead
en lo sucesivo *adv.* hereafter
en lugar de *n.* lieu
en medio de *prep.* among
en ningún sitio *adv.* nowhere
en parte *adv.* partly
en popa *adv.* aft
enseguida *adv.* straightway
en tierra *adv.* ashore
en vez de *adv.* instead
en voz alta *adv.* aloud
enagua *n.* petticoat
enajenar *v.t.* alienate
enamorar *v. t* enamour
enano *n.* dwarf, midget
encadenar *v.* interlink
encaje *n.* lace
encallado *adj.* aground
encallar *v.* strand
encantado *adj.* overjoyed
encantador *adj.* charming
encanto *n.* allure, charm
encaprichamiento *n.* infatuation
encapricharse *v.* infatuate

encapsular *v.* encapsulate
encarcelar *v.* imprison
encargado *n.* attendant
encarnación *n.* incarnation
encarnar *adj.* incarnate
encender *v.* ignite, kindle
encendido *adj.* aflame
encendido *n.* ignition
encerrar *v.* enclose
enchufe *n.* socket
encía *n.* gum
enciclopedia *n.* encyclopaedia
encima de *prep.* above
enclave *n.* enclave
enclenque *adj.* puny
encoger *v.* shrink
encoger los hombros *v.* shrug
encogimiento *n.* shrinkage
encolerizarse *v.* rave
encomiable *adj.* creditable
encontrar *v.* meet, encounter
encontrarse *v.r.* meet each other
encorvado *adj.* bent, crooked
encorvar *v.* hunch
encuentro *v.* encounter
encuestado *n.* respondent
encuestador *n.* pollster
endeble *adj.* infirm
endémico *adj.* endemic
enderezar *v.* straighten
endeudado *adj.* indebted
endogámico *adj.* inbred
endulzar *v.* sweeten
endurecer *v.* harden, toughen
enemigo *n.* enemy, foe
enemistad *n.* enmity, feud
enemistarse con *v.* antagonize
energético *adj.* energetic
energía *n.* energy
enérgico *adj.* brisk, spirited
Enero *n.* January
enfadado *adj.* angry

énfasis *n.* emphasis
enfático *adj.* emphatic
enfatizar *v.* emphasize
enfermedad *n.* disease, illness
enfermera *n.* nurse
enfermizo *adj.* ailing, sickly
enfermo *adj.* ill, sick
enfocar *v.* zoom
enfrentar *v.t.* confront, tackle
enfurecer *v.* enrage, infuriate
engalanar *v* deck
enganchado *adj.* hooked
engañar *v.* deceive, mislead
engaño *n.* deceit, trickery
engañoso *adj.* deceptive
engatusar *v.* cajole
engendrar *v.* beget, spawn
engualdrapar *v.* caparison
engullir *v.t.* gobble
enigma *n.* enigma
enjambre *n.* swarm
enjuagar *v.* rinse
enlace *n.* liaison
enlazar *v.* liaise
enloquecer *v.t.* go mad or insane
enmendar *v.* amend
enmienda *n.* amendment
ennegrecer *v.* blacken
enojo *n.* annoyance
enorme *adj.* enormous, huge
enormemente *adv.* greatly
enramada *n.* bower
enredado *adj.* knotty
enredar *v. t* entangle
enredo *n.* tangle
enrejado *n.* trellis, lattice
enriquecer *v.* enrich
enrollar *v.t.* wind
enroscadura *n.* kink
ensalada *n.* salad
ensamblaje *n.* assemblage
ensamblar *v.* assemble

ensanchar *v.* widen
ensangrentado *adj.* bloody
ensayar *v.* rehearse
ensayo *n.* essay, rehearsal
enseñanza *n.* tuition
enseñar *v.* teach
ensombrecer *v.* overshadow
ensordecedor *adj.* deafening
ensueño *n.* reverie
enteramente *adv.* altogether
entereza *n.* mettle
entero *adj.* entire
enterrar *v.* bury, embed
entidad *n.* entity
entierro *n.* burial
entomología *n.* entomology
entonar *v.* intone
entonces *adv.* then
entorno *n.* milieu
entrada *n.* entrance, entry
entramado *n.* lattice
entrante *n.* starter
entrañablemente *adv.* dearly
entrar *v.* enter
entrar en erupción *v.* erupt
entrar sin autorización *v.* trespass
entre *adv.* between
entre bastidores *adv.* backstage
entre *prep.* among
entreabierto *adj.* ajar
entrega *n.* delivery
entregar *v.* deliver
entrelazar *v.* interlock
entrenador *n.* trainer, coach
entrenamiento *n.* training
entrenar *v.* train
entresuelo *n.* mezzanine
entretela *n.* facing
entretener *v.t.* entertain, amuse
entretenerse *v.r.* tarry
entretenimiento *n.* entertainment

entrevista *n.* interview
entristecer *v.* sadden
entrometerse *v.r.* meddle, tamper
entrometido *adj.* nosy, intrusive
entronizar *v.* enthrone
entumecido *adj.* numb
entusiasmarse *v.r.* rave
entusiasmo *n.* enthusiasm, zeal
entusiasta *adj.* keen, zealous
enumerar *v. t* enumerate
enunciar *v.* enunciate
envalentonar *v.* embolden
envarar *v.* strand
envase de cartón *n.* carton
envergadura *n.* span
enviado *n.* envoy
enviar *v.* dispatch
envidia *n.* envy, jealousy
envidiable *adj.* enviable
envidioso *adj.* envious, jealous
envio *n.* shipment
envoltorio *n.* wrapper
envolver *v.* enfold, envelop
eón *n.* aeon
épico *n.* epic
epidémico *n.* epidemic
epidermis *n.* epidermis
epigrama *n.* epigram
epilepsia *n.* epilepsy
epílogo *n.* epilogue
episodio *n.* episode
epístola *n.* epistle
epitafio *n.* epitaph
epítome *n.* epitome
época *n.* epoch
equidad *n.* equity
equidistante *adj.* equidistant
equilátero *adj.* equilateral
equilibrio *n.* equilibrium
equipaje *n.* luggage
equipar *v.* equip
equiparar *v.* equate

equipo *n.* equipment
equipo (de personas) *n.* team
equitativo *adj.* equitable
equivalente *adj.* equivalent
equivalente *n.* counterpart
equivocado *adj.* mistaken, amiss
equívoco *adj.* equivocal
equívoco *n.* pun
era *n.* era
erguido *adj.* erect
erizo *n.* urchin
ermita *n.* hermitage
ermitaño *n.* hermit
erógeno *adj.* erogenous
erosión *n.* erosion
erosionar *v.* erode
erótico *adj.* erotic
erradicar *v.* eradicate
errante *adj.* roving
errar *v.* err
errata *n.* misprint
errático *adj.* erratic
erróneo *adj.* inaccurate
error *n.* error, mistake
error de cálculo *n.* miscalculation
error de imprenta *n.* misprint
error garrafal *n.* blunder
eructar *v.* belch
erudito *adj.* erudite, learned
erupción *n.* blotch
esbelto *adj.* slim, svelte
esbozo *n.* sketch
escabroso *adj.* scabrous, lurid
escabullirse *v.r.* sneak away
escala *n.* scale
escalar *v.t.* climb
escaldar *v.* scald
escalera *n.* ladder, staircase
escalera mecánica *n.* escalator
escalfar *v.* poach
escalón *n.* rung, stair
escama *n.* flake

escamoteo *n.* sleight
escandalizar *v.* scandalize
escandalo *n.* scandal
escandaloso *adj.* uproarious
escanear *v.* scan
escáner *n.* scanner
escapada *n.* escapade
escapar *v.i* escape
escaparate *n.* showcase
escapatoria *n.* elusion
escape *n.* leakage
escarabajo *n.* beetle
escaramuza *n.* scrimmage
escarapela *n.* cockade
escarbar *v.* scrabble
escarceo *n.* dalliance
escarcha *n.* frost
escarchado *adj.* frosty
escarificador *n.* harrow
escarlata *n.* scarlet
escarmentar *v.* chasten
escarpa *n.* scarp
escasez *n.* shortage
escaso *adj.* scarce, scant
escatimar *v.* scrimp
escena *n.* scene
escenario *n.* scenario, stage
escéptico *adj.* sceptic
esclavitud *n.* slavery
esclavizar *v.* enslave
esclavo *n.* slave
esclusa *n.* sluice
escoba *n.* broom
escocés *adj.* Scottish
escofina *n.* rasp
escoger *v.* pick
escolar *adj.* scholar
escollo *n.* pitfall
escolta *n.* escort
escombros *n.* debris, rubble, wreckage
esconder *v.t* hide

escoria *n.* scum, slag
escorpión *n.* scorpion
escotilla *n.* hatch
escriba *n.* scribe
escribir *v.* write
escritor *n.* writer
escritura (legal) *n.* deed
escritura *n.* writing, scripture
escritura de propiedad *n.* muniment
escrúpulo *n.* scruple, qualm
escrupuloso *adj.* scrupulous
escrutinio *n.* scrutiny
escuadra *n.* squad
escuadrón *n.* squadron
escuálido *adj.* squalid
escuchar *v.* listen
escudero *n.* squire
escudo *n.* shield
escudriñar *v.* scrutinize
escuela *n.* school
escueto *adj.* stark
esculpir *v.* scult, carve
escultor *n.* sculptor
escultura *n.* sculpture
escultural *adj.* sculptural
escupidera *n.* spittoon
escupitajo *n.* gob
escurridizo *adj.* elusive
esencia *n.* essence
esencial *n.* gist, crux
esencial *adj.* essential
esfera *n.* sphere, dial
esférico *adj.* spherical
esforzarse *v.r.* strive, spurt
esfuerzo *n.* effort
esfumarse *v.* decamp
esgrima *n.* fencing
eslabón *n.* link
eslogan *n.* slogan
esmalte *n.* enamel, gloss
esmeralda *n.* emerald

esmoquin *n.* tuxedo
esnob *n.* snob
esnob *adj.* snobbish
esnobismo *n.* snobbery
eso-esa *pron.* that
esófago *n.* gullet
esotérico *adj.* esoteric
espacial *adj.* spatial
espacio *n.* space
espacioso *adj.* spacious, roomy
espada *n.* sword
espadín *n.* sprat
espalda *n.* back
espantapájaros *n.* scarecrow
espantoso *adj.* awful, ghastly
español *adj.* Spanish
esparcido *adj.* sparse
esparcir *v.* scatter
esparrago *n.* asparagus
espasmo *n.* spasm
espasmódico *adj.* spasmodic
espástico *adj.* spastic
especia *n.* spice
especial *n.* flair
especial *adj.* special
especialidad *n.* speciality
especialista *n.* specialist
especialización *n.* specialization
especializarse *v.* specialize
especialmente *adv.* especially
especies *n.* species
especificación *n.* specification
especificar *v.* specify
especifico *adj.* specific
espécimen *n.* specimen
espectacular *adj.* spectacular
espectáculo *n.* show, spectacle
espectador *n.* onlooker
espectador *n.* spectator
espectral *adj.* spectral
espectro *n.* spectrum, wraith
especulación *n.* speculation

especular *v.* speculate
espejismo *n.* mirage
espejo *n.* mirror
esperanza *n.* hope
esperar *v.* wait, expect
esperma *n.* sperm
espesarse *v.* thicken
espeso *adj.* bushy
espetar *v.* blurt
espetón *n.* spit
espía *n.* spy
espina *n.* thorne, prickle
espinaca *n.* spinach
espinal *adj.* spinal
espinilla *n.* shin
espino *n.* hawthorn
espinoso *adj.* thorny
espionaje *n.* espionage
espiral *adj.* spiral
espíritu *n.* spirit
espiritual *adj.* spiritual
espiritualidad *n.* spirituality
espiritualismo *n.* spiritualism
espitar *v.* broach
esplendido *adj.* splendid, lavish
esplendor *n.* splendour
esponja *n.* sponge
esponjoso *adj.* puffy
espontaneidad *n.* spontaneity
espontáneo *adj.* spontaneous
espora *n.* spore
esporádico *adj.* sporadic
esposa manos *n.* wife, spouse
esposar *v.* handcuff
espray *n.* spray
espuela *n.* spur
espuma *n.* foam, froth
espumoso *adj.* sparkling
espurio *adj.* spurious
esputo *n.* sputum
esquelético *adj.* scrawny
esqueleto *n.* skeleton

esquemático *adj.* schematic
esquí *n.* ski
esquilar *v.* shear
esquina *n.* corner
esquivar *v. t* dodge, shun
esquizofrenia *n.* schizophrenia
esta noche *adv.* tonight
estabilidad *n.* stability
estabilización *n.* stabilization
estabilizar *v.* stabilize
estable *adj.* stable
establecer *v.* establish, set
establecimiento *n.* establishment
establo *n.* stable
estaca *n.* stake, peg
estación (del año) *n.* season
estación *n.* station
estacional *adj.* seasonal
estacionario *adj.* stationary
estadio *n.* stadium
estadista *n.* statistician
estadística *n.* statistics
estadístico *adj.* statistical
estado *n.* state
estafa *n.* scam
estafador *n.* trickster
estafar *v.* defraud
estallar *v.* burst, pop
estallido *n.* outbreak, bang
estambre *n.* stamen, worsted
estamina *n.* stamina
estampado *n.* pattern
estampida *n.* stampede
estancado *adj.* stagnant
estancamiento *n.* stagnation
estancarse *v.* stagnate
estancia *n.* sojourn
estándar *n.* standard
estandarización *n.* standardization
estandarizar *v.* standardize
estanque *n.* pond

estar cansado *v.* knacker
estar de pie *v.* stand
estáticamente *adv.* statically
estático *adj.* static
estatua *n.* statue
estatuario *adj.* statuary
estatuilla *n.* statuette
estatura *n.* stature
estatus *n.* status
estatutario *adj.* statutory
estatuto *n.* statute, charter
este *n.* east
estelar *adj.* stellar
estentóreo *adj.* stentorian
estepa *n.* steppe
estéreo *n.* stereo
estereofónico *adj.* stereophonic
estereoscópico *adj.* stereoscopic
estereotipo *n.* stereotype
estéril *adj.* sterile, infertile
esterilidad *n.* sterility
esterilización *n.* sterilization
esterilizar *v.* sterilize, spay
esterilla *n.* mat
esterlina *n.* sterling
esternón *n.* sternum
esteroide *n.* steroid
estertoroso *adj.* stertorous
estética *n.* aesthetics
esteticista *n.* beautician
estético *adj.* aesthetic
estetoscopio *n.* stethoscope
estiércol *n.* manure, muck
estigio *adj.* stygian
estigma *n.* stigma
estigmatizar *v.* stigmatize
estilista *n.* stylist
estilístico *adj.* stylistic
estilizado *adj.* stylized
estilo *n.* style
estima *n.* esteem
estimulante *adj.* stimulant

estimular *v.* stimulate, boost
estimulo *n.* stimulus
estipendio *n.* stipend
estipulación *n.* stipulation
estipular *v.* stipulate
estiramiento *n.* stretch
estirar *v.* stretch
esto, este *pron.* this
estofado *n.* stew
estoico *adj.* stoic
estola *n.* stole
estomago *n.* stomach
estoque *n.* rapier
estorbar *v.* hinder, impede
estorbo *n.* hindrance
estornino *n.* startling
estornudar *v.i.* sneeze
estrafalario *adj.* outlandish
estrago *n.* havoc
estrangulación *n.* strangulation
estrangular *v.* strangle
estratagema *n.* strategem
estratega *n.* strategist
estrategia *n.* strategy
estratégico *adj.* strategic
estratificar *v.* stratify
estrato *n.* stratum
estrechar *v.t.* tighten
estrecho *adj.* narrow
estrella *n.* star
estrellado *adj.* starry
estrellarse *v.r.* crash
estremecerse *v.* quiver, shudder
estreno *n.* premiere
estreñimiento *n.* constipation
estrés *n.* stress
estresar *v.t.* stress
estría *n.* stretch mark
estriación *n.* striation
estribo *n.* stirrup
estrictamente *adv.* strictly
estricto *adj.* strict

estridente *adj.* strident, raucous
estrobo *n.* strop
estroboscopio *n.* strobe
estrofa *n.* stanza
estropear *v.* spoil
estructura *n.* structure, frame
estructural *adj.* structural
estrúdel *n.* strudel
Estuardo *adj.* stuart
estuco *n.* stucco
estudiante *n.* student
estudiar *v.* study
estudio *n.* study
estudioso *adj.* studious
estupendo *adj.* stupendous
estupidez *n.* stupidity
estúpido *adj.* stupid, foolish
estupor *n.* stupor
etcétera *adv.* et cetera
eternidad *n.* eternity
eterno *adj.* eternal
ética *n* ethic
ético *adj.* ethical
etimología *n.* etymology
etiqueta *n.* label, tag
etiqueta (estar) *n.* etiquette
étnico *adj.* ethnic
euforia *n.* euphoria
eunuco *n.* eunuch
euro *n.* euro
europeo *adj.* European
eutanasia *n.* euthanasia
evacuar *v.* evacuate
evadir *v. t* evade
evaluación *n.* assessment
evaluar *v.t.* evaluate
evangelismo *n.* revivalism
evaporar *v.* evaporate
evasión *n.* evasion
evasivo *adj.* evasive
evento *n.* event
evidencia *n.* evidence

evidente *adj.* evident
evitación *n.* avoidance
evitar *v.* avoid
evocar *v.* evoke
evolución *n.* evolution
evolucionar *v.* evolve
exacto *adj.* exact
exageración *n.* exaggeration
exagerar *v.* exaggerate
exaltar *v.* exalt
examen *n.* exam
examinador *n.* examinee
examinar *v.* examine, peruse
exasperar *v.* exasperate
excavadora *n.* shovel
excavar *v.* excavate, gouge
exceder *v.* surpass, exceed
excederse *v.* overdo
excelencia *n.* excellence
excelente *adj.* excellent
excéntrico *adj.* eccentric
excepción *n.* exception
excepcional *adj.* exceptional
excepto *prep.* barring
excesivo *adj.* excessive
exceso *n.* excess
excitación *n.* excitement
excitar *v.t.* excite
exclamación *n.* exclamation
exclamar *v.* exclaim
excluir *v. t.* exclude
exclusivo *adj.* exclusive
excretar *v.* excrete
excursión *n.* excursion
exento *adj.* exempt
exhalar *v.* exhale
exhaustivo *adj.* exhaustive
exhortar *v.* exhort
exigencia *n.* exigency
exigente *adj.* demanding, fussy
exilio *n.* exile
existencia *n.* existence, being

existencias *n.* stock
existente *adj.* extant
existir *v.* exist
éxito *n.* success
exitoso *adj.* successful
exonerar *v.* exonerate
exorbitante *adj.* exorbitant
exótico *adj.* exotic
expandir *v.* expand
expatriado *adj.* expatriate
expectante *adj.* expectant
expedición *n.* expedition
expediente *n.* dossier
experiencia *n.* experience
experimental *adj.* tentative
experimento *n.* experiment
experto *adj.* accomplished
experto *n.* expert
expiación *n.* atonement
expiar *v.* atone, expiate
explicar *v.* explain
explícito *adj.* explicit
exploración *n.* exploration
explorador *n.* scout
explorar *v.* explore
explosión *n.* explosion, blast
explosivo *adj.* explosive
explotar *v. t* exploit
explotar *v.i.* explode
exponente *n.* exponent
exponer *v.* display, exhibit, expose
exportar *v. t.* export
exposición *n.* exhibition, exposure
expresar *v.* express
expresar dolor *v.* condole
expresión *n.* expression
expresivo *adj.* expressive

expreso *n.* espresso
expropiar *v.* expropriate
expulsar *v. t* expel, eject
expulsión *n.* expulsion
exquisito *adj.* delightful
extasiado *adj.* rapt
éxtasis *n.* ecstasy, rapture
extender *v.* extend, spread
extendido *adj.* widespread
extensión *n.* extension, extent
extenuante *adj.* strenuous
exterior *adj.* exterior, outer, outward
externalizar *v.* outsource
externo *adj.* external
extinguir *v.* extinguish
extinto *adj.* extinct
extirpar *v.* extirpate
extorsionar *v.* extort
extra *adj.* extra
extracción *n.* extraction
extraer *v. t* extract
extrafino *adj.* superfine
extralimitarse *v.* overreach
extranjero *adj.* foreign
extranjero *n.* foreigner
extraño *adj.* strange, bizarre
extraordinario *adj.* extraordinary
extrarradio *n.* outskirts
extravagancia *n.* extravagance
extravagante *adj.* extravagant
extraviar *v.t.* mislead
extraviarse *v.r.* astray
extremista *n.* extremist
extremo *adj.* extreme
extrovertido *n.* extrovert
exuberante *adj.* exuberant
exultante *adj.* jubilant
eyacular *v.* ejaculate

F

fabrica *n.* factory, warehouse
fabrica de cerveza *n.* brewery
fabricación *n.* manufacturer
fabricar *v.* manufacture
fábula *n.* fable
fabuloso *adj.* fabulous
facción *n.* faction
faccioso *adj.* factitious
faceta *n.* facet
fachada *n.* facade
facial *adj.* facial
fácil *adj.* easy
facilidad *n.* ease, facility
facilitar *v.* facilitate
fácilmente *adv.* readily
facsímil *n.* facsimile
factibilidad *n.* practicability
factible *adj.* feasible
factor *n.* factor
factura *n.* invoice
facultad *n.* faculty
facultativo *n.* practitioner
Fahrenheit *n.* Faherenheit
faja *n.* waistband, sash
fajo *n.* wad
falacia *n.* fallacy
falda *n.* skirt
falda escocesa *n.* kilt
falible *adj.* fallible
fallar *v.* fail, misfire
fallecimiento *n.* decease
falsificación *n.* forgery
falsificado *adj.* counterfeit
falsificar *v.t* forge
false *adj.* false, fake
falta de *n.* lack
falta (defecto) *n.* failling
fama *n.* fame

familia real *n.* royal family
familiar *adj.* familiar
familiar *n.* family
famoso *adj.* famous
fan *n.* fan
fanático *n.* fanatic, zealot
fanatismo *n.* fanaticism
fanfarrón *n.* swanky
fanfarronear *v.* swank
fangoso *adj.* slushy
fantasear *v.* fantasize
fantasía *n.* fantasy
fantasma *n.* ghost, phantom
fantástico *adj.* fantastic
fardo *n.* bale
farfullar *v.* gibber, mumble
farmacéutico *adj.* pharmaceutical
farmacéutico *n.* pharmacist
farmacia *n.* pharmacy
faro *n.* headlight
farol *n.* lantern
fárrago *n.* welter
farsa *n.* farce
fascinante *adj.* mesmeric
fascinar *v.* fascinate
fascismo *n.* fascism
fase *n.* phase
fastidioso *adj.* irksome
fatal *adj.* fatal
fatalidad *n.* fatality
fatídico *adj.* fateful
fatiga *n.* fatigue
fauna *n.* fauna
fausto *n.* pageantry
favor *n.* favour
favorable *adj.* favourable
favorecer *v.* befriend
favorito *adj.* favourite
fax *n.* fax
fe *n.* faith
fealdad *n.* ugliness
Febrero *n.* February

febril *adj.* febrile
fecha *n.* date
fecha atrasada *n.* backdate
fecha limite *n.* deadline
fechar *v.* date
fechoría *n.* misdeed
feculento *adj.* starchy
federación *n.* federation
federal *adj.* federal
federar *v.* federate
felicidad *n.* happiness
felicitación *n.* congratulation
felicitar *v.* congratulate
feliz *adj.* happy
felpa *n.* plush
femenino *adj.* feminine
feminismo *n.* feminism
feng shui *n.* feng shui
fénix *n.* phoenix
fenómeno *n.* phenomenon
feo *adj.* ugly
féretro *n.* bier
fermentación *n.* fermentation
fermentar *v.* ferment
ferocidad *n.* savagery
feroz *adj.* ferocious
ferrocarril *n.* railway
ferry *n.* ferry
fértil *adj.* fertile
fertilidad *n.* fertility
fertilizante *n.* fertilizer
fertilizar *v.* fertilize
ferviente *adj.* fervid
fervor *n.* fervour
festival *n.* festival
festividad *n.* festivity
festivo *adj.* festive
fetiche *n.* fetish
feto *n.* fetus
feudalismo *n.* feudalism
feudo *n.* manor
fiador *n.* guarantor

fianza *n.* bail
fiasco *n.* fiasco
fibra *n.* fibre
fibra de coco *n.* coir
fibroso *adj.* stringy
ficción *n.* fiction
ficha *n.* chip
fichero *n.* filings
ficticio *adj.* fictitious
fidedigno *adj.* reliable
fideicomisario *n.* trustee
fidelidad *n.* fidelity
fideos *n.* noodles
fiebre *n.* fever
fiel *adj.* faithful
fielato *n.* octroi
fiero *adj.* fierce
fiesta *n.* party
figura *n.* figure
figurativo *adj* figurative
filamento *n.* filament
filantropía *n.* philanthropy
filantrópico *adj.* philanthropic
filántropo *n.* philanthropist
filatelia *n.* philately
filete *n.* steak
filigrana *n.* watermark
filo *n.* edge
filología *n.* philology
filológico *adj.* philological
filólogo *n.* philologist
filosofía *n.* philosophy
filosófico *adj.* philosophical
filósofo *n.* philosopher
filtrado *n.* filtrate
filtrar *v.* leach
filtro *n.* filter
fin *n.* end
final *n.* end
final *adj.* final
finalista *n.* finalist
finalización *n.* completion

finalmente *adv.* eventually
financiero *adj.* financial
financiero *n.* financier
finanzas *n.* finance
fingir *v.* feign, pretend
finito *adj.* finite
fino *adj.* thin
fiordo *n.* fjord
firma *n.* signature
firmamento *n.* firmament
firme *adj.* firm
firmeza *n.* steadiness
fiscal *adj.* fiscal
fiscal *n.* prosecutor
física *n.* physics
físico *adj.* physical
físico *n.* physique
fisionomía *n.* physiognomy
fisioterapia *n.* physiotherapy
fisura *n.* fissure
flácido *adj.* flaccid
flaco *adj.* skinny
flacucho *adj.* spindly
flagelar *v.* flagellate
flagrante *adj.* flagrant
flanco *n.* flank
flatulento *adj.* flatulant
flauta *n.* flute
flecha *n.* arrow
flemático *adj.* phlegmatic
flequillo *n.* fringe
flexible *adj.* flexible, supple
flexionar *v.* flex
flirtear *v.i* flirt
flojo *adj.* floppy, slack
flor *n.* flower
flora *n.* flora
floral *adj.* floral
florecer *v.* flourish, bloom
florete *n.* rapier
florido *adj.* flowery
florista *n.* florist

florón *n.* finial
flota *n.* fleet
flotabilidad *n.* buoyancy
flotación *n.* flotation
flotante *adj.* buoyant, natant
flotar *v.* float, hover
fluctuar *v.* fluctuate
fluido *adj.* discursive
fluido *n.* fluid
fluir *v.i* flow
flujo *n.* flux
flúor *n.* flouride
fluorescente *adj.* flourescent
fluvial *adj.* fluvial
fobia *n.* phobia
foca *n.* seal
focal *adj.* focal
foco *n.* focus
foco de atención *n.* cynosure
fogonero *n.* stoker
folio *n.* folio
folklore *n.* folk
follaje *n.* foliage
folleto *n.* brochure, leaflet, booklet
fomentar *v.* boost
fondo común *n.* kitty
fondo *n.* fund
fondo (origen) *n.* background
fondo (trasero) *n.* bottom
fonético *adj.* phonetic
fontanero *n.* plumber
forastero *n.* outsider
fórceps *n.* forceps
forense *adj.* forensic
forestación *n.* afforestation
forma *n.* shape
forma (manera) *n.* manner
formación *n.* formation
formal *adj.* formal
formalidad *n.* formality
formato *n.* format

formidable *adj.* awesome, formidable
fórmula *n.* formula
formular *v.* formulate
fornido *adj.* hefty, beefy, strapping
foro *n.* forum
forro *n.* lining
fortalecer *v.* fortify , strengthen
fortaleza *n.* fortitude, fortress, stronghold
fortuito *adj.* haphazard
fortuna *n.* fortune
forzado *adj.* stilted
forzosamente *adv.* perforce
forzoso *adj.* forcible
fosfato *n.* phosphate
fosforoso *adj.* phosphorus
fósil *n.* fossil
foso *n.* moat
foto *n.* photo
fotocopia *n.* photocopy
fotocopiadora *n.* photostat
fotografía *n.* photography
fotográfico *adj.* photographic
fotógrafo *n.* photographer
fracasar *v.* flop
fracaso *n.* failure
fracción *n.* fraction
fracturar *v.t* fracture
fragancia *n.* fragrance
fragante *adj.* fragrant
frágil *adj.* fragile
fragmento *n.* fragment
frambuesa *n.* raspberry
francés *adj.* French
franco *adj.* frank, outspoken
franela *n.* flannel
franqueo *n.* postage
franqueza *n.* candour
franquicia *n.* franchise
frasco *n.* flask

frase *n.* phrase
fraseología *n.* phraseology
fraternal *adj.* fraternal
fraternidad *n.* fraternity
fraude *n.* fraud
fraudulento *adj.* fraudulent
frecuencia *n.* frequency
frecuente *adj.* frequent
fregadero *n.* sink
fregona *n.* mop
freír *v.* fry
frenesí *n.* frenzy
frenético *adj.* frenetic, frantic
freno *n.* brake
frente *n.* forehead
fresa *n.* strawberry
fresco *adj.* fresh
friable *adj.* friable
fricción *n.* friction
frígido *adj.* frigid
frigorífico *n.* fridge
friki *adj.* freak
frio *adj.* cold, chilly
frívolo *adj.* frivolous
frontera *n.* border, frontier
frotamiento *n.* rub
frotar *v.* rub
frugal *adj.* frugal
fruncir el ceño *v.i* frown
frustrar *v.* frustrate, thwart
fruta *n.* fruit
frutero *n.* greengrocer
fruto seco *n.* nut
fuego *n.* fire
fuelle *n.* bellows
fuente (de agua, letra) *n.* fountain
fuente *n.* source
fuera *n.* outside
fuera de juego *adj.* offside
fuera *adv.* out
fueraborda *n.* outboard

fuerte *adj.* strong, forceful
fuerte (lugar) *n.* fort
fuerte (sonido) *adj.* loud
fuerza *n.* strength, force
fuga *n.* leak, leakage
fugarse *v.* elope
fugitivo *n.* fugitive, runaway
fulcro *n.* fulcrum
fulgor *n.* refulgence
fumigar *v.* fumigate
función *n.* function
funcional *adj.* functional
funcionar *v.* function, work
funcionar mal *v.* malfunction
funcionario *n.* functionary
fundación *n.* foundation
fundador *n.* founder
fundamental *adj.* fundamental,
  pivotal
fundido *adj.* molten
fundir *v.* fuse
fundirse *v.* merge
funeral *n.* funeral
furgoneta *n.* van
furia *n.* fury
furioso *adj.* furious, irate
furor *n.* furore
fusión *n.* fusion, merger
fusionar *v.* meld, fuse
fútbol *n.* football
fútil *adj.* nugatory
futurístico *adj.* futuristic
futuro *n.* future

G

gaceta *n.* gazette
gacha *n.* gruel
gachas de avena *n.* porridge

gafas protectoras *n.* goggles
gafe *n.* jinx, gaffe
gaje *n.* perquisite
gala *n.* gala
galante *adj.* gallant
galantería *n.* gallantry
galardonado *n.* laureate
galaxia *n.* galaxy
galería *n.* pelmet
galgo *n.* greyhound
galimatías *n.* rigmarole
gallardo *adj.* dashing
galleta *n.* biscuit, cookie
galleta salada *n.* cracker
gallina *n.* hen
gallito *adj.* cocky
gallo *n.* rooster, cock
galón *n.* gallon
galope *n.* gallop
gama *n.* gamut
gamberro *n.* yob
ganado *n.* cattle
ganador *n.* winner
ganador *adj.* winning
ganancia *n.* revenue
ganancias *n.* pickings
ganar *v.* win, gain, earn
ganchillo *n.* crochet
gancho *n.* hook, crook
gandulear *v.* slouch
ganga *n.* bargain
ganso *n.* goose
gánster *n.* gangster
garabatear *v.* scribble
garaje *n.* garage
garante *n.* warrantor
garantía *n.* warranty
garantizar *v.t* guarantee
garbanzo *n.* chickpea
garbo *n.* panache
garboso *adj.* jaunty
garganta *n.* throat

gargantilla *n.* necklet
garra *n.* talon
garrafón *n.* carboy
garrapata *n.* tick
garrote *n.* cudgel
gárrulo *adj.* garrulous
gas *n.* gas
gasa *n.* gauze
gaseoso *adj.* fizzy
gasolina *n.* petrol
gastar *v.* spend
gastar (consumir) *v.* expend
gasto *n.* expense
gastos *n.* outlay
gástrico *adj.* gastric
gastronomía *n.* gastronomy
gatear *v.* scramble
gatillo *n.* trigger
gatito *n.* kitten, puss
gato *n.* cat
gato (enchufe) *n.* jack
gavilla *n.* sheaf
gaviota *n.* seagull
gay *adj.* gay
géiser *n.* geyser
gel *n.* gel
gelatina *n.* jelly
gema *n.* gem
gemelo *n.* twin
gemido *n.* moan, whine
gemir *v.* groan
generación *n.* generation
generador *n.* generator
general *adj.* general
generalizar *v.* generalize
generalmente *adv.* ordinarily
generar *v.* generate
género *n.* gender
generosidad *n.* generosity
generoso *adj.* generous
génesis *n.* genesis
genético *adj.* genetic

genial *adj.* terrific
genio *n.* genius
genio (carácter) *n.* temper
gente *n.* people
gentileza *n.* gentility
genuino *adj.* genuine
geografía *n.* geography
geográfico *adj.* geographical
geógrafo *n.* geographer
geología *n.* geology
geólogo *n.* geologist
geometría *n.* geometry
geométrico *adj.* geometric
gerencial *adj.* managerial
gerente *n.* manager
germen *n.* germ
germinación *n.* germination
germinar *v.* germinate
gerundio *n.* gerund
gestación *n.* gestation
gesto *n.* gesture
gigabyte *n.* gigabyte
gigante *n.* giant
gigante *adj.* jumbo
gigantesco *adj.* gigantic
gimnasio *n.* gymnasium
gimnasta *n.* gymnast
gimotear *v.* sniffle
ginecología *n.* gynaecology
girar *v.* turn, spin
giro *n.* giro
gitano *n.* gypsy
glacial *adj.* glacial
glaciar *n.* glacier
glamour *n.* glamour
glándula *n.* gland
glaseado *n.* icing
glasear *v.* glaze
glicerina *n.* glycerine
glicinia *n.* wisteria
global *adj.* global
globalización *n.* globalization

globo *n.* balloon
globo ocular *n.* eyeball
globo terráqueo *n.* globe
gloria *n.* glory
glorificación *n.* glorification
glorificar *v.* glorify
glorioso *adj.* glorious
glosario *n.* glossary
glotón *n.* glutton
glotonería *n.* gluttony
glucosa *n.* glucose
gobernabilidad *n.* governance
gobernador *n.* governor
gobernar *v.* govern, rule
gobierno *n.* government
golf *n.* golf
golfo *n.* gulf
golosina *n.* candy
golpe de estado *n.* coup
golpe *n.* stroke
golpear fuerte *v.* swipe
golpear *v.* knock, hit
golpecito *v.* flick
góndola *n.* gondola
gong *n.* gong
gordo *adj.* fat
gorgojo *n.* weevil
gorgotear *v.* gurgle
gorila *n.* gorilla
gorjear *v.* chirp, twitter
gorjeo *n.* tweeter
gorra *n.* cap
gorrión *n.* sparrow
gorrón *n.* gudgeon
góspel *n.* gospel
gota *n.* drop
gota enfermedad *n.* gout
gotear *v. i* drop, drip
gourmet *n.* gourmet
grabadora *n.* recorder
grabar *v.t.* engrave
gracia *n.* wit, grace

grácil *adj.* lissom
graciosísimo *adj.* hilarious
gracioso *adj.* funny, humorous
grada *n.* tier
gradación *n.* gradation
grado *n.* degree
grado (clase) *n.* grade
graduado *n.* graduate
gradual *adj.* gradual
grafa *n.* rook
gráfica *n.* graph
gráfico *adj.* graphic
grafiti *n.* graffiti
grafito *n.* graphite
gramática *n.* grammar
gramo *n.* gram
gramófono *n.* gramophone
gran ayuda *n.* boon
gran escala *n.* largesse
granada arma *n.* grenade
granada *n.* pomegranate
granate *n.* garnet, maroon
grande *adj.* big, large, great
grandioso *adj.* grandiose
granero *n.* barn, granary
granito *n.* granite
granizo *n.* hail
granja *n.* farm
granja porcina *n.* piggery
granjero *n.* farmer
grano *n.* grain
grano cuerpo *n.* pimple
gránulo *n.* granule
grapa *n.* staple
grapadora *n.* stapler
grapar *v.* staple
grasa *n.* grease
gratificación *n.* gratification
gratificar *v.* gratify
gratis *adv. &adj.* gratis
gratitud *n.* gratitude
gratuito *adj.* gratuitous

grava *n.* gravel
gravedad *n.* gravity
gravilla *n.* grit
gravitación *n.* gravitation
gravitar *v.* gravitate
graznar *v.* squawk
graznido *n* quack
gremio *n.* guild
grieta *n.* rift
grifo *n.* tap
grillete *n.* shackle
grillo *n.* cricket
griñón *n.* wimple
gripe *n.* flu, influenza
gripe aviar *n.* bird flu
gris *adj.* grey
gritar *v.* scream, shout
grito *n.* squeal, yell
grogui *adj.* groggy
grosella *n.* gooseberry
grosero *adj.* rude
grotesco *adj.* grotesque
grúa *n.* crane
grueso *adj.* thick, coarse
gruñido *v.t.* snarl
gruñir *v.t.* grunt, growl
gruñón *adj.* grumpy
grupo *n.* group
gruta *n.* grotto
guadaña *n.* scythe
guante *n.* glove, gauntlet
guapo (hombre) *adj.* handsome
guapo *adj.* beautiful
guardabosques *n.* ranger
guardaespaldas *n* bodyguard
guardería *n.* nursery
guardia *v.* guard
guardián *n.* guardian
guarida *n.* den
guarnición *n.* accoutrement
guayaba *n.* guava
guepardo *n.* cheetah

guerra *n.* war
guerrero *n.* warrior
guerrilla *n.* guerilla
guía *n.* guide
guía (de libro) *n.* guidebook
guijarro *n.* pebble
guillotina *n.* guillotine
guindilla *n.* chilli
guiño *v.* wink
guión ortografía *n.* hyphen
guión *n.* script
guirnalda *n.* garland
guisante *n.* pea
guitarra *n.* guitar
gusano *n.* worm
gusano de seda *n.* silkworm

H

hábil *adj.* skilled, skillful
habilidad *n.* ability, skill
habitable *adj.* habitable, inhabitable
habitación *n.* room
habitante *n.* inhabitant
habitar *v.* inhabit
hábitat *n.* habitat
habito *n.* habit
habitual *adj.* customary
hablador *adj.* talkative
hablar *v.* speak, talk
hacer *v.* do, make
hacer autostop *v.* hitch
hacer callar *v.i* hush
hacer cumplir *v.* enforce
hacer gárgaras *v.* gargle
hacer mímica *v.* mime
hacer pinitos *v.* toddle
hacer punto *v.* knit

hacer puré *v.* mash
hacer señas *v.* beckon
hacer teatro *n.* acting
hacerse querer *v.* endear
hacha *n.* axe, hatchet
hacia *prep.* to, towards
hacia allá *adv.* thither
hacia arriba *adv.* upward
hacia delante *adv* forward
hada *n.* fairy
halcón *n.* falcon
halcón *n.* hawk
halitosis *n.* halitosis
halógeno *n.* halogen
hamaca *n.* hammock
hambre *n.* hunger, famine
hambriento *adj.* hungry, famished
hamburguesa *n.* hamburger
hámster *n.* hamster
hándicap *n.* handicap
hangar *n.* hangar
haragán *n.* shirker
harén *n.* harem
harina *n.* flour
harinoso *adj.* mealy
harto *adj.* weary, jaded
hasta *prep.* till, until
hasta ahora *adv.* hitherto
haya *n.* beech
hazaña *n.* feat
hebilla *n.* buckle
hechicería *n.* sorcery, witchery
hechicero *n.* sorcerer, wizard
hechizado *adj.* spellbound
hechizar *v.* bewitch
hechizo *n.* charm
hecho *n.* fact
hectárea *n.* hectare
hedonismo *n.* hedonism
hedor *n.* stench
hegemonía *n.* hegemony

helada *n.* frost
helado *n.* icecream
helado *adj.* icy, frosty
helecho *n.* fern
hélice *n.* propeller
helicóptero *n.* helicopter
helipuerto *n.* heliport
hembra *n.* female
hemisferio *n.* hemisphere
hemoglobina *n.* haemoglobin
hemorragia *n.* haemorrhage
hendedura *n.* cleft
hender *v.* cleave
hendido *n.* riven
henna *n.* henna
heno *n.* hay
hepatitis *adj.* hepatitis
heptágono *n.* heptagon
hercúleo *adj.* herculean
heredar *v.* inherit
heredero *n.* heir
hereditario *adj.* hereditary
herencia *n.* heritage, inheritance
herida *n.* wound
herir *v.* hurt
hermana *n.* sister
hermandad *n.* brotherhood, sisterhood
hermano *n.* brother, sibling
hermético *adj.* hermetic
hernia *n.* hernia
héroe *n.* hero
heroico *adj.* heroic
heroína *n.* heroine
herpes *n.* herpes, shingle
herramienta *n.* tool
herrero *n.* blacksmith
herrumbre *n.* rust
hervidor *n.* kettle
hervir *v.i.* boil
hervir a fuego lento *v.* simmer
heterogéneo *adj.* heterogeneous

heterogéneo *adj.* miscellaneous
heterosexual *adj.* heterosexual
hexágono *n.* hexagon
híbrido *n.* hybrid
hidratar *v.* hydrate
hidráulico *adj.* hydraulic
hidrógeno *n.* hydrogen
hiedra *n.* ivy
hiel *n.* gall
hielo *n.* ice
hiena *n.* hyena
hierba *n.* grass
hierro *n.* iron
hígado *n.* liver
higiene *n.* hygiene
higo *n.* fig
hija *n.* daughter
hijo *n.* son
hilador *n.* spinner
hilaridad *n.* hilarity
hilo *n.* thread
hilo dental *n.* floss
himno *n.* hymn
himno nacional *n.* anthem
hinchar *v.t.* bloat, swell
hinchazón *n.* swelling
hinojo *n.* fennel
híper *pref.* hyper
hiperactivo *adj.* hyperactive
hipérbola *n.* hyperbole
hipermercado *n.* superstore
hipertensión *n.* hypertension
hipnosis *n.* hypnosis
hipnotismo *n.* hypnotism
hipnotizar *v.* hypnotize
hipo *n.* hiccup
hipocresía *n.* hypocrisy
hipócrita *adj.* hypocrite
hipoteca *n.* mortgage
hipótesis *n.* hypothesis
hipotético *adj.* hypothetical
hisopo *n.* swab

histeria *n.* hysteria
histérico *adj.* hysterical
histograma *n.* histogram
historia (anécdota) *n.* story
historia *n.* history
historiador *n.* historian
histórico *adj.* historical
hito *n.* milestone
hocico *n.* snout, muzzle
hockey *n.* hockey
hogar *n.* home
hogareño *adj.* homely
hoguera *n.* bonfire
hoja cuchilla *n.* blade
hoja (papel) *n.* sheet
hoja (planta) *n.* leaf
hoja de calculo *n.* spreadsheet
holgado *adj.* baggy
holgazanear *v.* laze
holístico *adj.* holistic
hollín *n.* soot
holmio *n.* holmium
holocausto *n.* holocaust
holograma *n.* hologram
hombre *n.* man
hombrera *n.* pad
hombro *n.* shoulder
homenaje *n.* homage
homeópata *n.* homoeopath
homeopatía *n.* homeopathy
homicidio *n.* homicide
homofobia *n.* homophobia
homogéneo *adj.* homogeneous
homónimo *adj.* namesake
homosexual *n.* homosexual
hondonada *n.* dell
honestidad *n.* honesty
honesto *adj.* honest
hongo *n.* fungus
honor *n.* honour
honorable *adj.* honourable
honorarios *n.* fee, emolument

honorífico *adj.* honorary
honrado *adj.* righteous
hora *n.* hour, time
horario flexible *n.* flexitime
horario *n.* schedule
horas extras *n* overtime
horca *n.* gallows
horda *n.* horde
horizontal *adj.* horizontal
horizonte *n.* horizon
hormiga *n.* ant
hormigón *n.* concrete
hormona *n.* hormone
hornada *n.* batch
hornear *v.* bake
horno *n.* oven, furnace
horóscopo *n.* horoscope
horrendo *adj.* horrendous
horrible *adj.* horrible
horror *n.* horror
horrorizado *adj.* aghast
horrorizar *v.* horrify
horroroso *adj.* horrid, horrific
hortera *adj.* tacky
horticultura *n.* horticulture
hosco *adj.* testy
hospicio *n.* hospice
hospital *n.* hospital
hospitalario *adj.* hospitable
hospitalidad *n.* hospitality
hostal *n.* hostel
hostil *adj.* hostile
hostilidad *n.* hostility
hotel *n.* hotel
hoy *adv.* today
hoyo *n.* hole, pit
hoz *n.* sickle
hueco *adj.* hollow
hueco *n.* gap
huelga *n* strike
huelguista *n.* striker
huella *n.* track

huérfano *n.* orphan
huerto *n.* orchard
hueso *n.* bone
huesudo *adj.* bony
huevo *n.* egg
huir *v.* flee
humanidad *n.* humanity, mankind
humanismo *n.* humanism
humanitario *adj.* humanitarian
humanizar *v.* humanize
humano *n.* human
humano *adj.* humane
humedad *n.* humidity
humedecer *v.* dampen, moisten
húmedo *adj.* humid, damp
humildad *n.* humility
humilde *adj.* humble
humillar *v.t.* humiliate
humo *n.* smoke, fume
humor *n.* mood
humorista *n.* humorist
hundido *adj.* sunken
hundir *v.* sink
huracán *n.* hurricane
hurgar *v.* scavenge
hurtar *v.* pilfer
hurto en tiendas *n.* shoplifting
husmear *v.* poke, sniff
huso *n.* spindle

I

iceberg *n.* iceberg
icono *n.* icon
ictericia *n.* jaundice
idea *n.* idea
idea falsa *n.* misconception
ideal *adj.* ideal

idealismo *n.* idealism
idealista *adj.* idealistic
idealizar *v.* idealize
ídem *n.* ditto
idéntico *adj.* identical
identidad *n.* identity
identificación *n.* indentification
identificar *v.* identity
ideología *n.* ideology
idilio *n.* idyll
idioma *n.* idiom
idiomático *adj.* idiomatic
idiosincrasia *n.* idiosyncrasy
idiota *n.* idiot
idiota *adj.* idiotic
idiotez *n.* idiocy
idolatrar *v.* idolize
idolatría *n.* idolatry
ídolo *n.* idol
idoneidad *n.* suitability
iglesia *n.* church
iglú *n.* igloo
ígneo *adj.* igneous
ignominia *n.* ignominy
ignominioso *adj.* ignominious
ignorancia *n.* ignorance
ignorante *adj.* ignorant
ignorar *v.* ignore
igual *adj.* equal
igual *n.* peer
igualar *v. t* equalize
ilegal *adj.* illegal
ilegibilidad *n.* illegibility
ilegible *adj.* illegible
ilegítimo *adj.* illegitimate
ileso *adj.* unscathed
ilícito *adj.* illicit
ilimitado *adj.* unlimited
ilógico *adj.* illogical
iluminación *n.* lighting
iluminar *v.* illuminate
ilusión *n.* illusion

ilusorio *adj.* illusory
ilustración *n.* illustration
ilustrar *v* illustrate
ilustre *adj.* illustrious
imagen *n.* image
imágenes *n.* imagery
imaginable *adj.* conceivable
imaginación *n.* imagination
imaginario *adj.* imaginary
imaginar *v.* imagine
imaginativo *adj.* imaginative
imán *n.* magnet
imbécil *adj.* imbecile, fool
imbuir *v.* imbue
imitación *n.* imitation
imitador *n.* impersonator
imitar *v.* impesonate
impaciente *adj.* impatient, eager
impactante *adj.* striking
impacto *n.* impact
impalpable *adj.* impalpable
impar *adj.* odd
imparcial *adj.* impartial
imparcialidad *n.* impartiality
impasible *adj.* impassive
impecable *adj.* impeccable
impedimento *n.* impediment
impedir *v.* impede, prevent
impeler *v.* impel
impenetrable *adj.* impenetrable
impensable *adj.* unthinkable
imperativo *adj.* imperative
imperecedero *adj.* undying
imperfección *n.* imperfection
imperfecto *adj.* imperfect
imperial *adj.* imperial
imperialismo *n.* imperialism
imperio *n.* empire
impermeable *adj.* waterproof
impersonal *adj.* impersonal
impertinencia *n* impertinence
impertinente *adj.* impertinent

ímpetu *n.* impetus
impetuoso *adj.* impetuous
impío *adj.* impious
implacable *adj.* implacable
implantar *v.* implant
implementar *n.* implement
implicación *n.* implication
implicar *v.* implicate, involve
implícito *adj.* implicit
implorar *v.* implode
imponente *adj.* impressive
imponer *v.* impose
imponible *adj.* taxable
impopular *adj.* unpopular
importador *n.* importer
importancia *n.* importance
importante *adj.* important, major
importar *v.* import
importunar *v.t.* intrude, nag
imposibilidad *n.* impossibility
imposible *adj.* impossible
imposición *n.* imposition
impostor *n.* imposter
impotencia *n.* impotence
impotente *adj.* impotent
impracticable *adj.* impracticable
imprescindible *adj.* requisite
impresión *n.* impression
impresionar *v.* impress
impresora *n.* printer
imprevisor *adj.* improvident
imprevisto *adj.* unforeseen
imprimación *n.* primer
imprimir *v.* print, imprint
improbable *adj.* unlikely
improvisado *adj.* unprepared
improvisar *v.* improvise
imprudente *adj.* imprudent
impuesto *n.* tax
impuestos *n.* excise, taxation
impugnación *n.* impeachment
impugnar *v.* impeach

impulsar *v.t.* impel
impulsivo *adj.* impulsive
impulso *n.* impulse
impunidad *n.* impunity
impureza *n.* impurity
impuro *adj.* impure
imputar *v.* impute
inacabado *adj.* undone
inactividad *n.* inaction, idleness
inactivo *adj.* inactive
inactivo *adj.* idle
inadaptado *adj.* misfit
inadecuado *adj.* inadequate, unfit
inadmisible *adj.* inadmissible
inagotable *adj.* inexhaustible
inalámbrico *adj.* wireless
inalterado *adj.* unadulterated
inamovible *adv.* immovable
inanimado *adj.* inanimate
inapelable *adj.* unemployable
inaplicable *adj.* inapplicable
inapropiado *adj.* innapropriate
inarticulado *adj.* inarticulate
inaudible *adj.* inaudible
inaugural *adj.* inaugural
inaugurar *v.* inaugurate
incalculable *adj.* incalculable
incapacidad *n.* inability, incapac-ity
incapacitado *adj.* handicapped
incapaz *adj.* incapable
incautar *v.* impound
incendiario *adj.* inflammatory
incendio provocado *n.* arson
incensario *n.* censer
incentivo *n.* incentive
incesante *adj.* ceaseless
incesto *n.* incest
incidencia *n.* incidence
incidental *adj.* incidental
incidente *n.* incident
incienso *n.* incense

incierto *adj.* uncertain
incineración *n.* cremation
incinerar *v.* cremate
incisivo *adj.* incisive
incitar *v.* incite, abet
inclinación *n.* inclination
inclinar *v.* incline, lean, tilt
incluir *v.* include
inclusión *n.* inclusion
inclusivo *adj.* inclusive
incoherente *adj.* incoherent
incoloro *adj.* colourless
incomodar *v.* disturb
incomodidad *n.* discomfort
incomodo *adj.* uncomfortable
incomparable *adj.* incomparable
incompatible *adj.* incompatible
incompetente *adj.* incompetent
incompleto *adj.* incomplete
inconcluyente *adj.* inconclusive
incondicional *adj.* unconditional
inconexo *adj.* disjointed
inconformista *adj.* nonconformist
inconfundible *adj.* unmistakable
inconsciente *adj.* unconscious
inconsciente de *adj.* oblivious
inconscientemente *adv.* unwittingly
inconsiderado *adj.* inconsiderate
inconsistente *adj.* inconsistent
inconsolable *adj.* inconsolable
inconstante *adj.* fickle
incontable *adj.* unaccountable
inconveniencia *n.* inconvenience
inconveniente *adj.* drawback
incorporación *n.* incorporation
incorporar *v.* incorporate
incorpóreo *adj.* disembodied
incorreción *n.* impropriety
incorrecto *adj.* incorrect, wrong
incorregible *adj.* incorrigible
incorruptible *adj.* incorruptible

incredulidad *n.* disbelief
increíble *adj.* incredible
incrementar *v.* increase
incremento *n.* increment
incriminar *v.t.* incriminate
incrustar *v.* stud
incubar *v.* incubate
inculcar *v.* inculcate, instil
inculpado *n.* culprit
incumplir *v.* infringe
incurable *adj.* incurable
incurrir *v.* incur
incursión *n.* incursion, raid
indecencia *n.* indecency
indecente *adj.* indecent
indecible *adj.* untold
indecisión *n.* indecision
indeciso *adj.* undecided
indecoroso *adj.* improper
indefectible *adj.* unfailling
indefensible *adj.* indefensible
indefenso *adj.* helpless
indefinido *adj.* indefinite
indemnización *n.* indemnity
independencia *n.* independence
independiente *adj.* independent
independientemente *adv.* irrespective
indescriptible *adj.* indescribable
indeseable *adj.* undesirable
indicación *n.* indication
indicador *n.* indicator, gauge
indicar *v.* indicate
indicativo *adj.* indicative
índice *n.* index
indiferencia *n.* indifference
indiferente *adj.* indifferent
indígena *n.* indigenous
indigente *adj.* indigent
indigestión *n.* indigestion
indigesto *adj.* indigestible
indignación *n.* indignation

indignado *adj.* indignant
indignidad *n.* indignity
indigno *adj.* unworthy
Indio *n.* Indian
indirecta *n.* hint
indirecto *adj.* indirect
indisciplina *n.* indiscipline
indiscreción *n.* indiscretion
indiscreto *adj.* indiscreet
indiscriminado *adj.* indiscriminate
indiscutible *adj.* indisputable
indispensable *adj.* indispensable
indispuesto *adj.* indisposed, unwell
indistinto *adj.* indistinct
individual *adj.* individual
individualidad *n.* individuality
individualismo *n.* individualism
indivisible *adj.* indivisible
indolente *adj.* indolent
indómito *adj.* indomitable
inducir *v.* induce, mislead
indulgencia *n.* indulgence
indulgente *adj.* indulgent
indultar *v.* reprieve
industria *n.* industry
industrial *adj.* industrial
ineficaz *adj.* ineffective
ineficiente *adj.* inefficient
inelegible *adj.* ineligible
ineludible *adj.* inescapable
inenarrable *adj.* unutterable
inercia *n.* inertia
inerte *adj.* inert
inescrupuloso *adj.* unscrupulous
inesperado *adj.* unexpected
inestabilidad *n.* instability
inestable *adj.* unstable
inevitable *adj.* unavoidable
inexacto *adj.* inexact
inexcusable *adj.* inexcusable

inexorable *adj.* inexorable
inexperiencia *n.* inexperience
inexplicable *adj.* inexplicable
inexpugnable *adj.* unassailable
inextricable *adj.* inextricable
infalible *adj.* infallible
infame *adj.* infamous, vile
infamia *n.* infamy
infancia *n.* childhood
infantería *n.* infantry
infanticidio *n.* infanticide
infantil *adj.* infantile
infección *n.* infection
infeccioso *adj.* infectious
infectar *v.* infect
infeliz *adj.* unhappy
inferencia *n.* inference
inferior *adj.* inner, lower
inferioridad *n.* inferiority
inferir *v.* infer
infernal *adj.* infernal
infestar *v.* infest
infidelidad *n.* infidelity
infiel *adj.* unfaithful
infierno *n.* hell
infiltrado *adj.* undercover
infiltrar *v.* infiltrate
infinito *adj.* infinite
infinito *n.* infinity
inflación *n.* inflation
inflamable *adj.* flammable
inflamación *n.* inflammation
inflamar *v.* inflame
inflamatorio *adj.* inflammatory
inflar *v.* inflate
inflexibilidad *n.* obduracy
inflexible *adj.* inflexible
influencia *n.* influence
influyente *adj.* influential
información *n.* information
informado *adj.* aware
informal *adj.* informal

informante *n.* informer
informar *v.* inform, report
informativo *adj.* informative
informe *n.* notice
infortunio *n.* mischance
infractor *n.* offender
infraestructura *n.* infrastructure
inframundo *n.* underworld
infranqueable *adj.* impassable
infravalorar *v.* understate
infrecuente *adj.* infrequent
infringir *v.* breach
infundado *adj.* unfounded
infundir *v.* infuse
infusión *n.* infusion
ingeniero *n.* engineer
ingenio *n.* witticism
ingenioso *adj.* resourceful, witty
ingenuidad *n.* naivety
ingerir *v.* imbibe
ingle *n.* groin
inglés *adj.* English
ingobernable *adj.* ungovernable
ingratitud *n.* ingratitude
ingrato *adj.* thankless
ingrediente *n.* ingredient
ingresos *n.* income, takings
inhalador *n.* inhaler
inhalar *v.* inhale
inherente *adj.* inherent
inhibición *n.* inhibition
inhibir *v.* inhibit
inhóspito *adj.* inhospitable
inhóspito *adj.* bleak
inhumano *adj.* inhuman
iniciación *n.* induction
inicial *adj.* initial
iniciar *v.* initiate
iniciativa *n.* initiative
inicio *n.* onset
inigualado *adj.* unequalled
inimitable *adj.* inimitable

injerto *n.* graft
injuriar *v.* revile
injurioso *adj.* scurrilous
injusticia *n.* injustice
injustificado *adj.* unwarranted
injusto *adj.* unfair, unjust
inmaculado *adj.* immaculate
inmadurez *n.* immaturity
inmaduro *adj.* immature
inmanente *adj.* immanent
inmediatamente *adv.* forthwith
inmediato *adj.* immediate
inmemorial *adj.* immemorial
inmencionable *adj.* unmentionable
inmensidad *n.* immensity
inmenso *adj.* immense
inmensurable *adj.* immeasurable
inmerecido *adj.* uncalled
inmersión *n.* immersion
inmigración *n.* immigration
inmigrante *n.* immigrant
inmigrar *v.* immigrate
inminente *adj.* imminent
inmoderado *adj.* immoderate
inmodestia *n.* immodesty
inmodesto *adj.* immodest
inmolar *v.* immolate
inmoral *adj.* immoral
inmoralidad *n.* immorality
inmortal *adj.* immortal
inmortalidad *n.* immortality
inmortalizar *v.* immortalize
inmóvil *adj.* motionless, still
inmune *adj.* immune
inmunidad *n.* immunity
inmunizar *v.* immunize
inmunología *n.* immunology
inmutable *adj.* immutable
innato *adj.* innate, inborn
innecesario *adj.* unnecessary
innegable *adj.* undeniable

innoble *adj.* ignoble
innovación *n.* innovation
innovador *n.* innovator
innovar *v.* innovate
innumerable *adj.* countless
inocencia *n.* innocence
inocente *adj.* innocent
inoculación *n.* inoculation
inocular *v.* inoculate
inocuo *adj.* unexceptionable
inofensivo *adj.* harmless
inolvidable *adj.* unforgettable
inoperante *adj.* inoperative
inoportuno *adj.* inopportune
inquietar *v.t.* fret
inquieto *adj.* anxious
inquietud *n.* disquiet
inquilino *n.* lodger, tenant
inquisición *n.* inquisition
inquisitivo *adj.* inquisitive
insaciable *adj.* insatiable
insalvable *adj.* insurmountable
inscribir *v.* inscribe
inscripción *n.* inscription
insecticida *n.* insecticide
insecto *n.* insect
inseguridad *n.* insecurity
inseguro *adj.* insecure
insensato *adj.* unwise, senseless
insensible *adj.* callous, insensible
inseparable *adj.* inseparable
inserción *n.* insertion
insertar *v.* insert
insignia *n.* badge
insignificancia *n.* insignificance
insignificante *adj.* insignificant
insincero *adj.* disingenuous
insinuación *n.* insinuation
insinuar *v.* insinuate
insípido *adj.* insipid, tasteless
insistencia *n.* insistence
insistente *adj.* insistent

insistir *v.* insist
insolencia *n.* insolence
insolente *adj.* insolent
insólito *adj.* unheard
insoluble *adj.* insoluble
insolvencia *n.* insolvency
insolvente *adj.* insolvent
insoportable *adj.* insupportable
inspección *n.* inspection
inspeccionar *v.t.* inspect, survey
inspector *n.* inspector
inspiración *n.* inspiration
inspirar *v.* inspire
instalación *n.* installation
instalador *n.* fitter
instalar *v.* install
instantáneo *adj.* instantaneous
instigar *v.* instigate
instintivo *adj.* instinctive
instinto *n.* instinct
institución *n.* institution
instituto *n.* institute
institutriz *n.* governess
instrucción *n.* instruction
instrucciones *n.* briefing
instructivo *adj.* monitory
instructor *n.* instructor
instruido *adj.* literate
instruir *v.* instruct
instrumental *adj.* instrumental
instrumentista *n.* instrumentalist
instrumento *n.* instrument
insubordinación *n.* insubordination
insubordinado *adj.* insubordinate
insuficiente *adj.* insufficient
insulina *n.* insulin
insultar *v.t.* insult
insurgente *n.* insurgent
insurrección *n.* insurrection
intacto *adj.* intact
intangible *adj.* intangible

integral *adj.* integral
integridad *n.* integrity
intelecto *n.* intellect
intelectual *adj.* intellectual
inteligencia *n.* intelligence
inteligente *adj.* intelligent, clever
inteligible *adj.* intelligible
intención *n.* intention
intencional *adj.* intentional
intensidad *n.* intensity
intensificar *v.* intensify
intensificar los esfuerzos *v.*
  redouble
intensivo *adj.* intensive
intenso *adj.* intense
intentar *v.* try, attempt, attempt
intento *n.* attempt, intent
interacción *n.* interplay
interactuar *v.* interact
intercambiar *v. t* exchange, swap
interceder *v.* intercede
intercepción *n.* interception
interceptar *v.* intercept
interconectar *v.* interconnect
interdependiente *adj.* interdependent
interés *n.* interest
interesante *adj.* interesting
interface *n.* interface
interferencia *n.* interference
interferir *v.* interfere
interfono *n.* intercom
interino *adj.* interim
interior *adj.* interior, indoor
interlocutor *n.* interlocutor
intermediario *n.* intermediary
intermedio *adj.* intermediate
intermedio *n.* intermission
interminable *adj.* endless
intermitente *adj.* intermittent
internacional *adj.* international
internet *n.* internet

interno *adj.* internal
interno *n.* intern, boarder
interponer *v.* interject
interpretar *v.* interpret
interprete *n.* interpreter
interracial *adj.* interracial
interrelacionarse *v.* interrelate
interrogar *v.* interrogate
interrogativo *adj.* interrogative
interrumpir *v.* interrupt
interrupción *n.* interruption
interruptor *n.* switch
intervalo *n.* interval
intervención *n.* intervention
intervenir *v.* intervene
intestino *n.* intestine, bowel
intestino *n.* gut
intimidación *n.* intimidation
intimidad *n.* intimacy
intimidar *v.* intimidate
intimo *adj.* intimate
intocable *adj.* untouchable
intolerable *adj.* intolerable
intolerancia *n.* intolerance
intolerante *adj.* intolerant
intoxicación *n.* intoxication
intoxicar *v.* intoxicate
intranet *n.* intranet
intransitivo *adj.* intransitive
intrépido *adj.* intrepid
intrigar *v.* intrigue
intrínseco *adj.* intrinsic
introducir *v.* stash
introspección *n.* introspection
introspectivo *adj.* introspective
introvertido *n.* introvert
intrusión *n.* intrusion
intruso *n.* interloper
intuición *n.* intuition
intuitivo *adj.* intuitive
inundación *n.* flood, deluge
inundar *v.* flood, inundate

inusual *adj.* unusual
inútil *adj.* useless, pointless
inutilidad *n.* futility
inutilizar *v.* disable
invadir *v.* invade, overrun
invalidar *v.* invalidate, override
inválido *n.* invalid
invalorable *adj.* invaluable
invariable *adj.* invariable
invasión *n.* invasion
invencible *adj.* invincible
invención *n.* figment
inventar *v.* invent
inventario *n.* inventory
inventiva *n.* contrivance
invento *n.* invention
inventor *n.* inventor
invernal *adj.* wintry
invernar *v.* hibernate
inverosímil *adj.* implausible
inversión *n.* investment
inverso *adj.* inverse
invertir *v.t.* invert, invest
investigación *n.* investigation
investigar *v.* investigate
investir *v.* induct
invierno *n.* winter
inviolable *adj.* inviolable
invisible *adj.* invisible
invitación *n.* invitation
invitado *n.* guest
invitar *v.* invite
invocación *n.* invocation
invocar *v.* invoke
involucrar *v.* involve
involuntario *adj.* involuntary
invulnerable *adj.* invulnerable
inyección *n.* injection
inyectar *v.* inject
ir *v.i.* go
ir a la deriva *v.* drift

ir a todo gas *v.* pelt
ir de compras *n.* shopping
ira *n.* ire
iracundo *adj.* splenetic
irascible *adj.* petulant
iris *n.* iris
irlandés *adj.* irish
ironía *n.* irony
irónico *adj.* ironical, wry
irracional *adj.* irrational
irradiar *v.* irradiate, radiate
irrazonable *adj.* unreasonable
irreconciliable *adj.* irreconcilable
irrefutable *adj.* irrefutable
irregular *adj.* irregular
irregularidad *n.* irregularity
irrelevante *adj.* irrelevant
irremediable *adj.* irredeemable
irremplazable *adj.* irreplaceable
irreprochable *adj.* unimpeachable
irresistible *adj.* irresistible
irresoluto *adj.* irresolute
irresponsable *adj.* irresponsible
irreversible *adj.* irreversible
irrevocable *adj.* irrevocable
irrigación *n.* irrigation
irrigar *v.* irrigate
irrisorio *adj.* risible
irritable *adj.* irritable, tetchy
irritante *n.* irritant
irritar *v.* irritate
irrupción *n.* irruption
irse corriendo *v.t.* scamper
isla *n.* island
Islam *n.* Islam
isleta *n.* islet
isobara *n.* isobar
iterar *v.* iterate
itinerario *n* itinerary
izquierda *n.* left
izquierdista *n.* leftist

J

jabalí *n.* boar
jabalina *n.* javelin
jabón *n.* soap
jabonoso *adj.* soapy
jacuzzi *n.* jacuzzi
jade *n.* jade
jadear *v.i* pant
jaleo *n.* ruckus
jamón *n.* ham
jaque mate *n* checkmate
jardín *n.* garden
jardín de infancia *n.* kindergarten
jardinero *n.* gardener
jarra *n.* jug, pitcher
jarrón *n.* vase
jaula *n.* cage
jazmín *n.* jasmine
jazz *n.* jazz
jeep *n.* jeep
jefe *n.* boss, chief
jefe de correos *n.* postmaster
jengibre *n.* ginger
jerarquía *n.* hierarchy
jerga *n.* jargon
jeringa *n.* syringe.
jersey *n.* jumper, jersey
jet lag *n.* jet lag
jinete *n.* rider
jirafa *n.* giraffe
jockey *n.* jockey
jocoso *adj.* jocose
joroba *n.* hump
joven *adj.* young
jovencito *adj.* youngster
jovial *adj.* jovial
jovialidad *adv.* joviality
joya *n.* jewel

joyero *n.* jeweller
jubilación *n.* retirement
jubilado *n.* pensioner
jubilarse *v.* retire
jubileo *n.* jubilee
judía *n.* bean
judicatura *n.* judiciary
judicial *adj.* judicial
judo *n.* judo
juego *n.* game
juego de naipes *n.* whist
juerga *n.* jamboree, binge, spree
Jueves *n.* Thursday
juez *n.* judge
jugador *n.* player, gambler
jugar *v.* play
jugoso *adj.* juicy
juguete *n.* toy
juguetear *v.i.* frolic
juguetón *adj.* wanton
juicio *n.* judgement
Julio *n.* July
jungla *n.* jungle
Junio *n.* June
junta *n.* gasket
juntar *v.* join
junto a *prep.* alongside
juntos *adv.* together
Júpiter *n.* jupiter
jurado *n.* jury
juramento *n.* oath
jurisdicción *n.* jurisdiction
jurisprudencia *n.* jurisprudence
jurista *n.* jurist
justicia *n.* justice
justificable *adj.* justifiable
justificación *n.* justification
justificar *v.* justify
justificado *adj.* righteous
justo *adj.* just, fair
juvenil *adj.* juvenile
juventud *n.* youth
juzgado *n.* court

K

karaoke *n.* karaoke
karate *n.* karate
karma *n.* karma
kebab *n.* kebab
keroseno *n.* kerosene
kétchup *n.* ketchup
kilo *n.* kilo
kilobyte *n.* kilobyte
kilómetro *n.* kilometre
kit *n.* kit
Kosher *adj.* kosher
kung fu *n.* kung fu

L

la *pron.* her
laberinto *n.* labyrinth, maze
labia *n.* blarney
labial *adj.* labial
labio *n.* lip
labio leporino *n.* harelip
laboratorio *n.* laboratory
laborioso *adj.* laborious
labrar *v.t.* plough
laca *n.* lacquer
lacayo *n.* lackey
lacerar *v.* lacerate
lacio *adj.* lank
lacónico *adj.* laconic
lacrimógeno *adj.* lachrymose
lacrosse *n.* lacrosse
lactancia *n.* suckling
lácteo *adj.* dairy
lactosa *n.* lactose
lado *n.* side

ladrido *n.* woof
ladrillo *n.* brick
ladrón *n.* thief, burglar
lagartija *n.* lizard
lagarto *n.* lizard
lago *n.* lake
lago de montaña *n.* tarn
lágrima *n.* tear
laguna *n.* lagoon
laico *n.* layman
lamentable *adj.* lamentable
lamentar *v.* mourn
lamento *n.* lament
lamer *v.* lick
laminar *v.* laminate
lámpara *n.* lamp
lana *n.* wool
lancero *n.* lancer
lanceta *n.* lancet
langosta *n.* lobster, locust
languidecer *v.* languish
lánguido *adj.* languid
lanza *n.* lance, spear
lanzadera *n.* shuttle
lanzar *v.* launch
lápiz *n.* pencil
lápiz de color *n.* crayon
lapso *n.* span
lapsus *n.* lapse
largo *adj.* long
larguirucho *adj.* gangling
laringe *n.* larynx
larva *n.* larva
lasaña *n.* lasagne
lascivo *adj.* lascivious, lewd
laser *n.* laser
lastimero *adj.* piteous, pitiful
lata *n.* tin, can
latente *adj.* latent
latigazos *n.* lashings
látigo *n.* whip
latir *v.* throb

latitud *n.* latitude
latón *n.* brass
laúd *n.* lute
laurel *n.* laurel
lava *n.* lava
lavable *adj.* washable
lavabo *n.* basin
lavadora *n.* washer
lavanda *n.* lavender
lavandera *n.* wagtail
lavandería *n.* launderette, laundry
lavar *v.* wash
laxante *n.* laxative
lazo *n.* bond
leal *adj.* loyal, trusty
lealtad *n.* allegiance
lección *n.* lesson
lechada *n.* grout
leche *n.* milk
lechoso *adj.* milky
lector *n.* reader
lectura *n.* reading
leer *v.* read
leer mal *v.* misread
legado *n.* legacy, bequest
legal *adj.* legal
legalidad *n.* legality
legalizar *v.* legalize
legar *v.* bequeath
legendario *adj.* legendary
leggings *n.* leggings
legible *adj.* legible
legión *n.* legion
legislación *n.* legislation
legislador *n.* legislator
legislar *v.* legislate
legislativo *adj.* legislative
legislatura *n.* legislature
legitimidad *n.* legitimacy
legitimo *adj.* legitimate
lejos *adv.* away, far

lema *n.* motto, slogan
lencería *n.* lingerie
lengua (idioma) *n.* language
lengua *n.* tongue
lenguaje *n.* language
lengüeta *n.* barb
lentamente *adv.* slowly
lente *n.* lens
lenteja *n.* lentil
lentitud *n.* slowness
lento *adj.* slow
Leo *n.* Leo
león *n.* lion
leopardo *n.* leopard
leotardos *n.* leggings
lepra *n.* leprosy
leproso *n.* leper
lesbiana *n.* lesbian
lesión *n.* injury
lesionar *v.* injure
letal *adj.* lethal
letárgico *adj.* lethargic
letargo *n.* lethargy
letrero *n.* placard
letrina *n.* latrine
letrista *n.* lyricist
levadura *n.* yeast
levantamiento *n.* uprising
levantar *v.t.* lift
léxico *adj.* lexical
léxico *n.* lexicon
ley *n.* law
leyenda *n.* leyend, caption
liberación *n.* liberation
liberal *adj.* liberal
liberar *v.* liberate, release
libertad *n.* freedom, liberty
libertad condicional *n.* parole
libertador *n.* liberator
libido *n.* libido
libra (peso) *n.* libra
libra *n.* pound, quid

libre *adj.* free, vacant
librea *n.* livery
librero *n.* bookseller
libresco *adj.* bookish
libro *n.* book
libro de contabilidad *n.* ledger
libro de pasta blanda *n.* paperback
libro de texto *n.* textbook
libro encuadernado *n.* hardback
licencia *n.* licence
licencioso *adj.* licentious
lichi *n.* lychee
licor *n.* liquor
licorera *n.* decanter
licuadora *n.* blender
licuar *v.* liquefy
líder *n.* leader
liderazgo *n.* leadership
liebre *n.* hare
liga (ropa) *n.* garter
liga *n.* league
ligamento *n.* ligament
ligeramente *adv.* slightly
ligereza *n.* levity
lignito *n.* lignite
lijadora *n.* sander
lila *n.* lilac
lima *n.* lime
limbo *n.* limbo
limitación *n.* limitation
limitado *adj.* limited
limitar *v.* limit
limite *n.* boundary, limit
limón *n.* lemon
limonada *n.* lemonade
limosna *n.* alms
limoso *adj.* slimy
limpiamente *adv.* fairly
limpiar *v.* cleanse
limpieza *n.* cleanliness
limpio *adj.* clean

limusina *n.* limousine
linaje *n.* lineage
linaza *n.* linseed
linchar *v.* lynch
lindar *v.* abut
línea de meta *n.* byline
línea lateral *n.* sideline
línea *n.* line
linfa *n.* lymph
lingotes de plata u oro *n.* bullion
lingual *n.* lingual
lingüista *n.* linguist
lingüístico *adj.* linguistic
linterna *n.* torch, flashlight
lío *n.* rumpus
liposucción *n.* liposuction
liquidación *n.* clearance
liquidar *v.* liquidate, settle
líquido *n.* liquid
lira *n.* lyre
lírica *n.* lyric
lírico *adj.* lyrical
lirio *n.* lily
lisiado *n.* cripple
lisiar *v.* maim
liso *adj.* smooth
lista *n.* list
lista negra *n.* blacklist
listado *n.* printout
listo para ir *adj.* ready
listo *adj.* smart
listón *n.* lath, slat
litera *n.* bunk
literal *adj.* literal
literario *adj.* literary
literatura *n.* literature
litigación *n.* litigation
litigante *n.* litigant
litigar *v.* litigate
litro *n.* litre
llaga *n.* blain
llama *n.* flame

llamada *n.* ring, call
llamamiento *n.* summons
llamar *v.* call
llamar teléfono *v.* ring
llamarada *n.* flare, blaze
llamativo *adj.* jazzy
llanura *n.* moor
llave *n.* key
llave inglesa *n.* spanner
llegada *n.* arrival
llegar *v.* arrive
llenar *v.* fill
lleno *adj.* full
lleno de humo *adj.* smoky
llevar *v.* bring, carry
llevar puesto *v.* wear
llorar *v.* cry, weep
lloriquear *v.* blub, whimper
lloro *n.* cry
llorón *adj.* weepy
lloroso *adj.* tearful
llovizna *n.* drizzle
lluvia *n* rain
lluvioso *adj.* rainy
lo ideal *adv.* ideally
lo *pron.* it
loable *adj.* laudable
loar *v.* laud
lobo *n.* wolf
lóbulo *n.* lobe
local *adj.* local
local *n.* premises
localidad *n.* locality
localización *n.* location
localizar *v.* localize, locate
loción *n.* lotion
loco *adj.* crazy, mad
locomoción *n.* locomotion
locomotora *n.* locomotive
locución *n.* locution
locura *n.* madness
lodo *n.* sludge

logaritmo *n.* logarithim
lógica *n.* logic
lógico *adj.* logical
logística *n.* logistics
logo *n.* logo
lograr *v.* achieve
logro *n.* achievement
loma *n.* hillock
lomo *n.* loin
lona *n.* canvas
longevidad *n.* longevity
longitud *n.* length, longitude
loro *n.* parrot
los *pron.* them
losa *n.* slab
lotería *n.* lottery
loto *n.* lotus
loza *n.* china
lubricación *n.* lubrication
lubricante *n.* lubricant
lubricar *v.* lubricate
lucha *n.* fight
luchador *n.* wrestler
luchar *v.* fight, struggle
luchas internas *n.* infighting
lucidez *adv.* lucidity
lúcido *adj.* lucid
luciente *adj.* lucent
lucrativo *adj.* lucrative
lucro *n.* lucre
lugar *n.* place, venue
lugar apartado *n.* backwater
lúgubre *adj.* dingy
lujo *n.* luxury
lujoso *adj.* luxurious
lujuria *n.* lust
lujurioso *adj.* lustful
luminaria *n.* luminary
luminoso *adj.* luminous
luna *n.* moon
luna de miel *n.* honeymoon
lunar *adj.* lunar

lunático *n.* lunatic
Lunes *n.* Monday
lupa *n.* lens
lustre *n.* lustre
lustroso *adj.* glossy
luto *n.* mourning
luz *n.* light
luz de luna *n.* moonlight

M

macabro *adj.* macabre
machacar *v.* crush
macho *adj.* macho
Macintosh *n.* mackintosh
macizo *adj.* stout
madeja *n.* hank, skein
madera *n.* wood, timber
madre *n.* mother
madriguera *n.* burrow, den
madrina *n.* godmother
madurar *v.* ripen
madurez *n.* maturity
maduro *adj.* ripe, mature
maestría *n.* mastery
mafia *n.* Mafia
mafioso *n.* racketeer
magenta *n.* magenta
magia *n.* magic
mágico *adj.* fey
magistrado *n.* magistrate
magistral *adj.* magisterial
magnánimo *adj.* magnanimous
magnate *n.* magnate, tycoon
magnético *adj.* magnetic
magnetismo *n.* magnetism
magnificencia *n.* grandeur
magnifico *adj.* magnificent,
  grand, superb

magnitud *n.* magnitude
mago *n.* magician
maíz *n.* corn
majara *adj.* gaga
majestuosidad *n.* majesty
majestuoso *adj.* majestic
mal *adv.* poorly, badly, awry
mal casamiento *n.* misalliance
mal humor *n.* petulance
mal ventilado *adj.* stuffy
mal (enfermedad) *n.* malady
mala administración *n.* mismanagement
mala conducta *n.* misconduct
mala práctica *n.* malpractice
malabarista *n.* juggler
malaria *n.* malaria
maldecir *v.* damn
maldición *n.* curse
maleable *adj.* malleable, pliable,
  pliant
maleante *n.* marauder
maleducado *adj.* impolite
malentendido *n.* misconception
malestar *n.* malaise
maletero *n.* porter
maleza *n.* weed
malformación *n.* malformation
malgastar *v.* waste
malhechor *n.* malefactor
malhumorado *adj.* moody, sullen, surly
malicia *n.* malice
malicioso *adj.* malicious, cunning
maligno *adj.* malign, malignant
malinformar *v.* misinform
malinterpretar *v.* misinterpret,
  misunderstand
malísimo *adj.* lousy
malla *n.* mesh
malo *adj.* bad
maloliente *adj.* smelly

malsano *adj.* unhealthy
malta *n.* malt
maltratar *v.* mistreat
malvado *adj.* villain, evil
malvavisco *n.* marshmallow
malversación *v.* misappropriation
malversar *v.* misconduct
mama *n.* mum
mamario *adj.* mammary
mamífero *n.* mammal
maná *n.* manna
mancha *n.* stain
manchar *v.t.* stain
mancillar *v.* sully
mandamiento judicial *n.* injunction
mandar *v.* command
mandar (enviar) *v.* send
mandarina *n.* tangerine
mandato *n.* mandate, writ
mandíbula *n.* jaw
mandón *adj.* bossy
mandril *n.* baboon
manejable *adj.* manageable
manejar *v.* wield
manera *n.* way
manga *n.* sleeve
manganeso *n.* manganese
mango *n.* handle, shank
mango (fruta) *n.* mango
mangosta *n.* mongoose
manguera *n.* hose
manía *n.* craze
maniaco *adj.* maniac
manicura *n.* manicure
manerismo *n.* mannerism
manifestación *n.* manifestation
manifiesto *adj.* manifest
manifiesto *n.* manifesto
maniobra *n.* manoeuvre
manipulación *n.* manipulation
manipular *v.* manipulate

maniquí *n.* dummy
mano *n.* hand
mano de obra *n.* manpower
manojo *n.* bunch
manosear *v.* tinker
manotada *n.* smack
mansión *n.* mansion
manso *adj.* tame
manta *n.* blanket
manteca *n.* lard
mantener *v.* maintain, keep
mantenimiento *n.* maintenance
mantequilla *n.* butter
manto *n.* mantle
mantra *n.* mantra
manual *n.* handbook
manual *adj.* manual
manumisión *n.* manumission
manuscrito *n.* manuscript
manzana *n.* apple
mañana *n.* morning
mañana *adv.* tomorrow
mapa *n.* map
maquillaje *n.* make-up
maquina *n.* machine
maquinaria *n.* machinery
mar *n.* sea
maratón *n.* marathon
maravillar *v.t.* amaze
maravilloso *adj.* wonderful, marvellous
marca *n.* brand, mark
marca de agua *n.* watermark
marca de fábrica *n.* trademark
marca *n.* hallmark
marcador *n.* bookmark, marker, scorer
marcapasos *n.* pacemaker
marcar *v.* score
marcha *n.* going
marchar *v.* march
marchitarse *v.* shrivel, wither

marchito *adj.* wizened
marcial *adj.* martial
marco *n.* frame, framework
marco de la ventana *n.* casement
marea *n.* tide
mareado *n.* tipsy
marejada *n.* swell
maremoto *n.* tsunami
marfil *n.* ivory
margarina *n.* margarine
margarita *n.* daisy
margen *n.* margin
marginado *n.* outcast
marginal *adj.* marginal
marido *n.* husband
marina *n.* navy
marinar *v.* marinate
marinero *n.* sailor
marino *adj.* marine
marioneta *n.* puppet
mariposa *n.* butterfly
mariquita *n.* ladybird
mariscal *n.* marshal
marítimo *adj.* maritime
marketing *n.* marketing
mármol *n.* marble
marquesina *n.* marquee
marrana *n.* slut
marrón *adj.* brown
marsupial *n.* marsupial
Marte *n.* Mars
Martes *n.* Tuesday
martillo *n.* hammer
mártir *n.* martyr
martirio *n.* martyrdom
marxismo *n.* Marxism
Marzo *n.* march
más *adv.* more
más *conj.* but, yet
más allá *adv.* beyond
más blanca *adv.* whither
más lejano *adj.& adv.* furthest

más lejos *adv.* further
más o menos *adv.* about
más que *adv.* rather
más recóndito *adj.* inmost
masa *n.* mass
masa (pasta) *n.* dough, pastry
masacre *n.* massacre
masaje *n.* massage
masajista *n.* masseur
mascar *v.* crunch, munch
máscara *n.* mask
mascarada *n.* masquerade
mascota *n.* mascot
mascota (animal) *n.* pet
masculino *adj.* masculine, male
masoquismo *n.* masochism
masticar *v.* chew, masticate
mástil *n.* mast
masturbar *v.* masturbate
mata *n.* sprig
matador *n.* matador
matanza *n.* slaughter
matar *v.* kill
matemáticas *n.* mathematics
matemático *adj.* mathematical
matemático *n.* mathematician
materia *n.* matter
material *n.* material, stuff
materialismo *n.* materialism
materializar *v.* materialize
maternal *adj.* maternal, motherly
maternidad *n.* maternity, mother-hood
matiz *n.* nuance, tinge
matón *n.* bully
matorral *n.* thicket
matriarca *n.* matriarch
matricidio *n.* matricide
matriculación *n.* matriculation
matricular *v.* enrol
matrimonial *adj.* marital
matrimonio *n.* marriage

matriz *n.* matrix
matrona *n.* matron, midwife
maullar *v.* mew
mausoleo *n.* mausoleum
maximizar *v.* maximize
máximo *adj.* maximum
máximo *n.* maximum
Mayo *n.* May
mayonesa *n.* mayonnaise
mayor *adj.* elder
mayor parte de *n.* most
mayordomo *n.* butler
mayoría *n.* majority
mayorista *n.* wholesaler
mazapán *n.* marzipan
mazmorra *n.* dungeon
mazo *n.* mallet
me *pron.* me
mecánica *n.* mechanics
mecánico *n.* mechanic
mecánico *adj.* mechanical
mecanismo *n.* mechanism
mecanógrafo *n.* typist
mecer sobre ruedas *v.* dandle
mecerse *v.* sway
mecha *n.* wick
mechero *n.* lighter
mechón *n.* tress, wisp
medalla *n.* medal
medallista *n.* medallist
medallón *n.* medallion
media *n.* stocking
mediación *n.* mediation
mediano *adj.* medium, middling
medianoche *n.* midnight
mediar *v.* mediate
medicación *n.* medication
medicina *n.* medicine
medicinal *adj.* medicinal
medición *n.* measurement
médico *n.* doctor, physician
médico *adj.* medical

medida *a.* measure
medidas *n.* proceedings
medieval *adj.* medieval
medio *adj.& n.* middle
medio *adv.* half
medio ambiente *n.* environment
medio camino *adv.* midway
medio galope *n.* canter
mediocre *adj.* mediocre
mediocridad *n.* mediocrity
mediodía *n.* midday, noon
medios *n.* means
medios de comunicación *n.* media
medir *v.* measure
meditación *n.* meditation
meditar *v.* meditate
meditativo *adj.* meditative
Mediterráneo *adj.* mediterranean
medusa *n.* jellyfish
mega *adj.* mega
megabyte *n.* megabyte
megáfono *n.* megaphone
megahercio *n.* megahertz
megalítico *adj.* megalithic
megalito *n.* megalith
megapíxel *n.* megapixel
mejilla *n.* cheek
mejillón *n.* mussel
mejor *adj.* best
mejor que *adj.* better
mejora *n.* improvement
mejorar *v.* improve
melamina *n.* melamine
melancolia *n.* melancholia
melancólico *adj.* melancholic
melaza *n.* treacle
mella *n.* notch
mellarse *v.* indent
melocotón *n.* peach
melodía *n.* melody, tune
melódico *adj.* melodic

melodioso *adj.* melodious
melodrama *n.* melodrama
melodramático *adj.* melodramatic
melón *n.* melon
membrana *n.* membrane
membranoso *adj.* webby
membrillo *n.* quince
memo *n.* memo
memorable *adj.* memorable
memorándum *n.* memorandum
memoria *n.* memory, memoir
memorización *n.* rote
mencionar *v.* mention
mendigo *n.* beggar
menear *v.* wag, wiggle
menguar *v.* wane
meningitis *n.* meningitis
menopausia *n.* menopause
menor *adj.* lesser, minor
menor *n.* infant
menos *adj. & pron.* less
menos *prep.* minus, except
menospreciar *v.* underrate
mensaje *n.* message
mensaje de voz *n.* voicemail
mensajero *n.* messenger, courier
menstruación *n.* menstruation
menstrual *adj.* menstrual
mensual *adj.* monthly
menta *n.* mint, pepermint
menta verde *n.* spearmint
mental *adj.* mental
mentalidad *n.* mentality
mente *n.* mind
mentir *v.* lie
mentira *n.* falsehood
mentiroso *adj.* liar
mentor *n.* mentor
menú *n.* menu
mercado *n.* market
mercancía *n.* merchandise

mercantil *adj.* mercantile
mercenario *n.* mercenary
mercurio *n.* mercury
merecerse *v.* deserve
meridiano *n.* meridian
mérito *n.* merit
meritorio *adj.* meritorious
mermelada *n.* jam, marmalade
mero *adj.* mere
merodear *v.* lurk
mes *n.* month
mesa *n.* table
meseta *n.* plateau
mesías *n.* messiah
meta *n.* goal
metabolismo *n.* metabolism
metafísica *n.* metaphysics
metafísico *adj.* metaphysical
metáfora *n.* metaphor
metal *n.* metal
metálico *adj.* metallic
metalurgia *n.* metallurgy
metamorfosis *n.* metamorphosis
metedura *n.* gaffe
meteórico *adj.* meteoric
meteorito *n.* meteor
meteorología *n.* meteorology
meter *v.* place
meter paja *v.* waffle
meticuloso *adj.* meticulous
metódico *adj.* methodical
método *n.* method
metodología *n.* methodology
metralla *n.* shrapnel
métrico *adj.* metric, metrical
metro *n.* metre
metro (transporte) *n.* underground, subway
metrópolis *n.* metropolis
metropolitano *adj.* metropolitan
mezcla *n.* mixture, medley
mezcladora *n.* mixer

mezclar *v. t* mix
mezclarse *v.r* mingle
mezcolanza *n.* concoction
mezquindad *n.* parsimony
mezquino *adj.* miserly
mezquita *n.* mosque
michelines *n.* flab
mi, mis *adj.* my
mialgia *n.* myalgia
miasma *n.* miasma
mica *n.* mica
microbio *n.* germ
microbiología *n.* microbiology
microchip *n.* microchip
microcirugía *n.* microsurgery
microfilme *n.* microfilm
micrófono *n.* microphone
micrómetro *n.* micrometer
microondas *n.* microwave
microprocesador *n.* microprocessor
microscópico *adj.* microscopic
microscopio *n.* microscope
miedo *n.* fear
miedoso *adj.* fearful
miel *n.* honey
miembro *n.* limb
miembro *n.* member
mientras *conj.* whilst, whereas
mientras tanto *adv.* meantime
Miércoles *n.* Wednesday
miga *n.* crumb
migración *n.* migration
migraña *n.* migraine
mijo *n.* millet
mil *adj. & n.* thousand
milagro *n.* miracle
milagroso *adj.* miraculous
milenio *n.* millennium
milicia *n.* militia
miligramo *n.* milligram
milímetro *n.* millimetre

militante *adj.* militant
militar *n.* army officer
militar *adj.* military
militar *v.* militate
milla *n.* mile
millón *n.* million
millonario *n.* millionaire
milpiés *n.* millipede
mimar *v.* pamper, spoil
mimbre *n.* wicker, withe
mímica *n.* mime
mina *n.* mine
mina de carbón *n.* colliery
minarete *n.* minaret
mineral *n.* mineral
mineralogía *n.* mineralogy
minero *n.* miner
minestrón *n.* minestrone
mini *adj.* mini
mini taxi *n.* minicab
miniatura *n.* miniature
minibús *n.* minibus
minifalda *n.* miniskirt
minimizar *v.* minimize
mínimo *adj.* minimal
mínimo *n.* minimum
ministerial *adj.* ministerial
ministro *n.* minister
minoría *n.* minority
minorista *n.* retailer
minucioso *adj.* thorough
minúsculo *adj.* minuscule
minuto *n.* minute
mio *pron.* mine
miope *adj.* myopic
miopía *n.* myopia
miosis *n.* myosis
mirada *n* look, glance
mirar *v.* look, browse
mirar fijo *v.* gaze
mirar de cerca *v.* peer
mirar fijo *v.* stare

miríada *n.* myriad
mirra *n.* myrrh
mirto *n.* myrtle
miserable *adj.* bleak, wretched
miseria *n.* misery
mísero *adj.* paltry, measly
misil *n.* missile
misión *n.* mission, assignment
misionario *n.* missionary
misiva *n.* missive
mismo *adv.* same
misterioso *adj.* mysterious
misticismo *n.* mysticism
místico *n.* mystic
místico *adj.* mystical
mítico *adj.* mythical
mitigar *v.* mitigate
mitin *n.* rally
mito *n.* myth
mitología *n.* mythology
mitológico *adj.* mythological
mitón *n.* mitten
mitra *n.* mitre
moca *n.* mocha
mochila *n.* backpack, rucksack
moda *n.* fashion
moda pasajera *n.* fad
modalidad *n.* modality
modelo *n.* model
módem *n.* modem
moderación *n.* moderation
moderado *adj.* moderate
moderador *n.* moderator
moderar *v.t.* abate
modernidad *n.* modernity
modernismo *n.* modernism
modernizar *v.* modernize
moderno *adj.* modern, trendy
modestia *n.* modesty
modesto *adj.* modest
modificación *n.* modification
modificar *v.t.* modify, alter

modo de andar *n.* gait
modo *n.* mode
modular *v.* modulate
módulo *n.* module
mofa *n.* mockery
mohoso *adj.* fusty, musty
mojado *adj.* wet
mojar en algo *v. t* dip
mojigato *adj.* prim, prude
molar *n.* molar
molde *n.* mould
moldura *n.* moulding
molécula *n.* molecule
molecular *adj.* molecular
moler *v.* grind, mince
molestar *v.* disturb, bother
molestia *n.* nuisance
molesto *adj.* troublesome
molinete *n.* whirligig
molino *n.* mill
molino de viento *n.* windmill
molla *n.* flab
momentáneo *adj.* momentary
momento *n.* moment, while
momia *n.* mummy
momificar *v.* mummify
monacato *n.* monasticism
monarca *n.* monarch
monarquía *n.* monarchy
monárquico *adj.* royalist
monasterio *n.* monastery
monástico *adj.* monastic
moneda *n.* coin, currency
monedero *n.* purse
monetario *adj.* monetary
monetarismo *n.* monetarism
monitor *n.* monitor
monja *n.* nun
monje *n.* monk
mono *n.* ape, monkey
mono *adj.* cute
monocromática *n.* monochrome

monocular *adj.* monocular
monóculo *n.* monocle
monodia *n.* monody
monofónico *adj.* monophonic
monogamia *n.* monogamy
monografía *n.* monograph
monograma *n.* monogram
monolito *n.* monolith
monólogo *n.* monologue
monólogo *n.* soliloquy
monopolio *n.* monopoly
monopolista *n.* monopolist
monopolizar *v.* monopolize
monorraíl *n.* monorail
monosílabo *n.* monosyllable
monoteísmo *n.* monotheism
monoteísta *n.* monotheist
monotonía *n.* monotony
monótono *adj.* monotonous
monstruo *n.* monster
monstruoso *adj.* monstrous
montaje *n.* assembly
montaña *n.* mountain
montaña rusa *n.* rollercoaster
montañero *n.* mountaineer
montañoso *adj.* mountainous
montar *v.* ride, mount
montículo *n.* mound, hump
montón *n.* heap, stack, pile
montura *n.* saddle
monumental *adj.* monumental
monumento *n.* monument
monzón *n.* monsoon
mopa *n.* mop
moqueta *n.* carpet
mora *n.* blackberry
morada *n.* dwelling
morado *adj.* purple
moral *adj.* moral
moral *n.* morale
moralidad *n.* morality
moralista *n.* moralist

moralizar *v.* moralize
morar *v.* dwell
mórbido *adj.* morbid
morbosidad *adv.* morbidity
mordaz *adj.* barbed, scathing
morder *v.* bite
morena *n.* brunette
moreno *adj.* swarthy
morera *n.* mulberry
morfina *n.* morphine
morfología *n.* morphology
morganático *adj.* morganatic
morgue *n.* morgue, mortuary
moribundo *adj.* moribund
morir *v.* die
morsa *n.* walrus
mortal *adj.* deadly, mortal
mortalidad *n.* mortality
mortero *n.* mortar
mortificar *v.* mortify
mosaico *n.* mosaic
moscovita *adj.* muscovite
mosquete *n.* musket
mosquetero *n.* musketeer
mosquito *n.* mosquito
mostaza *n.* mustard
mostrador *n.* counter
mostrar *v.* show, evince
mota *n.* mote, speckle
moteado *n.* mottle
moteado *adj.* dappled
motel *n.* motel
motín *n.* mutiny, riot
motivación *n.* motivation
motivar *v.* motivate
motivo *n.* motive
moto *n.* bike
motocicleta *n.* motorcycle
motor *n.* engine
motorista *n.* rider
mousse *n.* mousse
movedor *n.* mover

mover *v.t* move
movible *adj.* movable
móvil *adj.* mobile
movilidad *n.* mobility
movilizar *v.* mobilize
movimiento *n.* movement
moza *n.* wench
mozuelo *n.* stripling
mozzarella *n.* mozzarella
mucho *adj.* lot, much
mucho *adv.* much
mucílago *n.* mucilage
mucosidad *n.* mucus
mucoso *adj.* mucous
mudanza *n.* removal
mudar *v.* moult
mudo *adj.* mute
mueble *n.* furniture
muebles *n.* furnishing
mueca *n.* sneer
muelle *n.* dock, pier, quay
muérdago *n.* mistletoe
muerte *n.* death
muerto *adj.* dead
muesca *n.* nick, notch
muesli *n.* muesli
muestra *n.* sample
muestra *n.* token
muestrario *n.* sampler
mugir *v.* moo
mugre *n.* grime
mujer *n.* woman
mula *n.* mule
mulato *adj.* mulatto
muleta *n.* crutch
multicultural *adj.* multicultural
multiforme *adj.* multiform
multilateral *adj.* multilateral
multimedia *n.* multimedia
multimillonario *n.* billionaire
multípara *adj.* multiparous

múltiple *adj.* multiple
multiplicación *n.* multiplication
multiplicar *v.* multiply
multíplice *n.* multiplex
multiplicidad *n.* multiplicity
multitud *n.* multitude, crowd
mundano *adj.* mundane
mundo *n.* world
municiones *n.* ammunition
municipal *adj.* municipal
municipio *n.* municipality
munificente *adj.* munificent
muñeca *n.* doll
muñeca (cuerpo) *n.* wrist
muñón *n.* stump
mural *n.* mural
muralla *n.* wall
murciélago *n.* bat
murmurar *v.* murmur
muro *n.* wall
musa *n.* muse
musaraña *n.* shrew
muscular *adj.* muscular
músculo *n.* muscle
muselina *n.* muslin
museo *n.* museum
musgo *n.* moss
música *n.* music
musical *adj.* musical
músico *n.* musician
muslo *n.* thigh
mustang *n.* mustang
musulmán *adj.* muslim
mutable *adj.* mutable
mutación *n.* mutation
mutar *v.* mutate
mutilación *n.* mutilation
mutilar *v.* mutilate
mutuo *adj.* mutual
muy *adv.* very

N

nabo *n.* turnip
nacho *n.* nacho
nacido muerto *n.* stillborn
naciente *adj.* nascent
nacimiento *n.* birth
nación *n.* nation
nacional *adj.* national
nacionalidad *n.* nationality
nacionalismo *n.* nationalism
nacionalista *n.* nationalist
nacionalización *n.* nationalization
nacionalizar *v.* nationalize
nada *pron.* nothing
nada *n.* nil
nadador *n.* swimmer
nadar *v.* swim
nadie *pron.* nobody
naftalina *n.* napthalene
nalga *n.* buttock
naranja *n.* orange
narcisismo *n.* narcissism
narciso *n.* daffodil
narcótico *n.* narcotic
nariz *n.* nose
narración *n.* narration
narrador *n.* narrator
narrar *v.* narrate
narrativa *n.* narrative
nasal *adj.* nasal
nata *n.* cream
natal *adj.* natal
natillas *n.* custard
natividad *n.* nativity
nativo *n.* native
nato *adj.* born
natural *adj.* natural
naturaleza *n.* nature
naturalista *n.* naturalist

naturalización *n.* naturalization
naturalizar *v.* naturalize
naturalmente *adv.* naturally
naturismo *n.* naturism
naufragio *n.* shipwreck
náufrago *n.* castaway
nausea *n.* nausea
nauseabundo *adj.* nauseous
náutico *adj.* nautical
navaja *n.* penknife, razor
naval *adj.* naval, marine
nave *n.* nave
navegable *adj.* navigable
navegación *n.* navigation
navegador *n.* browser
navegante *n.* navigator
navegar *v.* navigate, sail
Navidad *n.* Christmas
Navidades *n.* Xmas
neblina *n.* haze
neblinoso *adj.* misty
nebulosa *n.* nebula
nebuloso *adj.* nebulous
necesariamente *adv.* necessarily
necesario *adj.* necessary
necesidad *n.* necessity
necesitado *adj.* needy
necesitar *v.* need, necessitate
necio *adj.* asinine, fatuous
necromancia *n.* necromancy
necrópolis *n.* necropolis
néctar *n.* nectar
nectarina *n.* nectarine
nefario *adj.* nefarious
nefasto *adj.* dire, ominous
negación *n.* denial, negation
negar *v.t.* deny
negarse *v.r.* refuse
negativa *n.* refusal
negatividad *n.* negativity
negativo *adj.* negative
negligencia *n.* negligence

negligente *adj.* negligent
negociable *adj.* negotiable
negociación *n.* negotiation
negociador *n.* negotiator
negociar *v.* negotiate
negocio *n.* trade
negocios *n.* business
negro *adj.* black
némesis *n.* nemesis
neoclásico *adj.* neoclassical
neófito *n.* neophyte
neolítico *adj.* neolithic
neón *n.* neon
nepotismo *n.* nepotism
Neptuno *n.* Neptune
nervio *n.* Nerve
nervios *n.* jitters
nervioso *adj.* nervous
nesciencia *n.* nescience
neumático *adj.* pneumatic
neumático *n.* tyre
neumonía *n.* pneumonia
neural *adj.* neural
neurología *n.* neurology
neurólogo *n.* neurologist
neurosis *n.* neurosis
neurótico *adj.* neurotic
neutral *adj.* neutral
neutralizar *v.* neutralize
neutrón *n.* neutron
nevado *adj.* snowy
nevera *n.* fridge
nevisca *n.* sleet
nexo *n.* nexus
ni, no *conj.&adv.* nor
nicho *n.* niche, alcove
nicotina *n.* nicotine
nidada *n.* brood
nido *n.* nest
niebla *n.* fog, mist
niebla tóxica *n.* smog

nieve *n.* snow
nihilismo *n.* nihilism
nimbo *n.* nimbus
nimiedad *n.* trifle
ninfa *n.* nymph
ninguna *adj.* neither
niña *n.* girl
niñera *n.* nanny
niñez *n.* childhood
niño *n.* boy, kid, child
niño pequeño *n.* toddler
níquel *n.* nickel
nirvana *n.* nirvana
nítido *adj.* spotless
nitrógeno *n.* nitrogen
nivel *n.* level
no *adv.* not
no alineado *n.* non-aligned
no aprobar *v.* disapprove
no calificado *adj.* unqualified
no cualificado *adj.* unskilled
no deseado *adj.* unsolicited
no obstante *a.* nonetheless
no tripulado *adj.* unmanned
noble *adj.* lofty, noble
nobleza *n.* nobility, peerage
noche *n.* night
noción *n.* notion
nocional *adj.* notional
nociones *n.* smattering
nocivo *adj.* deleterious
nocturno *adj.* nocturnal
nódulo *n.* node
nómada *n.* nomad
nómada *adj.* nomadic
nombramiento *n.* appointment
nombrar *v.* appoint, name
nombre *n.* name
nombre de pila *n.* nickname
nomenclatura *n.* nomenclature
nominación *n.* nomination
nominal *adj.* nominal

nominar *v.* nominate
nonagésimo *adj.* ninetieth
nórdico *adj.* Nordic
norma *n.* rule, norm
normal *adj.* normal
normalidad *n.* normality
normalizar *v.* normalize
normalmente *adv.* usually
normativo *adj.* normative
norte *n.* north
norteño *adj.* northerly
nosotros *pron.* we
nostalgia *n.* nostalgia, longing
nostálgico *adj.* wistful
nota *n.* note
nota (resonancia) *n.* overtone
notable *adj.* noteworthy
notación *n.* notation
notario *n.* notary, solicitor
noticias *n.* news
notificable *adj.* notifiable
notificación *n.* notification
notificar *v.* notify
notoriedad *n.* notoriety
notorio *prep.* notorious
novato *n.* novice
novedad *n.* novelty
novela *n.* novel
novela rosa *n.* novelette
novelista *n.* novelist
noveno *adj.* ninth
noventa *adj. & n.* ninety
novia *n.* bride
noviazgo *n.* courtship
Noviembre *n.* November
novio *n.* bridegroom
nube *n.* cloud
núbil *a.* nubile
nublado *adj.* cloudy
nuca *n.* nape
nuclear *adj.* nuclear
núcleo *n.* nucleus

nudillo *n.* knuckle
nudista *n.* nudist
nudo *n.* knot
nudoso *adj.* gnarled
nuera *n.* daughter-in-law
nuestro *adj.* our
nueve *adj. & n.* nine
nuevo *adj.* new
nuevo juicio *n.* retrial
nuez *n.* walnut
nulidad *n.* nonentity
nulo *adj.* void, null
numerador *n.* numerator
numérico *adj.* numerical
número *n.* number
numeroso *adj.* numerous
nunca *adv.* never
nupcial *adj.* nuptial, bridal
nutria *n.* otter
nutrición *n.* nutrition
nutriente *n.* nutrient
nutrir *v.* nourish
nutritivo *adj.* nutritious
nylon *n.* nylon
ñame *n.* yam
ñoño *adj.* soppy
ñu *n.* gnu

O

o *conj.* or
oasis *n.* oasis
obedecer *v.* obey
obediencia *n.* obedience
obediente *adj.* obedient
obertura *n.* overture
obesidad *n.* obesity
obeso *adj.* obese
obispo *n.* bishop

obituario *n.* obituary
objeción *n.* objection
objetar *v.* demur
objetivamente *adv.* objectively
objetivo *adj.* objective
objeto *n.* object
oblación *n.* oblation
oblicuo *adj.* oblique
obligación *n.* obligation
obligado *adj.* obliging, obligated
obligar *v.* oblige
obligatorio *adj.* obligatory, compulsory, mandatory
obliteración *n.* obliteration
obra *n.* play
obra maestra *n.* masterpiece
obra (trabajo) *n.* handiwork
obras viales *n.* roadworks
obrero *n.* workman
obscenidad *n.* obscenity
obsceno *adj.* obscene
observación *n.* observation
observador *adj.* observant
observancia *n.* observance
observar *v.* observe
observatorio *n.* observatory
obsesión *n.* obsession
obsesionar *v.* obsess
obsolescente *adj.* obsolescent
obsoleto *adj.* obsolete
obstaculizar *v.* stymie
obstáculo *n.* obstacle
obstinación *n.* perversity
obstinado *adj.* obstinate, wilful
obstinancia *n* obstinacy
obstrucción *n.* obstruction, blockage
obstruccionista *adj.* obstructive
obstruir *v.* obstruct
obtener *v.* get, obtain
obtuso *adj.* obtuse
obviar *v.* obviate

obviedad *n.* truism
obvio *adj.* obvious
ocasión *n.* occasion
ocasional *adj.* occasional
ocasionalmente *adv.* occasionally
occidental *adj.* occidental
occidental *n.* westerner
occidentalizar *v.* westernize
occidente *n.* west, occident
ociosidad *n.* idleness
oceánico *adj.* oceanic
océano *n.* ocean
ochenta *adj. & n.* eighty
ocho *adj. & n.* eight
ocioso *adj.* idler
ocluir *v.* occlude
octágono *n.* octagon
octava *n.* octave
octavo *n.* octavo
octogenario *n.* octogenarian
Octubre *n.* October
ocular *adj.* ocular
ocultar *v.* conceal
oculista *n.* optician
oculto *adj.* occult, hidden
ocupación *n.* occupation, occupancy
ocupacional *adj.* occupational
ocupado *adj.* busy
ocupante *n.* occupant
ocupar *v.* occupy
ocurrencia *n.* occurrence
ocurrente *adj.* droll
ocurrir *v.* occur
oda *n.* ode
odiar *v.t.* hate
odio *n.* hate
odioso *adj.* hateful, loathsome
odisea *n.* odyssey
oeste *n.* west
ofender *v.* offend, aggrieve
ofensa *n.* offence

ofensivo *adj.* offensive
oferta *n.* offer, tender
ofertar *v.* bid, offer
oficial *n.* officer
oficial *adj.* official
oficialmente *adv.* officially
oficiar *v.* officiate
oficina *n.* office
oficina correos *n.* postoffice
oficio *n.* craft
oficioso *adj.* officious
ofrecer *v.* dispense
ofrecimiento *n.* offering
ofuscar *v.* obfuscate
oído *n.* hearing
oír *v.* hear
oír sin querer *v.* overhear
ojeroso *adj.* haggard
ojo *n.* eye
ojo cerradura *n.* keyhole
oleada *n.* surge
oler *v.* reek
oligarquía *n.* oligarchy
olímpico *adj.* olympic
olla *n .* pot
olor *n.* smell, scent
oloroso *adj.* odorous
olvidadizo *adj.* forgetful
olvidado *adj.* unsung
olvidar *v.* forget
olvido *n.* oblivion
omisión *n.* omission, default
omitir *v.* omit
omnipotencia *n.* omnipotence
omnipotente *adj.* omnipotent
omnipresencia *n.* omnipresence
omnipresente *adj.* omnipresent
omnisciencia *n.* omniscience
omnisciente *adj.* omniscient
once *adj. & n.* eleven
onda *n.* wave, ripple
ondear *v.* undulate

ondulado *adj.* corrugated, wavy
ónice *n.* onyx
onomatopeya *n.* onomatopoeia
ontología *n.* ontology
onza *n.* ounce
opacidad *n.* opacity
opaco *adj.* opaque
ópalo *n.* opal
opción *n.* option
opcional *adj.* optional
opera *n.* opera
operación *n.* operation
operacional *adj.* operational
operador *n.* operator
operar *v.* operate
operativo *adj.* operative
opinar *v.* opine
opinión *n.* opinion
opio *n.* opium
oponer *v.* oppose
oponerse a *v.t.* counter
oportunidad *n.* opportunity
oportunismo *n.* opportunism
oportuno *adj.* opportune
oposición *n.* opposition
opositor *n.* opponent
opresión *n.* oppression
opresivo *adj.* oppressive
opresor *n.* oppressor
oprimir *v.* oppress
optar *v.* opt
óptico *adj.* optic
optimismo *n.* optimism
optimista *n.* optimist
optimista *adj.* optimistic
optimizar *v.* optimize
óptimo *adj.* optimum
opuesto *adj.* opposite
opulencia *n.* opulence, affluence
opulento *adj.* opulent, wealthy
oración *n.* prayer
oráculo *n.* oracle

orador *n.* speaker, orator
oral *adj.* oral
oratorio *n.* oratory
orbe *n.* orb
órbita *n.* orbit
orbital *adj.* orbital
orden judicial *n.* warrant
orden *n.* order
ordenado *adj.* tidy, orderly
ordenador *n.* computer
ordenanza *n.* ordinance
ordenar *v.* order, instruct
ordinario *adj.* crude
oreja *n.* ear
orfanato *n.* orphanage
orfebre *n.* goldsmith
orgánico *adj.* organic
organismo *n.* organism
organización *n.* organization
organizar *v.* organize
órgano *n.* organ
orgasmo *n.* orgasm
orgia *n.* orgy
orgullo *n.* pride
orgulloso *adj.* proud
oriental *adj.* eastern, oriental
orientar *v.* orientate
oriente *n.* orient
orificio nasal *n.* nostril
origami *n.* origami
origen *n.* origin
original *adj.* original
originalidad *n.* originality
originar *v.t.* originate
originarse *v.r.* originate
orilla *n.* shore
orilla del mar *n.* seaside
orillo *n.* selvedge
orina *n.* urine
orinal *n.* urinal
orinar *v.* urinate
ornamentación *n.* ornamentation

ornamentado *adj.* ornate
ornamental *adj.* ornamental
oro *n.* gold
oropel *n.* tinsel
orquesta *n.* orchestra
orquestal *adj.* orchestral
orquídea *n.* orchid
ortiga *n.* nettle
ortodoxia *n.* orthodoxy
ortodoxo *adj.* orthodox
ortografía *n.* spelling
ortopedia *n.* orthopaedics
oruga *n.* caterpillar
osado *adj.* daring
oscilación *n.* oscillation
oscilar *v.* oscillate, waver
oscurecer *v.* darken
oscuridad *n.* darkness
oscuro *adj.* dark
osificarse *v.* ossify
oso *n.* bear
ostentación *n.* ostentation
ostentar *v.* flaunt
osteopatía *n.* osteopathy
ostra *n.* oyster
otomano *n.* ottoman
otoño *n.* autumn
otorgar *v.* grant
otra vez *adv.* again
otro *pron.* another
otro *adj.* other
otro *adv.* else
ovación *n.* ovation
ovado *adj.* ovate
ovalado *adj.* oval
ovario *n.* ovary
oveja *n.* sheep
ovular *v.* ovulate
oxidado *adj.* rusty
óxido *n.* oxide
oxigeno *n.* oxygen
ozono *n* ozone

P

pabellón *n.* pavilion
pacana *n.* pecan
paciencia *n.* patience
paciente *adj.* patient
paciente *n.* patient
Pacífico *n.* Pacific
pacífico *adj.* peaceable, peaceful
pacifista *n.* pacifist
pacotilla *adj.* shoddy
pacto *n.* pact, bargain
paddock *n.* paddock
padre *n.* father
padrino *n.* godfather
pagable *adj.* payable
pagano *n.* pagan
pagar *v.* pay
página *n.* page
página web *n.* webpage
pago *n.* payment
pagoda *n.* pagoda
país *n.* country
paisaje *n.* landscape
paja *n.* straw
pajar *n.* rick
pájaro *n.* bird
pajita *n.* straw
pala *n.* spade
palabra *n.* word
palabras *n.* words, speech
palaciego *adj.* palatial
palacio *n.* palace
paladar *n.* palate
palanca *n.* lever
palatal *adj.* palatal
palet *n.* palette, pallet
paleta *n.* pallet
pálido *adj.* pale
palillo *n.* toothpick

palillos chinos *n.* chopsticks
paliza *adj.* spanking
palma *n.* palm
palmera *n.* palm
palo *n.* stick
paloma *n.* pigeon
palos *n.* wicket
palpable *adj.* palpable
palpitación *n.* palpitation
palpitar *v.* palpitate
pan *n.* bread
panacea *n.* panacea
panadería *n.* bakery
panadero *n.* baker
panal *n.* honeycomb
pancarta *n.* banner
páncreas *n.* pancreas
panda *n.* panda
pandemonio *n.* pandemonium
pandereta *n.* tambourine
pandilla *n.* gang
panegírico *n.* panegyric
panel *n.* panel
panfletista *n.* pamphleteer
panfleto *n.* pamphlet, leaflet
pánico *n.* panic
panorama *n.* panorama
pantalla *n.* screen
pantalón *n.* pantaloon
pantalones *n.* trousers
pantano *n* marsh, swamp
panteísmo *n.* pantheism
panteísta *adj.* pantheist
pantera *n.* panther
pantomima *n.* pantomime
pantorrilla *n.* calf
panza *n.* paunch
pañal *n.* nappy, diaper
pañuelo *n.* handkerchief
pañuelo de papel *n.* tissue
papa *n* dad
Papa *n.* pope

papado *n.* papacy
papal *adj.* papal
papel *n.* paper
papel de lija *n.* sandpaper
papel (rol) *n.* role
papelería *n.* stationery
paperas *n.* mumps
papilla *n.* mush
papiroflexia *n.* origami
paquete *n.* package, parcel
par *n.* pair
para *prep.* for
para siempre *adv.* forever
parábola *n.* parable
paracaídas *n.* parachute
paracaidista *n.* parachutist
parachoques *n.* bumper
parada *n.* standstill
paradero *adv.* whereabout
parado *adj.* unemployed
paradoja *n.* paradox
paradójico *adj.* paradoxical
parafernalia *n.* paraphernalia
parafina *n.* paraffin
paráfrasis *v.* paraphrase
paraguas *n.* umbrella
paraíso *n.* paradise
paralelo *n.* parallel
paralelogramo *n.* parallelogram
parálisis *n.* paralysis
paralitico *adj.* paralytic
paralizar *v.* paralyse
paramédico *n.* paramedic
parámetro *n.* parameter
páramo *n.* backwater
parar *v.* stop, halt
parásito *n.* parasite
parcial *adj.* partial
parcialidad *n.* partiality
parco *adj.* sparing
pareado *n.* couplet
parecer *n.* opinion

parecer *v.i.* appear, seem
parecerse *v.r.* resemble
parecido *n.* resemblance
parecido *adj.* similar
pared *n.* wall
pareja *n.* couple
parejo *adj.* even
parental *adj.* parental
parentesco *n.* kinship
paréntesis *n.* brackets
paria *n.* pariah
paridad *n.* parity
pariente *adj.* relative
parientes *n.* kin
parlamentario *n.* parliamentarian
parlamentario *adj.* parliamentary
parlamento *n.* parliament
parlotear *v.i.* chatter
parodia *n.* parody
parpadear *v.t* flicker
parque *n.* park
párrafo *n.* paragraph
parrandear *v.* roister
parricidio *n.* parricide
párroco *n.* vicar
parroquia *n.* parish
parte *n.* part, share
parte delantera *n.* front
parte trasera *n.* rear
parteluz *n.* mullion
partición *n.* partition
participación *n.* participation
participante *n.* participant
participar *v.* participate
partícula *n.* particle
partidario *n.* loyalist
partir *v.* depart
partir (algo) *v.* split
partisano *n.* partisan
pasa *n.* raisin
pasa de Corinto *n.* currant
pasable *adj.* passable

pasado *adj.* past, bygone
pasado de moda *adj.* outdated
pasaje *n.* excerpt
pasajero *n.* passenger
pasajero *adj.* passing
pasamanos *n.* banisters
pasaporte *n.* passport
pasar *v.* pass
pasar contrabando *v.* smuggle
pasar hambre *v.* starve
pasar por alto *v.* overlook
pasar un trapo *v.* wipe
pasar volando *v.* hurtle
pasatiempo *n.* pastime
Pascua *n.* easter
pasear *v.* ramble
pasillo *n.* aisle, corridor
pasión *n.* passion
pasivo *adj.* passive
pasmado *adj.* flabbergasted
paso *n.* step, pace, passage
paso de zebra *n.* zebra crossing
paso elevado *n.* overpass
pasta *n.* paste
pasta de dientes *n.* toothpaste
pastar *v.* graze
pastel *n.* cake, pie
pastelería *n.* patisserie
pasteurizado *adj.* pasteurized
pastilla *n.* pill, lozenge
pastor *n.* shepherd
pastoril *adj.* pastoral
pastos *n.* pasture
pata *n.* paw
pata delantera *n.* foreleg
pataleta *n.* tantrum
patán *n.* lout, slob
patata *n.* potato
patear *v.* kick
patente *n.* patent
paternal *adj.* paternal
paternidad *n.* paternity

patético *adj.* pathetic
patetismo *n.* poignancy
patín *n.* skate
patinazo *n.* gymnastic
patio *n.* courtyard, yard
pato *n.* duck
patología *n.* pathology
patriarca *n.* patriarch
patrimonio *n.* heritage
patriota *n.* patriot
patriótico *adj.* patriotic
patriotismo *n.* patriotism
patrocinador *n.* sponsor
patrocinio *n.* sponsorship
patrón *n.* pattern
patrono *n.* patron
patrullar *v.* patrol
pausa *n.* pause
pava real *n.* peahen
pavimentar *v.* pave
pavo *n.* turkey
pavo real *n.* peacock
pavonearse *v.* swagger
payasadas *n.* tomfoolery
payaso *n.* clown
paz *n.* peace
peaje *n.* toll
peatón *n.* pedestrian
peca *n.* freckle
pecado *n.* sin
pecador *n.* sinner
pecaminoso *adj.* sinful, unholy
pecho *n.* breast
peculiar *adj.* peculiar
peculiaridad *n.* quirk
pedagogía *n.* pedagogy
pedagogo *n.* pedagogue
pedal *n.* pedal, treadle
pedante *n.* pedant
pedante *adj.* pedantic
pedazo *n.* piece
pederasta *n.* paedophile

pedernal *n.* flint
pedestal *n.* pedestal
pediatra *n.* paediatrician
pediatría *n.* paediatrics
pedicura *n.* pedicure
pedido *n.* order
pedigrí *n.* pedigree
pedregoso *adj.* stony
pegadizo *adj.* catchy
pegajoso *adj.* sticky
pegamento *n.* glue
pegar (golpear) *v.* beat
pegar *v.t.* stick, glue
pegatina *n.* sticker
peinado *n.* hairstyle
peine *n.* comb
pelado *adj.* broke
pelar *v.* pare
pelea *n.* brawl
pelear *v.t* fight
peliagudo *adj.* tricky
pelícano *n.* pelican
película *n.* film
películas *n.* movies
peligro *n.* danger
peligroso *adj.* dangerous
pellizcar *v.* pinch, tweak
pellizco *n.* nip
pelo *n.* hair, fur
pelota *n.* ball
peluca *n.* wig
peludo *adj.* hairy
pelusa *n.* fluff
pelvis *n.* pelvis
pena *n.* pity, sorrow
pena (castigo) *n.* penalty
penal *adj.* penal
penalizar *v.* penalize
penas *n.* hardship
pendenciero *adj.* quarrelsome
pendiente *n.* gradient
pendiente *adj.* pending

péndulo *n.* pendulum
pene *n.* penis
penetración *n.* penetration
penetrar *v.* penetrate
península *n.* peninsula
penique *n.* penny
penitencia *n.* penance
penitente *adj.* penitent
penoso *adj.* grievous
pensador *n.* thinker
pensar *v.* think
pensativo *adj.* thoughtful, pensive
pensión *n.* pension
pentágono *n.* pentagon
penúltimo *adj.* penultimate
peñasco *n.* tor
peón *n.* labourer, pawn
peor *adj.* worse
pepino *n.* cucumber
pepita *n.* nugget
péptico *adj.* peptic
pequeñito *n.* tot
pequeño *adj.* little, small, tiny
pera *n.* pear
peralte *n.* camber
perca *n.* perch
percance *n.* mishap
percepción *n.* perception
perceptible *adj.* perceptible
perceptor *adj.* percipient
percha *n.* coat hanger
percibir *v.* apprehend, perceive
perder *v.* lose, forfeit
perdición *n.* perdition, downfall
perdida *n.* loss
perdigón *n.* pellet
perdón *n.* pardon
perdonable *adj.* pardonable
perdonar *v.* forgive
perdurable *adj.* abiding
perecedero *adj.* perishable
perecer *v.* perish

peregrinación *n.* pilgrimage
peregrino *n.* pilgrim
perenne *adj.* perennial
pereza *n.* sloth
perezoso *adj.* slothful, sluggard
perfección *n.* perfection
perfecto *adj.* perfect
pérfido *adj.* perfidious
perfil *n.* profile
perforar *v.* perforate
perfumar *v.* perfume
perfume *n.* perfume
pericia *n.* expertise
periferia *n.* periphery, suburbia
periódico *adj.* periodic, periodical
periodismo *n.* journalism
periodista *n.* journalist
periodo *n.* period
periquete *n.* trice
perjudicar *v.* impair
perjudicial *adj.* harmful
perjurar *v.* perjure
perjurio *n.* perjury
perla *n.* pearl
permanencia *n.* permanence
permanente *adj.* permanent
permeable *adj.* permeable
permisible *adj.* permissible
permisivo *adj.* permissive
permiso *n.* permission
permitir *v.* allow, permit
permitir a alguien hacer algo *v.*
  enable
permutación *n.* permutation
pernicioso *adj.* pernicious
pero *conj.* but
perpendicular *adj.* perpendicular
perpetrar *v.* perpetrate
perpetuar *v.t.* perpetuate
perpetuo *adj.* perpetual
perplejidad *n.* perplexity
perra *n.* bitch

perrera *n.* kennel
perro *n.* dog
perro cobrador *n.* retriever
perro de caza *n.* hound
persecución *n.* persecution
perseguir *v.* chase, persecute
perseverancia *n.* perseverance
perseverar *v.i.* persevere
persistencia *n.* persistence
persistente *adj.* persistent
persistir *v.* persist
persona *n.* person
personaje *n.* character
personal *n.* personnel
personal *adj.* personal
personalidad *n.* personality
personalizar *v.* customize
personificación *n.* personification
personificar *v.* personify
perspectiva *n.* perspective,
  overview
perspicacia *n.* insight
perspicuo *adj.* perspicuous
persuadir *v.* persuade
persuasión *n.* persuasion
pertenecer *v.* belong, pertain
pertenencias *n.* belongings
pertinente *adj.* pertinent
perturbar *v.t.* perturb
perversión *n.* perversion
perverso *adj.* perverse
pervertir *v.* pervert, debauch
pesadilla *n.* nightmare
pesado *adj.* heavy, turgid
pesar *v.* weigh
pesca *n.* fishing
pescado *n.* fish
pescadilla *n.* whiting
pescador *n.* fisherman
pescar *v.* fish
pesebre *n.* manger
pesimismo *n.* pessimism

pesimista *n.* pessimist
pesimista *adj.* pessimistic
peso *n.* weight
pesquisa *n.* inquest
pestaña *n.* tab
pestañear *v.* blink
peste *n.* pest
pesticida *n.* pesticide
pestilencia *n.* pestilence
pestillo *n.* latch
pétalo *n.* petal
petardo *n.* cracker, squib
petición *n.* petition, request
peticionario *n.* petitioner
petrificar *v.* petrify
petróleo *n.* petroleum
petulante *adj.* smug
peyorativo *adj.* pejorative
pez *n.* fish
pezón *n.* nipple
pezuña *n.* hoof
piadoso *adj.* devout, pious
pianista *n.* pianist
piano *n.* piano
piar *v.* peep, tweet
pica *n.* pike
picadura *n.* sting
picante *adj.* spicy, pungent
picante *n.* pungency
picar *v.* itch, bite, sting
picotear *v.* nibble
pícaro *adj.* cheeky, roguish
picnic *n.* picnic
pico *n.* beak
pica *adj.* itchy
picotazo *n.* tingle
picotear *v.i.* peck
pictografía *n.* pictograph
pictórico *adj.* pictorial
pie *n.* foot
piedad *n.* piety
piedra *n.* stone

pelo *n.* fur
piel *n.* skin
piel (cáscara) *n.* peel
pienso *n.* fodder
pierna *n.* leg
pigmento *n.* pigment
pigmeo *n.* pygmy
pija *adj.* posh
pijama *n.* pyjamas
pila *n.* battery
pilar *n.* pillar
píldora *n.* pill
pillería *n.* roguery
pillo *n.* rascal
piloto *n.* pilot
pimentón *n.* capsicum
pimienta *n.* pepper
pináculo *n.* pinnacle
pinchar *v.* puncture, prick
pinchazo *n.* puncture
pingüino *n.* penguin
pinta *n.* pint
pintarrajear *v.* deface
pinto *adj.* brindle
pintor *n.* painter
pintoresco *adj.* picturesque,
  scenic
pintura *n.* paint
pinzas de depilar *n.* tweezers
piña *n.* pineapple
piojo *n.* louse
pionero *n.* pioneer
piorrea *n.* pyorrhoea
pipeta *n.* pipette
piquete *n.* picket
pira *n.* pyre
pirámide *n.* pyramid
pirata *n.* pirate
piratería *n.* piracy
piromanía *n.* pyromania
pisada *v.* tread
pisando fuerte *v.* stomp

piso *n.* storey
pisotear *v.* trample
pista *n.* clue, track
pistola *n.* pistol
pistolera *n.* holster
pistón *n.* piston
pitido *n.* beep
pitón *n.* python
pivote *n.* pivot
pixel *n.* pixel
pizarra *n.* blackboard
pizca *n.* pinch, dash
pizza *n.* pizza
placa *n.* plate, hob
placa base *n.* motherboard
placer *n.* pleasure
plácido *adj.* placid
plaga *n.* plague
plan *n.* plan
plancha *n.* iron, griddle
planeador *n.* glider
planeta *n.* planet
planetario *adj.* planetary
plano *adj.* flat
plano *n.* mapa
planta *n.* plant
plantación *n.* plantation
plantear *v.* posit
plantilla *n.* template
plaqueta *n.* platelet
plástico *n.* plastic
plata *n.* silver
plataforma *n.* platform
plátano *n.* banana
platillo *n.* saucer
platino *n.* platinum
plato *n.* plate, dish
platónico *adj.* platonic
playa *n.* beach
plaza *n.* square
plazo *n.* instalment
plebeyo *n.* commoner

plebeyo *adj.* plebeian
plebiscito *n.* plebiscite
plegado *adj.* folding
plegar *v.t* fold
pleito *n.* trial
pleno verano *adj.* midsummer
plétora *n.* plethora
pliegue *n.* crease
plinto *n.* plinth
plomizo *adj.* leaden
plomo *n.* lead
pluma *n.* feather
plumaje *n.* plumage
plumero *n.* duster
plumín *n.* nib
plural *adj.* plural
pluralidad *n.* plurality
pluviosidad *n.* rainfall
población *n.* population
poblar *v.* populate
pobre *adj.* poor, penniless
pobreza *n.* poverty
pocilga *n.* hovel, sty
poco a poco *adv.* slowly
pocos *adj.* few
podar *v.* lop
podcast *n.* podcast
poder *v.* can, may
poder *n.* power
poder hacerlo *v.* cope
poderoso *adj.* powerful
podio *n.* podium
podómetro *n.* pedometer
podrido *adj.* rotten
poema *n.* poem
poesía *n.* poetry
poeta *n.* poet
polar *adj.* polar
polea *n.* pulley
polémico *adj.* controversial
polen *n.* pollen
poliandria *n.* polyandry

policía *n.* police
poligamia *n.* polygamy
polígamo *adj.* polygamous
poliglota *adj.* polyglot
polilla *n.* moth
politécnico *n.* polytechnic
politeísmo *n.* polytheism
politeísta *adj.* polytheistic
política *n.* politics
político *adj.* political
político *n.* politician
póliza *n.* policy
pollo *n.* chicken
polluelo *n.* nestling
polo *n.* lolly
polvo *n.* dust, powder
pomada *n.* ointment
pompa *n.* bubble, pomp
pompón *n.* pompon
pomposidad *n.* pomposity
pomposo *adj.* pompous
poner *v.* put
poni *n.* pony
pontífice *n.* pontiff
popelina *n.* poplin
popular *adj.* popular
popularidad *n.* popularity
popularizar *v.* popularize
populoso *adj.* populous
poquer *n.* poker
por *prep.* per
por aquí *adv.* hereabouts
por la noche *adv.* overnight
por la presente *adv.* hereby
por lo tanto *adv.* hence
por qué *adv.* why
por otra parte *adv.* moreover
por separado *adv.* asunder
por todo *prep.* throughout
por último *adv.* ultimately
por vía de *prep.* via
porcelana *n.* porcelain

porcentaje *n.* percentage
porche *n.* porch
porción *n.* portion, serving
pornografía *n.* pornography
poro *n.* pore
porque *conj.* because
porra *n.* truncheon, baton
portafolio *n.* portfolio
portal *n.* portal
portarse mal *v.* misbehave
portátil *adj.* portable
portavoz *n.* spokesman
porte *n.* poise
porteador *n.* porter
porteo *n.* portage
portero *n.* goalkeeper
portero automático *n.* intercom
pórtico *n.* portico
posar *v.* pose
posavasos *n.* coaster
poseer *v.* possess
posesión *n.* possession
posesivo *adj.* possessive
posibilidad *n.* possibility
posible *adj.* possible
posición *n.* position
positivo *adj.* positive
postal *adj.* postal
postal *n.* postcard
postdata *n.* postscript
poste *n.* post, pole
poster *n.* poster
posteridad *n.* posterity
posterior *adj.* posterior
postgraduado *n.* postgraduate
postor *n.* bidder
postración *n.* prostration
postrado *adj.* prostrate
postre *n.* dessert
postre dulce *n.* pudding
postular *v.* propound
póstumo *adj.* posthumous

postura *n.* posture, stance
potencia *n.* potency
potencial *adj.* potential
potentado *adj.* nabob
potente *adj.* mighty
pozo *n.* well
practica *n.* practice
practicar *v.* practise
práctico *adj.* practical
pradera *n.* meadow
prado *n.* meadow
pragmático *adj.* pragmatic
pragmatismo *n.* pragmatism
praliné *n.* praline
preámbulo *n.* preamble
precario *adj.* precarious
precaución *n.* precaution
precedencia *n.* precedence
precedente *adj.* foregoing
precedente *n.* precedent
preceder *v.* precede
precepto *n.* precept
precio *n.* price
precioso *adj.* precious
precipicio *n.* cliff
precipitado *adj.* rash
precipitar *v.* precipitate
precisión *n.* precision
preciso *adj.* precise
precognición *n.* precognition
precursor *n.* precursor
predecesor *n.* predecessor
predecir *v.* predict, foretell
predestinación *n.* predestination
predeterminar *v.* predetermine
predicado *n.* predicate
predicador *n.* preacher
predicción *n.* prediction
predominante *adj.* predominant
predominar *v.* predominate
predominio *n.* predominance
preestreno *n.* preview

prefabricado *adj.* prefabricated
prefacio *n.* preface, foreword
preferencia *n.* preference
preferencial *adj.* preferential
preferir *v.* prefer
prefijo *n.* prefix
pregonado *adj.* vaunted
pregunta *n.* question
preguntar *v.* ask
prehistórico *adj.* prehistoric
prejuicio *n.* prejudice
prejuzgar *v.* prejudge
prelado *n.* prelate
preliminar *adj.* preliminary
preliminares del acto sexual *n.* foreplay
preludio *n.* prelude
prematrimonial *adj.* premarital
prematuro *adj.* premature
premeditación *n.* premeditation
premeditar *v.* premeditate
premiar *v.* award
preminencia *n.* pre-eminence
preminente *adj.* pre-eminent
premio gordo *n.* jackpot
premisa *n.* premise
premonición *n.* premonition
prenda de vestir *n.* garment
preocupación *n.* preoccupation, concern
preocupado *adj.* worried
preocupante *adj.* worrisome
preocupar *v.* preoccupy, worry
preparación *n.* preparation
preparar *v.* prepare, brew
preparatorio *adj.* preparatory
preponderancia *n.* preponderance
preponderar *v.* preponderate
preposición *n.* preposition
prepotente *adj.* pushy

prerrogativa *n.* prerogative
presa (agua) *n.* dam
presa *n.* prey
presagiar *v.* foreshadow
presagio *n.* omen
presciencia *n.* prescience
prescindible *adj.* dispensable
presencia *n.* presence
presentación *n.* introduction
presentador *n.* compere
presentar *v.t.* introduce
presentarse a *v.r.* apply
presente *adj.* present
preservación *n.* preservation
presidencial *adj.* presidential
presidente *n.* president
presidir *v.* preside
presión *n.* pressure
presionar *v.* pressurize
preso *n.* prisoner, inmate
prestamista *n.* pawnbroker
préstamo *n.* loan
prestar *v.t.* lend, loan
presteza *n.* alacrity
prestigio *n.* prestige
prestigioso *adj.* prestigious
presumir *v.* boast
presunción *n.* presumption
presuntuoso *adj.* overweening
presuponer *v.* presuppose
presupuestar *v.* quote
presupuesto *n.* budget
pretencioso *adj.* pretentious
pretender *v.* pretend
pretendido *adj.* ostensible
pretendiente *n.* suitor
pretensión *n.* pretension
pretexto *n.* pretence, pretext
pretzel (galleta salada) *n.* pretzel
prevalecer *v.* prevail
prevención *n.* prevention
prevenir *v.* prevent

preventivo *adj.* preventive
prever *v.* foresee
previo *adj.* prior, previous
previsión *n.* foresight
previsor *adj.* provident
prima (familia) *n.* cousin
prima *n.* premium, bonus
primacía *n.* supremacy
primario *adj.* primal
primate *n.* primate
primera sesión *n.* matinee
primero *adj. & n.* first
primeros auxilios *n.* first aid
primigenio *adj.* primeval
primitivo *adj.* primitive
primo *n.* cousin
primordial *adj.* paramount
princesa *n.* princess
principal *adj.* main, prime
principalmente *adv.* primarily
príncipe *n.* prince
principesco *adj.* princely
principiante *n.* novice
principio *n.* beginning
pringar *v.* baste
priorato *n.* priory
prioridad *n.* priority
prisa *n.* haste
prisión *n.* prison
prisionero *n.* prisoner
prisma *n.* prism
privacidad *n.* privacy
privación *n.* privation
privado *adj.* private, privy
privar *v.* deprive
privatizar *v.* privatize
privilegio *n.* privilege
proactivo *adj.* proactive
probabilidad *n.* probability
probabilidades *n.* odds
probable *adj.* likely, probable
probable *n.* prospective

probablemente *adv.* probably
probación *n.* probation
probar *v.* prove
probar (sabor) *v.* taste
probidad *n.* probity
problema *n.* problem, trouble
problemático *adj.* problematic
procedencia *n.* provenance
proceder *v.* proceed
procedimiento *n.* procedure
procesable *adj.* actionable
procesión *n.* parade
proceso *n.* process
proclamación *n.* proclamation
proclamar *v.* proclaim
proclive *adj.* prone
proclividad *n.* proclivity
procrear *v.* procreate
procuración *n.* care
procurar *v.* procure
prodigio *n.* prodigy
prodigioso *adj.* prodigious
pródigo *adj.* prodigal
producción *n.* production
producir *v.* produce
producir leche *v.* lactate
productividad *n.* productivity
productivo *adj.* productive
producto *n.* product
productor *n.* producer
profanar *v. t* profane
profano *adj.* profane
profecía *n.* prophecy
profesión *n.* profession
profesional *adj.* professional
profesor *n.* professor
profeta *n.* prophet
profético *adj.* prophetic
profundamente *adv.* sorely
profundidad *n.* depth
profundo *adj.* deep, profound
profusión *n.* profusion

profuso *adj.* profuse
progenie *n.* progeny
programa *n.* programme
progresivo *adj.* progressive
progreso *n.* progress
prohibición *n.* prohibition
prohibir *v.* prohibit, forbid
prohibitivo *adj.* prohibitive
prolapso *n.* prolapse
proliferación *n.* proliferation
proliferar *v.* proliferate
prolífico *adj.* prolific
prólogo *n.* prologue
prolongación *n.* prolongation
prolongado *adj.* lengthy
prolongar *v.* prolong
promedio *n.* average
promesa *n.* promise, pledge
prometedor *adj.* promising
prometido *n.* fiance
prominencia *n.* prominence
prominente *adj.* prominent
promiscuo *adj.* promiscuous
promover *v.* promote
promulgar *v.* promulgate, enact
pronombre *n.* pronoun
pronosticador *n.* tipster
pronosticar *v.* prognosticate
pronóstico *adj* forecast
pronóstico *n.* prognosis
pronto *adv.* soon
pronunciación *n.* pronunciation
pronunciar *v.* pronounce
propagación *n.* propagation
propaganda *n.* propaganda
propagar *v.* propagate
propenso *adj.* prone
propiciar *v.* propitiate
propicio *adj.* auspicious
propiedad *n.* property, ownership
propietario *n.* proprietor

propina *n.* tip
propio *adj. & pron.* own
proponer *v.* propose
proporción *n.* proportion
proporcional *adj.* proportional
proposición *n.* proposition, proposal
propósito *n.* purpose
propuesta *n.* proposal
propulsar *v.* propel
prorrogar *v.* prorogue
prosa *n.* prose
prosaico *adj.* prosaic
proscrito *n.* outlaw
prospecto *n.* prospectus
prosperar *v.* prosper, thrive
prosperidad *n.* prosperity
próspero *adj.* prosperous
próstata *n.* prostate
prostitución *n.* prostitution
prostituta *n.* prostitute
protagonista *n.* protagonist
protección *n.* protection, safeguard
protector *adj.* protective
protectorado *n.* protectorate
proteger *v.* protect
proteína *n.* protein
protesta *n.* protest
protestar *v.* protest
protocolo *n.* protocol
prototipo *n.* prototype
provecho *n.* profit
provechoso *adj.* fruitful
proveer *v.* provide
proverbial *adj.* proverbial
proverbio *n.* proverb
providencia *n.* providence
providencial *adj.* providential
provincia *n.* province
provincial *adj.* provincial
provinciano *adj.* parochial

provisión *n.* provision
provisional *adj.* provisional
provocación *n.* provocation
provocador *adj.* provocative
provocar *v.t.* provoke
proximidad *n.* proximity, vicinity
próximo *adj.* next
proyección *n.* projection
proyectar *v.* project
proyectil *n.* projectile
proyecto *n.* project
proyector *n.* projector
prudencia *n.* prudence
prudencial *adj.* prudential
prudente *adj.* prudent
prueba *n.* proof, test
psicología *n.* psychology
psicológico *adj.* psychological
psicólogo *n.* psychologist
psicópata *n.* psychopath
psicosis *n.* psychosis
psicoterapia *n.* psychotherapy
psique *n.* psyche
psiquiatra *n.* psychiatrist
psiquiatría *n.* psychiatry
psíquico *adj.* psychic
pub *n.* pub
pubertad *n.* puberty
púbico *adj.* pubic
publicación *n.* publication
publicar *v.* publish
publicidad *n.* publicity
público *adj.* public
pudrirse *v.* rot
pueblerino *adj.* yokel
pueblo *n.* village
puente *n.* bridge
puerco espín *n.* porcupine
pueril *adj.* puerile
puerro *n.* leek
puerta *n.* door

puerto *n.* harbour, port
puesto *n.* stall
pulcro *adj.* sleek, neat
pulga *n.* flea
pulgada *n.* inch
pulgar *n.* thumb
pulla *n.* quip
pulmón *n.* lung
pulpa *n.* pulp
púlpito *n.* pulpit
pulpo *n.* octopus, squid
pulsación *n.* pulsation
pulsar *v.* press, push
pulsera *n.* bracelet
pulso *n.* pulse
punitivo *adj.* punitive
punta *n.* spike, end
punta de lanza *n.* spearhead
puntal *n.* strut, stanchion
puntear *v.* stipple
puntería *n.* aim
puntiagudo *adj.* spiky
puntilla *n.* lace
puntilloso *adj.* stickler
punto (dictado) *n.* dot
punto *n.* point
punto (médico) *n.* stitch
punto de vista *n.* outlook, standpoint
punto muerto *n.* deadlock, impasse
punto y coma *n.* semicolon
puntuación *n.* punctuation, score
puntual *adj.* punctual
puntualidad *n.* punctuality
puntuar *v.* punctuate
punzada *n.* pang, twinge
punzante *adj.* piquant
puñado *n.* handful
puñalada *v.* stab
puñal *n.* dagger
puño *n.* fist, cuff

pupitre *n.* desk
pureza *n.* purity
purgación *n.* purgation
purgante *adj.* purgative
purgar *v.* purge
purgatorio *n.* purgatory
purificación *n.* purification
purificar *v.* purify
purista *n.* purist
puritano *n.* puritan
puritano *adj.* puritanical
puro *n.* cigar
puro *adj.* pure
pus *n.* pus
puta *n.* whore, bitch
putrefacto *adj.* putrid

Q

quad *n.* quad
quark *n.* quark
que *pron. & adj.* what
quebradizo *adj.* brittle, frail
quebrado *adj.* broken
quebrar *v.t.* break, bend
quebrarse *v.t.* become ruptured
quedar *v.t.* remain
quedarse *v.r.* stay
quedarse atrás *v.* lag
queja *n.* complaint
quejarse *v.r.* complain
quejumbroso *adj.* fractious
quemador *n.* burner
quemar *v.* burn
querer *v.* want
querido *adj.* dear, darling
querido *n.* lover
queso *n.* cheese
quien *pron.* who

quietud *n.* quietude
quijotesco *adj.* quixotic
quilate *n.* carat
quilla *n.* keel
quimera *n.* chimera
química *n.* chemistry
químico *adj.* chemical
químico *n.* chemist
quimioterapia *n.* chemotherapy
quimono *n.* kimono
quince *adj. & n.* fifteen
quincena *n.* fortnight
quincha *n.* wattle
quinina *n.* quinine
quintaesencia *n.* quintessence
quintillizo *n.* quin
quinto *n.* filth
quiromancia *n.* palmistry
quiromántico *adj.* palmist
quirúrgico *adj.* surgical
quisquilloso *adj.* pettish
quiste *n.* cyst
quiste sebáceo *n.* wen
quitar *v.* remove
quizás *adv.* maybe, perhaps
quórum *n.* quorum

R

rábano *n.* radish
rabia *n.* anger, rage
rabia (enfermedad) *n.* rabies
rabieta *n.* tantrum
rabioso *adj.* rabid
rácano *n.* scrooge
racha *n.* streak
racial *adj.* racial
racimo *n.* cluster
ración *n.* portion, ration

racional *adj.* rational
racionalismo *n.* rationalism
racionalizar *v.* rationalize
racismo *n.* racialism
radar *n.* radar
radiación *n.* radiation
radial *adj.* radial
radiante *adj.* radiant
radical *adj.* radical
radio *n.* radio
radioactivo *adj.* radioactive
radiografía *n.* radiography
radiología *n.* radiology
radioyente *n.* listener
ráfaga *n.* gust
raído *adj.* shabby
raíz *n.* root
raja *n.* slit
rallador *n.* grater
rama *n.* branch
ramificación *n.* ramification
ramificar *v.* ramify
ramita *n.* twig
ramo *n.* bouquet
rampa *n.* ramp
rana *n.* frog
rancho *n.* ranch
ranciedad *n.* staleness
rancio *adj.* rancid
rango *n.* rank
ranura *n.* slot, groove
rapaz *adj.* rapacious
rápidamente *adj.* fast
rapidez *n.* fastness, rapidity
rápido *adj.* quick, rapid
rapsodia *n.* rhapsody
raqueta *n.* racket
raquitismo *n.* rickets
rara vez *adv.* seldom
rareza *n.* oddity
raro *adj.* rare, weird
rasar *v.* skim

rascacielos *n.* skyscraper
rascar *v.t.* scratch
rasgar *v.* tear, rip
rasgo *n.* trait
rasguñar *v.* scrape
raso *adj.* clear
raso *n.* satin
rastreado *adj.* traceable
rastrillo *n.* rake
rastro *n.* trail, spoor
rata *n.* rat
ratificar *v.* ratify
ratio *n.* ratio
ratón *n.* mouse
raya *n.* line, stripe
rayado *adj.* streaky
rayo *n.* ray
razón *n.* reason
razonable *adj.* reasonable
reacción *n.* reaction
reaccionar *v.* react
reaccionario *adj.* reactionary
reacio *adj.* reluctant
reacondicionar *v.* recondition
reactor *n.* reactor, jet
reafirmar *v.* reaffirm
reajustar *v.* readjust
real *adj.* real, royal
realidad *n.* reality
realismo *n.* realism
realista *adj.* realistic
realización *n.* fulfilment
realizar *v.* conduct
realmente *adv.* really
reanudación *n.* resumption
reanudar *v.* resume
reaparecer *v.* reappear
reavivar *v.* vitalize
rebanada *n.* slice
rebaño *n.* herd, flock
rebeca *n.* cardigan
rebelarse *v.r.* rebel, revolt

rebelde *adj.* rebellious
rebelión *n.* rebellion
rebobinar *v.* rewind
rebotar *v.* rebound, bounce
rebuznar *v.* bray
recado *n.* errand
recaer *v.i.* relapse
recaída *n.* relapse
recámara *n.* breech
recapitular *v.* recapitulate
recargar *v.* recharge
recargo *n.* surtax
recatado *adj.* demure
recaudar *v.* raise
recelo *n.* misgiving
receloso *adj.* suspicious
recepción *n.* reception
recepcionista *n.* receptionist
receptáculo *n.* receptable
receptivo *adj.* receptive
receptor *n.* receiver
recesión *n.* recession
recesivo *adj.* recessive
receta *n.* recipe
recetar *v.* prescribe
rechazar *v.* reject
rechazo *n.* rejection
rechinar *v.* squeak
recibir *v.* receive
recibo *n.* receipt
reciclar *v.* recycle
recién *adv.* newly
reciente *adj.* recent
recientemente *adv.* recently
recinto *n.* enclosure
recíproco *adj.* reciprocal
recital *n.* recital
recitar *v.* recite
reclamación *n.* reclamation
reclamar *v.t.* claim
reclinar *v.t.* lean
reclinarse *v.r.* recline

recluido *adj.* secluded
recluir *v.* seclude, detain
reclusión *n.* confinement
recluso *n.* recluse
reclutar *v.* recruit
recobrar *v.t.* recover
recoger *v.* collect, reap
recolección *n.* recollection
recomendable *adj.* commendable
recomendación *n.* recommendation
recomendar *v.* recommend
recompensa *n.* reward
recompensar *v.* recompense
reconciliación *n.* reconciliation
reconciliar *v.* reconcile
reconocer *v.t.* recognize
reconocimiento *n.* recognition
reconquistar *v.* recapture
reconsiderar *v.* reconsider
reconstituir *v.t.* reconstitute
reconstruir *v.t.* rebuild, reconstruct
recopilar *v.* compile
recordar *v.* remember, recall
recordar a alguien *v.* remind
recordar viejas historias *v.* reminiscence
recordatorio *n.* reminder
recorrer a pie *v.* tramp
recortar *v.* trim
recorte *n.* cutting, cutback
recostado *adj.* recumbent
recreación *n.* recreation
recrear *v.t.* recreate
recriminación *n.* recrimination
rectangular *adj.* rectangular
rectángulo *n.* rectangle
rectificación *n.* rectification
rectificar *v.* rectify
rectitud *n.* rectitude
recto *n.* rectum

recto *adj.* straight
recuerdo *n.* memory, reminder
recuerdo (regalo) *n.* souvenir
recular *v.* blench
recuperación *n.* recovery
recuperar *v.t.* recover, reclaim, regain
recuperarse *v.r.* recuperate
recurrencia *n.* recurrence
recurrente *adj.* recurrent
recurrir *v.* betake
recurso *n.* resource, resort
red *n.* net, network
red (telaraña) *n.* web
redacción *n.* wording, essay
redada *n.* raid
redención *n.* redemption
redes *n.* netting
redimir *v.* redeem
redomado *adj.* arrant
redondeado *adj.* rounded
redondo *adj.* round
reducción *n.* reduction
reducir *v.* reduce
reducir poco a poco *v.* whittle
reductor *adj.* reductive
reembolsar *v.* reimburse, repay
reembolso *n.* refund, repayment
reemplazar *v.* replace
reemplazo *n.* replacement
reencarnar *v.* reincarnate
referencia *n.* reference
referéndum *n.* referendum
referir *v.* refer
refinado *adj.* refined
refinamiento *n.* refinement
refinar *v.* refine
refinería *n.* refinery
reflector *adj.* reflective
reflejar *v.* reflect
reflejo *n.* reflex
reflexión *n.* reflection

reflexivo *adj.* reflexive
reflexología *n.* reflexology
reflujo *n.* ebb
reformación *n.* reformation
reformador *n.* reformer
reformar *v.* reform
reforzar *v.* reinforce
refracción *n.* refraction
refrán *n.* saying, say
refrenar *v.* restrain
refrescar *v.* refresh
refresco *n.* beverage
refriega *n.* scuffle
refrigeración *n.* refrigeration
refrigerador *n.* refrigerator
refrigerante *n.* coolant
refrigerar *v.* refrigerate
refuerzo *n.* reinforcement
refugiado *n.* refugee
refugio *n.* shelter, refuge
refulgente *adj.* refulgent
refundir *v.* conflate
refunfuñar *v.* grumble, growl
refutación *n.* refutation
refutar *v.* refute
regalar *v.t.* treat, give away
regalo *n.* present, gift
regatear *v.* haggle
regeneración *n.* regeneration
regenerar *v.* regenerate
regente *n.* regent
reggae *n.* reggae
regicidio *n.* regicide
régimen *n.* regime
regimiento *n.* regiment
regio *adj.* regal
región *n.* region
regional *adj.* regional
registrar *v.* register, search
registro *n.* register, registry
reglamento *n.* regulation
regocijo *n.* glee

regocijarse *v.r.* rejoice
regulador *n.* regulator, setter
regular *v.* regulate
regularidad *n.* regularity
regularizar *v.* regularize
rehabilitación *n.* rehabilitation
rehabilitar *v.* rehabilitate
rehén *n.* hostage
reincidencia *n.* relapse
reincidir *v.i.* relapse
reimprimir *v.* reprint
reina *n.* queen
reinar *v.* reign
reincorporar *v.t.* reincorporate
reincorporarse *v.r.* rejoin
reino *n.* kingdom, realm
reír *v.* laugh
reírse tontamente *v.* giggle
reiteración *n.* reiteration
reiterar *v.* reiterate
reja *n.* grid, fence
rejilla *n.* grating, rack
rejuvenecer *v.* rejuvenate
rejuvenecimiento *n.* rejuvenation
relación *n.* relationship
relacionado con *adj.* akin
relacionar *v.* relate
relajación *n.* relaxation
relajarse *v.* relax, unwind
relatividad *n.* relativity
relegar *v.* relegate
relevancia *n.* relevance
relevante *adj.* relevant
relevo *n.* relay
relicario *n.* locket
religión *n.* religion
religioso *adj.* religious
relincho *n.* neigh, whinny
reliquia *n.* relic
rellenar *v.* refill, replenish
rellenito *adj.* plump
relleno *n.* filling, padding

reloj *n.* clock
relucir *v.* shimmer, sparkle
remache *n.* rivet
remedio *n.* remedy
rememorativo *adj.* redolent
remesa *n.* consignment
remiendo *n.* patch
reminiscente *adj.* reminiscent
remisión *n.* remission, remit
remo *n.* rowing
remo (pala) *n.* oar
remodelación *v.* reshuffle
remolacha *n.* beetroot
remolcador *v.* tug
remolcar *v.* tow
remolino *n.* whirlpool
remolque *n.* trailer
remontar *v.t.* remount
remordimiento *n.* regret, remorse
remoto *adj.* remote
remover *v.* stir
remuneración *n.* remuneration
remunerado *adj.* remunerative
remunerar *v.* remunerate
renacimiento *n.* renaissance
rencor *n.* rancour, spite
rencoroso *adj.* spiteful
rendición *n.* surrender
rendirse *v.* surrender
renegado *n.* renegade
renegar *v.* disown
renombrado *adj.* renowned
renombre *n.* renown
renovación *n.* renovation, renewal
renovar *v.* renew, renovate
renta *n.* annuity
renuncia *n.* renunciation
renunciar *v.* resign, renounce
reorganizar *v.* reorganize
reparar *v.* mend, repair
repartición *n.* division
repartir *v.* allocate
reparto *n.* allocation
reparto (artistas) *n.* casting
repasar *v.* overhaul
repatriación *n.* repatriation
repatriar *v.* repatriate
repelente *adj.* repellent
repentino *adj.* sudden
repercusión *n.* repercussion
repetición *n.* repetition
repetidor *n.* booster
repetir *v.t.* repeat, replay
repique *n.* chime
repisar *v.* retread
replegar *v.t.* redouble
replegarse *v.r.* fall back
repleto *adj.* replete
réplica *n.* replica
reportaje *n.* reportage
reposo *n.* repose
reprender *v.t.* reprimand
reprensible *adj.* reprehensible
represalia *n.* reprisal
represalias *n.* retaliation
representación *n.* representation
representante *adj.* representative
representar *v.* represent
represión *n.* repression
reprimir *v.* repress
reprobación *n.* reproof
reprobar *v.* reprove
réprobo *n.* reprobate
reprochar *v.t.* reproach
reproche *n.* reproach
reproducción *n.* reproduction
reproducir *v.* reproduce
reproductor *adj.* reproductive
reptil *n.* reptile
república *n.* republic
republicano *adj.* republican
repudiación *n.* repudiation
repudiar *v.* repudiate

repugnancia *n.* repugnance
repugnante *adj.* repugnant
repugnar *v.* repel
repujar *v.* emboss
repulsar *v.* repulse
repulsión *n.* repulsion
repulsivo *adj.* repulsive
reputación *n.* reputation
requerimiento *n.* solicitation
réquiem *n.* requiem
requisición *n.* requisition
requisito *n.* requirement, prerequisite
resaca *n.* hangover
resaltar *v.* highlight
resbaladizo *adj.* slippery
resbalón *v.* slip
rescatar *v.* rescue
rescate *n.* ransom
rescindir *v.* rescind
reseco *adj.* parched
resentimiento *n.* resentment
resentirse *v.* resent
reseña *n.* review
reserva *n.* reservation
reservado *adj.* aloof, secretive
reservar *v.* reserve
residencia *n.* residence
residencial *adj.* residential
residente *n.* resident
residir *v.* reside
residual *adj.* residual
residuo *n.* residue
resistencia *n.* resistance
resistente *adj.* resistant, hardy
resistir *v.* resist
resma *n.* ream
resollar *v.* wheeze
resolución *n.* resolution
resolver *v.* resolve, solve
resonancia *n.* resonance
resonante *adj.* resonant

resonar *v.* resonate
resoplar *v.* snuffle
respectivo *adj.* respective
respecto a *prep.* regarding
respetable *adj.* respectable
respeto *n.* respect
respetuoso *adj.* respectful
respiración *n.* respiration
respiradero *n.* vent
respirador *n.* respirator
respirar *v.* breathe, respire
respiro *n.* breath
resplandeciente *adj.* resplendent
responder *v.* reply, respond
responsabilidad *n.* responsibility
responsable *adj.* responsible
respuesta *n.* answer, response
resta *n.* subtraction
restablecimiento *n.* reinstatement
restar *v.* subtract
restaurado *adj.* restoration
restaurador *n.* restaurateur
restaurante *n.* restaurant
restaurar *v.* refurbish, restore
restitución *n.* restitution
restituir *v.* reinstate
resto *n.* remnant
restos *n.* wreck, remains
restregar *v.* scrub, scour
restricción *n.* restriction
restrictivo *adj.* restrictive
resucitar *v.* resurrect
resuelto *adj.* resolute, steadfast
resultado *n.* outcome, result
resultante *adj.* resultant
resumen *n.* summary
resumir *v.* summarize
resurgente *adj.* resurgent
resurgimiento *a.* resurgence
retablo *n.* tableau
retardar *v.t.* retard
retazo *n.* snippet

retención *n.* retention
retener *v.* retain, withhold
retentivo *adj.* retentive
reticencia *n.* reluctance
reticente *adj.* reluctant
retina *n.* retina
retirada *n.* withdrawal
retirar *v.t.* withdraw
retirarse *v.r.* retreat
retiro *n.* retreat
reto *n.* challenge
retocar *v.* retouch
retomar el camino *v.* wend
retoño *n.* offshoot
retorcer *v.t.* twist
retorcerse *v.r.* squirm, writhe
retórica *n.* rhetoric
retórico *adj.* rhetorical
retorno *n.* return
retozar *v.* frisk, gambol
retozo *n.* romp
retrasado *adj.* belated, late
retrasar *v. t* delay
retraso *n.* retardation
retratar *v.* depict
retrato *n.* portrait
retribución *n.* retribution
retribuir *v.t.* requite
retro *adj.* retro
retroactivo *adj.* retroactive
retroceder *v.* recoil, reced
retrogrado *adj.* retrograde
retrospección *n.* retrospect
retrospectiva *n.* hindsight
retrospectivo *adj.* retrospective
retumbar *v.* reverberate
reubicar *v.* relocate
reumático *adj.* rheumatic
reumatismo *n.* rheumatism
reunión *n.* meeting, reunion
reunir *v.* reunite, collect
reusar *v.* reuse

revaluación *n.* reappraisal
revaluar *v.* reassess
revelación *n.* revelation
revelador *adj.* telling
revelar *v.t.* reveal, disclose
reverencia *n.* reverence, bow
reverencial *adj.* reverential
reverenciar *v.* revere
reverendo *adj.* reverend
reverente *adj.* reverent
reversible *adj.* reversible
reverso *n.* back
revertir *v.* regress
revés *n.* backhand
revestimiento *n.* coating, casing
revestir *v.* encase
revirar *v.* check
revisar *v.* revise
revisión *n.* revision
revista *n.* magazine
revivir *v.* revive
revocable *adj.* revocable
revocación *n.* revocation
revocar *v.* revoke
revolcar *v.t.* roll over
revolcarse *v.r.* wallow
revolotear *v.* flit, flutter
revolución *n.* revolution
revolucionar *v.* revolutionize
revolucionario *adj.* revolutionary
revolver *v.* rummage
revólver *n.* revolver
rey *n.* king
reyerta *n.* affray
rezagado *adj.* laggard
rezagarse *v.* straggle
rezar *v.* pray
rezumar *v.i.* ooze
riachuelo *n.* stream
ricamente *adv.* richly
rico *adj.* rich, wealthy
ridiculizar *v.* deride

ridículo *n.* ridicule
ridículo *adj.* ridiculous
rienda *n.* rein
riesgo *n.* risk, hazard
rifa *n.* raffle
rifle *n.* rifle
rígido *adj.* rigid, stiff
rigor *n.* rigour
riguroso *adj.* rigorous
rima *n.* rhyme
rimbombante *adj.* flamboyant
rímel *n.* mascara
rincón *n.* nook
rinoceronte *n.* rhinoceros
riña *n.* quarrel
riñón *n.* kidney
rio *n.* river
riqueza *n.* wealth
riquísimo *adj.* delicious, rich
risa *n.* laughter
risa disimulada *n.* snigger
risible *adj.* laughable
risueño *adj.* cheery
rítmico *adj.* rhythmic
ritmo *n.* rhythm
rito *n.* rite
ritual *n.* ritual
rival *n.* rival
rivalidad *n.* rivalry
rizar *v.* curl
robar *v.* steal, rob
roble *n.* oak
robo *n.* burglary, theft
robot *n.* robot
robusto *adj.* robust, stocky
roca *n.* rock
roce *n.* rub
rociar *v.t.* sprinkle
rocío *n.* dew
rocoso *adj.* rocky
rodaja *n.* slice
rodapié *n.* skirting

rodar *v.* roll
rodear *v. t* encircle
rodeo *n.* rodeo
rodilla *n.* knee
rodillo *n.* roller
rodio *n.* rhodium
roedor *n.* rodent
roer *v.* gnaw
rogar *v.* beg
rojizo *adj.* reddish
rojo *adj.* red
rollo *n.* roll, scroll
romanticismo *n.* romance
romántico *adj.* romantic
romanticón *adj.* soppy
rombo *n.* rhombus
rompecabezas *n.* jigsaw
romper *v.* break
ron *n.* rum
ronco *adj.* hoarse, husky, throaty
ronquido *n.* snore
ronronear *v.* purr
ropa *n.* clothes, clothing
ropa de cama *n.* bedding, linen
ropa interior *n.* underwear
rosa *adj.* pink
rosa (flor) *n.* rose
rosado *adj.* rosy
rosario *n.* rosary
roseta *n.* rosette
rostro *n.* visage
rotación *n.* rotation
rotar *v.* rotate
rotatorio *adj.* rotary
roto *adj.* broken
rotonda *n.* roundabout
rotor *n.* rotor
rótulo *n.* label, rubric
rotundamente *adv.* outright,
  roundly
rotura *n.* breakage
rubí *n.* ruby

rubio *adj.* blonde
ruborizarse *v.r.* blush
rúbrica *n.* rubric
rudimentario *adj.* rudimentary
rudimento *n.* rudiment
rueda *n.* wheel
rueda de molino *n.* treadmill
ruedecilla *n.* castor
ruedo *n.* arena
rufián *n.* ruffian
rugbi *n.* rugby
rugido *n.* roar
rugir *v.* roar
ruido *n.* noise
ruidoso *adj.* noisy
ruin *adj.* dastardly
ruina *n.* wrack
ruinoso *adj.* dilapidated
ruiseñor *n.* nightingale
ruleta *n.* roulette
rumiar *v.* ruminate
rumiante *n.* ruminant
rumor *n.* rumour
ruptura *n.* severance
rural *adj.* rural
rusticidad *n.* rusticity
rustico *adj.* rustic
ruta *n.* route
rutina *n.* routine
rutinario *adj.* workaday

S

sábado *n.* Saturday
sábana *n.* sheet
saber *v.* know
saber *n.* learning
sabiduría *n.* wisdom
sabio *adj.* wise

sable *n.* sabre
sabor *n.* flavour, taste
sabor fuerte *n.* tang
saborear *v.* relish, saviour
sabotaje *v.* sabotage
sabroso *adj.* tasty, savoury
sabueso *n.* sleuth
sacar *v.* remove
sacarina *n.* saccharin
sacerdocio *n.* priesthood, ministry
saciable *adj.* satiable
saciar *v.* satiate
saciedad *n.* satiety
saco *n.* sack
sacramento *n.* sacrament
sacrificado *adj.* halal
sacrificar *v.* sacrifice
sacrificio *n.* sacrifice
sacrilegio *n.* sacrilege
sacrílego *adj.* sacrilegious
sacristán *n.* sexton
sacristía *n.* vestry
sacrosanto *adj.* sacrosanct
sacudir *v.* shake, jiggle
sádico *n.* sadist
sadismo *n.* sadism
safari *n.* safari
saga *n.* saga
sagacidad *n.* sagacity, acumen
sagaz *adj.* sagacious, vulpine
sagrado *adj.* holy, sacred
sagrario *n.* sanctum
sal *n.* salt
sala *n.* ward, hall
salado *adj.* salty
salario *n.* salary
salchicha *n.* sausage
salchicha alemana *n.* frankfurter
salero *n.* panache
salida *n.* exit, departure
saliente *adj.* retiring
salinidad *n.* salinity

salino *adj.* saline
salir *v.t.* leave
salir a chorros *v.* squirt
salir ileso *adv.* scot-free
saliva *n.* saliva
salmo *n.* psalm
salmón *n.* salmon
salmuera *n.* brine
salón *n.* lounge, parlour
salpicaduras *n.* sprinkling
salpicar *v.* dash, splatter
salsa *n.* sauce, gravy
saltar *v.t.* jump, skip
saltador *n.* jumper
saltamontes *n.* grasshopper
salto mortal *n.* somersault
salud *n.* health
saludable *adj.* healthy
saludar *v* greet
saludo *n.* salutation, salute, greet-ing
salva *n.* salvo
salvación *n.* salvation
salvaje *adj.* wild, savage, feral
salvamanteles *n.* trivet
salvamento *v.* salvage
salvar *v.* save
salvia *n.* sage
samaritano *n.* samaritan
samuera *n.* pickle
sanatorio *n.* sanatorium
sanción *n* demerit
sancionar *v.* sanction
sandalia *n.* sandal
sándalo *n.* sandalwood
sandía *n.* watermelon
sándwich *n.* sandwich
saneamiento *n.* sanitation
sangrar *v.* bleed
sangre *n.* blood
sangre fría *n.* sangfroid
sangriento *adj.* gory

sanguijuela *n.* leech
sanguinario *adj.* sanguinary
sanitario *adj.* sanitary
sano *adj.* wholesome
santidad *n.* sanctity
santificación *n.* sanctification
santificar *v.* sanctify
santo *n.* saint
santo *adj.* saintly
santuario *n.* sanctuary
sapo *n.* toad
saquear *v.* plunder, maraud
sarampión *n.* measles
sarcasmo *n.* sarcasm
sarcástico *adj.* sarcastic
sarcófago *n.* sarcophagus
sardónico *adj.* sardonic
sarga *n.* serge
sargento *n.* sergeant
sari *n.* sari
sarna *n.* scabies
sarro *n.* tartar
sartén china *n.* wok
sartorial *adj.* sartorial
sastre *n.* tailor
satanás *n.* satan
satánico *adj.* satanic
satanismo *n.* satanism
satélite *n.* satellite
satinado *adj.* silken
sátira *n.* satire
satírico *adj.* satirical
satírico *n.* satirist
satirizar *v.* satirize
satisfacción *n.* satisfaction
satisfacer *v.* satisfy, fulfil
satisfactorio *adj.* satisfactory
satisfecho *adj.* satisfied
saturación *n.* saturation
saturado *adj.* sated
saturar *v.* saturate
saturnino *adj.* saturnine

sauce *n.* willow
sauna *n.* sauna
savia *n.* sap
saxófono *n.* saxophone
sebo *n.* tallow
secador *n.* dryer
sección *n.* section, platoon
secesión *n.* secession
seco *adj.* dry
secreción *n.* secretion
secretaria *n.* secretary
secretariado *n.* secretariat
secretario *n.* registrar
secreto *n.* secret
secreto *adj.* secret
sectario *n.* sect
sectario *adj.* sectarian
sector *n.* sector
secuaz *n.* henchman
secuela *n.* sequel
secuencia *n.* sequence
secuencial *adj.* sequential
secuencias *n.* footage
secuestrar *v.t.* kidnap
secuestro *n.* kidnapping
secular *adj.* secular
secundario *adj.* secondary
sed *n.* thirst
seda *n.* silk
sedación *n.* sedation
sedán *n.* sedan
sedante *n.* sedative
sede central *n.* headquarters
sedentario *adj.* sedentary
sedición *n.* sedition
sedicioso *adj.* seditious
sediento *adj.* thirsty
sedimento *n.* sediment, silt
sedoso *adj.* silky
seducción *n.* seduction
seducir *v.* seduce
seductor *adj.* alluring, seductive

segadora *n.* reaper
segar *v.* reap
segar el césped *v.* mow
segmento *n.* segment
segregación *n.* segregation
segregar *v.* segregate
seguidor *n.* follower
seguir *v.* follow, ensue
segundo *adj.* second
seguramente *adv.* surely
seguridad *n.* safety, security
seguro *adj.* safe, secure, sure
seguro *n.* insurance
seis *adj.& n.* six
selección *n.* selection
seleccionar *v.* select
selectivo *adj.* selective
sellante *n.* sealant
sellar *v.* stamp
sello *n.* stamp
selva tropical *n.* rainforest
semana *n.* week
semanal *adj.* weekly
semántico *adj.* semantic
semblante *n.* semblance
sembrar *v.* wreak
semejantes *adj.* alike
semejanza *n.* likeness
semen *n.* semen
semental *n.* stallion
semestral *adj.* biannual
semestre *n.* semester
semicírculo *n.* semicircle
semilla *n.* seed
seminario *n.* seminar, tutorial
semítico *adj.* semitic
senado *n.* senate
senador *n.* senator
senatorial *adj.* senatorial
sencillez *n.* simplicity
sencillo *adj.* plain, simple
senda *n.* path

sendero *n.* path
senil *adj.* senile
senilidad *n.* senility
senior *adj.* senior
seno *n.* bosom, sinus
sensación *n.* sensation
sensacionalista *adj.* sensational
sensato *adj.* sensible
sensibilidad *n.* sensibility
sensibilizar *v.* sensitize
sensible *adj.* sensitive
sensiblero *adj.* maudlin
sensor *n.* sensor
sensorial *adj.* sensory
sensual *adj.* sensual
sensualidad *n.* sensuality
sentar *v.t.* sit
sentencia *n.* sentence
sentenciar *v.* sentence
sentencioso *adj.* sententious
sentido *n.* sense
sentimental *adj.* sentimental
sentimiento *n.* feeling
sentir *v.* feel
sentirse atrapado *v.* trammel
seña *n.* sign
señal *n.* signal
señalación *n.* pointing
señalar *v.* pinpoint
señor *n.* sir
señor feudal *n.* liege
señor noble *n.* lord
señor amo *n.* master
señora *n.* lady, madam
señorita *n.* miss
señuelo *n.* decoy
separación *n.* separation
separado *adj.* separated
separar *v.t.* separate
separarse *v.r.* separate
separatista *n.* separatist
sepsis *n.* sepsis

séptico *adj.* septic
Septiembre *n.* September
séptimo *adj. & n.* seventh
septuagésimo *adj. & n.* seventieth
sepulcral *adj.* sepulchral
sepulcro *n.* sepulchre
sepultura *n.* sepulture
sepulturero *n.* undertaker
sequía *n.* drought
séquito *n.* entourage
ser incapaz *adj.* unable
ser mayor que *v.* outweigh
ser mujeriego *v.* womanize
ser suficiente *v.* suffice
ser *v.* be
serenidad *n.* serenity
sereno *adj.* serene
seres queridos *adj.* nearest
series *n.* series
serio *adj.* serious, earnest
sermón *n.* sermon
sermonear *v.* preach
serpentear *v.* crankle, wriggle
serpentina *n.* streamer
serpentino *adj.* serpentine
serpiente *n.* snake
serrar *v.* saw
serrín *n.* sawdust
servicio *n.* service
servidor *n.* server
servil *adj.* servile, slavish
servilismo *n.* servility
servilleta *n.* napkin
servir *v.* serve
sésamo *n.* sesame
sesenta *adj. & n.* sixty
sesgado *adj.* biased
sesgar *v.* skew
sesgo *n.* bias
sesión *n.* session
setenta *adj. & n.* seventy
seto *n.* hedge

seudónimo *n.* pseudonym
severidad *n.* severity
severo *adj.* severe, stern
sexagésimo *adj. & n.* sixtieth
sexismo *n.* sexism
sexo *n.* sex
sextillo *n.* sextuplet
sexto *adj. & n.* sixth
sexual *adj.* sexual
sexualidad *n.* sexuality
sexy *adj.* sexy
si *conj.* if, whether
si *excl.* yes
si no *adv.* otherwise
sibarita *n.* sybarite
sibilante *adj.* sibilant
sicomoro *n.* sycamore
sida *n.* aids
sidra *n.* cider
sidra de pera *n.* perry
siempre *adv.* always
siempre joven *adj.* ageless
sierra *n.* saw
siervo *n.* serf
siesta *n.* nap, siesta
siete *adj. & n.* seven
sifón *n.* siphon
sigilosamente *adv.* stealthily
siglo *n.* century
signatario *n.* signatory
significación *n.* signification
significado *n.* meaning
significancia *n.* significance
significar *v.* signify, mean
significativo *n.* significant
signo & *n.* ampersand
sílaba *n.* syllable
silábico *adj.* syllabic
silbar *v.* whiz
silbato *n.* whistle
silbido *n.* zing
silenciador *n.* silencer

silencio *n.* silence
silencioso *adj.* silent
sílfide *n.* sylph
silicona *n.* silicon
silla *n.* chair
sillita de paseo *n.* buggy
silogismo *n.* syllogism
silueta *n.* silhouette
silvestre *adj.* sylvan
silvicultura *n.* forestry
simbiosis *n.* symbiosis
simbólico *adj.* symbolic
simbolismo *n.* symbolism
simbolizar *v.* symbolize
símbolo *n.* symbol
simetría *n.* symmetry
simétrico *adj.* symmetrical
símil *n.* simile
similitud *n.* similarity
simpático *adj.* friendly
simplificación *n.* simplification
simplificar *v.* simplify
simplón *n.* simpleton
simposio *n.* symposium
simular *v.* simulate
simultaneo *adj.* simultaneous
sin *prep.* without
sin corazón *adj.* heartless
sin costura *adj.* seamless
sin embargo *adv.* however
sin forma *adj.* shapeless
sin hogar *n.* waif
sin más *n.* ado
sin miedo *adj.* fearless
sin nacer *adj.* unborn
sin par *adj.* nonpareil
sin precedentes *adj.* unprecedented
sin principios *adj.* unprincipled
sin proposito *adj.* aimless
sin valor *adj.* worthless
sinceridad *n.* sincerity

sincero *adj.* sincere, truthful
sincronizado *adj.* synchronous
sincronizar *v.* synchronize
sindicalista *n.* unionist
sindicato *n.* syndicate
síndrome *n.* syndrome
sinecura *n.* sinecure
sinergia *n.* synergy
sinfonía *n.* symphony
singular *adj.* singular
singularidad *n.* singularity
siniestro *n.* damage
siniestro *adj.* sinister
sino *n.* doom
sinónimo *n.* synonym
sinónimo *adj.* synonymous
sinopsis *n.* synopsis
sintaxis *n.* syntax
síntesis *n.* synthesis
sintético *adj.* synthetic
sintetizar *v.* synthesize
síntoma *n.* symptom
sintomático *adj.* symptomatic
sinuoso *adj.* sinuous
sirena cuento *n.* mermaid
sirena *n.* siren
sirope *n.* syrup
sirvienta *n.* maid
sirviente *adj.* menial
sirviente *n.* servant
sisear *v.i* hiss
sísmico *adj.* seismic
sistema *n.* system
sistemático *adj.* systematic
sistematizar *v.* systematize
sistémico *adj.* systemic
sitiar *v.* besiege
sitio web *n.* website
sitio *n.* place, site
situación *n.* situation
situación difícil *n.* plight
situar *v.* situate

skateboard *n.* skateboard
soberanía *n.* sovereignty
soberano *n.* sovereign, ruler
sobornar *v. t.* bribe
sobre *prep.* about, over
sobre *n.* envelope
sobre ascuas *n.* tenterhook
sobreactuar *v.* overact
sobrealimentar *v.* overefeed
sobrecarga *n.* surcharge
sobrecargar *v.* overload
sobrecargo *n.* purser
sobredosis *n.* overdose
sobreescrito *adj.* superscript
sobrehumano *adj.* susperhuman
sobrepasar *v.* overstep, exceed
sobreponer *v.* superimpose
sobrepujar *v.* outbid
sobrerreacionar *v.* overreact
sobresalir *v.* excel, protude
sobrestimar *v.* overestimate
sobrevenir *v.* supervene
sobrevivir *v.* outlive, survive
sobrexcitado *adj.* overwrought
sobriedad *n.* sobriety
sobrina *n.* niece
sobrino *n.* nephew
sobrio *adj.* sober
socavar *v.* undermine
sociabilidad *n.* sociability
sociable *adj.* sociable, outgoing
social *adj.* social
socialismo *n.* socialism
socialista *n. & adj.* socialist
socializar *v.* socialize
sociedad *n.* society
sociología *n.* sociology
socorro *n.* succour
soda *n.* soda
sodomía *n.* sodomy
sofá *n.* sofa, couch, settee
sofisma *n.* sophism

sofista *n.* sophist
sofisticación *n.* sophistication
sofisticado *adj.* sophisticated
sofocante *adj.* sultry
sofocar *v.t.* suffocate, choke
sofocarse *v.r.* suffocate
soga *n.* noose
sol *n.* sun
solapa *v.* flap
solapado *adj.* underhand
solapar *v.* overlap
solar *adj.* solar
soldado *n.* soldier
soldar *v.* weld
soleado *adj.* sunny
soledad *n.* loneliness, solitude
solemne *adj.* solemn
solemnidad *n.* solemnity
solemnizar *v.* solemnize
solicitar *v.* solicit
solícito *adj.* solicitious
solicitud *n.* solicitude
solidaridad *n.* solidarity
sólido *adj.* solid
solista *n.* soloist
solitario *adj.* lone, solitary
solitario *n.* loner
sollozar *v.* sob
sólo *adv.* only, just
solo *adj.* alone
solo *n.* solo
soltar *v.* release
soltero *n.* bachelor
soltero *adj.* single
solterón *n.* singleton
solterona *n.* spinster
solubilidad *n.* solubility
soluble *adj.* soluble
solución *n.* solution
solvencia *n.* solvency
solvente *n.* solvent
sombra *n.* shade, shadow

sombreado *adj.* shady
sombrerero *n.* milliner
sombrero *n.* hat
sombrilla *n.* parasol
sombrío *adj.* bleak, sombre
somero *adj.* perfunctory
somnolencia *n.* somnolence
sonambulismo *n.* somnambulism
sonámbulo *n.* somnambulist
sonar *v.* rattle
sonda *n.* probe
soneto *n.* sonnet
sónico *adj.* sonic
sonido *n.* sound
sonoridad *n.* sonority
sonreír *v.* smile
sonrisa falsa *n.* smirk
sonsacar *v.* wheedle
soñoliento *adj.* somnolent
sopa *n.* soup
soplar *v.* blow
soplo *n.* puff
soporífero *adj.* soporific
soportable *adj.* tolerable
sorber *v.* sip, slurp
sorbete *n.* sorbet
sordidez *n.* sleaze
sórdido *adj.* seamy
sordo *adj.* deaf, mute
sorprender *v.* astound
sorpresa *n.* surprise
soso *adj.* bland
sospecha *n.* suspicion
sospechar *v.* suspect
sospechoso *adj.* suspicious
sospechoso *n* suspect
sostener *v.* sustain
sostenible *adj.* sustainable
sotana *n.* cassock
sótano *n.* basement, cellar
su *adj.* his, her, their
suave *adj.* soft, gentle

suavemente *adv.* lightly
suavizar *v.t.* smooth, soften
subalterno *n.* subaltern
subarrendar *v.t.* sublet
subasta *n.* auction
subconsciente *adj.* subconscious
subcontrato *n.* subcontract
subestimar *v.* underestimate
subíndice *n.* subscript
subir *v.* climb, raise
subjetivo *adj.* subjective
subjuntivo *adj.& n.* subjunctive
sublimar *v.* sublimate
sublime *adj.* sublime
subliminal *adj.* subliminal
submarino *n.* submarine
subordinación *n.* subordination
subordinado *adj.* subordinate
subordinado *n.* underling
subrayar *v.t.* underline
subrepticio *adj.* surreptitious
subsecuente *adj.* subsequent
subsidiaria *adj.* subsidiary
subsidio *n.* allowance
subsistencia *n.* subsistence
subsónico *adj.* subsonic
subsumir *v.* subsume
subterfugio *n.* subterfuge
subterráneo *adj.& n.* underground
subtítulo *n.* subtitle
subtotal *n.* subtotal
subtropical *adj.* subtropical
suburbano *adj.* suburban
suburbio *n.* suburb
subvención *n.* subsidy
subvencionar *v.* subsidize
subversión *n.* subversion
subversivo *adj.* subversive
subyugación *n.* subjugation
subyugar *v.* subjugate
succión *n.* suction

suceder *v.* happen
sucesión *n.* succession
sucesivo *adj.* successive
suceso *n.* event
sucesor *n.* successor
suciedad *n.* dirt
sucinto *adj.* succint
sucio *adj.* dirty
suculento *adj.* succulent
sucumbir *v.* succumb
sucursal *n.* branch
sudar *v.* swear
sudario *n.* shroud
sudoku *n.* sudoku
sudor *n.* sweat
suegra *n.* mother-in-law
sueldo *n.* wage
suelo *n.* floor, ground
suelto *adj.* loose
sueño *n.* dream
suero *n.* whey
suerte *n.* luck
suéter *n.* sweater
suficiencia *n.* sufficiency
suficiente *adj.* sufficient
sufijo *n.* suffix
sufragar *v.* defray
sufragio *n.* suffrage
sufrimiento *n.* ordeal
sufrir *v.* suffer
sugerencia *n.* suggestion
sugerente *adj.* suggestive
sugerir *v.* suggest
sugestionable *adj.* suggestible
suicida *adj.& n.* suicidal
suicidio *n.* suicide
suite *n.* suite
suizo *adj.* swish
sujeción *n.* subjection
sujetador *n.* bra
sujetar *v.t* hold
sultana *n.* sultana

suma *n.* sum
sumamente *adv.* highly
sumariamente *adv.* summarily
sumario *n.* summary
sumergible *adj.* submersible
sumergir *v.* immerse
suministrar *v.* supply
sumisión *n.* submission
sumiso *adj.* submissive
suntuoso *adj.* sumptuous
súper *adj.* super
superar *v.* overcome
superávit *n.* surplus
superficial *adj.* shallow, superficial
superficialidad *n.* superficiality
superficie *n.* surface
superfluidad *n.* superfluity
superfluo *adj.* superfluous
superior *adj.* superior, upper
superioridad *n.* superiority
superlativo *adj.* superlative
supermercado *n.* supermarket
supernatural *adj.* supernatural
superpotencia *n.* superpower
supersónico *adj.* supersonic
superstición *n.* superstition
supersticioso *adj.* superstitious
supervalorar *v.* overrate
supervisar *v.* supervise, oversee
supervisión *n.* supervision
supervisor *n.* supervisor
supervivencia *n.* survival
suplantación *n.* impersonation
suplantar *v.* supersede
suplementario *adj.* supplementary
suplemento *n.* supplement
suplicante *n.* suppliant
suplicar *v.* plead, beg
suponer *v.* presume, suppose

suposición *n.* supposition
supositorio *n.* suppository
supremacía *n.* supremacy
supremo *adj.* supreme
suprimir *v.t.* suppress, delete
supuesto *adj.* putative
supurar *v.* suppurate
sur *n.* south
surco *n.* furrow
sureño *adj.* southern
surf *n.* surf
surgir *v.* arise
surreal *adj.* surreal
surrealismo *n.* surrealism
surtido *adj.* assorted
surtido *n.* assortment
susceptible *adj.* susceptible
suscitar *v.* rouse, arouse
suscribir *v.* subscribe
suscripción *n.* subscription
suspender *v.* suspend, fail
suspense *n.* suspense, thriller
suspensión *n.* suspension
suspirar *v.i.* sigh
sustancia *n.* substance
sustancial *adj.* substantial
sustancialmente *adv.* substantially
sustantivo *adj.* substantive
sustantivo *n.* noun
sustento *n.* sustenance
sustitución *n.* substitution
sustituir *v.* supplant
sustituto *n.* substitute
susto *n.* fright
susurrar *v.* whisper
sutil *adj.* subtle
sutileza *n.* finesse, subtlety
sutilezas *n.* nicety
sutura *n.* suture
suya, suyo *pron.* hers

T

tabaco *n.* tobacco
taberna *n.* tavern, saloon, inn
tabilla *n.* splint
tabla *n.* plank
tablas *n.* stalemate
tablero *n.* board
tableta *n.* tablet
tabloide *n.* tabloid
tablón de anuncios *n.* notice-board
tabú *n.* taboo
tabulación *n.* tabulation
tabulador *n.* tabulator
tabular *adj.* tabular
taburete *n.* stool
tacaño *adj.* stingy
tachuela *n.* tack
tácito *adj.* tacit
taciturno *adj.* taciturn
taco *n.* stud
taco de billar *n.* cue
tacómetro *n.* tachometer
tacón de aguja *n.* stiletto
táctica *n.* tactic
táctico *adj.* tactical
táctil *adj.* tactile
tacto *n.* tact
taimado *adj.* devious
tal *adv.& pron.* such
talabartero *n.* saddler
taladradora *n.* drill
taladro *n.* drill
talar *v.* fell
talco *n.* talc
talento *n.* talent
talentoso *adj.* talented
talismán *n.* talisman
talla *n.* size

taller *n.* workshop
tallo *n.* stalk, stem
talón *n.* heel, stub
tamarindo *n.* tamarind
tambalearse *v.* wobble, stagger
también *adv.* also, too
tambor *n.* drum
tampoco *adv.* either
tampón *n.* tampon
tal *adj.* such
tan *adv.* so
tanda *n.* bout
tándem *n.* tandem
tangente *n.* tangent
tangible *adj.* tangible
tapa *n.* lid
tapas *n.* tapas
tapicería *n.* upholstery
tapicero *v.* upholster
tapiz *n.* tapestry
tapón *n.* plug, bung, stopper
taquígrafa *n.* stenographer
taquigrafía *n.* stenography
taquilla *n.* locker
tarde *n.* evening
tardío *adj.* tardy
tarea *n.* task
tarifa *n.* tariff, fare
tarima *n.* dais
tarjeta *n.* card
tarot *n.* tarot
tarro *n.* jar
tarta *n.* tart
tartamudear *v.* stutter, stammer
tasa *n.* rate
tasación *n.* rating
tatarear *v.* hum
tatuaje *n.* tattoo
taxi *n.* taxi, cab
taxonomía *n.* taxonomy
taza *n.* cup
taza grande *n.* mug

té *n.* tea
teatral *adj.* theatrical
teatro *n.* theatre
teca *n.* teak
techo *n.* ceiling
techumbre *n.* roofing
teclado *n.* keyboard
técnica *n.* technique
tecnicidad *n.* technicality
técnico *adj.* technical
técnico *n.* technician
tecnología *n.* technology
tecnológico *adj.* technological
tecnólogo *n.* technologist
tedio *n.* tedium
tedioso *adj.* tedious, wearisome
teísmo *n.* theism
tejado *n.* roof
tejedor *n.* weaver
tejer *v.* weave
tejido *n.* fabric
tejo *n.* yew
tela *n.* cloth
telar *n.* loom
telaraña *n.* cobweb
teléfono *n.* telephone
teléfono móvil *n.* cellphone
telegrafía *n.* telegraphy
telegráfico *adj.* telegraphic
telégrafo *n.* telegraph
telegrama *n.* telegram
telepatía *n.* telepathy
telepático *adj.* telepathic
telescopio *n.* telescope
teletexto *n.* teletext
teletipo *n.* teleprinter
televisar *v.t.* telecast, televise
televisión *n.* television
tema *n.* subject, issue
temario *n.* theme
temático *adj.* thematic
temblar *v.* tremble, shiver

temblor *n.* tremor
tembloroso *adj.* tremulous
temer *v.t* dread
temerario *adj.* reckless
temeridad *n.* temerity
temeroso *adj.* afraid
temor *n.* trepidation
témpano *n.* floe
temperamental *adj.* temperamental
temperamento *n.* temperament
temperatura *n.* temperature
tempestad *n.* tempest
tempestuoso *adj.* tempestuous, stormy
templo *n.* temple
temporal *adj.* temporal
temporizar *v.* temporize
temprano *adj.* early
tenacidad *n.* tenacity
tenaz *adj.* tenacious
tenazas *n.* tongs
tendencia *n.* trend, tendency
tendencioso *adj.* tendentious
tender a *v.* tend
tendero *n.* shopkeeper
tendón *n.* tendon
tenedor *n.* fork
tener *v.* have
tener cuidado *v.* beware
tener en cuenta *v.* keep in mind
tener éxito *v.* succeed
tener mohíno *v.* sulk
teniente *n.* lieutenant
tenis *n.* tennis
tenor *n.* tenor
tensión *n.* tension
tenso *adj.* tense, edgy
tentación *n.* temptation
tentáculo *n.* tentacle
tentador *adj.* tempting
tentar *v.* tempt

tentempié *n.* snack
tenue *adj.* tenuous
teñir *v.* dye, stain
teocracia *n.* theocracy
teodolito *n.* theodolite
teología *n.* theology
teólogo *n.* theologian
teorema *n.* theorem
teoría *n.* theory
teórico *adj.* theoretical
teórico *n.* theorist
teorizar *v.* theorize
teosofía *n.* theosophy
terapeuta *n.* therapist
terapéutico *adj.* therapeutic
terapia *n.* therapy
tercero *adj.* third
terciario *adj.* tertiary
terciopelo *n.* velvet
tergiversar *v.* misrepresent
termal *adj.* thermal
terminación *n.* termination
terminal *adj.* terminal
terminar *v.* finish, terminate
término *n.* term
terminología *n.* terminology
terminológico *adj.* terminological
termita *n.* termite
termo *n.* thermos
termodinámico *n.* thermodynamics
termómetro *n.* thermometer
termostato *n.* thermostat
ternera *n.* beef, veal
terracota *n.* terracotta
terraplén *n.* rampart
terraza *n.* terrace
terremoto *n.* earthquake
terrenal *adj.* earthly, worldly
terreno *n.* terrain
terreno ondulado *n.* wold
terrestre *adj.* terrestrial

terrible *adj.* terrible, dreadful
terrier *n.* terrier
territorial *adj.* territorial
territorio *n.* territory
terror *n.* terror
terrorismo *n.* terrorism
terrorista *n.* terrorist
tesis *n.* thesis
tesorería *n.* treasury, bursary
tesorero *n.* treasurer, bursar
tesoro *n.* treasure
tesoro público *n.* exchequer
testado *adj.* testate
testamento *n.* testament
testarudo *adj.* stubborn
testículo *n.* testicle
testificar *v.* testify
testigo *n.* witness
testimonial *adj.* attesting
testimonio *n.* testimony
testosterona *n.* testosterone
tetina *n.* teat
textil *n* textile
texto *n.* text
texto largo *n.* screed
textual *adj.* textual
textualmente *adv.* verbatim
textura *n.* texture
tía *n.* aunt
tibio *adj.* tepid, lukewarm
tiburón *n.* shark
tic-tac *n.* ticking
tiempo *n.* weather
tiempo libre *n.* leisure
tienda *n.* shop, store
tienda de campaña *n.* tent
tierno *adj.* tender
tierra *n.* earth, land, soil
tifoideo *n.* typhoid
tifón *n.* typhoon
tifus *n.* typhus
tigre *n.* tiger

tijeras *n.* scissors
tijeretear *v.* snip
timar *v.* cheat
timbre *n.* buzzer
timidez *n.* timidity
tímido *adj.* shy, timid
timón *n.* rudder, helm
timorato *adj.* timorous
tinieblas *n.* gloom
tinta *n.* ink
tinte *n.* dye
tintinear *v.* tinkle
tintineo *n.* clink
tintura *n.* tincture
tiña *n.* ringworm
tío *n.* bloke, guy
tío (familiar) *n.* uncle
típico *adj.* typical
tipificar *v.* typify
tipo *n.* type
tira *n.* band
tirabuzón *n.* ringlet
tirador *n.* knob
tiranía *n.* tyranny
tiranizar *v.* tyrannize
tirano *n.* tyrant
tirante *adj.* taut
tirar *v.t.* throw
tirar (lanzar) *v.* flip
tiro *n.* shot
tiroides *n.* thyroid
tirón *n.* jerk
tiroteo *n.* shooting
titánico *adj.* titanic
títere *n.* stooge
titubeante *adj.* halting
titulado *adj.* titled
titular *adj.* titular
titular (noticia) *n.* headline
título *n.* title, heading
tiza *n.* chalk
tizón *n.* blight

toalla *n.* towel
tobillo *n.* ankle
tocado *adj.* touching
tocar *v.* touch
todavía *adv.* yet
todo *adj.* every, whole
todopoderoso *adj.* almighty
todos *adj.* all
toga *n.* toga, gown
tolerancia *n.* tolerance
tolerante *adj.* tolerant
tolerar *v.* tolerate
tomar el sol *v.* sunbathe
tomar *v.* take
tomate *n.* tomato
tomo *n.* tome
tonel *n.* barrel
tonelada *n.* ton, tonne
tonelaje *n.* tonnage
tonelero *n.* cooper
tóner *n.* toner
tónico *n.* tonic
tono *n.* tone
tonsura *n.* tonsure
tontería *n.* nonsense
tonto *n.* fool
tonto *adj.* silly, zany, daft
topacio *n.* topaz
topiario *n.* topiary
tópico *n.* topic
topless *adj.* topless
topo *n.* mole
topografía *n.* topography
topográfico *adj.* topographical
topógrafo *n.* topographer
toque de queda *n.* curfew
toque de trompetas *n.* fanfare
torbellino *n.* whirlwind
torcedura *n.* strain
torcer *v.t.* strain, sprain, twist
torcerse *v.r.* to be twisted
torcido *adj.* crooked, lopsided, strained

torero *n.* toreador
tormenta *n.* storm
tormento *n.* torment
tornado *n.* tornado
torneo *n.* tournament
tornero *n.* turner
tornillo *n.* screw, bolt
torno *n.* winch
toro *n.* bull
torpe *adj.* clumsy
torpedo *n.* torpedo
torre *n.* tower
torre (ajedrez) *n.* rook
torrencial *adj.* torrential
torrente *n.* torrent
tórrido *adj.* torrid
torsión *n.* torsion
torso *n.* torso
tortilla *n.* omelette
tortuga *n.* turtle, tortoise
tortuoso *adj.* tortuous
tortura *n.* torture
torturador *n.* torturer
tosco *adj.* artless
toser *v.* cough
tostada *n.* toast
tostadora *n.* toaster
total *adj.* total, utter, overall
total *n.* total
totalidad *n.* totality
totalitario *adj.* totalitarian
totalmente *adv.* wholly
totalmente empapado *adj.* sopping
tóxico *adj.* toxic
toxicología *n.* toxicology
toxina *n.* toxin
tozudo *adj.* mulish
trabajador *adj.* industrious
trabajador *n.* worker
trabajo *n.* job, labour, work
trabajos duros *n.* toils

tracción *n.* traction
tractor *n.* tractor
tradición *n.* tradition
tradicional *adj.* traditional
tradicionalista *n.* traditionalist
traducción *n.* translation
traducir *v.* translate
traer *v.* bring
traficante *n.* trafficker
traficar *v.* trafficking
trafico *n.* traffic
tragaluz *n.* skylight
tragar *v.* swallow
tragar saliva *v.* gulp
tragedia *n.* tragedy
trágico *adj.* tragic
trago *n.* mouthful
traición *n.* treason, betrayal, treachery
traicionar *v.* betray
traidor *n.* traitor
traidor *adj.* treacherous
traje *n.* suit
trajinar *v.* potter
trama *n.* plot
tramar *v.* contrive
tramitar *v.* transact
trampa *n.* trap
trampolín *n.* trampoline
tramposo *n.* cheat
trance *n.* trance
tranquilidad *n.* tranquility
tranquilizar *v.* reassure
tranquilizar *v.* tranquillize
tranquilo *adj.* tranquil
transacción *n.* transaction
transatlántico *adj.* transatlantic
transcendente *adj.* transcendent
transcender *v.* transcend
transcontinental *adj.* transcontinental
transcribir *v.* transcribe

transcripción *n.* transcription
transcurrir *v.* elapse
transeúnte *n.* bystander
transexual *n.* transsexual
transferible *adj.* transferable
transferir *v.* transfer
transfiguración *n.* transfiguration
transfigurar *v.* transfigure
transformación *n.* transformation
transformador *n.* transformer
transformar *v.* transform
transfundir *v.* transfuse
transfusión *n.* transfusion
transgredir *v.* transgress
transgresión *n.* transgression
transición *n.* transition
transistor *n.* transistor
transitivo *adj.* transitive
transito *n.* transit
transitorio *adj.* transitory
transliterar *v.* transliterate
translucido *adj.* translucent
transmigración *n.* transmigration
transmisión *n.* transmission
transmisor *n.* transmitter
transmitir *v.* transmit
transmutar *v.* transmute
transparencia *n.* transparency
transparente *adj.* transparent
transpiración *n.* perspiration
transpirar *v.i.* transpire
transportación *n.* transportation
transportador *n.* transporter
transportar *v.* convey
transporte *n.* transport
transportista *n.* carrier
transversal *adj.* transverse
tranvía *n.* tram
trapecio *n.* trapeze
trapo *n.* cloth, rag, duster
trascendental *adj.* transcendental

trasero *n.* backside
trasfondo *n.* background
trasplante *v.* transplant
trasponer *v.* transpose
trastabillar *v.* bumble
trastornar *v.t.* upset, mess up
tratable *adj.* tractable
tratado *n.* treaty
tratamiento *n.* treatment
trauma *n.* trauma
travesía *n.* crossing
travesti *n.* transvestite
travesura *n.* mischief, prank
travieso *adj.* naughty
trayectoria *n.* trajectory
trazar *v.t.* trace
trece *adj. & n.* thirteen
tregua *n.* truce
treinta *adj. & n.* thirty
tremendo *adj.* tremendous
trementina *n.* turpentine
trémulo *adj.* shaky
tren *n.* train
trenza *n.* plait
tres *adj. & n.* three
tres veces *adv.* thrice
treta *n.* ploy
triangular *adj.* triangular
triangulo *n.* triangle
triatlón *n.* triathlon
tribal *adj.* tribal
tribu *n.* tribe
tribulación *n.* tribulation
tribuna *n.* rostrum
tribunal *n.* court, tribunal
tributario *adj.* tributary
tributo *n.* tribute
tríceps *n.* triceps
triciclo *n.* tricycle
tricolor *adj.* tricolour
tridente *n.* trident
trigo *n.* wheat

trigonometría *n.* trigonometry
trigueño *adj.* wheaten
trillado *adj.* trite
trillar *v.* thresh
trillizo *n.* triplet
trillón *adj & n.* trillion
trilogía *n.* trilogy
trimestral *adj.* quarterly
trinar *v.* warble
trinchera *n.* trench
trineo *n.* sledge, sleigh
trinidad *n.* trinity
trino *n.* trill
trinquete *n.* ratchet
trío *n.* trio
tripa *n.* gut
tripartita *adj.* tripartite
triple *adj.* treble, triple
triplicado *adj.* triplicate
trípode *n.* tripod
tríptico *n.* triptych
tripulación *n.* crew
triste *adj.* sad
tristeza *n.* sadness
triturador *n.* grinder
triunfal *adj.* triumphal
triunfante *adj.* triumphant
triunfo *n.* triumph
triunfo (cartas) *n.* trump
trivial *adj.* trivial
trivialidad *n.* trivia, trivialness
triza *n.* shred
trofeo *n.* trophy
trol *n.* troll
trompeta *n.* trumpet
tronco *n.* trunk, log
trono *n.* throne
tropezar *v.* stumble
tropical *adj.* tropical
trópico *n.* tropic
trotamundos *n.* globetrotter
trotar *v.* lope

trote *n.* trot
Troya *n.* troy
trozo *n.* hunk, chunk
trucha *n.* trout
truco *n.* trick, gimmick
trueno *n.* thunder
trufa *n.* truffle
truhan *n.* knave
truncar *v.* truncate
tú mismo *pron.* yourself
tú *pron.* you
tuberculosis *n.* tuberculosis
tubo *n.* tube, pipe
tubular *adj.* tubular
tugurio *n.* slum
tuitear *v.* tweet
tulipán *n.* tulip
tumba *n.* tomb, grave
tumbar *v* take down
tumescente *adj.* tumescent
tumor *n.* tumour
tumulto *n.* tumult, mayhem
tumultuoso *adj.* tumultuous
túnel *n.* tunnel
túnica *n.* tunic
tupé *n.* quiff
turba *n.* turf
turbante *n.* turban
turbina *n.* turbine
turbio *adj.* turbid, murky
turbulencia *n.* turbulence
turbulento *adj.* turbulent
turismo *n.* tourism
turista *n.* tourist
turno *n.* innings
turquesa *n.* turquoise
turrón *n.* nougat
tutela *n.* tutelage
tutor *n.* tutor
tweed *n.* tweed

U

uadi *n.* wadi
ualabí *n.* wallaby
ubicar *v.* locate
ubicuo *adj.* ubiquitous
ubre *n.* udder
úlcera *n.* ulcer
ulcerar *v.t.* ulcerate
últimamente *adv.* lately
ultimátum *n.* ultimatum
último *adj.* last, latter, ultimate
ultra *pref.* ultra
ultrajar *v.t.* outrage
ultramarino *n.* ultramarine
ultramarinos *n.* grocery
ultrasónico *adj.* ultrasonic
ultrasonido *n.* ultrasound
umbilical *adj.* umbilical
umbral *n.* threshold
un *art.* an
un atisbo de *n.* modicum
un rato *adv.* awhile
una *n.* one (femenine)
una barra *n.* loaf
una vez *adv.* once
unánime *adj.* unanimous
unanimidad *a.* unanimity
únicamente *adv.* solely
único *n.* sole
único *adj.* unique
unidad *n.* unit, unidad
unificación *n.* unification
unificar *v.* unify
uniforme *adj.* uniform
unilateral *adj.* unilateral
unión *n.* union

unir *v.* unite
unisex *adj.* unisex
unísono *n.* unison
universal *adj.* universal
universalidad *adv.* universality
universidad *n.* university
universo *n.* universe
uno *n. & adj.* one
uno mismo *pron.* oneself
untar *v.* spread
untuoso *adj.* unctuous
uña *n.* nail
urbanidad *n.* urbanity
urbano *adj.* urban
urgente *adj.* urgent
urgir *v.* urge
urinario *adj.* urinary
urna *n.* urn
urraca *n.* magpie
usar *v.t.* use
uso *n.* usage
usual *adj.* usual
usuario *n.* user
usura *n.* usury
usurpación *n.* usurpation
usurpar *v.* usurp
utensilio *n.* utensil
utensilios *n.* ware
útero *n.* womb, uterus
útil *adj.* useful, helpful
utilidad *n.* utility
utilitario *adj.* utilitarian
utilizable *adj.* usable
utilización *n.* utilization
utilizar *v.* utilize
utópia *n.* utopia
utópico *adj.* utopian
uva *n.* grape

V

vaca *n.* cow
vacaciones *n.* holidays
vacante *n.* vacancy
vaciar *v.* vacate
vacilación *n.* vacillation
vacilar *v.* hesitate
vacío *adj.* empty, vacuous
vacío *n.* emptiness
vacuna *n.* vaccine
vacunación *n.* vaccination
vacunar *v.* vaccinate
vagabundo *n.* tramp
vagar *v.* wander, roam
vagina *n.* vagina
vago *adj.* lacy
vagón *n.* wagon
vaguedad *n.* vagueness
vaina *n.* pod, sheath
vajilla *n.* crockery
vale *n.* voucher, coupon
valencia *n.* valency
valentía *n.* bravery, valour
valetudinario *n.* valetudinarian
validar *v.* validate
validez *n.* validity
válido *adj.* valid
valiente *adj.* brave, valiant
valija *n.* valise
valioso *adj.* valuable
valla *n.* hurdle
valle *n.* valley
valor *n.* value
valor (coraje) *n.* courage
valores *n.* values
vals *n.* waltz
valuación *n.* valuation
válvula *n.* valve
vampiro *n.* vampire

vanaglorioso *adj.* vainglorious
vandalizar *v.* vandalize
vándalo *n.* vandal, hooligan
vanguardia *n.* vanguard
vanidad *n.* vanity
vanidosamente *adv.* vainly
vanidoso *adj.* vain
vano *adj.* futile
vapor *n.* steam, vapour
vaporizar *v.* vaporize
vapulear *v.* maul
vaqueros *n.* jeans
vara *n.* rod
variable *adj.* variable
variación *n.* variation
variado *adj.* varied, miscellaneous
variante *n.* variant
variar *v.* vary
variedad *n.* variety
variopinto *adj.* motley
varios *adj.* various
varios *pron.* several
varita *n.* wand
variz *adj.* varicose
varonil *adj.* manly
vasallo *n.* vassal
vascular *adj.* vascular
vasectomía *n.* vasectomy
vasija *n.* vessel
vaso *n.* glass
vasto *adj.* vast
vaticinar *v.* prophesy
vatio *n.* watt
vecindario *n.* neighbourhood
vecino *n.* neighbour
vector *n.* vector
vegetación *n.* vegetation
vegetar *v.* vegetate
vegetariano *n.* vegetarian
vegetativo *adj.* vegetative
vehemente *adj.* vehement

vehicular *adj.* vehicular
vehículo *n.* vehicle
veinte *adj.&n.* twenty
vejación *n.* vexation
vejiga *n.* bladder
vela *n.* candle
vela (barco) *n.* sail
veleta *n.* vane
vellón *n.* fleece
velo *n.* veil
velocidad *n.* speed, velocity
veloz *adj.* speedy, swift
velvetón *n.* velour
vena *n.* vein
venal *adj.* venal
venalidad *n.* venality
vencedor *n.* victor
vencer *v.* beat, defeat
vencido *adj.* due, overdue
vencimiento *n.* expiry
vendaje *n.* bandage
vendar los ojos *v.* blindfold
vendaval *n.* gale
vendedor *n.* salesman, seller, vendor
vender *v.* sell
vendetta *n.* vendetta
vendible *adj.* saleable
vendimia *n.* vintage
veneciano *adj.* venetian
veneno *n.* poison, venom
venenoso *adj.* poisonous, venomous
venerable *adj.* venerable
veneración *n.* veneration
venerar *v.* venerate
venganza *n.* revenge, vengeance
vengar *v.* avenge
vengativo *adj.* vengeful
venial *adj.* venial
venir *v.* come
venoso *adj.* venous

venta *n.* sale
ventaja *n.* advantage
ventana *n.* window
ventilación *n.* ventilation
ventilado *adj.* airy
ventilador *n.* ventilator
ventilar *v.* ventilate
ventisca *n.* blizzard
ventosa *n.* sucker
ventoso *adj.* windy
ver *v.* see
veracidad *n.* veracity
veranda *n.* verandah
verano *n.* summer
veraz *adj.* veracious
verbal *adj.* verbal
verbalizar *v.* verbalize
verbalmente *adv.* verbally, orally
verbo *n.* verb
verborrea *n.* verbosity
verboso *adj.* verbose, wordy
verdad *n.* truth
verdaderamente *adv.* verily
true *adj.* true
verde *adj. & n.* green
verdeante *adj.* verdant
verdor *n.* greenery
verdugón *n.* welt
verdulero *n.* greengrocer
verdura *n.* vegetable
veredicto *n.* verdict
verga *n.* cock
vergonzoso *adj.* shameful
vergüenza *n.* shame, disgrace
verificación *n.* verification
verificar *v.* verify
verja *n.* gate
vernáculo *n.* vernacular
vernal *adj.* vernal
verosímil *adj.* plausible
verosimilitud *n.* verisimilitude
verruga *n.* wart

versado *adj.* versed
versátil *adj.* versatile
versatilidad *n.* versatility
versificación *n.* versification
versificar *v.* versify
versión *n.* version
verso *n.* verse
vértebra *n.* vertebra
vertebrado *n.* vertebrate
vertedero *n.* dump
verter *v.* pour
vertical *adj.* vertical, upright
vértice *n.* vertex
vertido *n.* spillage
vertiginoso *adj.* vertiginous
vértigo *n.* vertigo
vesícula *n.* vesicle
vestíbulo *n.* hall, lobby
vestido *adj.* clad
vestido *v.* dress, frock
vestidura *n.* vestment
vestigio *n.* vestige
vestimenta *n.* garb
vestir *v.* dress, clothe
veterano *n.* veteran
veterinario *adj.* veterinary
veto *n.* veto
viable *adj.* viable
viaducto *n.* viaduct
viaje *n.* journey, travel
viajero *n.* traveller
vial *n.* vial
vibración *n.* vibe, vibration
vibrador *n.* vibrator
vibráfono *n.* vibraphone
vibrante *adj.* vibrant
vibrar *v.* vibrate
vice *n.* vice
viceversa *adv.* vice-versa
viciar *v.* vitiate
vicisitud *n.* vicissitude
victima *n.* victim

victoria *n.* victory
victorioso *adj.* victorious
vid *n.* vine
vida *n.* life
vidente *n.* seer
video *n.* video
videocámara *n.* camcorder
vidriero *n.* glazier
vieira *n.* scallop
viejo *adj.* old
viento *n.* wind
viento del oeste *adv.* westerly
vientre *n.* belly
viernes *n.* Friday
viga *n.* beam
vigésimo *adj.&n.* twentieth
vigilancia *n.* surveillance
vigilante *n.* watchman
vigilante *adj.* vigilant
vigilia *n.* vigil
vigor *n.* vigour
vigoroso *adj.* vigorous
vikingo *n.* viking
vilipendiar *v.* vilify
villancico *n.* carol
vinagre *n.* vinegar
vinatero *n.* vintner
vinculo *n.* bond
vindicación *n.* vindication
vindicar *v.* vindicate
vinilo *n.* vinyl
vino *n.* wine
viñeta *n.* vignette
violación *n.* violation
violador *n.* rapist
violar *v.* rape, violate
violencia *n.* violence
violento *adj.* violent, rampant
violeta *n.* violet
violín *n.* violin, fiddle
violinista *n.* violinist
virago *n.* virago

viraje *n.* veer
virar *v.* yaw
virgen *n.* virgin
virgen (de fogueo) *adj.* blank
virginidad *n.* virginity
vírico *adj.* viral
viril *adj.* virile
virilidad *n.* virility
virrey *n.* viceroy
virtual *adj.* virtual
virtud *n.* virtue
virtuoso *adj.* virtuous
viruela *n.* smallpox
virulencia *n.* virulence
virulento *adj.* virulent
virus *n.* virus
visado *n.* visa
viscosa *n.* viscose
viscoso *adj.* viscous
visera *n.* visor
visibilidad *n.* visibility
visible *adj.* visible
visión *n.* vision
visionario *adj.* visionary
visita *n.* visitation
visitante *n.* visitor
visitar *v.* visit
visitas turísticas *n.* sightseeing
visón *n.* mink
víspera *n.* eve
vista *n.* sight, view, vista
vistazo *n.* glimpse
visual *adj.* visual
visualizar *v.* visualize
vital *adj.* vital
vitalidad *n.* vitality
vitamina *n.* vitamin
viticultura *n.* viticulture
vítreo *adj.* vitreous
vitrificar *v.* vitrify
vitrina *n.* cabinet
vitriolo *n.* vitriol

vituallas *n.* victuals
vituperio *n.* vituperation
viuda *n.* widow
viudo *n.* widower
vivacidad *n.* vivacity, zest
vivaz *adj.* vivacious
vivero *n.* vivarium
vívido *adj.* vivid
vivificar *v.* vivify
vivir *v.* live
vivo *adj.* alive
vivo *n.* living
vizconde *n.* viscount
vizcondesa *n.* viscountess
vocabulario *n.* vocabulary
vocación *n.* vocation
vocal *adj.* vocal
vocal *n.* vowel
vocalista *n.* vocalist
vocalizar *v.* vocalize
vocinglero *adj.* vociferous
vodevil *n.* vaudeville
volante *n.* wheel
volar *v.i* fly
volátil *adj.* volatile
volcán *n.* volcano
volcánico *adj.* volcanic
volcar *v.* capsize
volición *n.* volition
voltaje *n.* voltage
voltear *v.* overturn
voltio *n.* volt
voluble *adj.* voluble, volatile
volumen *n.* volume
voluminoso *adj.* voluminous
voluntariamente *adv.* voluntarily
voluntario *adj.* voluntary
voluntario *n.* volunteer
voluntarioso *adj.* wayward
voluptuoso *adj.* voluptuous
volver *v.* return
volver a *v.* revert

vomitar *v.* vomit
voraz *adj.* voracious
vórtice *n.* vortex
votación *n.* ballot
votación *n.* poll
votante *n.* voter
votivo *adj.* votive
voto (elección) *n.* vote
voto *n.* vow
voz *n.* voice
vudú *n.* voodoo
vuelo *n.* flight
vuelta *n.* lap
vulcanizar *v.* vulcanize
vulgar *adj.* vulgar
vulgaridad *n.* vulgarity
vulnerable *adj.* vulnerable

W

whisky *n.* whisky

X

xenofobia *n.* xenophobia
xenón *n.* xenon
Xerox *n.* xerox
xilófago *adj.* xylophagous
xilófono *n.* xylophone

Y

y *conj.* and
ya *adv.* already

ya lo creo *adv.* indeed
yak *n.* yak
yate *n.* yacht
yegua *n.* mare
yema *n.* yolk
Yen *n.* Yen
yesca *n.* tinder
yeso *n.* plaster
yeti *n.* yeti
Yo *pron.* I
yo mismo *pron.* myself
yodo *n.* iodine
yoga *n.* yoga
yogui *n.* yogi
yogur *n.* yogurt
yunque *n.* anvil
yunta *n.* yoke
yute *n.* jute

Z

zafio *n.* boor
zafiro *n.* sapphire
zagual *n.* paddle
zambullirse *v.* dive
zampar *v.* quaff
zanahoria *n.* carrot
zanco *n.* stilt
zanja *n.* ditch
zapatero *n.* cobbler
zapatilla *n.* slipper
zapatilla de deporte *n.* sneaker
zapato *n.* shoe
zarpa *n.* claw
zigzag *n.* zigzag
zinc *n.* zinc
zodiaco *n.* zodiac
zombi *n.* zombie
zona *n.* zone, district

zonal *adj.* zonal
zoo *n.* zoo
zoología *n.* zoology
zoológico *adj.* zoological
zoólogo *n.* zoologist
zopenco *adj.* dullard, jackass
zoquete *adj.* oaf

zorra *n.* vixen
zorro *n.* fox
zumbido *n.* buzz, whir
zumo *n.* juice
zurcir *v.* darn
zurrar *v.* spank, wallop